EMPLOYER'S GUIDE TO

The Americans With Disabilities Act

To keep abreast of ongoing developments on the Americans with Disabilities Act and related issues, refer to *BNA's Americans with Disabilities Act Manual,* a two-binder monthly information service from The Bureau of National Affairs, Inc. For more information, call BNA Customer Relations at 800-372-1033.

EMPLOYER'S GUIDE TO

The Americans With Disabilities Act

James G. Frierson

The Bureau of National Affairs, Inc.

Copyright © 1992
The Bureau of National Affairs, Inc.
All Rights reserved

Second Printing October 1992

Library of Congress Cataloging-in-Publication Data

Frierson, James G.
    Employer's guide to the Americans with Disabilities Act / James G.
Frierson.
        p.   cm.
    Includes bibliographical references and index.
    ISBN 0-87179-728-3
    1.   Handicapped—Employment—Law and legislation—United States.
    2.   Discrimination against the handicapped—Law and legislation-
-United States.   I. Title.
    KF3469.F75   1992
    344.73'0159—dc20
    [347.304159]   92-7275
                                                                       CIP

Authorization to photocopy items for internal or personal use, or the internal or personal
use of specific clients, is granted by BNA Books for libraries and other users registered
with the Copyright Clearance Center (CCC) Transactional Reporting Service, provided
that $0.50 per page is paid directly to CCC, 27 Congress St., Salem, MA 01970.
0-87179-728-3/92/$0 + .50.

Published by BNA Books
1250 23rd St., NW, Washington, D.C. 20037-1165

Dedication

To R. Page Powell, M.D., whose skill and dedication allowed life, and to Lynn, who makes life worth living.

Preface

This book is intended to be a practical guide to compliance with the Americans with Disabilities Act (ADA). It is the first book on the ADA that combines a coverage of the law's requirements with extensive materials explaining various disabilities, methods of possible accommodations including example costs, and numerous sources of additional information.

However, effective compliance with the letter and spirit of the ADA will not occur by using the correct forms, learning the technical law, and knowing more about accommodations. Instead, attitudes must change. Emphasis must be placed upon discovering the abilities of workers, disabled or not. Because most legally disabled workers are current employees, many of whom hide their disability because of a fear of discrimination, employers must encourage employees to identify their disabilities. In many cases, reasonable accommodations that are free or very inexpensive can be found to improve each employee's disability.

When most people hear the word disability, or a reference to the Americans with Disabilities Act, they immediately think of people who are blind, deaf, or in a wheelchair. However, the law and effective business practice must recognize that there are many disabilities. For example, only about 800,000 Americans are completely blind, while some eight million have mental disabilities, with I.Q.'s under 70. Only two million are deaf, but 12 million are hearing-impaired. Millions more have hidden disabilities such as diabetes, cancer, learning disabilities, epilepsy, and mental illness.

Although employers express fear that the ADA will result in many excessive demands for accommodations and unfounded lawsuits, the largest financial losses will occur when employers fail to discover employee disabilities and make reasonable accommodations. There will be excessive demands and unfounded lawsuits that will cost management time and company money. However, these losses will be insignificant when compared to the loss of productivity caused by employees failing to work at peak efficiency because of hidden disabilities and lack of minor accommodations.

This book is designed not only to be read, but also to be used as a reference source. Numerous cross-references are given to allow one to research precise issues. Chapter 1 gives a summary of the law with extensive citations to later chapters for more in-depth coverage of specific issues under the ADA. Chapter 2 contains some of the key changes that employers must take as soon as possible to comply with the law, while chapters 3 and 4 contain many of the legal rules necessary to understand when an individual is a qualified, disabled person who is legally protected under the ADA.

Chapter 5 contains the legal rules concerning the duty to make reasonable accommodations for disabled workers. More importantly, it gives practical examples of accommodations and their costs, and lists some major sources of information concerning devices and techniques to accommodate employee disabilities.

Chapters 6 and 7 discuss the legal standards for determining if a disabled person can be denied a job because of the threat of injury or death to the worker, co-workers, or customers and other outsiders. Specific coverage of the conditions that have caused the greatest number of successful lawsuits under the federal Rehabilitation Act of 1973 and state handicapped laws are covered. In these areas—AIDS, bad backs, diabetes, and epilepsy—employers need to be very careful in denying jobs based upon a perception that employment will cause danger.

Chapter 8 contains a number of sample company policies, job applications, and other forms that may be used in compliance with the ADA. Chapter 9 discusses the legal procedures of an ADA lawsuit, including damages, attorneys fees, and the changes made by the Civil Rights Act of 1991. Chapter 10 presents some ideas on managing disabilities in a manner that maximizes compliance with the law, while minimizing health and workers' compensation insurance claims.

Part II lists many potential disabilities in alphabetical order, giving brief descriptions of the mental or physical disorder, hints on dealing with people with the medical condition, sample accommodations (including representative prices for accommodation devices), and sources of additional information. It is designed to be used as reference material that will help employers in making accommodations.

The appendixes present the ADA law as written by Congress, as well as the Equal Employment Opportunity Comission's first regulations under the law. The final appendix may be used to order catalogs or inquire about various accommodation devices.

Since this is the first book that attempts to go beyond a legal explanation of the ADA by giving medical information concerning various disabilities and emphasizing practical accommodation methods and devices, the author would appreciate hearing of your suggestions, especially concerning additional accommodation ideas you might discover. Please write or phone your ideas to: James G. Frierson, Dept. of Management & Marketing, P.O. Box 70625, East Tennessee State University, Johnson City, TN 37614; phone (615) 929-5384.

In preparing this book extensive use was made of CCH's Employment Practices Decisions Looseleaf and Case Service, BNA's Policy and Practice Looseleaf Service, materials supplied by various disability and health-related organizations listed in Part II of this book, and the President's Committee on Employment of People with Disabilities. The author is especially appreciative of the company materials furnished by IBM, Sears, Dupont, Honeywell, AT&T, and General Motors.

The author would also like to express his appreciation to the people who, among others, offered their comments and advice. While the author is solely responsible for any mistakes that appear in this book, the people listed below are responsible for correcting mistakes and supplying additional information. Individuals who checked for medical mistakes in Part II and offered advice based on general knowledge as of June 1991, include Dean Paul Stanton of the James H. Quillen College of Medicine, East Tennessee State University; his assistant, Kim Blevins; and faculty members who reviewed sections of Part II: Drs. Felix Sarubbi, James Evans, May L. Votaw, Barbara Kimbrough, Louis Modica, Richard Jordan, Bradley Arbogast, Eapen Thomas, William Browder, William Messerschmidt, and Louis Cancellaro.

Physicians in private practice who also checked sections of Part II and offered helpful advice include Drs. Stephen Kimbrough, David Lurie, Horace B. Cupp, Jr., Thomas Borthwick, Franklin Montenegro, and Art Harris.

Individuals and groups helpful in aiding general research include Steven Patrick, Sherrod Library; the Office of Graduate Affairs; the Department of Management & Marketing, and College of Business; all of East Tennessee State University.

Individuals who offered practical business advice or supplied information concerning their company's activities include Robert C. Dryer, Martin Marietta Company; Paul L. Scher, Sears, Roebuck & Co.; W. Kenneth Tregenza, General Motors; J.A. Honeck, IBM;

Reed Welke, Honeywell, Inc.; Elizabeth P. Dixon, AT&T; H.G. Smith, DuPont; and Mac Macdonald, Sesco Management Consultants.

Others who kindly provided aid and information include Gary Grom, Vice-President of Human Resources, Sara Lee Corporation; Zeke Scher, Editor, Preventive Law Reporter, University of Denver College of Law; Joe Johns, Personnel Director with the Harris-Tarkett Company; John P. Pincince, Director of Personnel, Nuclear Fuel Services; Catherine Bellecci, Sensory Aid Foundation; W.G. Zilleti; Mary Ellen Ross, President's Committee on Employment of People with Disabilities; Lana Smart, Industry-Labor Council; and Robert Brabham, National Rehabilitation Association.

Contents

Part I. Understanding and
Complying With the ADA

Part II. Accommodating Specific Disabilities

Part I

Understanding and Complying
With the ADA

Chapter 1

A Summary of the Law

The Americans with Disabilities Act (ADA) is one of the most significant employment laws in American history. The preamble to the law states that it covers 43,000,000 Americans. However, because of the expansive definition of who is disabled, it may cover even more. Unlike previous equal employment laws, the ADA may require the purchase of equipment and modification of a company's physical facilities. Businesses and professional firms that make major renovations to their facilities or build new structures are subject to detailed accessibility rules. Other sections of the ADA not covered in this book apply to retail and service businesses, transportation companies, phone companies, and governmental agencies.

This chapter outlines the basic employment provisions of the ADA with references to later chapters in Part I that contain more detailed information. Part II of the book lists and describes a number of possible disabilities, along with ideas for accommodation and sources of additional information.

Employment Discrimination Outlawed

Title I of the ADA prohibits discrimination against a "qualified individual with a disability" with regard to job application procedures, hiring, training, compensation, fringe benefits, advancement, or any other term or condition of work.[1] An employer cannot discriminate in any aspect of employment because of a job applicant's or employee's disability.

In addition to the overall prohibition against discrimination, the ADA lists the following acts as discriminatory and illegal:

1. *Limiting, segregating, or classifying a job applicant or employee based upon a disability that in any way adversely affects*

the employment opportunities or status of the individual.[2] This rule applies to all job-related activities. For example, limiting the type of work that is offered to disabled people based on an employer's assumptions concerning the abilities of a disabled person is a violation of law. Placing disabled workers in a special section of the workplace or on a separate assembly line will usually violate the law. The use of separate pay or promotion tracts for disabled and non-disabled workers violates the ADA. The law also forbids separate lunch, break, or rest rooms, unless necessary as a reasonable accommodation. Even social and recreational activities provided to employees must be made accessible to all, if possible.

2. *Entering into contracts or other arrangements with third parties that have the effect of subjecting an employer's workers to discrimination based upon disability.*[3] Although this does not require a company to protect a subcontractor's or supplier's employees, it does mandate that employers insure that subcontractors or other outsiders used by the company do not discriminate against the firm's own workers. For instance, a company that hires outside consultants to conduct a supervisory training program is legally responsible if the consultants discriminatorily segregate a disabled supervisor, or fail to provide a reasonable accommodation for a supervisor's known disability. Company liability can also result when outside employment recruiters, testing consultants, performance evaluation experts, or any other contractors violate the law when dealing with the company's own employees or job applicants.

3. *Utililization of any standards, criteria, or administrative methods that have the effect of discriminating based upon disability, or that perpetuate the discrimination of others.*[4] This provision outlaws a type of discrimination that lawyers call "disparate impact," and it follows the disparate impact principles of Title VII of the Civil Rights Act of 1964. In nonlegal language, this phrase refers to discrimination resulting from a company policy or action that is not intended to be discriminatory, but (1) results in different treatment of a disabled person, as compared to a nondisabled person, and (2) is not based upon a business necessity. To avoid accidentally violating the ADA by using policies that disproportionally impact disabled workers adversely and are not essential to the business, employers must review and make necessary changes in job descriptions, pre-employment procedures, personnel recordkeeping, job evaluations, and many other aspects of employment. Of particular importance are the ADA's rules concerning hiring and testing. See

Chapter 2, "Major Changes to Conform to the Law," and Chapter 4, "Determining if a Disabled Person is Qualified" for more detail on these important subjects.

4. *Excluding or otherwise discriminating against a job applicant or employee because of that person's association with a disabled person or group.*[5] Employers must not base employment decisions upon the disability of an individual's spouse, family member, friend, or live-in mate. Nor can employment decisions be based upon a person's relationship with disability-related groups, charities, or social clubs. For example, it is illegal for an employer to refuse to hire or retain an individual because he or she lives with a person with AIDS or is active in AIDS-related organizations.

5. *Not making reasonable accommodations for the known disabilities of job applicants and employees.* Failure to make accommodations will be discussed later in this chapter, with a more extensive discussion given in Chapter 5, "Making Accommodations for Disabled Employees."

Almost as significant as what the law requires is what it does not require. The ADA does not require affirmative action plans, preferential treatment of disabled job applicants and employees, or expensive accommodations or modifications of current workplaces. Nor does the law require new recordkeeping or governmental reporting requirements. Furthermore, the Act does not require the hiring or retention of unqualified individuals, and it does not provide an excuse for poorly performing or disruptive employees. Once necessary and reasonable accommodations are provided, the ADA provides that disabled workers be treated just like nondisabled workers.

Effective Dates and Coverage

Effective July 26, 1992, the ADA employment law provisions apply to private employers of 25 or more employees, all city and state governments, employment agencies, labor organizations, and joint labor-management committees. On July 26, 1994, coverage is extended to private employers with 15 to 24 employees. An employer is covered if the requisite number of employees are employed for at least 20 weeks in the current or preceding calendar year. The rules for counting the number of employees follow the requirements of Title VII of the Civil Rights Act of 1964.[6] Once a business is subject to the ADA, all employees come under the protection of the Act, including high ranking management officers. Despite the inclusion of the word "Americans" in the title, the law protects aliens authorized to work in the United States as well as American citizens. Rules concerning renovations and newly built places of employment apply to all employers, no matter how small, and are briefly covered later in this chapter and in Chapter 2, "Major Changes to Conform to the Law." See the end of this chapter for a summary of effective dates for implementation of the ADA.

The Definition of Disabled

A disabled person is one who has a physical or mental impairment that substantially limits a major life activity, a person who has a past record of such an impairment, or a person who is regarded by other people as having such an impairment.[7] This definition matches the definition of a handicapped person under the Federal Rehabilitation Act of 1973. Many state handicapped employment laws also use this definition. The ADA refers to "disabled" people, while the Rehabilitation Act and most state laws use the term "handicapped." The two terms are synonymous.

When the term disabled person is used, most people immediately think of individuals who are blind, deaf, in a wheelchair, or have other serious and obvious medical conditions. These individuals have a condition that easily meets the definition of a physical or mental impairment that substantially limits a major life activity. However, many more people are covered by the definition. Individuals with serious, but nonobvious impairments such as cancer, diabetes, mental illness, AIDS or the HIV virus, and bad backs are legally disabled. Other individuals with physical or mental conditions that may not be obvious, and may be thought by some to be less serious, may be legally disabled, including individuals with mental depression, colon resections, learning disabilities, and sensitivity to cigarette smoke. See Chapter 3, "Determining Who is Disabled," for a detailed discussion as to who is a disabled person, and Chapter 6, "Risk of Future Injury: Epilepsy, Diabetes, and Bad Backs," and Chapter 7, "Aids, Infectious Diseases, Drug and Alcohol Problems, and Weight Problems," for a discussion of some specific medical problems.

The ADA specifically excludes several physical and mental conditions from coverage. The following conditions are not disabilities:[8]

1. Homosexuality, bisexuality, transvestism, transsexualism, pedophilia, exhibitionism, voyeurism, and gender identity disorders, if not caused by a physical impairment.
2. Sexual behavior disorders.
3. Compulsive gambling, kleptomania, pyromania, and psychoactive substance use disorders resulting from the illegal use of drugs.

Drug and Alcohol Use

The ADA specifically excludes current users of illegal drugs from protection as a disabled person.[9] It also amends sections 503 and 504 of the Rehabilitation Act applicable to federal contractors and recipients of federal aid by excluding current users of illegal drugs.[10] The ADA states that "[n]othing in this title shall be construed to encourage, prohibit, or authorize the conducting of drug testing for the illegal use of drugs by job applicants or employees or making employment decisions based upon such test results."[11]

The ADA allows companies to prohibit the illegal use or possession of drugs in the workplace. It also allows employers to demand that employees meet company requirements developed under the Drug-Free Workplace Act of 1988.[12] Furthermore, the ADA specifically permits the Department of Defense, Nuclear Regulatory Commission, and the Department of Transportation to continue issuing and enforcing drug and alcohol regulations for businesses covered by their rules.[13]

Despite the prohibition against coverage for current drug users, the ADA provides protection for individuals who are past users of illegal drugs. A user of illegal drugs who has successfully completed a rehabilitation program (formal, informal, or even self-imposed) and is no longer using illegal drugs is a person with a history of an impairment and must be considered disabled. Also, any past user of illegal drugs who is currently not using drugs and is participating in a supervised rehabilitation program is a disabled person who is entitled to the protection of the law.[14] Employers are free to use drug testing to insure that such an individual is not continuing to use illegal drugs.

Alcoholism is treated differently. The ADA allows employers to prohibit the use of alcohol in the workplace, and allows employers to discipline or discharge workers if their alcoholism or alcohol consumption creates a safety risk or unsatisfactory performance. However, unlike an individual's use of illegal drugs, alcohol problems created by off-the-job consumption may be the basis of employment decisions only if the problems affect job performance.[15] See Chapter 7, "AIDS, Infectious Diseases, Drug and Alcohol Problems, and Weight Problems."

Qualified Disabled Individuals

Only "qualified" individuals with disabilities are protected by the ADA. A qualified individual with a disability is one who can successfully perform all the essential functions of the job in question, once reasonable accommodations are provided by the employer.[16] Upon furnishing reasonable accommodations, employers should treat disabled employees just like other employees. No additional special treatment is required. If, after accommodation, the employee's job performance would lead to the discharge of a nondisabled worker, then it may lead to the discharge of a disabled worker. If, after reasonable disability leave accommodations, a disabled employee has excessive absenteeism, the employee should be treated just like a nondisabled worker with a similar record.

The most difficult assessment of a disabled person's qualifications may occur in the original hiring process. After allowing for or providing reasonable accommodations, the disabled applicant should compete equally with nondisabled applicants. For example, assume that two people apply for the position of typist. One applicant is visually impaired and needs a $35 magnifier to read the material to be keyed into the word processor. The other applicant is not disabled. The company's job description for typists requires typing or keyboard skills of 60 words per minute (wpm), corrected. A typing test is given in which the disabled applicant is provided an adequate magnifier. The disabled person types 55 wpm and the nondisabled applicant types 80 wpm. The nondisabled applicant should be hired. Even if the disabled applicant types the required minimum of 60 wpm, the nondisabled applicant is still more qualified and should be hired, assuming added speed increases job performance.

Qualifications are more difficult to judge in job positions that do not have specific, numerical standards. Is a blind person able to adequately perform a sales job where new customers are constantly coming into the store? Can a person with cerebral palsy who is in a wheelchair successfully serve as a trial court attorney who must enter various courthouses? Should a person with a history of back problems be employed as a truck driver? In answering these questions, employers must be very careful to avoid stereotypes and misunderstandings.

Many disabled people can perform functions that seem almost impossible. Individuals with the same medical condition often vary in the types of physical actions they can perform. Moreover, many job descriptions unfairly exclude persons with disabilities by listing job duties that are outdated or nonessential. Changes in job testing, job descriptions, and placement—as well as the removal of stereotypes and increased knowledge of legal guidelines—are vital steps in complying with the ADA. See Chapter 2, "Major Changes to Conform to the Law," and Chapter 4, "Determining if a Disabled Person is Qualified," for coverage of this important subject.

Threat to Health and Safety

The ADA states that a qualified disabled individual does not include one whose disability creates a "direct threat to the health or safety of other individuals in the workplace."[17] However, employers must not interpret this language too literally. Court decisions interpreting the Rehabilitation Act and state laws with provisions similar to the ADA show that a person becomes unqualified only if there is a *substantial* risk of *serious* harm to the employee, co-workers, or other people.

The language of the ADA quoted above appears to disqualify a disabled person only if there is a threat of health or safety danger to "other people." However, Equal Employment Opportunity Commission (EEOC) regulations apply the disqualification to people who pose "a significant risk of substantial harm to the health or safety of the individual or others that cannot be eliminated or reduced by reasonable accommodation."[18] This interpretation is consistent with case decisions issued under the Federal Rehabilitation Act. The EEOC regulations also require that "[t]he determination that an individual poses a 'direct threat' shall be based on an individualized assessment of the individual's present ability to safely perform the essential functions of the job," and the assessment must be "based upon a reasonable medical judgment that relies on the most current medical knowledge."[19] Past court decisions covered in Chapter 6, "Risk of Future Injury: Epilepsy, Diabetes, and Bad Backs," and Chapter 7, "AIDS, Infectious Diseases, Drug and Alcohol Problems, and Weight Problems," have found a lack of a sufficient probability of substantial harm in case situations such as a

meatcutter with epilepsy, an elementary schoolteacher with tuberculosis, various people with AIDS, truck drivers and manual
laborers with back problems, and in almost all jobs, people with
diabetes.

The Hiring Process and Testing

The most immediate changes many businesses must make to
conform to the ADA involve the hiring process. The ADA prohibits
employers from asking job applicants disability or health-related
questions. It also prohibits preemployment medical or physical
examinations.[20] Even if a job applicant's disability is obvious, the
law prohibits asking such an applicant about the severity of the
disability. However, job applicants may be asked about their ability
to perform job-related functions.[21] Although these two provisions of
the ADA appear contradictory, they are not.

Job applicants cannot be asked questions such as "Are you
disabled?" or "Are you in good health?" They also cannot be asked to
list any past or present diseases or medical problems. However, if a
disabled applicant applies for a position involving driving a vehicle,
the employer may ask if that individual has a driver's license. If the
job involves lifting 50-pound sacks, the employer may ask if the
applicant can lift 50-pound sacks or give a test to see if the applicant
can lift 50 pounds. The EEOC's interpretive guidance states that
physical agility tests can also be given to job applicants, if the test is
directly related to the skills needed in the job for which an individual
has applied.[22]

Once a tentative offer of employment is made, the employer
may ask health questions and require a medical examination, as long
as all tentatively hired employees are treated the same and the
resulting information is kept confidential.[23] However, the information gathered in asking health questions or giving physical exams to
tentatively hired employees cannot be used to disqualify a person
unless the reason for disqualification is job-related and based upon a
business necessity.[24]

Physical or medical exams, medical questions, and medical
history questions may be given to current employees only as part of a
wellness program or other employee health program,[25] if participation is voluntary. Physical or mental testing may also be required if
an employer has reasonable doubt about an employee's current

ability to perform job duties because of changing health conditions. See Chapter 2, "Major Changes to Conform to the Law," and Chapter 4, "Determining if a Disabled Person is Qualified," for additional information.

Reasonable Accommodations

The ADA requires employers to make "reasonable accommodations to the known physical or mental impairments of an otherwise qualified, disabled job applicant or employee," unless the employer can prove the accommodation would create an "undue hardship" on the business.[26]

Examples of possible accommodations listed in the ADA include making existing facilities accessible to a disabled applicant or employee, job restructuring, part-time or modified work schedules, reassignment of an employee to a vacant position, adjustment of testing and training materials, purchase of devices to accommodate a person's disability, or the provision of qualified readers or interpreters.[27] Thousands of additional accommodations exist, many of which are inexpensive or free. See Chapter 5, "Making Accommodations for Disabled Employees," and Part II for additional information and examples of reasonable accommodations.

No employer is required to furnish an accommodation that creates an undue hardship. The ADA defines an undue hardship as an action requiring significant difficulty or expense, when considered in light of the following:[28]

1. the nature and cost of the accommodation;
2. the overall financial resources of the specific facility where the accommodation is considered, including a consideration of the number of employees at the job site and the effect of the accommodation on the expenses and resources of the company facility;
3. the overall financial resources of the company, including the total size of the parent company, the number of employees, and type of company; and
4. the type of operations of the business, including the business's structure, administrative organization, geographic separateness, and fiscal relationship of the facility to the entire company.

Although the Federal Rehabilitation Act of 1973 and many state laws have required accommodations unless they create an undue hardship, there is little case precedent or regulatory guidance available to distinguish required accommodations from those that create an undue hardship. Congress refused to place a specific ceiling on accommodation costs. In fact, it rejected an amendment that would have limited the cost of reasonable accommodations to 10 percent of the employee's annual salary. What is—and is not—an undue hardship will have to be determined on a case-by-case basis. See Chapter 5, "Making Accommodations for Disabled Employees," for a more detailed discussion of accommodations and undue hardship.

Fringe Benefits

The ADA's prohibition against discrimination includes the requirement that employers provide disabled workers with the same fringe benefits as other employees. The provisions of a company pension plan, health insurance, disability benefits, life insurance, sick leave, and other benefits must apply equally to disabled and nondisabled employees. Employers are also prohibited from changing the availability or type of fringe benefits because of a disability of a member of an employee's family.[29]

The prohibition against discrimination in fringe benefits does not require an employer to extend a full range of benefits to all employees. The ADA simply requires that any fringe benefits the employer provides must be offered equally to all employees, disabled or not. Additionally, the law does not require that all medical conditions be covered in health, life, disability, or other benefit plans. Employers and insurance companies continue to be free to exclude certain illnesses, causes of death, or types of coverage, if consistent with insurance underwriting practices and applied consistently to all employees.[30] For example, the ADA permits employee health insurance coverage that excludes preexisting conditions (medical conditions that arise before the employee is hired), as well as policies that exclude certain types of claims such as psychological counseling or alcoholism.

The ADA does prohibit different benefits for disabled employees. For example, a new employee who is diagnosed as having diabetes prior to the start of employment cannot be denied the same insurance coverage given to other employees. However, if the insurance plan denies coverage for preexisting medical problems, the new employee's medical expenses for diabetes are not covered. If the diabetic employee later has medical claims based upon cancer that was diagnosed after the beginning of employment, the employee's cancer-related claims should be covered, assuming cancer is not excluded from policy coverage.

If a company's health or disability benefit plan excludes coverage of mental health treatment, an employee who develops problems requiring such medical treatment will not be covered by the employer's benefit plan. However, an employee with mental problems cannot be denied the same benefits coverage as nondisabled employees. Therefore, the employee can collect payments for any physical health claims covered by the insurance policy such as cancer, heart attack, and accidental injury.

Workers' Compensation

In an attempt to control workers' compensation claims, many companies ask about past workers' compensation claims on job application forms or in interviews. Others have used the services of firms that specialize in checking on job applicants' past claims. The ADA appears to prohibit these acts as an illegal preemployment health inquiry.[31] Interpretive guidance issued as an appendix to the EEOC's regulations states that an employer cannot "inquire at the preoffer stage about an applicant's workers' compensation history."[32]

Employers have also declined to hire applicants with certain types of disabilities upon the grounds that another accident may cause a large workers' compensation claim. For example, an applicant who is blind in one eye may be denied a job because the company is concerned that an accident to the other eye may produce a workers' compensation claim based upon total blindness—a costly claim. This practice constitutes illegal discrimination under the ADA. Increased costs of workers' compensation, health insurance, or other insurance such as disability, cannot be used as a reason to discriminate against a disabled job applicant or employee.[33]

Fortunately, there is a method available in all states to reduce the costs incurred where an on-the-job accident or job-related illness aggravates a preexisting medical problem. State programs, usually referred to as a "second injury fund," limit workers' compensation insurance payments to the amount that would have been payable without the preexisting medical problem. For instance, if a new worker is blind in one eye and later suffers blindness in the remaining good eye because of an on-the-job injury, the employer or employer's insurance company need pay only the compensation required for the loss of one eye, not both.

Regulations concerning second injury funds vary from state to state. In some states, an employer must notify a state agency when hiring or retaining a worker with a preexisting injury. In other states, the company only has to note the preexisting injury on company records, while in a few states no recordkeeping or reporting is required—the second injury fund automatically applies to all employees with preexisting disabilities. Employers should check with the state workers' compensation commission or their workers' compensation insurance carrier for additional information.

Physical Facilities

Modification of an employer's current work sites to make the premises accessible to disabled employees is not required unless it is a reasonable accommodation for a specific disabled employee or group of employees. As with other accommodations, physical changes in accessibility to accommodate a disabled individual need not be undertaken if such changes create an undue hardship. However, current facilities that are used by customers or clients must be made accessible if the changes are "readily achievable."[34] Readily achievable changes include only those changes that can be carried out without much difficulty or expense where the cost of change may be recouped by the increased business resulting from attracting disabled customers or clients.[35]

All "commercial facilities," that are renovated or newly built are subject to much stricter physical accessibility requirements. The term "commercial facilities" includes all places of employment, retail and service businesses, and professional offices, as well as any section of any facility that employees, customers, or clients are expected to use. This provision applies to all employers, not just those with 15 or more employees.[36]

Renovations

Renovations to physical facilities begun after January 26, 1992, must be made "in such a manner that, to the maximum extent feasible, the altered portions of the facility are readily accessible to and usable by individuals with disabilities, including individuals who use wheelchairs."[37]

New Buildings

Newly built facilities designed for first occupancy after January 26, 1993, must be fully accessible to disabled people, including those using wheelchairs, unless it is structurally impractical to do so.[38] Both renovations to existing facilities and newly built structures will be required to meet regulations issued by the United States Attorney General's Office. These regulations parallel previous regulations issued by the United States Architectural and Transportation Barriers Compliance Board applicable to federal and federally funded buildings.[39] See Chapter 2, "Major Changes to Conform to the Law," for additional information concerning the accessibility of commercial facilities.

Regulations and Enforcement

Employment-related regulations contained in Title I of the ADA are issued by the Equal Employment Opportunity Commission (EEOC). Both the EEOC and individuals can bring lawsuits to enforce the law, following the same rules promulgated under Title VII of the Civil Rights Act of 1964.[40] See Chapter 9, "Legal Enforcement Procedures," for more detailed information.

Claims of violation of the physical accessibility rule for renovated and new structures may be brought by individuals.[41] Additionally, the United States Attorney General may conduct compliance reviews, which include certification that state or local building codes comply with the ADA,[42] and institute lawsuits for violation of the physical accessibility standards.[43] The courts may issue injunctions requiring building modifications, the adoption of auxiliary aids or new company policies. In addition, the courts may award monetary damages and a civil penalty of up to $50,000 for a first violation and $100,000 for subsequent violations. Punitive damages are not allowed.[44]

Additional ADA Employment Law Provisions

Religious Organizations

Religious organizations are allowed to give preference to individuals of their particular religion, even if this practice results in denying a job to a disabled person.[45] These organizations may also require all job applicants and employees to conform to the religious tenets of their faith.[46]

Posting Notice

All employers subject to the ADA and all employment agencies, labor organizations, and joint labor-management committees must post notices in an accessible format likely to be seen by job applicants, employees, and members.[47] Failure to do so may subject the organization to an almost limitless time period in which a disabled person can file a lawsuit. The new Consolidated EEO Poster that meets the requirements of the ADA is available from the EEOC, 1801 L Street, NW, Washington, DC 20507, phone (202) 663-4900 or (800) USA-EEOC.

Retaliation

Individuals who file complaints or lawsuits under the ADA, as well as any persons who testify, assist, or participate in any investigation or lawsuit charging a violation of the ADA, are legally protected. An employer cannot discriminate, interfere, coerce, or intimidate any such person.[48]

Alternative Dispute Methods Encouraged

Alternative methods to settle disputes under the ADA are specifically encouraged, including negotiations, conciliation, mediation, minitrials, and arbitration.[49]

PRACTICAL TIPS

Sources of General Information About the ADA

1. BNA's Americans with Disabilities Act Manual, 1231 25th St., NW, Washington, DC 20037-1165, phone (202) 452-4200.

2. President's Committee on the Employment of People with Disabilities, 1111 20th Street, NW, Washington, DC 20037, phone (202) 376–6200.
3. Equal Employment Opportunity Commission, Public Information Office, 1801 L Street, NW, Washington, DC 20507, phone (202) 663-4900 or (800) 669–EEOC. When using the toll free number, dial 2 after the recorded voice begins speaking if you desire to speak to a person, rather than hearing a lengthy prerecorded program.
4. Department of Justice, Civil Rights Division, 320 First Street, NW, Washington, DC 20530. Phone the ADA Information Line at (202) 514-0301.
5. Clearinghouse on Disability Information, Program Information and Coordination Staff, U.S. Department of Education, Room 3132, Switzer Building, Washington, DC 20202, phone (202) 732-1723.
6. National Center on Employment and Disability, Industry-Labor Council, 201 I.U. Willets Road West, Albertson, NY 11507, phone (516) 747-5400.
7. Institute for Rehabilitation and Disability Management, Washington Business Group on Health, 777 North Capitol Street, NE, Suite 800, Washington, DC 20002, phone (202) 408-9320.
8. National Easter Seal Society, 70 East Lake Street, Chicago, IL 60601, phone (312) 726-6200.

Employer Problems Under the ADA

Although business problems in compliance with any new law are to be expected, the ADA and the regulations and interpretive guidance issued under the authority of the ADA on July 26, 1991 create some special problems.

1. **Employers are restricted from informing co-workers or unions of accommodations made for a disabled employee.** The ADA's confidentiality requirement concerning an individual's medical information and disability allows only three exceptions under which others may be told of a disability: supervisors and managers who need to know in order to make accommodations, first aid and safety personnel, and government officials investigating compliance with the ADA.[50] EEOC interpretive guidance states that the collection and disclosure of information under state workers' compensation laws are also allowed.[51] This exception should allow disclosure

of employees' preexisting medical conditions to use a state second injury fund. However, two major groups are not exempted from the confidentiality requirement: co-workers and unions.

When an individual's disability is not obvious, such as in diabetes, many cancers, bad backs and numerous other conditions, co-worker knowledge of the disability may be vital in obtaining cooperation in making accommodations. For example, many accommodations involve trading some nonessential duties between the disabled worker and nondisabled workers. However, no provision has been made for informing co-workers of an employee's disability to implement these accommodations.

Even when accommodations do not directly involve other workers, they can cause an appearance of unfairness, leading to worker dissatisfaction, discrimination claims, and union problems. For example, assume a newly hired 30-year-old disabled warehouse worker is restricted from loading dock duties as a reasonable accommodation for a back problem. Loading dock duties continue to be performed by other employees of greater seniority and the duty is considered to be more unpleasant than inside duties. The other employees become upset with the apparent favoritism shown the new worker. Even worse, an employee over the age of 40 alleges age discrimination, or even files a discrimination charge or lawsuit. Changing job duties, even nonessential ones, may also cause serious and more immediate problems under the terms of a collective bargaining agreement.

The following steps should offer a partial or full remedy to the problems discussed above:

a. EEOC regulations or enforcement guidance may be changed in the future to allow co-workers to be informed of the reason for changes in job duties because of an individual's disability.

b. The employer may provide an employee education program on the ADA before such problems arise. The law should be explained, and employees should be specifically told that under the law the company will occasionally make reasonable accommodations, including modifications of job duties, without being able to explain why they have done so.

c. Disabled employees may be encouraged to voluntarily inform co-workers of their disability and the fact that changes in job duties are a result of a reasonable accommodation. However, be careful not to require or pressure a disabled employee to disclose his or her disability. This practice violates the ADA. Simply explain to the disabled employee the personal advantages of informing co-workers (avoiding the appearance of favoritism and helping make the accommodations workable) and suggest that he or she voluntarily inform co-workers of the need for accommodations.

d. When co-worker cooperation must be obtained as a reasonable accommodation, such as switching of job duties, inform the relevant co-workers that they are being asked to switch duties to provide other aid as a reasonable accommodation for a disabled worker, without disclosing the exact disability. Although the ADA and EEOC regulations do not state that this type of limited disclosure can be made, informing co-workers whose cooperation is vital in making an accommodation work is simply compliance with the legal duty of providing a reasonable accommodation. Asking the disabled employee to sign a written statement agreeing to inform relevant co-workers and promising not to charge a violation of the ADA (a legal release) may be helpful in ensuring the disabled person has been informed of the action and agrees with it. However, the release may not be legally binding.

e. New collective bargaining agreements should provide for the right to make reasonable accommodations under the ADA, even if this otherwise violates provisions of the contract. Unions as well as employers are subject to the ADA.

2. **Except for government contractors taking affirmative action under section 503 of the Rehabilitation Act, employers may not ask job applicants to voluntarily identify their disabilities and request accommodations.**[52] Progressive companies may wish to establish a program to actively recruit disabled workers and take special measures to work out necessary accommodations. However, this recruitment cannot be done if disabled people cannot be identified as a target group for recruiting and hiring. The following steps may be useful in an outreach program to the disabled community without violating the ADA:

a. Give prominence to notices that the employer desires to hire, accommodate, and promote disabled individuals. This notice should appear in job advertisements, notices to employment agencies, job application forms, and other communications.

    b. Recruit potential new workers by contacting local disability organizations such as local branches of the American Cancer Society, American Diabetes Association, and the Disabled American Veterans. Contact governmental agencies such as local vocational rehabilitation agencies or job placement specialists at Veterans Administration facilities.

    c. Immediately upon hiring an individual, ask each new employee if they desire to voluntarily disclose a disability and ask for a reasonable accommodation. A form that may be used for this purpose appears at the end of Chapter 8, "Company Policies and Forms."

    3. **The difference between a reasonable accommodation that must be provided and an accommodation that creates an undue hardship is not clearly defined.** Although past case decisions, EEOC regulations, and interpretive guidance provide some factors to consider in deciding when an accommodation becomes an undue hardship, much of this area of the law will have to be determined on a case-by-case basis. Until additional information becomes available in the form of case decisions under the ADA and future EEOC regulations or guidance, employers should err on the side of providing accommodations, rather than refusing to provide them because of an undue hardship.

    4. **Readily achievable changes required in areas used by customers or clients are not clearly defined.**[53] Although some guidance exists, this term is new and has not appeared in previous laws. Therefore, unlike the undue hardship standard, no case precedent exists for determining what is and is not readily achievable.

    5. **Employers cannot refuse to employ a disabled person because of increased costs of providing workers' compensation, health, or disability insurance, or because insurance coverage is not available.**[54] This issue may appear to be more of a problem than it really is. See the discussion is Chapter 2, "Major Changes to Conform to the Law," showing costs should not increase.

    6. **The effect of the ADA on the emerging trend of charging employees an extra premium if they smoke, drink, have high blood pressure, or have other risk factors that may increase health or disability insurance claims is uncertain.** The ADA prohibits discrimination in all terms and conditions of employment based upon an individual's disability, including discrimination in providing fringe benefits.[55] An employer's program requiring disabled

employees to pay more or receive less coverage, as compared to other employees, is illegal. Therefore, requiring employees to pay a surcharge because they have high blood pressure, a high cholesterol reading, or other medical problems violates the ADA. However, imposing a surcharge based upon employees' acts not related to a disability, such as smoking, should be legal. Imposing such a charge on drinking may violate the ADA as applied to alcoholics because alcoholism is a disability.

Other ADA Provisions

In addition to the employment law provisions covered in this book, the ADA contains major rules governing retail, service, and professional firms; transportation companies; and telecommunications companies. The most significant of these provisions concern the rules governing businesses that serve the public. In addition to the physical accessibility requirements given earlier in this chapter, the ADA requires retailers, service businesses, and professional firms to refrain from discriminating against disabled customers and clients. Furthermore, these businesses and professional firms must take measures to accommodate the needs of disabled customers and clients. See Chapter 2, "Major Changes to Conform to the Law," for additional information.

EFFECTIVE COMPLIANCE DATES
for
EMPLOYERS, PUBLIC ACCOMMODATIONS &
COMMERCIAL FACILITIES

Title I. EMPLOYMENT

Effective Dates:

Employers of 25 or more employees	July 26, 1992
Employers of 15 to 24 employees	July 26, 1994
Employers of 14 or fewer employees	Law Does Not Apply

Title III. PUBLIC ACCOMMODATIONS OPERATED BY PRIVATE ENTITIES

Rules Concerning Customers and Clients

Effective Date:	January 26, 1992

However, smaller companies may be
sued only for acts occurring on or after
the following dates:

Firms with 25 or fewer employees and
annual gross receipts of $1,000,000
or less   July 26, 1992
Firms with 10 or fewer employees and
annual gross receipts of $500,000 or less   January 26, 1993

Renovations of Public Accommodations and Commercial Facilities

Effective Date: Renovation work beginning after January 26, 1992

New Construction of Public Accommodations and Commercial Facilities

Applicable to all construction of facilities designed for any commercial use by any business or professional firm, if:

(1) Final building permit or extension of
    building permit is granted after   January 26, 1992
                    and
(2) First certificate of occupancy occurs
    after   January 26, 1993

Notes

1. Americans with Disabilities Act §102(a), 42 U.S.C.A. §12112 (West 1991).
2. *Id.* at §102(b)(1), 42 U.S.C.A. §12112 (West 1991).
3. *Id.* at §102(b)(2), 42 U.S.C.A. §12112 (West 1991).
4. *Id.* at §102(b)(3), 42 U.S.C.A. §12112 (West 1991).
5. *Id.* at §102(b)(4), 42 U.S.C.A. §12112 (West 1991).
6. *Id.* at §101(5), 42 U.S.C.A. §12111 (West 1991).
7. *Id.* at §2(2), 42 U.S.C.A. §12101 (West 1991).
8. *Id.* at §511, 42 U.S.C.A. §12211 (West 1991).
9. *Id.* at §104, 42 U.S.C.A. §§12114, 12210 (West 1991).
10. *Id.* at §512, 42 U.S.C.A. §12111 (West 1991).
11. *Id.* at §104(d)(1), 42 U.S.C.A. §12114 (West 1991).
12. 41 U.S.C. §§701 et seq.
13. Americans with Disabilities Act §104(c)(5), 42 U.S.C.A. §12114 (West, 1991).
14. *Id.* at §104(b), 42 U.S.C.A. §12114 (West 1991).
15. *Id.* at §104(c), 42 U.S.C.A. §12114 (West 1991).
16. *Id.* at §101(8), 42 U.S.C.A. §12111 (West 1991).
17. *Id.* at §103(b), 42 U.S.C.A. §12113 (West 1991).
18. EEOC Regulations on the Americans with Disabilities Act, 56 Fed. Reg. 35,736 (1991) (to be codified at 29 C.F.R. §1630.2(r)).
19. *Id.*

20. Americans with Disabilities Act, §102(c)(2)(A), 42 U.S.C.A. §12112 (West 1991).
21. *Id.* at §102(c)(2)(B), 42 U.S.C.A. §12112 (West 1991).
22. EEOC Interpretive Guidance on Title I of the Americans with Disabilities Act, 56 Fed. Reg. 35,750 (1991).
23. Americans with Disabilities Act, §102(c)(3), 42 U.S.C.A. §12112 (West 1991).
24. *Id.* at §102(c)(4)(A), 42 U.S.C.A. §12112 (West 1991).
25. *Id.* at §102(c)(4)(B), 42 U.S.C.A. §12112 (West 1991).
26. *Id.* at §102(b)(5)(A), 42 U.S.C.A. §12112 (West 1991).
27. *Id.* at §101(9), 42 U.S.C.A. §12111 (West 1991).
28. *Id.* at §102(b)(1), 42 U.S.C.A. §12111 (West 1991).
29. *Id.* at §102, 42 U.S.C.A. §12112 (West 1991).
30. *Id.* at §501(c), 42 U.S.C.A. §12201 (West 1991).
31. *See id.* at §42 U.S.C.A. §12112 (West 1991).
32. EEOC Interpretive Guidance on Title I of the Americans with Disabilities Act, 56 Fed. Reg. 35,750 (1991).
33. *See id.* at 35,751. *See also* S. Rep. No. 116, 101st Cong., 1st Sess., 85.
34. Americans with Disabilities Act, §301(9), 42 U.S.C.A. §12181 (West 1991).
35. H.R. Rep. Nos. 101-485, 101st Cong., 2d Sess., pt. 4, at 56–57 (1990).
36. *Id.* at §301(2), 42 U.S.C.A. §12181 (West 1991).
37. *Id.* at §303(a)(2), 42 U.S.C.A. §12183 (West 1991).
38. *Id.* at §303(a)(1), 42 U.S.C.A. §12183 (West 1991).
39. Minimum Guidelines and Requirements for Accessible Design (MGRAD), 36 C.F.R. Part 1190.
40. Americans with Disabilities Act, §107, 42 U.S.C.A. §12117 (West 1991).
41. *Id.* at §308(a), 42 U.S.C.A. §12188 (West 1991).
42. *Id.* at §308(b), 42 U.S.C.A. §12188 (West 1991).
43. *Id.* at §308(b)(1)(B), 42 U.S.C.A. §12188 (West 1991).
44. *Supra* note 40.
45. Americans with Disabilities Act, §103(c)(1), 42 U.S.C.A. §12113 (West 1991).
46. *Id.* at §103(c)(2), 42 U.S.C.A. §12113 (West 1991).
47. *Id.* at §105, 42 U.S.C.A. §12115 (West 1991).
48. *Id.* at §503, 42 U.S.C.A. §12203 (West 1991).
49. *Id.* at §513, 42 U.S.C.A. §12212 (West 1991).
50. EEOC Regulations on the Americans with Disabilities Act, 56 Fed. Reg. 35,736 (1991) (to be codified at 29 C.F.R. §1630.2(r)).
51. EEOC Interpretive Guidance on Title I of the Americans with Disabilities Act, 56 Fed. Reg. 35,751 (1991).
52. *Id.* at 35,750.
53. Department of Justice Regulations on the Americans with Disabilities Act, 56 Fed. Reg. 35,597 (1991) (to be codified at 28 C.F.R. §36.304).
54. See the Americans with Disabilities Act, §102, 42 U.S.C.A. §12112 (West 1991); EEOC Regulations on the Americans with Disabilities Act, 56 Fed. Reg. 35,736 (1991) (to be codified at 29 C.F.R. §1630.4).
55. *Id.*

Chapter 2

Major Changes to Conform to the Law

Three major areas of change businesses must undertake to conform to the Americans with Disabilities Act (ADA) are (1) developing a new understanding about disabled people, (2) reforming the hiring process, and (3) meeting the ADA's physical accessibility rules, especially when making major renovations or constructing new buildings.

Understanding Disabilities and Disabled Workers

Many disabled people say that the largest barriers to employment are the myths and false information that most people have about disabilities and disabled individuals. Therefore, the first step a business must take to effectively comply with the ADA is to increase management's understanding of the capabilities of disabled workers and to remove the common myths concerning disabled persons.[1]

Myth #1. Disabled employees are less productive than nondisabled employees. Ninety-one percent of disabled workers are rated average or above average by their employers.

Myth #2. Disabled employees have higher than average absenteeism. A survey by the United States Office of Vocational Rehabilitation confirms the findings of other researchers. Compared to nondisabled employees, 55 percent of disabled workers have a better than average attendance record, while only 5 percent have worse than average attendance.

Myth #3. Disabled employees have high job turnover rates. The study cited above shows that 88 percent of disabled workers have a lower than average turnover rate. Because job turnover expenses are costly, this statistic illustrates a key reason to actively recruit disabled job applicants.

Myth #4. Disabled employees create a safety risk. The Office of Vocational Rehabilitation survey found that 57 percent of disabled workers have better than average safety records, while only 2 percent are worse than average.

Myth #5. Insurance rates will skyrocket if disabled employees are hired. A United States Chamber of Commerce study of 279 companies found that 90 percent of the companies incurred no increased insurance expenses because of hiring disabled workers. In fact, insurance costs may be less. Because disabled employees have higher than average safety records they will cause fewer on-the-job accidents—leading to a possible reduction in workers' compensation claims and negligence lawsuits by customers or other outsiders. Many seriously disabled people such as those who are blind, deaf, or paralyzed are in stable condition and will not use medical insurance or disability leave benefits any more than nondisabled workers. Workers' compensation second injury funds, and, if necessary, limitations or exclusion of preexisting conditions in company health insurance, may be used to insure that no added costs are incurred by hiring disabled workers.

Myth #6. Co-workers' attitudes make effective placement of a disabled employee impractical. Although fear, misunderstanding, and resentment may occur if a disabled worker is arbitrarily injected into the work force without proper education of co-workers, most co-workers will accept, understand, and even help disabled employees if they are educated as to the facts of the disability and the need for reasonable accommodations. However, because of the ADA's prohibition against disclosing a worker's disability, educational efforts should not be in reference to specific disabled individuals, but rather an overall program explaining the law and the need to accommodate disabled employees. Even if there is co-worker dissatisfaction, the law does not allow co-worker (or customer) preference to be used to make employment decisions. In other words, employee resistance is not an excuse for failure to comply with the law. It is the employer's obligation to educate co-workers and obtain their acceptance of the disabled person.

Myth #7. Disabled employees are too demanding. Secretly and sometimes subconsciously, managers may avoid hiring disabled people because they feel that the worker may have a bad attitude and may demand too many special favors. Although some disabled people may make unreasonable demands, some nondisabled employees also make unreasonable demands. There is no evidence that disabled workers have different attitudes than nondisabled employees.

Myth #8. Placing disabled employees in positions that deal with the public will be an embarrassment to the company. The opposite is probably true. Changing public attitudes show that most customers and clients will look with favor upon companies hiring and accommodating disabled workers. In particular, the tens of millions of disabled Americans who are potential customers and clients will favor companies who actively hire and accommodate disabled workers. Several companies such as McDonald's, IBM, and DuPont have recognized this advantage and advertised their use of disabled workers.

Myth #9. Making accommodations for disabled workers is too expensive. According to a 1987 Harris Poll, 74 percent of top management respondents reported that accommodations for disabled workers were not expensive.[2] The Job Accommodation Network's 1986 statistics on the thousands of accommodations in their files reveal that 31 percent involve no cost (moving office furniture, adjusting work schedule, etc.), 38 percent cost between $1 and $500, while another 19 percent cost between $500 and $1,000. Only 12 percent cost over $1,000.[3] See Chapter 5, "Making Accommodations for Disabled Employees," and Part II for additional examples of accommodations and their costs.

Who Are the Disabled

Some disabilities are severe, creating a substantial mental or physical impairment that has a major effect on day-to-day living and employment (e.g., blindness, deafness, and extreme cases of cerebral palsy or paralysis). Other disabilities may cause moderate impairments and fewer work-related problems (e.g., typical cases of diabetes, epilepsy, or arthritis). Disabilities may also be classified as obvious (wheelchair user, amputee, etc.) or hidden (digestive disease, heart problems, diabetes, etc.).

However, all employment decisions—including hiring, placement, performance evaluations, and pay—should be based upon the individual and his or her capabilities, rather than the type or classification of disability. As is true in the general population, disabled people vary greatly in personality, intelligence, ability, work performance, and skill.

Each person's physical or mental impairment is different, even if the medical diagnosis is the same. Therefore, employers should not think in terms of classes of people such as diabetics, epileptics, or crippled people, but rather should treat each disabled person as an individual. When the disability must be considered, such as when determining reasonable accommodations, the employer should think of the person as *an individual* with diabetes, *an employee* with epilepsy, or *a person* with a mobility impairment.

Each individual with diabetes will have different symptoms and different problems than other individuals with diabetes. Each person with epilepsy will have different strengths and weaknesses. Even people in wheelchairs must not be grouped together as a class because their physical skills differ. For example, some people in wheelchairs are experts in maneuvering them. Others never become skilled in handling the wheelchair. Dozens of different wheelchairs are used. Some are narrow, others are too wide to fit into small door openings. Some are electric, others are not. Some allow the paralyzed user to stand up, most do not. Some people who use wheelchairs can leave the wheelchair and walk short distances, others are unable to move from the chair to bed without help.

Disabled people are simply individuals. Each will bring different skills and imperfections to the workplace, just as all employees do. Except for the segregation imposed upon them by lack of accessibility, and sometimes a lack of equal education and equal opportunity, they are the same as anyone else. They are not courageous for having "overcome" their disabilities—they had no choice. Different treatment, whether favorable or unfavorable, is discrimination. The only special treatment that disabled employees should receive is the provision of reasonable accommodations, if necessary.

However, offering reasonable accommodations is not really special treatment. Businesses often offer accommodations for employees. For example, women's restrooms were provided when females were first hired into workplaces that were previously male only. Special provisions for Spanish-speaking employees have been made. Extra education and job training have been provided to

disadvantaged workers. Unpaid leave and job protection were given
to reservists who were called to active duty during the Persian Gulf
war. All these actions were reasonable accommodations.

A final word about who is disabled. When the subject of disabled persons in employment arises, most managers think in terms
of hiring disabled people. However, it is more likely that the majority of disabled workers will become disabled after they are
employed. On- and off-the-job accidents, diabetes, heart conditions, and other disabilities are most likely to occur when one is an
adult and already employed. Therefore, employers should not limit
consideration of disabilities only when hiring workers. Effective
management dictates that employers identify current employees
who are disabled so that reasonable accommodations can be given to
allow those employees to work at peak efficiency. See Chapter 10,
"Managing Disabilities," for a discussion of a disability management
program for identifying and handling disabled employees.

Disabled Adults: An Untapped Pool of Workers

Although most employees become disabled after being hired,
companies may find disabled job seekers to be an excellent source of
new employees. Partly because of the myths listed above, millions
of disabled Americans who desire to work—and who can work
effectively—are unemployed. While 78.5 percent of nondisabled,
working-age adults are in the labor force, only 33.6 percent of
disabled adults are employed.[4] Additionally, only 19.7 percent of
severely impaired American adults are employed full-time, while
59.4 percent of nondisabled adults are so employed.[5]

A 1987 survey of 280 members of the United Handicapped
Federation found that 83 percent of the unemployed disabled people wanted to work, but 53 percent were unemployed and another
21 percent worked only part-time. As a result, only 63 of the 127
working respondents had incomes greater than $5,000.[6] A 1987
Bureau of the Census report found that disabled employees had a
median income of $6,434, compared to $13,403 for nondisabled
workers.[7]

The 1987 Harris Poll referenced above found that although the
great majority of employers who employed disabled workers rated
the disabled employees' job performance as good or excellent,
virtually none of the employers reported disabled workers do poor
work. Nevertheless, this experience with disabled employees has
not resulted in the widespread hiring of disabled workers.[8] Not

surprisingly, the survey found that large employers with 10,000 or more employees are the most likely to hire disabled employees. The key barriers to the employment of disabled people were found to be the lack of company policies on hiring disabled persons and the lack of company programs to recruit and train disabled job applicants.

Changing the Hiring Process

For many employers, the most important and immediate change that must be made to comply with the ADA is a revision in the procedures used in interviewing, testing, and hiring new employees.

Identifying Disabilities of Applicants

Employers are prohibited from asking job applicants health or disability questions or requiring medical examinations. The law also prohibits preemployment questions about the nature and extent of the person's disability, even if the impairment is obvious.[9] However, applicants can be asked about their ability to perform job-related functions.[10]

Questions or requests for information from job applicants such as the following are illegal:

1. Are you handicapped? Do you have a disability?
2. Have you seen a physician or received medical treatment in the past five years?
3. Do you have any of the following conditions: diabetes, heart problems, hypertension, etc.?
4. Do you have any physical or mental problems that limit your ability to do the job?
5. Have you ever made a claim for workers' compensation?

Whether employers should be allowed to obtain information concerning an applicant's past workers' compensation claims is a controversial area under the ADA. The EEOC did not address the issue in its final regulations issued in 1991. However, in an interpretive guidance appendix to those regulations, the EEOC states that employers cannot "inquire at the preoffer stage about an applicant's workers' compensation history."[11] This interpretation appears to be consistent with the ADA's prohibition against asking health- and disability-related questions before hiring. Obtaining such information from firms who specialize in keeping workers' compensation records results in acquisition of the same information an employer might obtain by asking job applicants. Therefore, pending any changes in future regulations, employers should not obtain workers' compensation claim information from any source.

Asking job applicants to volunteer information concerning their disabilities and needed accommodations is not allowed under EEOC regulations and interpretive guidance, except in two situations:

1. Government contractors taking affirmative action to hire and accommodate disabled people under section 503 of the Rehabilitation Act of 1973 may ask job applicants to voluntarily identify themselves as disabled so that reasonable accommodations can be considered.[12] See Chapter 8, "Company Policies and Forms," for a form that can be used by government contractors.
2. Employers who will conduct testing of job applicants may ask applicants to request any necessary accommodations needed to take the tests.[13] This inquiry can be made orally, in a written announcement, or as part of a job application form.

Upon learning of an applicant's disability, an employer is prohibited from asking questions about the extent of the disability, how the person became disabled, when the disability occurred, whether it will cause absences from work, the extent of physical or mental limitations created, and other similar questions. However, there is one exception; the employer may ask about and discuss reasonable job accommodations.

Questions and discussions concerning possible accommodations must be approached in a positive, problem-solving manner. For example, "Do we have to give an accommodation?" is inappropriate. Rather, "Is there anything we can do to accommodate your problem?" is an acceptable means of inquiry. An even better question is, "What modifications might help you effectively perform the job?"

Determining if an Applicant is Qualified

Both disabled and nondisabled applicants can be asked about their ability to perform essential functions of the job for which they have applied.[14] For example, applicants for a job that involves driving an automobile may be asked if they have a driver's license (but not whether they have a visual impairment). People applying for a job that involves heavy lifting may be asked if they can lift 75 pounds, if the lifting of 75 pounds is an essential part of the job (but not whether they have a back problem). Applicants for a word processing job that requires typing 60 words per minute may be asked if they can type at that speed (but not whether they have a physical problem that limits their typing ability). Applicants can also be asked if they can meet the employer's stated job attendance policy (but not whether any health condition will cause attendance problems).

An employer may also ask a job applicant to describe or demonstrate how, with or without reasonable accommodation, the applicant will be able to perform job-related functions. The EEOC interpretive guidance states that the question may be asked of all applicants, or individually to a person with a known disability, even if other applicants are not asked.[15]

The EEOC's interpretive guidance also provides that applicants may be given a job-related physical agility test.[16] For example, applicants for a position that requires difficult assembly of minute electrical parts onto a circuit board may be given a test to see if they can perform the work. In the alternative, the employer may explain the job tasks and ask the applicants how they will perform the work. A fire department can require job applicants to undergo a realistic test concerning climbing ladders, handling equipment, and performing other essential tasks required of a firefighter. Other job-related tests are permissible, assuming a reasonable accommodation is given to allow a disabled person to take the exam. See Chapter 4, "Determining if a Disabled Person is Qualified," for more detail on conducting valid prehire testing.

Health and Medical Information

Medical or physical exams, health questionnaires, and other health-related data may be obtained only after a tentative offer of employment is made and certain conditions are met.[17] This requirement demands that employers choose applicants without regard to their health or disability. But it does not mean employees must begin work if they have job-related impairments. Employers who desire to ask health questions or require a medical exam simply do so after a tentative offer is made, and before actual work begins.

The tentative hiring decision can be made conditional upon meeting valid medical requirements.[18] An applicant may be informed in advance that a job offer is tentative and may be withdrawn if the posthiring questions or medical exam disclose job-related problems that make the applicant unqualified, even with reasonable accommodations.[19] Chapter 8, "Company Policies and Forms," gives a format for announcing this requirement on a job application form. It may also be stated orally.

To give a medical examination, ask health-related questions, or take a medical history, the following conditions must be met:[20]

1. The exam must be given only after a tentative offer of employment is extended.
2. All newly hired employees in the same job category must be asked the same health questions or given the same type of medical exam—not just those who appear to be disabled.
3. The information obtained from the examination or medical history must be collected and maintained in confidential files, separate from normal personnel files.
4. The information must not be disclosed to anyone other than managers and supervisors who need to know of any work restrictions or accommodations, first aid and safety personnel who need to know in order to render emergency services, government officials who are investigating compliance with the ADA, and workers' compensation offices in accordance with state workers' compensation laws. The latter provision will allow employers to notify workers' compensation agencies when such notice is required in order to gain protection under a workers' compensation second injury fund.

Although the medical examination or health history can be comprehensive, an employer cannot withdraw a tentative offer of employment unless the decision is based upon valid medical evidence that the employee cannot perform the essential functions of the job, after reasonable accommodations are given.[21] For example, while it is permissible for the examination or health history to determine if an individual has diabetes, the employer normally will not be allowed to withdraw an offer of employment based upon this fact. Almost all people with diabetes are able to effectively perform almost all types of jobs. On the other hand, if the physical examination discloses that a new truck driver has a visual impairment that prevents safe driving and that cannot be reasonably accommodated, the tentative offer of employment may be withdrawn. See Chapter 4, "Determining if a Disabled Person is Qualified," and Chapter 6, "Risk of Future Injury: Epilepsy, Diabetes, and Bad Backs," concerning the restrictive rules that apply in denying jobs based on a risk of future injury or health problems.

The ADA also allows periodic voluntary medical exams or health screening of current employees, if such exams are part of an employee health program available to all employees at a work site,[22] and the ADA's confidentiality provisions are followed.[23] Employers may also ask current employees about their ability to perform job-related functions.[24]

PRACTICAL TIPS
Dealing With Health and Disability Information

1. When dealing with job applicants, reserve the right to ask health questions or give a medical examination. See Chapter 8, "Company Policies and Forms," for forms to use.

2. Inform physicians conducting company medical examinations of the ADA's requirements of confidentiality, as well as the legal standards concerning who is qualified. See Chapter 4, "Determining if a Disabled Person is Qualified," Chapter 6, "Risk of Future Injury: Epilepsy, Diabetes, and Bad Backs," and Chapter 7, "AIDS, Infectious Diseases, Drug and Alcohol Problems, and Weight Problems."

3. Ask physicians to refrain from forwarding medical information that is obviously not job related such as abortion records, past cancer, HIV or AIDS findings, sexual history, and other information that cannot be used to withdraw a job offer. In this area, ignorance is a defense. An employer cannot be proven to have discriminated based upon facts the employer did not know.

4. Be sure each withdrawal of a job offer because of information derived from a medical exam or health questionnaire is based upon an *individual* determination of ability to work. See Chapter 4, "Determining if a Disabled Person is Qualified," Chapter 6, "Risk of Future Injury: Epilepsy, Diabetes, and Bad Backs," and Chapter 7, "AIDS, Infectious Diseases, Drug and Alcohol Problems, and Weight Problems."

5. If health or medical records are kept in a computer data base, be sure it is secured by use of a password known only to those authorized under the ADA to be informed of disabilities.

6. If health or medical records are kept in paper files, establish separate files that are locked and can be opened only by those authorized by the ADA to be told of disabilities.

7. Transfer old medical information, including copies of health insurance claims or payments, from existing personnel files into new, secure health and medical files.

8. When conducting wellness programs or other plans requiring company health screening programs, be sure employee participation is voluntary.

9. If an employee is singled out for medical examination, be confident of proving a valid reason for doing so, such as decreased work performance.

Structural Modifications

The ADA imposes rules on physical accessibility of business facilities under three categories: existing facilities, alterations of existing facilities, and new construction. Little change in existing structures may be necessary, but much stricter rules apply when making renovations and building new facilities. The latter categories are governed by Title III of the ADA concerning public accommodations and commercial facilities.[25] While existing facilities are governed by Title I, which applies only to companies with 25 or more workers prior to July 26, 1994, and 15 or more workers thereafter, Title III applies to all employers, retailers, service businesses, and professional firms, regardless of size.

Existing Facilities

Physical modifications of existing workplaces are required only if the changes are a reasonable accommodation to meet the needs of a specific disabled job applicant or employee. Decisions to modify the physical premises should be given the same consideration as other accommodations. Changes that will allow a qualified individual to perform the essential task of the job must be made if they can be accomplished without undue hardship on the employer. See Chapter 5, "Making Accommodations for Disabled Employees," for more information on accommodations and undue hardship.

However, if the work site is used by customers or clients, companies are required to consider modifications to increase accessibility of existing structures and adopt those that are "readily achievable."[26] Modifications are readily achievable if they are easy to accomplish and can be done without much expense. Examples of changes that should be readily achievable include the following:[27]

1. The simple ramping of a few steps to allow use by people in wheelchairs
2. The addition of raised letters and numerals on elevator controls, if there is an elevator
3. Rearrangement of office furniture, shelves, display racks, and equipment to improve access by disabled persons, and to prevent injuries caused by nonobvious protrusions
4. The installation of "grab bars" in rest rooms
5. The rearrangement of furniture in professional offices to allow movement by those in wheelchairs and others with mobility problems
6. The marking of handicapped parking spaces in off-street parking lots furnished for customers or clients
7. Making curb cuts
8. Removing a turnstile or other obstacle to entry

To determine if modifications of existing structures are readily achievable, the overall size and type of business should be balanced with the cost involved in making the changes that will accommodate disabled persons. The Senate Committee on Labor and Human Resources reported that the ADA requirement to modify existing structures should involve only "minimal" expense and businesses should focus on changes where costs can be recouped by increased patronage of customers and clients.[28]

In determining what changes are readily achievable, Department of Justice regulations "urge" that the following priorities for change be used:[29]

First Priority: Measures to provide access to a place of public accommodation from public sidewalks, streets, parking, or public transportation.

Second Priority: Measures to provide access to those areas where goods and services are made available.

Third Priority: Measures to provide access to restroom facilities.

Fourth Priority: Other measures to increase access and use by people with disabilities.

The public accommodations requirements of Section III of the ADA apply to retailers, service providers, professional firms, and others serving customers and clients. The law and regulations are extensive,[30] and beyond the scope of this book. However, the legal rules imposed on employers are covered below.

Access for Job Applicants

Although preexisting work sites need not be altered except as a reasonable accommodation to a known disability of a specific person, the company personnel office, human relations department, or other similar locations used by job seekers to apply, interview, or test for jobs must be accessible.[31] The following guidelines may be helpful in providing access to disabled applicants, including those in wheelchairs.

1. If possible, at least one guest handicapped parking spot should be available that is on level ground, 12 feet wide, leading to access to the company employment office. If the parking space is in a garage, the minimum height should be eight feet, if possible, to allow access by raised-roof vans. If no accessible parking is feasible, there should be a drop-off zone near the entrance to the office.

2. Signs or other markings should direct persons to the nearest accessible entrance.

3. Walkways from the handicapped parking to the entrance to the building should be at least 48 inches wide. Curbs should be cut and sloped with a gradient of no more than eight degrees, with a lip or bump of no more than five-eighths of an inch. Curb cuts should have a textured, nonslip surface.

4. A ramp should be provided on any walking area that rises 12 inches or more in 12 feet of length. Ramps should also be used if there are any steps. Ramps should have at least one handrail, and a nonslip surface (possibly a rubber overlay). Long ramps should have a level surface of 5 feet in length every 30 feet or so. Any door that is near either end of a ramp should be fronted by a level area of at least 5 feet.

5. Doors accessible to disabled people should be prominently marked as handicapped. Each door should give an unencumbered opening of no less than 32 inches. Users should be able to operate the doors by a single effort that does not require the use of more than 12 pounds of pressure. Door sills should be level, or be no higher than five-eighths of an inch.

6. Thick carpeting makes it difficult for people to operate wheelchairs, while smooth floors are sometimes dangerous

to people using crutches or those who have other walking problems. If the path job applicants must take causes either problem, a rubber or nonslip, vinyl walkway overlay should be installed.

7. If a job applicant must use an elevator, be sure it is accessible. It should have a call button and inside controls that are no more than 50 inches from the floor, with an opening into the elevator that is at least 36 inches wide. If modifications of existing elevators are unreasonable, either place the personnel office on the ground floor, or have a person near the elevator who is available to help disabled people.

8. All sections of the human relations department or personnel office that job applicants must use should be examined for accessibility. Are the floor coverings proper? Are the doors at least 32 inches wide? Is the door threshold no more than five-eighths of an inch high?

9. A final check should be made to ensure that appropriate handicapped access signs lead the job seeker to the correct offices.

A simple-to-follow, but more detailed explanation of making premises accessible is the *Revised Manual for Accessibility*, published by the National Rehabilitation Association, 633 South Washington Street, Alexandria, Va. 22314, phone (703) 836-0850.

Partial Renovations

The ADA requires that major structural alterations of the premises of "commercial facilities" (employers, retailers, service businesses, professional firms, or other businesses)[32] that are made to areas to be used by employees, customers, or clients be designed to maximize accessibility by disabled people.[33] This requirement applies to major structural alterations of buildings, walkways, parking lots, sidewalks, and any other part of the premises that might be used by disabled people.

Major structural alterations occur when physical changes or renovations are made that will become a permanent, fixed part of a building or its surroundings. Normally this includes alterations to expand the size of the structure, replace load-bearing walls, build new walls or rooms, create new doorways, or replace floors or ceilings. Renovations of outside walkways, entrances, and parking lots are also covered by this section of the law if they constitute major alterations. Normal maintenance, reroofing, painting, wallpapering, asbestos removal, and changes to mechanical and electrical systems, standing alone, are not considered to be alterations or renovations subject to the accessibility rules.[34]

The law requires that such alterations be done in a "manner that, to the maximum extent feasible," makes the altered portions "readily accessible" to disabled persons.[35] Although the term "feasible" may eliminate the need for very expensive modifications for disabled persons, there is no balancing test of costs versus benefits that is applied for partial renovations. The altered part of a building must include all known, feasible designs and modifications that will materially aid disabled persons in utilizing the altered sections of the premises.

Department of Justice regulations state that an alteration to a part of a facility normally used by customers or clients should, to the maximum extent possible, ensure that the path of travel to the newly renovated area be made accessible for disabled people.[36] For example, if a retail store renovates a back room that will be used by customers, the store must ensure that the path of travel from the entrance of the store (or even from the parking lot, if there is one) to the newly renovated room is accessible to disabled people. However, business and professional firms need not incur disproportionate expenses in altering the path of travel. Department of Justice regulations state that the cost will be considered "disproportionate to the overall alteration when it exceeds 20 percent of the cost of the alteration."[37] Therefore, when complete accessibility alterations to a path of travel exceed 20 percent of the cost of renovation, the ADA requires only partial measures costing 20 percent of renovation costs.

How to Correctly Plan and Construct Partial Renovations

The ADA requirements concerning partial renovations and alterations of commercial facilities apply to renovations and alterations that begin after January 26, 1992.[38] Businesses that use architects to plan building modifications may wish to include a statement similar to the following in their contracts with architects:

> (Name of architect or architectural firm) agrees that all plans and designs submitted under this agreement will conform to the architectural and accessibility regulations issued by the United States Attorney General under the authority of Title III of the Americans with Disabilities Act, and to the current Minimum Guildelines and

Requirements for Accessible Design (MGRAD) issued by the Federal Architectural and Transportation Barriers Compliance Board. In any area of direct conflict with the regulations issued by the Attorney General and the MGRAD, (name of architect or architectural firm) agrees to follow the requirements of the Attorney General.

(Name of architect or architectural firm) agrees to reimburse and indemnify (name of company) for any expenses incurred due to the (name of architect or architectural firm's) failure to follow the architectural regulations and standards listed above, including the costs of making later renovations to structural alterations designed by (name of architect or architectural firm) in order to comply with the Americans with Disabilities Act and the above-mentioned regulations or standards; profits lost due to decreased business during any such later renovations; any and all fines, civil penalties, and damages awarded against (name of company) because of (name of architect or architectural firm's) noncompliance with the Americans with Disabilities Act and the regulations listed above; and all reasonable legal expenses incurred in defending such claims, including reasonable attorneys' fees.

Businesses should have an attorney draft the statement so that it complies with the laws and regulations of the state where the project is located.

New Structures

Any new structure designed for use by employees, customers, or clients where a final building permit or extension of a building permit is certified as complete (granted) after January 26, 1992, *and* the first certificate of occupancy occurs after January 26, 1993, must be designed and constructed so that it is "readily accessible to and usable by individuals with disabilities."[39] This requirement applies to all commercial facilities, including all places of employment, regardless of size. The only exception to this requirement occurs where it is structurally impracticable to meet the requirements of the ADA and the regulations issued by the United States Attorney General.[40]

To be "readily accessible to, and usable by individuals with disabilities," new structures must be designed and constructed so that people with disabilities can get to, enter, and use the facility. The intent of the ADA is to create a high degree of convenient accessibility in parking lots, routes to and from the building, entrances, public use areas within the structure, rest rooms, and water fountains, among other items.[41]

The exemption from the accessibility rules because of structural impracticability is very limited. Congressional committee reports show an intent to limit the exception to cases where it is almost impossible, not just impractical, to make the premises accessible. [42] The fact that a building lot is hilly, small, or has unusual features normally will not justify an exception.

The rules concerning building new places of accommodation and commercial facilities are extensive and very detailed. For additional information concerning these standards, see the Department of Justice regulations on the ADA and the appendix to the regulations, entitled *ADA Accessibility Guidelines for Buildings and Facilities.* [43]

How to Correctly Plan and Construct New Facilities

New commercial facilities must be designed and constructed in conformance with the regulations issued by the United States Attorney General. [44] Local or state building codes may be followed if they have been certified by the Attorney General to meet the ADA's requirements. [45]

Whether an architect is used to design a new structure, or a building contractor is employed to build without professional architectural designs, businesses may include in their contract(s) for the design or construction of a new structure a statement similar to the following:

(Name of architect, architectural firm or contractor) agrees that all plans, designs, and construction submitted or performed under this agreement will conform to the architectural and accessibility regulations issued by the United States Attorney General under the authority of the Americans with Disabilities Act, and the current Minimum Guidelines and Requirements for Accessible Design (MGRAD) issued by the Federal Architectural and Transportation Barriers Compliance Board. In cases of direct conflict with the regulations issued by the United States Attorney General and the MGRAD, (name of architect, architectural firm or contractor) agrees to comply with the regulations issued by the United States Attorney General.

(Name of architect, architectural firm or contractor) agrees to reimburse and indemnify (name of company) for any expenses incurred due to a failure of (name of architect or architectural firm) to follow the architectural regulations and standards listed above, including the costs of making renovations to the structure designed or constructed by (name of architect or architectural firm) in order to comply with the Americans with Disabilities Act and the above-mentioned regulations and standards; profits lost due to decreased business during any such renovations; and all fines, civil penalties, and damages awarded against (name of company) because of (name of architect or architectural firm's) noncompliance with the Americans with Disabilities Act and the regulations issued thereunder; and all reasonable legal expenses incurred in defending such claims, including reasonable attorneys' fees.

Businesses should have an attorney draft the statement so that it complies with the laws and regulations of the state where the project is located. The attorney may desire to add language concerning relevant state or city legal requirements.

Rental or Lease of Structures

Several difficult problems arise when modifications of an employer's facilities involve buildings or other property that is owned by another. Neither the ADA nor the EEOC regulations on employment allocate the responsibilities. However, regulations on public accommodations issued under Title III of the ADA have been issued by the Department of Justice,[46] and some assumptions can be reasonably made concerning Title I on employment.

Structural Modifications as a Reasonable Accommodation

If modifications of an existing physical structure are necessary as a reasonable accommodation for a specific disabled person, the legal duty of accommodation remains with the employer. If the rental agreement prohibits the employer from making the modifications, the employer must engage in a good faith attempt to gain permission from the landlord to allow an exception. If the landlord refuses, what was a reasonable accommodation may become an undue hardship. In such a case, the modification need not be made.

General Lack of Accessibility

A more difficult problem may arise when leased premises are not accessible to job applicants. Employers must make modifications to allow access to their employment office, if the lease allows it. If not, the employer should make a determined effort to obtain the landlord's permission to modify the premises. If permission cannot be obtained, the employer should consider alternative methods— such as moving the employment office—that would allow disabled people to apply for jobs.

Newly Built Commercial Facilities

In the construction of new buildings, the owner-landlord has the legal duty to meet accessibility requirements. However, if the construction results from a preexisting contract between the employer-tenant and the owner-landlord, the employer may also have a legal duty to insure the facility meets the requirements of the ADA. Such a situation may exist when the landlord builds the structure after obtaining the employer's agreement to rent the premises.

Existing Leases and Rental Contracts

As between landlords and tenants, Justice Department regulations provide that the lease or rental agreement should control who must furnish auxiliary devices and make readily achievable structural modifications in areas used by customers or clients.[47] Existing leases will often be unclear regarding each party's responsibilities. However, in a typical lease agreement that does not specifically provide for an allocation of responsibilities under the ADA, traditional legal principles will probably divide them as follows:

1. If the rental contract or lease states who is responsible for making alterations, the ADA's duty is on the named entity. For example, if a lease agreement between a physician and an office building owner specifies that no modifications or alterations may be made by the tenant, the duty is upon the landlord. However, the physician does have the legal responsibility to request that modifications be made, if necessary, to meet the intent of the ADA requirements.
2. If the rental contract or lease provides that the tenant may not make alterations without the landlord's permission, the tenant is required to attempt to obtain the landlord's permission to make modifications to comply with the ADA. If the landlord refuses, the landlord may be liable for violation of the ADA, but not the tenant. If the landlord approves of the alterations, but they are not completed, the tenant is in violation of the ADA.
3. Generally, the tenant is responsible only for alterations in the leased premises, while the landlord is responsible for making readily achievable alterations in the common use areas such as the parking lot, building entrance, or hallways.

It remains the duty of the employer, professional firm, or business tenant to provide any required auxiliary devices that are not a part of the leased structure, nor commonly provided as part of a leased premises.

New Leases and Rental Agreements

In compliance with the Department of Justice regulations[48] and to avoid confusion about the relative duties of landlord and tenant, new leases and rental contracts should clearly establish each party's responsibility for complying with the ADA. Employers, professional firms, retail and service businesses, and others who rent or lease their facilities may have their legal counsel prepare a clause for all rental or lease contracts similar to the following:

> The lessor (or landlord) promises and warrants that the leased offices, rooms, buildings, structures, and facilities covered by this rental or lease agreement comply with Title III of the Americans with Disabilities Act and the regulations issued thereunder by the United States Department of Justice concerning accessibility of places of public accommodation and commercial facilities. The lessor (or landlord) further promises and warrants that any common use areas or adjacent property owned or controlled by the lessor (or landlord) that might be used by employees, customers, clients, and the general public such as parking lots, walkways, entrances, hallways, elevators, and other devices or pathways for egress and exit to the leased property, conform to the requirements of the Americans with Disabilities Act and all regulations issued thereunder by the Department of Justice or other authorized agencies under the authority of the Americans with Disabilities Act.
>
> The lessor (or landlord) promises to reimburse and indemnify the lessee (or renter) for any expenses incurred because of the failure of the leased premises and adjacently owned property to conform to Title III of the Americans with Disabilities Act and the regulations issued thereunder, including the costs of making any alterations, renovations, or structural accommodations required under the Americans with Disabilities Act, or by any governmental enforcement agency or any court acting pursuant to Title III of the Americans with Disabilities Act. The lessor (or landlord) also promises to reimburse and indemnify the lessee (or tenant) for all fines, civil penalties, and damages awarded against the lessee (or renter) resulting from a violation or violations of the above-cited law and regulations concerning the accessibility of commercial facilities, and all reasonable legal expenses incurred in defending claims made under the above-cited law and regulations, including reasonable attorneys' fees.

Businesses should have an attorney draft the statement so that it complies with the laws and regulations of the state where the facilities are located. The attorney may wish to add additional language concerning state or city legal requirements.

The example lease or rental provision given above does not mean that each leased or rented facility has to be fully accessible. It only means that the premises must comply with the ADA. If the office, store, building, or other facilities were constructed and first occupied before January 26, 1993, the rented premises need not be fully accessible. However, new buildings designed for first occupancy after January 26, 1993, and major modications begun after January 26, 1992, must have maximized accessibility for disabled persons under the rules explained earlier in this chapter.

PRACTICAL TIPS

Designing Accessible Facilities

Modifications to make existing structures more accessible, or techniques used during alterations of present structures and the building of new structures to ensure accessibility, can best be done as a joint effort. Although the suggested contract clauses provided above place the major burden of providing accessibility upon architects and landlords, businesses can be best assured of practical, useful designs by following these guidelines:

1. Be sure the architect or architectural firm is well versed on the requirements of the ADA and other accessibility standards. Ask direct questions as to their knowledge, training, and experience in designing accessible structures.
2. If an architect is not used, be sure the contractor knows the law and practice of providing accessibility to disabled persons, using the same types of questions that should be asked of architects.
3. Apply the same criteria used in choosing architects or building contractors when employing interior designers, landscape architects, and others who will design or construct the inside, outside, or surrounding area of any commercial facility.
4. Assemble a team to make suggestions and offer ideas to make the premises accessible. Team members might vary from one project to another, but should always include one or more disabled persons (one of whom should be a wheelchair user), the architect or builder, and one or more members of management. If the business has no employees with major disabilities, and no

employees who use wheelchairs, hire one or more local disabled people as consultants to assist the team.

5. Discuss the team's suggestions or plans with city building code officials to see that they are permissible under local law.

6. If possible, check with rehabilitation or disability specialists for added input. Specific ideas and suggestions might be made by local vocational rehabilitation agency personnel or by other interested organizations such as the National Rehabilitation Association or others listed in Part II.

7. Be sure that suggestions made by the team are forwarded to any architect or other person involved in the design or construction of alterations or new facilities. It is best to formally present the suggestions, even if the architect or contractor was part of the team.

Notes

1. Much of the material concerning myths is adapted from Lester & Caudill, *The Handicapped Worker: Seven Myths*, TRAINING AND DEV. J., Aug. 1987, at 50-1; Stevens, *Exploding the Myths About Hiring the Handicapped*, PERSONNEL, Dec. 1986, at 57–60.

2. Watts, *Capabilities*, EXECUTIVE FEMALE, May-June 1990, at 36.

3. *Id.*

4. KRAUS AND STODDARD, CHARTBOOK ON DISABILITY IN THE UNITED STATES National Institute on Disability and Rehabilitation, U.S. Department of Education, Washington, D.C. (1989), p. 37.

5. *Id.* at 38.

6. United Handicapped Fed'n Newsl., St. Paul, Minn. (May 1, 1987).

7. KRAUS & STODDARD, *supra* note 4, at 45.

8. BNA Policy and Practice Series, *Fair Employment Practices*, February 19, 1987.

9. Americans with Disabilities Act §102(c), 42 U.S.C.A. §12112 (West 1991).

10. *Id.*

11. Interpretive Guidance on Title I of the Americans with Disabilities Act, 56 Fed. Reg. 35,750 (1991) [hereinafter Interpretive Guidance].

12. *Id.*

13. *Id.*

14. EEOC Regulations on the Americans with Disabilities Act, 56 Fed. Reg. 35,737 (1991) (to be codified at 29 C.F.R. §1630.14(a)) [hereinafter EEOC Regulation].

15. *Supra* note 11.

16. Interpretive Guidance on Title I of the Americans with Disabilities Act, 56 Fed. Reg. 35,750 (1991).

17. Americans with Disabilities Act of 1990, §102(c)(3), 42 U.S.C.A. §12112 (West 1991).

18. *Id.*

19. EEOC Regulation on the Americans with Disabilities Act, 56 Fed. Reg. at 35,737 (1991) (to be codified at 29 C.F.R. §1630.14. *See also* Interpretive

Guidance on Title I of the Americans with Disabilities Act, 56 Fed. Reg. at 35,750 (1991)).

20. *Id.*
21. *Id.*
22. Americans with Disabilities Act of 1990, §42 U.S.C. §12112; EEOC Regulation on the Americans With Disabilities Act, 56 Fed. Reg. at 35,738. (1991) (to be codified at 29 C.F.R. sec. 1630.14).
23. *Id.*
24. *Id.*
25. Americans with Disabilities Act, Title III, 42 U.S.C.A. §12181 (West, 1991); Department of Justice Regulations on the Americans with Disabilities Act, 56 Fed. Reg. 35,543-35,691 (1991) (to be codified at 28 C.F.R. Part 36).
26. Americans with Disabilities Act of 1990, §302(b)(2)(A)(iv), 42 U.S.C. §12182.
27. Department of Justice Regulation on the Americans with Disabilities Act, 56 Fed. Reg. 35,597 (1991) (to be codified at 28 C.F.R. §304).
28. S. REP. NO. 116, 101st Cong., 1st Sess. (1989).
29. Department of Justice Regulation on the Americans with Disabilities Act, 56 Fed. Reg. 35,597 (1991) (to be codified at 28 C.F.R. §36.304(c)).
30. *Supra* note 25.
31. Section 102(b)(1) of the Americans with Disabilities Act prohibits limiting a job applicant in a way that adversely affects job opportunities, and section 102(b)(6) outlaws selection criteria that tends to screen out disabled applicants. Neither section provides the defense of undue hardship.
32. Americans with Disabilities Act of 1990, §301(2), 42 U.S.C.A. §12181 (West 1991).
33. *Id.* at §303(a)(2), 42 U.S.C.A. §12183.
34. Department of Justice Regulation on the Americans with Disability Act, 56 Fed. Reg. 35,600 (1991) (to be codified at 28 C.F.R. §36,402).
35. *Supra* note 33.
36. Department of Justice Regulation on the Americans with Disabilities Act, 56 Fed. Reg. 35,601 (1991) (to be codified at 28 C.F.R. §403).
37. Department of Justice Regulation on the Americans with Disabilities Act, 56 Fed. Reg. 35,601 (1991) (to be codified at 28 C.F.R. §36.403(f)).
38. 42 U.S.C.A. §12112 (West 1991).
39. Department of Justice Regulation on the Americans with Disabilities Act, 56 Fed. Reg. 35,599 (1991) (to be codified at 28 C.F.R. §36.401(a)).
40. Department of Justice Regulation on the Americans with Disabilities Act, 56 Fed. Reg. 35,601 (1991) (to be codified at 28 C.F.R. §36.403(f)).
41. 42 U.S.C.A. §12181 (West 1991).
42. S. REP. NO. 116, 101st Cong., 1st Sess. Aug 30, 1989, H. REP. NO. 485; 101st Cong., 2d Sess. May 16, 1990.
43. *Supra* note 25.
44. *Id.*
45. Americans with Disabilities Act of 1990, §42 U.S.C.A. §12188 (West 1991).
46. *Supra* note 25.
47. Department of Justice Regulation on the Americans with Disabilities Act, 56 Fed. Reg. 35,595 (1991) (to be codified at 28 C.F.R. §36.201(b)).
48. *Id.*

Chapter 3

Determining Who Is Disabled

The definition of a disabled person is so broad that employers should usually treat any person with an obvious physical or mental impairment, or any person who claims an impairment, as a legally disabled individual. However, if expensive or unreasonable demands for accommodations are made, it may become necessary to determine if an employee or job applicant meets the legal requirements of a disabled person. The definition also becomes important when an individual claims he or she was discriminated against because of a disability and files a complaint with the Equal Employment Opportunity Commission (EEOC) or a private lawsuit. A complete defense to such a claim is to show that the individual is not legally disabled. Simply put, an employer violates the law only with respect to a disabled person. If the individual is not legally disabled, the ADA does not apply.

This chapter will discuss the definition of a disabled person under the Americans with Disabilities Act (ADA), EEOC regulations and interpretative guidance, the Rehabilitation Act of 1973, and state laws that have similar definitions of a disability or handicap.

To be entitled to the legal protections of the ADA:

1. An employee or job applicant must be legally disabled.
2. The disability must be known by the employer, personnel department, immediate supervisor, or someone else in authority. It is known if the disability is obvious (missing limb(s), blind, etc.), or the job applicant or employee informs any of the above-mentioned people of his or her disability. Actual knowledge of the disability is also present if it comes to the attention of the company or its manage-

47

ment in any other manner (such as hearing about the disability from someone other than the disabled person).

3. The individual must be qualified to perform the essential tasks of the job in question, once reasonable accommodations are made. See Chapter 4, "Determining if a Disabled Person is Qualified," and Chapter 5, "Making Accommodations for Disabled Employees."

Disability Defined

The ADA defines a disabled person as an individual who has:

"(A) a physical or mental impairment that substantially limits one or more of the major life activities of such individual;
 (B) a record of such an impairment; or
 (C) being regarded as having such an impairment."[1]

The ADA's definition of disability is the same as the Rehabilitation Act of 1973 and many state handicapped laws. Therefore, past legal decisions covered in this chapter help illustrate how the ADA is applied. Furthermore, congressional committees of the Senate and House of Representatives[2] expressly state that the Rehabilitation Act and regulations adopted under the Rehabilitation Act by various federal agencies[2] should apply to the ADA.

The congressional committee reports (following various agency interpretations of the Rehabilitation Act) and EEOC regulations state that a physical or mental impairment includes:

> (1) any physiological disorder or condition, cosmetic disfigurement, or anatomical loss affecting one or more of the following body systems: neurological; musculoskeletal; special sense organs; respiratory, including speech organs; cardiovascular; reproductive; digestive; genito-urinary; hemic and lymphatic; skin; and endocrine; or (2) any mental or psychological disorder, such as mental retardation, organic brain syndrome, emotional or mental illness; and specific learning disabilities.[3]

Although the types of physical or mental problems are too numerous to list, the congressional committees' reports note that the above-stated definition includes, among others: orthopedic problems; visual, speech and hearing impairments; cerebral palsy; epilepsy; muscular dystrophy; multiple sclerosis; heart disease; diabetes; mental retardation; emotional illness; specific learning disabilities; past drug addiction; and alcoholism.[4]

What is Not a Disability

Physical or mental characteristics that are not legal disabilities include simple physical features such as eye color, hair color, or "height, weight and muscle tone that are in the 'normal' range and are not the result of a physiological disorder."[5] Most temporary nonchronic impairments with little or no future impact such as a simple broken leg or arm, sprained ankle, appendicitis, pregnancy, or influenza are also not considered to be legal disabilities.[6] The EEOC interpretive guidance issued as an appendix to EEOC regulations also states that obesity is not considered to be a handicap, except in rare circumstances.[7]

Other characteristics that are not considered to be disabilities under the ADA include the following:

1. Common personality traits such as poor judgment or quick temper that are not the result of a mental or physiological disorder[8]
2. Environmental, cultural, or economic disadvantages such as poverty, lack of an education, or having a prison record[9]
3. Other common physical characteristics such as being a little shorter than average, red-headed, or even ugly (unless caused by an injury or medical problem)
4. Advanced age by itself. However, many medical and physical problems associated with advancing age such as arthritis, heart disease, and others may be disabilities[10]

The ADA specifically eliminates from the definition of a disabled person the following conditions:

1. Compulsive gambling
2. Kleptomania
3. Pyromania
4. Psychoactive substance use disorders resulting from *current* illegal use of drugs
5. Transvestism
6. Homosexuality
7. Bisexuality
8. Transsexualism
9. Pedophilia
10. Exhibitionism
11. Voyeurism

12. Gender identity disorders not resulting from physical impairments
13. Other sexual behavior disorders[11]

Impairments That May Be A Disability

Almost any physical or mental impairment, other than the ones excluded above, can be a legal disability if it substantially limits a major life activity. The various regulations under the Rehabilitation Act and the ADA define major life activities as functions such as caring for one's self, performing manual tasks, walking, seeing, hearing, speaking, breathing, learning, or working.[12] For example, an individual with serious arthritis is legally disabled if such person is unable to accomplish simple tasks such as opening bottles or picking up commonly used objects. A person with dyslexia is disabled because the inability to adequately read creates a learning problem. The list of major life activities is not an exhaustive one. Nonlisted activities such as sitting, climbing, or reaching, among others, may also be major life activities.

EEOC regulations define the term "substantially limits" as:

(i) Unable to perform a major life activity that the average person in the general population can perform; or
(ii) Significantly restricted as to the condition, manner or duration under which an individual can perform a particular major life activity as compared to the condition, manner or duration under which the average person in the general population can perform. . . .[13]

EEOC regulations state that the following factors should be considered in determining whether an individual is substantially limited in a major life activity:

(i) The nature and severity of the impairment,
(ii) The duration or expected duration of the impairment, and
(iii) The permanence or long term impact or the expected permanent or long term impact of or resulting from the impairment.[14]

The EEOC states that "if an individual is substantially limited in any other major life activity, no determination should be made as to whether the individual is substantially limited in working."[15] Such a person is legally disabled; therefore, no finding of a substantial limitation in working is necessary.

A Record of Impairment

Any job applicant or employee who has a past record of an impairment that substantially limits a major life activity is considered disabled, even though the impairment does not currently cause a limitation. For example, individuals with diabetes who keep the disease in good control by diet, pills, or injections may not currently suffer a major impairment. However, in addition to having a condition affecting the endocrine system, diabetics have a record of impairment. At one time (at least before they were diagnosed as having diabetes), the diabetes affected their major life activity of continued life since untreated diabetes can lead to complete disability and death.

A person who was diagnosed as having cancer 20 years ago, but who was successfully treated with no recurrence, further treatment, or limitations for the past 15 years, continues to have a record of an impairment that substantially limits a major life activity (staying alive), and thus is entitled to the protection of the ADA. A job applicant or employee who was diagnosed and successfully treated for a manic-depressive mental illness years ago is also protected by the law because of a record of impairment.

The primary purpose of covering people with records of past impairment is to avoid discrimination against individuals based solely on stereotypical, false beliefs concerning their past physical or mental problems. A secondary purpose is to make clear that a person with a disabling condition does not cease to be disabled just because medicine or other treatment alleviates the impairment and allows the individual to act without restrictions.

Regarded as Impaired

Also considered to be legally disabled are people who have no current or past physical or mental impairment, but who are thought by others to be impaired or disabled. This provision is intended to cover individuals who are denied jobs or benefits because others treat them as impaired, even when they are not. An example is a victim of serious burn injuries. Although the person may have never experienced any permanent physical or mental limitations, the burn scars may create in others an impression of disability.

The prohibition against discrimination based upon an incorrect belief that a person is impaired also applies to people with cancer, hearing problems, epilepsy, and other problems. Stereotypical, untrue, negative reactions by employers to specific physical or mental conditions are illegal.

In practical terms, anytime an employer fails to hire, retain, or promote a person—or otherwise treats the individual differently—because the employer believes the person has a disability, the employer's action, by itself, may prove the individual is regarded as impaired. In other words, treating a person as if he or she is disabled may *create* a legal disability, giving the individual legal rights under the ADA.

The Extent of the Disability

One of the first cases under the Rehabilitation Act to decide the issue of whether an individual's physical or mental impairment substantially limited the major life activity of working was a 1980 United States District Court case, *E.E. Black, Ltd. v. Marshall*.[16] In *E.E. Black*, the Department of Labor argued that the rejection of a job applicant with a bad back automatically proved the person was disabled because it showed that a job was denied upon the basis of an impairment. However, the administrative law judge found that to be disabled a person must have an impairment that is likely to "generally" affect a person's employment chances. The *E.E. Black* decision rejected both of these approaches.

The Department of Labor's argument was too broad. It would include within the law's coverage any individual with a real or perceived impairment who was rejected for one particular job because of the impairment. *E.E. Black* illustrated the fallacy of this approach by stating:

> Thus, for example, a worker who was offered a particular job by a company at all of its plants but one, but was denied employment at that plant because of the presence of plant matter to which the employee was allergic, would be covered by the Act. An individual with acrophobia who was offered 10 deputy assistant accountant jobs with a particular company, but was disqualified from one job because it was on the 37th floor, would be covered by the Act. An individual with some type of hearing sensitivity who was denied employment at a location with very loud noise, but was offered positions at other locations, would be covered. The Court does not believe this was the result intended by Congress.[17]

However, the court also rejected the concept that to be disabled an individual must be generally unemployable.

> [T]his type of definition drastically reduces the coverage of the Act, and undercuts the purposes for which the Act was intended. A

person, for example, who has obtained a graduate degree in chemistry, and is then turned down for a chemist's job because of an impairment is not likely to be heartened by the news that he can still be a streetcar conductor, an attorney or a forest ranger. A person who is disqualified from employment in his chosen field has a substantial handicap to employment, and is substantially limited in one of his major life activities. The definitions contained in the Act are personal and must be evaluated by looking at the particular individual. A handicapped individual is one who "has a physical or mental disability *which for such individual* constitutes or results in a substantial handicap to employment . . . ." It is the impaired individual that must be examined, and not just the impairment in the abstract.[18]

EEOC regulations follow the approach of the court in the *E.E. Black* decision by stating that an individual is substantially limited in the activity of working only if there is a significant restriction "in the ability to perform either a class of jobs or a broad range of jobs in various classes as compared to the average person having comparable training, skills and abilities."[19]

In determining if an individual is disabled, each case must be examined upon its own facts. However, it may be helpful to examine past case decisions in which courts decided if an individual was legally disabled.

Cases Where A Disability Was Found

A legal disability was found in the following lawsuits, each using a definition of disability that is the same or similar to the ADA's definition:

1. A dentist with chronic hepatitis who worked in a prison system was found legally disabled.[20] Chronic hepatitis is an infection of the liver that is normally, but not always, preceded by acute hepatitis B (formerly called serum hepatitis) over a period of one year. It is a communicable disease. See Chapter 7 "AIDS, Infectious Diseases, Drug and Alcohol Problems, and Weight Problems," for additional information on communicable diseases.

2. A person with AIDS or the HIV Virus.[21] A more complete discussion of AIDS and the HIV virus is contained in Chapter 7, "AIDS, Infectious Diseases, Drug and Alcohol Problems, and Weight Problems."

3. A person with Crohn's disease, a chronic digestive disorder.[22]

4. A discharged employee suffering from cluster migraine headaches for several years.[23]

5. A rehabilitated drug or alcohol abuser.[24] See Chapter 7, "AIDS, Infectious Diseases, Drug and Alcohol Problems, and Weight Problems," for additional information on drug and alcohol abuse.

6. A member of a hospital's housekeeping department who injured her back while on the job and had continuing problems to the extent that a doctor recommended against her continuation as a housekeeper.[25]

7. A glass factory worker who underwent a back operation, even though physicians testified that he would have no future back problems and he was able to do strenuous work.[26] The court found proof that the employer regarded the worker as disabled in the employer's refusal to offer the individual a job because of problems found in a back X-ray.[27] See Chapter 6, "Risk of Future Injury: Epilepsy, Diabetes, and Bad Backs," for a discussion of bad backs.

8. A person who continued to experience pain after knee surgery, where his physician diagnosed his present condition as severe.[28]

9. A pregnant employee. The court found her to be disabled because the employer perceived her condition as one that substantially limited her work activities.[29] This decision is questionable because a legal disability is seldom found when the condition is temporary. However, this may offer little solace to employers since discrimination based on pregnancy is illegal under the Pregnancy Discrimination Act's amendments to Title VII of the Civil Rights Act of 1964.

10. A deaf postal worker.[30]

11. A person with dyslexia.[31]

12. A telephone installer whose physician advised her to stay away from dust and heavy exercise.[32]

13. A Postal Service employee diagnosed as suffering from paranoid schizophrenia.[33]

14. An individual with physical problems that included being tongue-tied, a left hand with only three digits, and no right hand.[34] The court found it "obvious" that she was disabled.

15. A female typist who had undergone cancer surgery to remove a breast and substantial amounts of muscle from one shoulder and upper arm.[35]

16. A meat cutter suffering a mild form of epilepsy.[36] Additional material on epilepsy is given in Chapter 6, "Risk of Future Injury: Epilepsy, Diabetes, and Bad Backs."
17. An achondroplastic dwarf who was four feet, five inches tall.[37]
18. A man whose cerebral palsy was very mild and caused no dysfunction. The court found a disability because he was perceived as having a physical impairment.[38] He was also found to be disabled because he had a record of an impairment—hospitalization for mental depression, and was found to have a learning disability.
19. An employee with a variety of health problems, including a heart condition and severe depression.[39]
20. An applicant for the position of a county deputy sheriff who had uncorrected vision of 20/400.[40] The court stated that even if not impaired, the applicant was entitled to the protection of the law because he was perceived as being disabled due to his rejection on the basis of vision problems. However, this decision may not meet the requirement of the *E.E. Black* decision and accompanying EEOC regulations that to be substantially impaired in the major life activity of working, one must have a significant restriction in the ability to perform a range of jobs, rather than being disqualified from only one narrow type of job.
21. A federal employee who had been medically retired because the employer's job description required that an employee's hearing be sufficient to understand normal conversation without a hearing aid.[41]
22. An office worker with a neurological disorder that caused difficulty in concentrating and reading when the worker was subject to normal office noise and lighting.[42]

Cases Where No Disability Was Found

There are recent cases under the Rehabilitation Act and state laws with the same or similar definitions of disability as the ADA in which no disability was found.

Personality Traits Not a Mental Condition

An applicant for a position as a New York City policeman was denied employment as a result of information derived from the

California Psychological Inventory Test, the Minnesota Multiphasic Personality Inventory, a job application form, and a psychiatrist's interview finding the applicant to be unsuitable for a police officer position because of poor judgment, irresponsible behavior, and poor impulse control.[43] The psychiatrist found no mental illness, but rather "significant personality traits" that would prevent the applicant from effectively functioning as a police officer. Both parties to the lawsuit agreed there was no actual disability, nor a record of disability. However, the applicant claimed the police department regarded him as disabled. The court disagreed.

In finding no disability the court pointed out that the applicant was simply disqualified from being a police officer—a specific job— and that the disqualification was not a significant limitation on work because the applicant was still able to obtain almost any other type of job. The court said that poor judgment, irresponsible behavior, and poor impulse control—without additional mental illness—are not mental conditions intended by Congress to be covered by the Rehabilitation Act.

Only One Job Prohibited

A telephone installer for AT&T in Oregon whose employment contract called for travel was diagnosed as having asthma and a sensitivity to heat.[44] His physician recommended against working in over 90 degree heat or in damp, cold climates. After his work unit was assigned to work in Arizona, the installer experienced heat problems and could not work, resulting in his discharge by the employer. He then found work in Oregon as a telephone installer with another company.

In a lawsuit for violation of the Oregon handicapped discrimination law with provisions similar to the ADA, the court found he was not disabled. The court explained: "An impairment which only interferes with an individual's ability to do one particular job with one particular employer, but which does not significantly decrease the individual's ability to obtain satisfactory employment otherwise is not 'substantially' limiting. . . . "[45] The fact the installer found another job in the same line of work helped to show that he was not substantially impaired in the major life activity of working. The court added: "An employer does not necessarily regard an employee as handicapped simply by finding that the employee is incapable of satisfying the singular demands of a particular job."[46]

No Defense to Sexual Harassment

A male supervisor who was discharged for sexual harassment of females claimed that his behavior was an aberration from normal behavior, and that he was therefore regarded by the employer as having a mental disability. The court rejected this argument by deciding he was not disabled.[47]

Major Life Activities Not Affected

A federal government employee with hypertension and sinusitis was found not disabled where no creditable medical testimony was presented to prove that the medical conditions placed any limitation on any major life activity.[48] The employee was not even able to prove the medical conditions limited his ability to work.

In a similar ruling, an applicant for a deputy sheriff's position with uncorrected distance vision of less than 20/100 and with a slight hearing loss in one ear was held not to be disabled under the Minnesota Human Rights Act.[49] The court reasoned that these problems had not affected the applicant's ability to obtain other jobs, and thus were not substantial impairments.

In a West Virginia case,[50] a woman with psoriatic lesions on her legs was denied a job as a coal miner because the job conditions of working in a damp, dirty coal mine would seriously aggravate her medical condition. The court found the applicant was not disabled because there was no proof the medical condition restricted her ability to find other employment.

An employee of a food store who developed a chronic susceptibility to bronchitis that prevented her from working around chemical fumes, dust, or in poorly ventilated areas was found not to be disabled under Iowa law.[51] The court decided that the employee's physical condition did not limit her from working in most types of jobs for which she was qualified.

A postal worker with strabismus, commonly known as crossed-eyes, who claimed his inability to operate a mail sorting machine resulted from his physical condition, was found not to be disabled.[52] There was no proof his physical condition substantially impaired his ability to find and keep employment.

Drinking is Not Alcoholism

Although a New Jersey court ruled that alcoholism is a legal disability, a discharged salesman fired for poor performance who claimed he was an alcoholic was found not to be disabled.[53] There was no medical proof he actually suffered from medically diagnosed alcoholism. See Chapter 7, "AIDS, Infectious Diseases, Drug and Alcohol Problems, and Weight Problems," for additional material on alcoholism.

No Disability if No Restrictions

An employee with varicose veins was found not to be disabled because the condition was mild and did not prevent her from doing the typist/clerk job she held.[54]

A letter carrier discharged for falsification of medical records and excessive absenteeism was found not to be disabled where her only complaint was about low back pain that had only caused two short periods of absenteeism.[55] The court found that the employee had never asked for, nor was given, work restrictions. Her continued ability to do her job, which consisted of heavy lifting and walking six to eight miles per day, proved that her back problem did not substantially limit a major life activity.

A utility engineer whose job description included climbing stairways and ladders was discharged when he informed management that he could not climb to certain heights required by the job. In denying the engineer the protection of the Rehabilitation Act, the court found that his acrophobia only disqualified him from this one job, and did not substantially affect his employment in his chosen field.[56]

Common Conditions Not Disabling

A left-handed mail sorter was discharged for poor job performance. He claimed this violated the Rehabilitation Act because he was perceived as disabled because his left-handedness resulted in slow work performance. The court found left-handedness not to be a disability because the employee was not substantially limited in his employability.[57] While being left-handed is a physiological condition affecting the neurological and musculoskeletal systems, the court said it is such a common condition that it cannot be considered to be a disability.

A city employee who was suspended without pay for failure to lose 37 pounds in 19 weeks was held not to be disabled because obesity, by itself, is not a substantially limiting disability.[58] However, see the discussion of obesity in Chapter 7, "AIDS, Infectious

Diseases, Drug and Alcohol Problems and Weight Problems," for a prediction of possible future court rulings.

Voluntary Physical Condition No Disability

A federal court in California found that an overweight person was not disabled.[59] The extra weight of the job applicant appeared to be the result of his bodybuilding activities that caused a large amount of muscle mass, compared to a small amount of fat. Therefore, the court found the condition was not the result of physiological disorders or other medical problems. The court stated: "For good or evil, private employers are generally free to be arbitrary and even capricious in determining whom to hire, unless the employer somehow discriminates on the basis of race, national origin, alienage, age, sex, or handicapped status, considerations which Congress has determined to be prohibited."[60] See Chapter 7, "AIDS, Infectious Diseases, Drug and Alcohol Problems, and Weight Problems," for a discussion of weight problems.

The United States Supreme Court Speaks

The only United States Supreme Court decision directly involving a definition of a disability for employment purposes under the Rehabilitation Act of 1973 is *School Board of Nassau County v. Arline*,[61] decided in 1987. Arline was hospitalized for treatment of tuberculosis (TB) in 1957. For the next 20 years she was in remission, with no TB symptoms. However, she had a relapse of TB in the spring of 1978 and another one in the fall of that year. The local school board dismissed her from employment as an elementary school teacher solely on the grounds of her TB. A United States District Court upheld the school board's decision by declaring that the Rehabilitation Act was not intended to apply to contagious diseases. The district court added that even assuming Arline was handicapped, a person with a contagious disease is not qualified to teach in an elementary school.

The United States Court of Appeals reversed the lower court,[62] and the United States Supreme Court affirmed the Court of Appeals decision for Arline by a seven-to-two majority. The majority opinion quickly came to the conclusion that Arline was a disabled person. The court stated:

Arline suffered tuberculosis in "an acute form in such a degree that it affected her respiratory system," and was hospitalized for this condition. . . . Arline thus has a physical impairment as that term is defined by the regulations . . . . This impairment was serious enough to require hospitalization, *a fact more than sufficient* to establish that one or more of her major life activities were substantially limited by her impairment. Thus Arline's hospitalization for tuberculosis in 1957 suffices to establish that she has a "record of impairment" within the meaning of the Rehabilitation Act (emphasis added).[63]

By the above-stated language, the Supreme Court appears to expand the coverage of the Rehabilitation Act, and thus automatically the Americans with Disabilities Act, to include many people who have been hospitalized for a physical (and possibly mental) health problem, at least if the problem involved a chronic impairment or one that typically may have long-range effects. The statement that hospitalization at some time in the past is "more than sufficient" to prove a record of impairment that substantially limits a major life activity applies to many millions of Americans.

The remaining issue in *Arline* involved whether Arline was qualified to teach elementary school students while having a contagious disease. Although this issue is discussed in Chapter 4, "Determining if a Disabled Person is Qualified," some of the Supreme Court's reasoning provides good general instruction concerning the approach employers should take toward disabled job applicants and employees, especially in AIDS cases and other diseases that prompt fear or discrimination. In discussing contagious diseases, the Court said:

Allowing discrimination based upon the contagious effects of a physical impairment would be inconsistent with the basic purpose of . . . [the Rehabilitation Act], which is to ensure that handicapped individuals are not denied jobs or other benefits because of prejudiced attitudes or the ignorance of others. By amending the definition of "handicapped" to include not only those who are actually physically impaired, but also those who are regarded as impaired and who, as a result are substantially limited in a major life activity, Congress acknowledged that *society's accumulated myths and fears about disability and disease are as handicapping as are the physical limitations that flow from the actual impairment* (emphasis added). Few aspects of a handicap give rise to the same level of public fear and misapprehension as contagiousness. Even those who suffer or have recovered from such noninfectious diseases as epilepsy or cancer have faced discrimination based on the irrational fear that they might be contagious. The Act is carefully structured to replace such reflexive reactions to actual or perceived handicaps with actions based upon reasoned and medically sound judgments . . . . The fact that *some* persons who have contagious diseases may pose a serious health threat to others under certain circumstances does not justify excluding from the coverage of the Act *all* persons with actual or perceived contagious diseases.

[T]he remaining question is whether Arline is otherwise qualified for the job of elementary school teacher. To answer this question in most cases the District Court will need to conduct an individualized inquiry and make appropriate findings of fact.[64]

The issue of whether Arline was qualified as an elementary school teacher is discussed in Chapter 4, "Determining if a Disabled Person is Qualified," and *Arline's* impact on AIDS or HIV virus cases is discussed in Chapter 7, "AIDS, Infectious Diseases, Drug and Alcohol Problems, and Weight Problems."

PRACTICAL TIPS

Determining Disabled Status

1. Any person with a physical or mental problem that substantially limits any major life activity, including general employability in his or her chosen line of work, is disabled.
2. Any individual with a past history of physical or mental impairment that substantially limits a major life activity, especially if hospitalized for the condition, comes under the protection of the law.
3. Any person who is treated by employers or others as disabled comes under the protections of the law if such treatment results in a limitation of a major life activity, particularly if it results in problems in gaining or retaining employment.
4. When an employer is not sure whether a job applicant's or employee's known impairment is significant enough to constitute a legal disability, the safer course of action is to consider the person as disabled under the provisions of the ADA or other relevant law.

Notes

1. Americans with Disabilities Act §3(2), 42 U.S.C.A. §12102 (West, 1991).
2. S. REP. NO. 116, 101st Cong., 1st Sess. (1989); H. REP. No. 485, 101st Cong., 2d Sess. pt. 1 (1990); H. REP. No. 488, 101st Cong., 2d Sess. (1990).
3. 42 Fed. Reg. 22685; 45 C.F.R. §84.3; 28 C.F.R. Part 41.3; 34 C.F.R. Part 104.3; EEOC Regulations on the Americans with Disabilities Act, 56 Fed. Reg. 35,735 (1991) (to be codified at 29 C.F.R. §1630.2).
4. *Supra* note 2.

5. Interpretive Guidance on Title I of the Americans with Disabilities Act, 56 Fed. Reg. 35,741 (1991).
6. *Id.*
7. *Id.*
8. *Id.*
9. *Id.*
10. *Id.*
11. Americans with Disabilities Act, §508, 42 U.S.C.A. §§12208, 1221 (West 1991); §511, 42 U.S.C.A. §1221 (West 1991).
12. *Supra* note 3.
13. EEOC Regulations on the Americans with Disabilities Act, 56 Fed. Reg. 35,735 (1991) (to be codified at 29 C.F.R. §1630.2) [hereinafter EEOC Regulations].
14. *Id.*
15. *Id.*
16. 497 F. Supp. 1088 (D. Haw. 1980).
17. *Id.* at 1099.
18. *Id.*
19. *Supra* note 13.
20. Lussier v. Dugger, 904 F.2d 661, 53 FEP Cases 443 (11th Cir. 1990).
21. Cain v. Hyatt, 734 F. Supp. 671, 50 FEP Cases 195 (E.D. Pa. 1990).
22. Antonsen v. Ward, 556 N.Y.S. 2d 479, 161 A.2d 378 (N.Y. 1989).
23. Kimbro v. Atlantic Richfield Co., 889 F.2d 869 (9th Cir. 1989).
24. Nisperos v. Buck, 720 F. Supp. 1424 (N.D. Cal. 1989).
25. Coffman v. W. Va. Bd. of Regents, 386 S.E.2d (W. Va. 1988).
26. Fourco Glass Company v. W. Va. Human Rights Comm'n, 383 S.E.2d 64 (W. Va. 1989).
27. *Id.*
28. Casteel v. Consol. Coal Co., 383 S.E.2d 305 (W. Va. 1989).
29. Melvin v. Kim's Restaurant, 776 P.2d 1286 (Or. 1989).
30. Davis v. Polk, 50 EPD §39,157 (N.D. Ill. 1989).
31. DiPompo v. West Point Military Academy, 708 F. Supp. 540, 49 FEP Cases 587 (S.D.N.Y. 1989).
32. Ackerman v. Western Elec. Co., 860 F.2d 1154 (9th Cir. 1988).
33. Franklin v. United States Postal Service, 687 F. Supp. 1214, 46 FEP Cases 1734 (S.D. Ohio 1988).
34. Recanzone v. Washoe County School Dist., 696 F. Supp. 1372, 48 FEP Cases 299 (D. Nev. 1988).
35. Harrison v. Marsh, 691 F. Supp. 1223, 46 FEP Cases 971 (W.D. Mo. 1988).
36. Jansen v. Food Circus Supermarkets, 541 A.2d 682, 52 FEP Cases 1632 (N.J. 1988).
37. Dexler v. Tisch, 660 F. Supp. 1418, 43 FEP Cases 1661 (D. Conn. 1987).
38. Pridemore v. Rural Legal Aid Soc'y of W. Cent. Ohio, 625 F. Supp. 1180 (S.D. Ohio 1985).
39. Carty v. Carlin, 623 F. Supp. 1181, 39 FEP Cases 1217 (D. Md. 1985).
40. Brown County v. Labor & Indus. Rev. 369 N.W.2d 735, 47 FEP Cases 1235 (Wis. 1985).
41. Crane v. Dole, 617 F. Supp. 156, 37 FEP Cases 255 (D.D.C. 1985).
42. Arneson v. Heckler, 879 F.2d 393, 50 FEP Cases 451 (8th Cir. 1989).
43. Daley v. Kock, 892 F.2d 212, 51 FEP Cases 1077 (2d Cir. 1989).

44. Miller v. AT & T Network Sys., 722 F. Supp. 633 (D. Or. 1989).
45. *Id.*
46. *Id.*
47. Blanton v. AT & T Communications, 52 FEP Cases 19 (D. Mass. 1990).
48. Thomas v. General Servs. Admin., 49 FEP Cases 1602, 51 EPD §39,221 (D.D.C. 1989).
49. State v. Cooper, 441 N.W.2d 106, 51 FEP Cases 166 (Minn. 1989). *See also* Chevron v. Redmon, 745 S.W. (2d) 314, 56 FEP Cases 870 (Tex. 1987).
50. Ranger Fuel v. W. Va. Human Rights Comm'n, 51 EPD §39,391 (W. Va. 1988).
51. Probasco v. Iowa Civil Rights Comm'n, 420 N.W.2d 432, 48 FEP Cases 1587 (Iowa 1988).
52. Jasany v. United States Postal Service, 755 F.2d 1244, 37 FEP Cases 210 (6th Cir. 1985).
53. Clowes v. Terminix Int'l, 538 A.2d 794, (N.J. 1988).
54. Oesterling v. Walters, 760 F.2d 859, 37 FEP Cases 865 (8th Cir. 1985).
55. Diaz v. United States Postal Service, 658 F. Supp. 484, 44 FEP Cases 743 (E.D. Cal. 1987).
56. Forrisi v. Bowen, 794 F.2d 931, 41 FEP Cases 190 (4th Cir. 1986).
57. Torres v. Bolger, 610 F. Supp. 503 (N.D. Tex. 1985).
58. Civil Serv. Comm'n of Pittsburgh v. Pennsylvania as reported in BNA Policy and Practice Series, *Fair Employment Practices*, June 6, 1991, p. 65.
59. Tudyman v. United Airlines, 608 F. Supp. 739, 38 FEP Cases 732 (C.D. Cal. 1984).
60. *Id.*, 608 F. Supp. at 746–47.
61. 480 U.S. 273, 43 FEP Cases 81 (1987).
62. Arline v. School Bd. of Nassau County, 772 F.2d 759, 39 FEP Cases 9 (11th Cir. 1985).
63. *Id.*, 480 U.S. at 281 (1985) (emphasis added).
64. *Id.*, 480 U.S. at 283 (emphasis added).

Chapter 4

Determining if a Disabled Person is Qualified

The Americans with Disabilities Act (ADA), as well as the Federal Rehabilitation Act and many state handicapped laws, extend the protection of the law only to "qualified" individuals with disabilities. The ADA states:

> QUALIFIED INDIVIDUAL WITH A DISABILITY.—The term "qualified individual with a disability" means an individual with a disability who, *with or without reasonable accommodations*, can perform the *essential* functions of the employment position that such individual holds or desires (emphasis added). For the purposes of this title, consideration shall be given to the employer's judgment as to what functions of a job are essential, and if an employer has prepared a written (job) description before advertising or interviewing applicants for the job, this description shall be considered evidence of the essential functions of the job.[1]

This definition follows the concept of the Rehabilitation Act of 1973, except for addition of the section about the employer's judgment or written job description. However, it should be emphasized that the new section only provides that the employer's judgment or job description will be considered as evidence by the court, not that it will automatically be followed. For example, if an employer rejects a job applicant because the employer's written job description states that an essential task of the job is to lift 30 pounds to a height of five feet, and the applicant is unable to do this because of confinement to a wheelchair, a court may still find illegal discrimination. If the evidence presented in court shows that despite the job description, workers must lift objects to a height of five feet only once or twice every few days, and it would be easy for the person in the wheelchair to do some minor job swapping with co-workers in order to have them lift the objects, the court should find that the

64

lifting requirement is not an essential task, regardless of the written description.

Equal Employment Opportunity Commission (EEOC) regulations provide that a determination of whether a function is essential may be made, in part, by determining if the job exists specifically to perform the function in question, how many other employees are available to perform the function, and how much expertise or specialization is required to perform the function. Evidence of whether a particular function is essential may be based, in part, on the employer's judgment, job descriptions prepared before advertising the job or interviewing applicants, the amount of time spent on the job performing the function, the terms of a collective bargaining agreement, and the work experience of past or present employees in the job under consideration.[2]

Essential Functions

The phrase "essential functions" means job tasks that are fundamental and not marginal. Individuals with disabilities may not be denied jobs simply because of a physical or mental requirement that is not really necessary for the effective performance of the basic tasks of a particular job.

Hire the Most Qualified

Employers remain free to select the most qualified person for a job or a promotion, just as long as each decision is based upon a practical, realistic determination of what the job entails. For example, if two applicants apply for a position as a typist, and one types 80 words per minute, but the other can type only 50 words per minute because of a physical disability, the employer is allowed to, and should, hire the person who can type 80 words per minute, assuming other things are equal. Granting a preference to disabled individuals is not required.

On the other hand, if two job applicants apply for a position that involves substantial use of a telephone, where one applicant has a hearing impairment that requires an amplifier (which costs only a few dollars), the employer should not choose the nondisabled employee solely because of the other's disability. If hearing over the telephone is an essential task of the job, but it can be successfully accomplished by the disabled applicant, with or without reasonable accommodations, the disability should play no part in the employer's decision regarding whom to hire. The decision should be based upon which of the two applicants is best, considering other factors such as ability to speak over the phone, quality of voice, and other relevant factors.

In determining whether a person with a disability is qualified, employers must avoid making blanket rules that result in the automatic disqualification of people with certain disabilities. Instead, each disabled person must be examined in light of his or her own qualifications, not a medical condition. For example, a company may violate the law if it refuses to consider all blind persons for employment as secretaries. Although the essential tasks of a specific secretary's job may be difficult for many blind people to effectively perform, this decision should be made on a case-by-case basis. Some blind secretaries may better perform the essential tasks of the job than some sighted workers.

There are a few exceptions where a blanket rule might be reasonable, such as prohibiting blind persons from jobs where it is essential to drive a car or refusing to consider paralyzed individuals for a position as a firefighter. However, one must be sure to restrict blanket rules to jobs where there is no doubt that *all* people with certain physical conditions cannot effectively and safely perform.

Health and Safety Risks

The problem of risk of future injury will be discussed in detail in Chapter 6, "Risk of Future Injury: Epilepsy, Diabetes, and Bad Backs." However, it was also the issue in the now famous United States Supreme Court case of *School Board of Nassau County v. Arline*,[3] discussed in part at the end of the Chapter 3, "Determining Who is Disabled."

In *Arline*, the United States Supreme Court had determined that Arline had a record of a physical impairment because of her hospitalization for tuberculosis (TB) twenty years earlier, and therefore was a legally disabled person. The Supreme Court decided that the lower court must determine whether Arline's tuberculosis, a contagious disease, disqualified her from teaching elementary school students.

The Supreme Court then gave the following guidelines to be applied in determining if Arline was qualified:

[T]he District Court will need to conduct an individualized inquiry and make appropriate findings of fact. Such an inquiry is essential if . . . [the law] is to achieve its goal of protecting handicapped individuals from deprivations based upon prejudice, stereotypes, or unfounded fear, while giving appropriate weight to such legitimate concerns of . . . [the employer in] avoiding exposing others to significant health and safety risks. . . . We agree with *amicus* American Medical Association that this inquiry should include:

[Findings of] fact based on reasonable medical judgments given the state of medical knowledge about (a) the nature of the risk (how the disease is transmitted), (b) the duration of the risk (how long the carrier is infectious), (c) the severity of the risk (what is the potential harm to third parties), and (d) the probabilities the disease will be transmitted and will cause varying degrees of harm.[4]

Upon remand of the *Arline* case,[5] the District Court found that Arline was qualified to be an elementary school teacher, even during the 1977-78 period when medical tests showed she had an active case of TB. The medical evidence showed that once a person with TB has begun antibiotic treatment, the chance of infecting others is quite low.

Arline was awarded back pay, attorneys' fees, and reinstatement to her teaching position. Because almost all the facts of this case are identical to AIDS and HIV virus cases, this decision has been used to prove that people with AIDS or the HIV virus are both disabled and otherwise qualified to work. A discussion of AIDS appears in Chapter 7, "AIDS, Infectious Diseases, Drug and Alcohol Problems, and Weight Problems."

Food Service Workers

Additional evidence proving individuals with AIDS or the HIV virus are under the protection of the ADA is shown by the actions taken regarding food service workers. An amendment to the ADA that would have allowed employers to refuse to hire food service workers and transfer current food service employees who have AIDS was defeated in Congress. Instead, Congress provided that employers may refuse to assign or to continue to assign individuals with infectious diseases to food service jobs if the disease is listed by the Secretary of Health and Human Services and the risk of transmission to others cannot be eliminated by reasonable accommodations.[6]

As expected, the regulations issued by the Secretary of Health and Human Services did not include AIDS or the HIV virus.[7]

Therefore, employers cannot refuse to hire applicants with AIDS or related conditions for food service jobs, and they cannot even transfer such individuals out of food service jobs into other areas (unless there is full and voluntary agreement by the worker).

The Secretary's regulations include somewhat common diseases such as hepatitis A, streptococcus, and salmonella, as well as less known infections such as Shigella species.[8] Warning symptoms of these infections include diarrhea, vomiting, open skin sores, fever, dark urine, or jaundice. However, the Secretary's interim list states that all the diseases listed can be accommodated by measures such as washing hands; wearing gloves; and not handling food after using the toilet, cleaning spills, or handling raw chicken. Therefore, the refusal to hire or reassign a food service worker because of the worker's contagious disease is not an alternative, even if the disease is on the Secretary's list.

Past Court Cases

The following examples taken from actual lawsuits illustrate the rules in determining whether disabled people are qualified for jobs, despite their individual disabilities. Like a determination of whether one is disabled, each decision must be made on a case-by-case basis. However, examples may help distinguish the legal principles involved.

Use Evidence Not Assumptions

An employee whose main duty involved office work and telephoning individuals who were delinquent in making loan repayments underwent brain surgery that left him legally blind. After a disability leave during which some vision returned and the employee received rehabilitation training that included the use of several accommodation devices, the employee returned to work. However, he was discharged. The employer said that his job performance did not meet company standards. The trial court ruled that the individual's vision problems made him unqualified because the job required reading. The Michigan Court of Appeals reversed.[9] The appeals court found the trial court had simply assumed the employee could not do his job. However, there was no evidence introduced to establish whether the employee's vision problem, with reasonable accommodations, actually prevented him from performing the essential tasks of the job.

Beware of Statistics

A probationary police officer with Crohn's disease (a serious, chronic intestinal problem) underwent surgery for removal of the diseased portion of his intestine. Upon return to work it was found he was in good health with no Crohn's disease symptoms. However, the probationary officer was terminated upon a police department physician's finding that the recurrence rate for Crohn's disease is from 13.5 percent to 50-percent. The court found a violation of the New York Human Rights Act because the decision was made upon a statistical likelihood of recurrence and inability to perform the duties of a police officer, rather than determining whether there was a *substantial probability* that the specific *individual* would suffer a recurrence.[10]

Poor Employees Not Protected

A paraplegic employee was found not to be "otherwise qualified" to retain his job because he "systematically abused leave privileges, performed poorly, was insubordinate, refused to be trained, was generally unavailable to work (which forced his supervisors to assign back-up employees to all of his assignments), and tended to make unsubstantiated accusations concerning his supervisors whenever any attempt was made to discipline him."[11] Disabled employees must abide by the same work standards as other workers. If the disabled person's attendance or job performance record would result in discipline or discharge of a nondisabled worker, it should result in the same outcome if the worker is disabled.

Employee Absences

A Temple University Hospital patient care attendant was absent from work for 49 days in less than two years, many resulting from alleged medical problems. After repeated warnings and suspensions, he was discharged. The United States Court of Appeals affirmed the lower court's decision that the excessive absences made the worker unqualified for the job.[12] The court stated that "[o]ne of the fundamental requirements of a patient care attendant is that he must be present when scheduled."[13]

In a similar case,[14] the Postal Service terminated a disabled employee after imposing disciplinary measures for excessive absences 14 times over a seven-year period. The court found that the individual was not discharged because of her disability, but rather for her failure to come to work and perform the essential tasks of the job.

Employers, however, must make reasonable accommodations for disabled employees. For instance, a case decided under the law of the state of Washington found the employer had unlawfully discharged an employee suffering from a back injury and cluster migraine headaches.[15] Although the employee was absent for several weeks, late for work on a number of days, and had received several warnings, he had unused sick leave equivalent to 10 weeks of full salary and 36 weeks of part-time salary. The court found that the company should have allowed him to use these benefits.

Essential Function

A utility company employee whose job was to give energy conservation demonstration programs throughout the state of New York was discharged after he lost his driver's license because of drunk driving offenses. Although the employee may have been legally disabled as an alcoholic under the Federal Rehabilitation Act, the court decided he was no longer qualified to perform the essential duties of his job because he was unable to drive to the locations where he was to give demonstration programs.[16]

An applicant for an entry level job in a paper mill was refused employment because laminotomy (back) surgery prevented him from meeting a 50-pound lifting test. The court found the lifting test to be a valid qualification test because the job in question frequently required the lifting of 50-pound loads.[17]

Not Qualified

An employee had wrist pain resulting from a repetitive motion disability (carpal tunnel syndrome) that caused him to be limited to sedentary work for no more than four hours per day without using his right hand. The court agreed with the United States Postal Service that he was not qualified to perform any available postal jobs.[18] Each open job position required full-time, physically active work performance. Therefore, the employee's discharge did not violate the law.

In another case involving the federal government, an employee who used physical violence against a supervisor and went on a rampage destroying office equipment was found not to be a qualified employee even if his actions resulted from a mental disability.[19] All employees, whether or not mentally disabled, must conform to reasonable workplace behavior.

Promote the Best

An employee of the Smithsonian Institution who had serious stuttering problems was denied a promotion to a managerial position in favor of a nondisabled employee. However no discrimination based upon his disability was found because the other employee was more qualified for the promotion.[20] For instance, the disabled employee submitted an application for promotion that was sloppy and incomplete, while the nondisabled employee submitted a neat, complete form indicating 35 years of experience. When asked during an oral interview how he would motivate employees and handle employee absences, the disabled candidate refused to expound beyond repeating, "I am the supervisor." The nondisabled applicant gave complete, thoughtful answers. These facts, among others, showed the nondisabled person to be more qualified.

Blanket Rules Normally Invalid

A nursing supervisor discovered that she had multiple sclerosis and attempted to return to work after a medical leave of absence. The only work restriction advised by her physician was that she not be on her feet for prolonged periods of time. The essential duties of the nursing supervisor did not require prolonged standing. However, the hospital demanded a medical examination showing she was free from the illness. When the supervisor refused to undergo such an examination, the hospital hired a permanent replacement. The court found the nursing supervisor to be fully qualified to perform the essential tasks of the job, and concluded the hospital had violated the Rehabilitation Act.[21]

The Exception to Invalid Blanket Rules

A person otherwise qualified for the position of special agent of the FBI was refused the position because of a rule disqualifying persons with insulin-dependent diabetes. Noninsulin-dependent diabetics were hired as special agents, and insulin-dependent employees were allowed in other job categories at the FBI. The court noted that blanket rules of disqualification are normally unacceptable. However, the court said a blanket rule may be imposed if valid medical evidence proves it to be necessary for the protection of the health or safety of the individual or others.[22]

In this case, medical evidence showed that it is impossible to predict with certainty which insulin-dependent diabetics may suffer hypoglycemia (low blood sugar), and that the seriousness of the hypoglycemic reaction cannot be predicted.[23] In severe cases, such a reaction can include mental confusion and even blackouts. Furthermore, the reaction is often caused by irregular meal periods and failure to follow a restricted diet, among other reasons. Because special agents often work irregular hours in remote places, such as a stake-out of a rural house, loading docks and the like, the court held that an individual with insulin-dependent diabetes is unqualified for the job.

Not Qualified

A longtime stenographer with a good work and attendance record began suffering emotional problems that were later diagnosed as a manic-depressive illness. Her job performance became erratic, disruptive, and insubordinate. Her attendance record began to suffer, and finally she left work without notice for over one-fourth of a year. After several warnings she was discharged. The court found that her job performance and lack of attendance showed the employee was not qualified for the job and could be discharged without violating the Rehabilitation Act.[24]

In another case, a probationary employee of the Postal Service with hemophilia and chronic arthritis completed an 89-day training period as a Multiple Letter Sorting Machine (MPLSM) operator. After five failed attempts to pass a standard proficiency test using the MPLSM—required of all permanent employees—he was discharged. The court had little trouble finding the disabled person to be unqualified for the job.[25]

Do Not Speculate

An applicant for admission to the Pennsylvania State Police Academy was rejected because the police physician concluded her allergies would *probably* be aggravated by the cadet training and that *perhaps* she would be unable to carry out her duties as a police officer. At trial, the medical evidence showed the applicant's allergies were unlikely to be aggravated by the academy training, and even if they were, the reaction would be minor (e.g., stopped up nose and sneezing). Therefore the applicant was qualified.[26]

Hire the Best

Three women applied for the position of junior eligibility counselor with a state department of human services. The first applicant, diagnosed as having a manic-depressive mental disease, had no formal training in social work (her college degree was in art and fashion) and no past experience in social work. During the applicant's interview, job stress was mentioned, whereupon the applicant demanded assurances that her mental condition not be considered. The interviewer tried to assure her, but stated that the fact could not be totally erased from his mind. In response, the applicant suffered a seizure of weeping and screaming. The second and third applicants handled the stress question without any apparent problems. The second job seeker had a master's degree in health and safety and had taught the subject at the university level. She had additional education in psychology and work experience in social services. The third applicant had taken 36 semester hours of psychology and several semester hours in social work, child welfare, and the American family. She had also worked as a social worker in a nursing facility.

The first applicant was rejected, but the second two were hired. Responding to a claim of handicapped discrimination under the Tennessee Human Rights Act, the court found that the job applicant simply was not qualified for the job in question. Therefore, there was no violation of law in refusing to hire her.[27]

PRACTICAL TIPS

"Otherwise Qualified Individuals"

1. In determining if a disabled person can perform the job, consider only *essential* tasks of the job.
2. Consider all reasonable accommodations.

3. After applying 1 and 2, treat disabled job applicants the same as nondisabled applicants.

4. Hire the person who is most qualified.

5. Avoid blanket rules. Look at each applicant as an individual. Decide if the individual is the most qualified to perform the essential job tasks, after reasonable accommodations are considered.

Practical Steps in Hiring Disabled Persons

To hire qualified disabled people and effectively comply with the ADA, employers may need to alter their practices in recruitment, interviewing, testing, and placing employees. The first step is to review or develop job descriptions for each job position within the company.

Job Descriptions

Lawrence Pencak, Mainstream, Inc.'s Executive Director, concludes that disabled people can perform 95 percent of most jobs.[28] A good job description can help determine whether the essential functions of the job fall in the 95 percent of the tasks the disabled person can do, with reasonable accommodations. Companies that do not have written job descriptions should develop them, while those with preexisting ones should examine them with an eye toward possible revision.

Job descriptions may be developed or revised by conducting a job analysis process that involves seven steps:[29]

1. *Determining the Essential Duties.* If possible, describe what must be accomplished, not how it is done. For example, describe a task as "communicating information," rather than "writing information." A disabled person might not be able to write on paper, but may perform the essential duty of communicating information by tape recorder or word processor.

   Remove all references to duties not required by the job. For example, some companies include the requirement in a job description that the employee have a driver's license, even though the job does not require driving. Other job descriptions retain listed duties that are out-of-date.

One company's job description for warehouse workers stated the job required lifting 150 pounds. However, unknown to the human relations department, the company had replaced human lifting of heavy amounts several years earlier with mechanical lifters.

2. *Estimate Time Spent in Each Duty.* This is an important step toward making reasonable accommodations in the future. For example, if a job requires heavy lifting, does it constitute 1 percent, 10 percent, or 50 percent of the job? If the job involves typing and filing, what is the proportion of time spent performing each task?

   If only a small part of the job involves duties that cannot be performed by an individual with a disability, job swapping can be a reasonable accommodation. However, if a disabled person cannot perform a major part of the job, the individual is not qualified and, thus, need not be hired or retained in the position.

3. *Mental Functions.* List elements required in the job such as calculating, cataloging, and inspecting.

4. *Methods.* Describe the currently used procedures for accomplishing the essential duties of the job. For example, the amount of reaching, lifting, carrying, or bending; or the amount of talking, writing, planning, calculating, or cooperating with other employees.

5. *Output.* List the results that prove good job performance such as typed words per minute, number of units assembled, or number of sales presentations per week.

6. *Working Conditions.* List factors such as temperatures at the work site, dry or humid conditions, noise, fumes, and possible hazards.

7. *Equipment, Tools, and Materials.* List the current types of equipment, machines, computers, and tools used in the job and the types of materials or information that must be handled.

Job descriptions that conform to these guidelines allow the company to determine if an applicant is qualified, and what reasonable accommodations should be considered. For example, without use of an accurate job description, a person with epilepsy who has no driver's license may be denied a job as a counselor at a juvenile hall because the job duties include driving juveniles to hospitals and to court appearances.

An accurate job description may show that only 1 to 2 percent of a counselor's time is spent driving. Therefore, an obvious accommodation is to provide minor adjustments to the job by which another counselor does the applicant's driving in exchange for the applicant doing some of that counselor's work. Instead of facing the risk of a successful ADA lawsuit for refusing to hire the individual, the company gains a qualified worker.

Recruiting Disabled Workers

Because of the excellent results many firms have had in hiring disabled employees, companies may desire to actively recruit disabled workers. However, such recruitment is not always easy. Many disabled people have encountered discrimination in the past and, as a result, are no longer actively seeking work. Vocational rehabilitation specialists sometimes appear to be more concerned with dealing with the personal problems of disabled people than in making contacts with business to place disabled workers.

Employers who desire to recruit disabled workers need to contact both standard and nonstandard recruiting sources, including:

1. State and city vocational rehabilitation agencies. Local agencies are usually listed in the telephone book under the state government listing. An additional source is a listing of 3,000 agencies in the *Rehabilitation Facility Sourcebook*, published by the National Association of Rehabilitation Facilities, P.O. Box 17675, Washington, DC 20041, phone: (703) 648-9300.
2. A local Job Training Partnership Act agency, sometimes called a Private Industry Council. Look in the telephone book under United States Government.
3. State employment agencies.
4. Veterans Administration Vocational Rehabilitation Office. Look in the telephone book under United States Government, Veterans Administration.
5. Private rehabilitation and disability groups. Look in the telephone book yellow pages under rehabilitation, vocational rehabilitation, disability, handicapped, or rehabilitative or occupational medicine.
6. Local universities (ask for the special student services or handicapped services office). For a directory of colleges with

special services for disabled students, contact the Association on Handicapped Student Service Personnel in Postsecondary Education, P.O. Box 21192, Columbus, OH 43221.
7. Local chapters of organizations such as the American Diabetes Foundation, American Cancer Society, Paralyzed Veterans of American, and the Easter Seal Society.

Job Applications and Interviews

As covered in Chapter 2, "Major Changes to Conform to the Law," the ADA does not allow employers to ask job applicants about a disability, either on a job application form or in an oral interview. However, if the job applicant voluntarily notes a disability, or the disability is obvious, for example, blind or in a wheelchair, the interviewer may, and should, discuss it. Failure to do so will give the applicant the impression that the company is not really interested in the individual.

There are some areas into which the interviewer should not delve, even if the disability is known. Do not ask about the severity of the disability, how long the person has had it, how it occurred, the personal transportation used by the individual, or any other non-job-related question.

Do not be afraid to ask job-related questions, including questions to determine if the person is qualified for the job. For example, if an applicant whose right arm has been amputated is applying for a job as a secretary, it is permissible to ask about training, previous experience, and even how the applicant can meet the typing and filing requirements of the job. Keep the interview positive. Do not dwell on the applicant's disability. Instead, discuss the applicant's abilities.

Once a disability is known, always discuss accommodations. Show a willingness to offer reasonable accommodations to allow the applicant to effectively perform the job. Ask the applicant about the accommodations needed. As an employer, you do not have to follow the applicant's suggestions if they create an undue hardship or if an alternative, effective accommodation would be less costly. See Chapter 5, "Making Accommodations for Disabled Employees," and Part II for more information on accommodations.

Try to avoid preconceived ideas about disabled persons. Deaf people do not necessarily make good printers, nor do blind people always make good piano tuners. Avoid placing yourself in the applicant's shoes and asking questions such as "If I had this disability, could I perform the job?" Such questions are unfair because the disabled person usually has been disabled for numerous years and has found methods of dealing with it that a nondisabled person cannot imagine.

Avoid slotting disabled applicants into "handicapped jobs" that offer low pay and little chance for promotion. At the other extreme, do not treat the applicant as a "supercrip," a derisive name given to the practice of overcomplementing or unduly praising disabled people, that is, "I am amazed at how well you get around," or "I really admire how you have overcome your handicaps."[30]

Specific guidelines for interviewing applicants who are blind or visually impaired, deaf or hearing impaired, and those with spinal injury or other wheelchair users are given in Part II.

Testing Job Applicants

The ADA prohibits using any employment tests, qualification standards, or other selection criteria "that screen out or tend to screen out an individual with a disability or a class of individuals with disabilities unless the standard, test or other selection criteria . . . is shown to be job related for the position in question and is consistent with business necessity."[31] Furthermore, the ADA requires that employment tests be given in the most effective manner to ensure that, when such test is administered to a job applicant or employee who has a disability that impairs sensory, manual, or speaking skills, such test results accurately reflect the skills, aptitude, or whatever other factor . . . that such test purports to measure, rather than reflecting the impaired sensory, manual or speaking skills of such employee or applicant (except where such skills are the factors that the tests purports to measure).[32]

In plain English, qualification tests must measure job applicants' or employees' abilities to do the job, not their abilities to take a certain type of test. For example, deaf job applicants whose deafness does not disqualify them from the job for which they applied cannot be denied a job because they were unable to pass an oral preemployment examination. Nor may blind applicants be denied jobs for which they are otherwise qualified simply because they were unable to take and pass a written honesty or integrity examination.

The rule that the method of testing must not disqualify an applicant for a job or promotion is absolute. There is no undue hardship exception. Employers must assure that disabled people are not denied jobs simply because of the format of the employment tests.

Sometimes alternatives are easy to find. If job applicants must pass an honesty or integrity examination the tester can accommodate a blind applicant by reading the questions aloud. These exams are rather simple and straightforward, thus easy to understand orally. However, a test based upon mathematics can be very difficult to take orally.

Timed tests can create special problems. For instance, whether a deaf applicant can successfully complete a written exam in a specified time period may depend upon when the applicant became deaf. If deafness occurred at birth, the person will usually have much lower language skills than if deafness occurred during adulthood. Even if both deaf applicants have the same intelligence, the prelingual deaf person has never developed the same capacity for understanding language as has the deaf person who grew up hearing verbal language. Furthermore, the prelingual deaf person may be trained in sign language—a system that uses different syntax and construction than verbal and written English uses.

A timed, written test of driving skills and highway laws given to truck driver applicants may be very difficult for an applicant with the learning disability of dyslexia (whereby the applicant often sees transposed letters or even words spelled backward). The applicant may be the most qualified truck driver, but still fail the written test. The solution may be to give the applicant extra time to complete the written examination. However, the need for extra time raises two questions. First, how much extra time is reasonable? Second, does the extra time give the disabled applicant an advantage over non-disabled applicants?[33]

Two alternatives that avoid testing bias problems have been used by the federal government. If the job applicant or employee has an educational and work record, use the past record as a judgment for ability, rather than a test. Another alternative is to waive the test and substitute a probationary length of employment of approximately one to six months. Such an on-the-job trial period is the best way of determining a person's qualifications. However, when using the latter idea, it is wise to have a complete understanding about the probationary or trial period of employment. New employees must realize that they have not obtained a permanent job, but rather are being evaluated for permanent employment.

Although generalized examinations such as IQ, aptitude, honesty, personality, and other written and verbal tests must be adjusted to accommodate disabled people, nothing in the ADA prevents or limits the use of relevant job skill tests. If an employer is hiring word processors and has a requirement that all employees be able to type 60 wpm, a typing or keyboarding skills test may be given and those applicants not able to meet the job requirements may be refused employment. Additionally, a trucking company may give all applicants, disabled and nondisabled, a reasonable driving test. Those applicants who do not pass should not be hired.

However, there is one major condition to the freedom to use job skill examinations. Disabled persons must be tested on direct job skills while using any reasonable accommodations they would be entitled to as an employee. Therefore, a visually impaired computer processor applicant may require a computer with a magnified screen to take the test if such a screen would be a reasonable accommodation. Also, a disabled truck diver applicant must be furnished accommodations that would normally be used on the job. Often these devices may be borrowed from a state vocational rehabilitation agency or private organization such as the Easter Seal Society or the Paralyzed Veterans of America.

Specific suggestions concerning administering job-related tests to people who are blind or vision impaired, deaf or hearing impaired, those with spinal cord injuries and other paralysis, as well as those with learning disabilities, are covered in Part II.

The Job Matching Process

By combining an accurate job description with an individual's functional limitations, an employer can determine what accommodations must be considered, and whether the applicant is qualified, once accommodations are given. A format that allows a comparison of job duties and possible physical and mental limitations, leading to questions that must be answered in order to decide upon reasonable accommodations and to make a final judgment as to an applicant's qualifications is given below. This Job Matching Check Sheet is modified from one developed by Ruth Bragman and Joyce Couch Cole.[34]

Three examples showing the use of the Job Matching Check Sheet are given below. In each case the job tasks are matched with possible disability problems, leading to questions to ask or areas to investigate.

Exhibit 4.1

JOB MATCHING CHECK SHEET

Name of Applicant: Disability:

Job Position:

Job Description:

POSSIBLE JOB DEMANDS	TYPICAL ESSENTIAL JOB TASKS	POSSIBLE DISABILITY RELATED PROBLEMS	QUESTIONS TO ASK
Physical Demands XXXXXXXXXXXXXXX	XXXXXXXXXX	XXXXXXXXXX	XXXXXXXXXX
Walking			
Lifting, Reaching, Carrying			
Stooping, Bending, Squatting			
Climbing, Balancing			
Handling, Fingering			
Physical Coordination			
Prolonged Standing or Sitting			
Vision			
Eye-Hand Coordination			
Unusual Degree of Stamina			
Communication Skills XXXXXXXXXXXX	XXXXXXXXXX	XXXXXXXXXX	XXXXXXXXXX
Writing			
Speaking			
Hearing			
Reading			
Interpersonal Relationships			
Receiving Instructions			
Giving Instructions			
Intellectual Skills XXXXXXXXXXXXXXX	XXXXXXXXXX	XXXXXXXXXX	XXXXXXXXXX
Short Term Memory			
Long Term Memory			
Abstract Reasoning			
Decision Making			
Directing Others			
Mathematical Calculations			

continues

Exhibit 4.1 *Continued*

POSSIBLE JOB DEMANDS	TYPICAL ESSENTIAL JOB TASKS	POSSIBLE DISABILITY RELATED PROBLEMS	QUESTIONS TO ASK
Work Situations XXXXXXXXXXXXXXXX	XXXXXXXXXX	XXXXXXXXXX	XXXXXXXXXX
Irregular Hours			
Out-of-Town Travel			
Working Alone			
Working as Part of a Group			
Working with the Public			
High-Speed Performance			
Constant High Stress			
Stress of Meeting Frequent Deadlines			
Emergency Stress Situations			
Leadership Skills			
Performing a Variety of Duties			
Performing Routine, Repetitive Duties			
Driving Vehicles			
Operating Machinery			
Environmental Conditions XXXXXXXXX	XXXXXXXXXX	XXXXXXXXXX	XXXXXXXXXX
Extreme Heat or Cold			
Wet or Humid			
Noise or Vibration			
Safety Hazards			
Fumes, Dust, or Odors			
Equipment with Moving Parts			

Exhibit 4.2

JOB MATCHING CHECK SHEET

Name of Applicant: Jane Johnson   Disability: Diabetes

Job Position:Traveling Sales Representative

Job Description: Sells products to business and industrial customers over a three state area. Requires extensive driving (about 45% of work time), and overnight stays in various cities. Requires carrying a ten pound sample case from car to various offices. Demonstrates company products, solicits and takes orders, quotes prices, and calculates discounts. Writes sales contracts, keeps expense account, and writes weekly summary of sales and expenses. Thirty-five percent of time spent in customer offices. Remaining time spent in doing paperwork. Sometimes works long hours to comply with customer availability.

POSSIBLE JOB DEMANDS	TYPICAL ESSENTIAL JOB TASKS	POSSIBLE DISABILITY RELATED PROBLEMS	QUESTIONS TO ASK
Physical Demands XXXXXXXXXXXXXX	XXXXXXXXXX	XXXXXXXXXX	XXXXXXXXXX
Walking	X		
Lifting, Reaching, Carrying	X	X	(1)
Stooping, Bending, Squatting			
Climbing, Balancing			
Handling, Fingering	X		
Physical Coordination			
Prolonged Standing or Sitting	X		
Vision	X		
Eye-Hand Coordination			
Unusual Degree of Stamina	X	X	(2)
Communication Skills XXXXXXXXXXXX	XXXXXXXXXX	XXXXXXXXXX	XXXXXXXXXX
Writing	X		
Speaking	X		
Hearing	X		
Reading	X		
Interpersonal Relationships	X		
Receiving Instructions			
Giving Instructions			
Intellectual Skills XXXXXXXXXXXXXX	XXXXXXXXXX	XXXXXXXXXX	XXXXXXXXXX
Short Term Memory	X		
Long Term Memory	X		
Abstract Reasoning	X		
Decision Making	X		
Directing Others			
Mathematical Calculations	X		

continues

Exhibit 4.2 *Continued*

POSSIBLE JOB DEMANDS	TYPICAL ESSENTIAL JOB TASKS	POSSIBLE DISABILITY RELATED PROBLEMS	QUESTIONS TO ASK
Work Situations XXXXXXXXXXXXXXXX	XXXXXXXXXX	XXXXXXXXXX	XXXXXXXXXX
Irregular Hours	X	X	(2)
Out-of-Town Travel	X		
Working Alone	X		
Working as Part of a Group			
Working with the Public	X		
High-Speed Performance			
Constant High Stress			
Stress of Meeting Frequent Deadlines			
Emergency Stress Situations			
Leadership Skills			
Performing a Variety of Duties			
Performing Routine, Repetitive Duties			
Driving Vehicles	X	X	(3)
Operating Machinery			
Environmental Conditions XXXXXXXX	XXXXXXXXXX	XXXXXXXXXX	XXXXXXXXXX
Extreme Heat or Cold			
Wet or Humid			
Noise or Vibration			
Safety Hazards			
Fumes, Dust, or Odors			
Equipment with Moving Parts			

Questions to Ask:

1. Does your physical condition allow you to lift and carry the 10-pound sample case into and out of various locations? If not, do you know of anything that may be used to accommodate your problem, such as a wheeled luggage carrier?
2. Do you expect any problems in working irregular hours requiring extra stamina, sometimes delaying meals and staying in out-of-town locations? If so, how can we accommodate the problem?
3. Do you have any problems driving?

Exhibit 4.3

JOB MATCHING CHECK SHEET

Name of Applicant: Jean Peterson   Disability: Lower Extremities Paralyzed; Wheelchair User

Job Position: Registered Industrial Nurse

Job Description: Provides nursing services to ill or injured workers or others on the premises with medical problems. Gives first aid, attends to subsequent dressing of employee injuries, keeps records of patients treated, prepares accident reports for insurance, OSHA, and other purposes, assists with physical examinations, plans and conducts health information programs for employees, evaluates plant environment for health and safety problems. Ninety percent of time spent in medical office or seminar room. Ten percent of time spent in rendering first aid at the location of an accident or evaluating health and safety factors.

POSSIBLE JOB DEMANDS	TYPICAL ESSENTIAL JOB TASKS	POSSIBLE DISABILITY RELATED PROBLEMS	QUESTIONS TO ASK
Physical Demands XXXXXXXXXXXXXX	XXXXXXXXXX	XXXXXXXXXX	XXXXXXXXXX
Walking	X	X	(1)
Lifting, Reaching, Carrying	X	X	(2)
Stooping, Bending, Squatting	X	X	(2)
Climbing, Balancing			
Handling, Fingering	X		
Physical Coordination			
Prolonged Standing or Sitting			
Vision	X		
Eye-Hand Coordination	X		
Unusual Degree of Stamina			
Communication Skills XXXXXXXXXXXX	XXXXXXXXXX	XXXXXXXXXX	XXXXXXXXXX
Writing	X		
Speaking	X		
Hearing	X		
Reading	X		
Interpersonal Relationships	X		
Receiving Instructions			
Giving Instructions	X		
Intellectual Skills XXXXXXXXXXXXXX	XXXXXXXXXX	XXXXXXXXXX	XXXXXXXXXX
Short Term Memory	X		
Long Term Memory	X		
Abstract Reasoning	X		
Decision Making	X		
Directing Others	X		
Mathematical Calculations			

continues

Exhibit 4.3 *Continued*

POSSIBLE JOB DEMANDS	TYPICAL ESSENTIAL JOB TASKS	POSSIBLE DISABILITY RELATED PROBLEMS	QUESTIONS TO ASK
Work Situations XXXXXXXXXXXXXXXX	XXXXXXXXXX	XXXXXXXXXX	XXXXXXXXXX
Irregular Hours			
Out-of-Town Travel			
Working Alone			
Working as Part of a Group			
Working with the Public			
High-Speed Performance			
Constant High Stress			
Stress of Meeting Frequent Deadlines			
Emergency Stress Situations	X		
Leadership Skills			
Performing a Variety of Duties	X		
Performing Routine, Repetitive Duties			
Driving Vehicles			
Operating Machinery			
Environmental Conditions XXXXXXXXX	XXXXXXXXXX	XXXXXXXXXX	XXXXXXXXXX
Extreme Heat or Cold			
Wet or Humid			
Noise or Vibration			
Safety Hazards			
Fumes, Dust, or Odors			
Equipment with Moving Parts			

Questions to Ask:

1. Do you envision any problems in getting around the plant in order to render first aid or examine for health and safety problems. If so, what do you need to overcome any problem(s)?
2. Can you bend, lean over, or otherwise get into positions to render medical aid to a person on the floor? Do you have enough mobility to adequately treat patients in the office or assist in physical exams? If not, what accommodations would help?

Exhibit 4.4

JOB MATCHING CHECK SHEET

Name of Applicant: Frank Mills   Disability: Epilepsy

Job Position: Maintenance Electrician

Job Description: Performs a variety of electrical repair and maintenance jobs in various locations throughout the plant. Work includes installing and repairing generators, transformers, switchboards, controllers, circuit breakers, motors, heating units, and transmission systems. Must work from blueprints, drawings, and instruction manuals. Must locate and diagnose trouble. Work locations both inside and outside plant, in low and high places. Must be able to use a variety of tools, measuring devices, and testing instruments under a variety of conditions. Some work is on an emergency basis.

POSSIBLE JOB DEMANDS	TYPICAL ESSENTIAL JOB TASKS	POSSIBLE DISABILITY RELATED PROBLEMS	QUESTIONS TO ASK
Physical Demands XXXXXXXXXXXXXX	XXXXXXXXXX	XXXXXXXXXX	XXXXXXXXXX
Walking	X		
Lifting, Reaching, Carrying	X		
Stooping, Bending, Squatting	X		
Climbing, Balancing	X	X	(1)
Handling, Fingering	X		
Physical Coordination	X		
Prolonged Standing or Sitting			
Vision	X		
Eye-Hand Coordination	X		
Unusual Degree of Stamina			
Communication Skills XXXXXXXXXXXX	XXXXXXXXXX	XXXXXXXXXX	XXXXXXXXXX
Writing			
Speaking	X		
Hearing	X		
Reading	X		
Interpersonal Relationships			
Receiving Instructions			
Giving Instructions			
Intellectual Skills XXXXXXXXXXXXXXX	XXXXXXXXXX	XXXXXXXXXX	XXXXXXXXXX
Short Term Memory	X		
Long Term Memory	X		
Abstract Reasoning	X		
Decision Making	X		
Directing Others			
Mathematical Calculations	X		

continues

Exhibit 4.4 *Continued*

POSSIBLE JOB DEMANDS	TYPICAL ESSENTIAL JOB TASKS	POSSIBLE DISABILITY RELATED PROBLEMS	QUESTIONS TO ASK
Work Situations XXXXXXXXXXXXXXXX	XXXXXXXXXX	XXXXXXXXXX	XXXXXXXXXX
Irregular Hours			
Out-of-Town Travel			
Working Alone	X		
Working as Part of a Group			
Working with the Public			
High-Speed Performance			
Constant High Stress			
Stress of Meeting Frequent Deadlines			
Emergency Stress Situations	X	X	(2)
Leadership Skills			
Performing a Variety of Duties	X		
Performing Routine, Repetitive Duties			
Driving Vehicles			
Operating Machinery			
Environmental Conditions XXXXXXXXX	XXXXXXXXXX	XXXXXXXXXX	XXXXXXXXXX
Extreme Heat or Cold	X		
Wet or Humid	X		
Noise or Vibration	X		
Safety Hazards	X	X	(1)
Fumes, Dust, or Odors			
Equipment with Moving Parts	X	X	(1)

Questions to Ask:

1. Will your epilepsy cause you or others any danger, considering the fact that you will have to climb and balance yourself at times, work around dangerous working parts, and experience fumes, dust, and the like? How many daytime seizures have you had in the past few years? Were they serious? Is your physician able to recommend this type of work for you?
2. Will occasional stressful situations cause any increased chance of a seizure? Are there any job alterations or modifications that could help you safely perform the job?

The key to using the Job Matching Check Sheet is knowing enough about the disability so that the possible disability-related problems can be marked, and knowing enough to ask intelligent questions. Part II lists some of the symptoms and problems created by various medical conditions and may be an aid in conducting job matches. The Job Matching Check Sheet may also be used with current employees who become disabled to determine if they can still perform their job, with or without accommodations, or possibly to determine if they might qualify for another job.

Notes

1. Americans with Disabilities Act §101(8), 42 U.S.C.A. §12111 (West 1991) (emphasis added).
2. EEOC Regulations on the Americans with Disabilities Act, 56 Fed. Reg. 23,735 (1991) (to be codified at 29 C.F.R. §1630.2(n)).
3. 480 U.S. 273, 43 FEP Cases 81 (1987).
4. *Id.*, 480 U.S. at 274.
5. Arline v. School Bd. of Nassau County, 692 F.Supp. 1286, 47 FEP Cases 530 (M.D. Fla. 1988).
6. Americans with Disabilities Act, §103(d)(2), 42 U.S.C.A. §12113 (West 1991).
7. ADA List of Infectious Diseases, United States Dep't of Health and Human Services, 56 Fed. Reg. 40,897 (1991).
8. The complete list is as follows: "(1) Diseases often transmitted by infected food handlers: Hepatitis A virus, Norwalk and Norwalk-like viruses, Salmonella typhi, Shigella species, Staphylococcus aureus, Streptococcus pyogenes. (2) Diseases occasionally transmitted by infected food handlers: Campylobacter jejuni, Entamoeba histolytica, Enterohemorrhagic Escherichia coli, Enterotoxigenic Escherichia coli, Giardia lamblia, Nontyphoidal Salmonella, Rotavirus, Vibrio cholarae 01, Yersinia entercolitica." United States Dep't of Health and Human Services, 56 Fed. Reg. 40,897 (1991).
9. Mitchell v. General Motors Acceptance Corp. 439 N.W. 2d 261 (1989).
10. Antonsen v. Ward, 556 N.Y. 2d 479, 161 A.2d 378 (1989).
11. Thomas v. General Servs. Admin., 49 FEP Cases 1602, EPD §39,221 (D.D.C. 1989).
12. Santiago v. Temple Univ., 928 F.2d 396 (3d Cir. 1991).
13. *Id.* at 402.
14. Holmes v. Frank, 54 EPD §40,136 (E.D. Mich. 1990).
15. Kimbro v. Atlantic Richfield Co., 889 F.2d 869, 57 FEP Cases 363 (9th Cir. 1989).
16. O'Keefe v. Niagara Power Corp., 714 F.Supp. 622 (N.D. N.Y. 1989).
17. Plourde v. Scott Paper Co. 532 A.2d 1257, 48 FEP Cases 1452 (Me. 1989).
18. Black v. Frank, 730 F. Supp. 1087 (S.D. Ala. 1990).
19. Adams v. Alderson, 723 F. Supp. 1531, 51 FEP Cases 647 (D.D.C. 1989).
20. Solomon v. Smithsonian Inst., 509 FEP Cases 386, 53 EPD §39,968 (D.D.C. 1989).
21. Carter v. Casa Central, 849 F.2d 1048, 47 FEP Cases 257 (7th Cir. 1988).

22. Davis v. Meese, 692 F. Supp. 505, 47 FEP Cases 828 (E.D. Pa. 1988).
23. *Id.*
24. Matzo v. Postmaster General, 685 F. Supp. 260, 46 FEP Cases 869 (D.D.C. 1987). For a similar set of facts and outcome, *see* Franklin v. United States Postal Service, 687 F. Supp. 1214, 46 FEP Cases 1734 (S.D. Ohio 1988).
25. Davis v. United States Postal Service, 675 F. Supp. 225, 44 FEP Cases 1299 (M.D. Pa 1987).
26. Pennsylvania State Police v. Pennsylvania Human Relations Commission, 457 A.2d 584, 36 FEP Cases 602 (1983).
27. Peebles v. Puett, 39 EPD section 36,068 (Tenn. Ct. App. 1985). For a similar case of a less qualified disabled person in competition with a nondisabled person, *see* Norcross v. Sneed, 755 F.2d 113, 37 FEP Cases 77 (8th Cir. 1985).
28. "Performing Job Analysis and Making Reasonable Accommodations," IN THE MAINSTREAM, Jan.–Feb. 1989, at 3.
29. This material taken in part from Bragman & Cole, *Job-Match: A Process for Interviewing and Hiring Qualified Handicapped Individuals*, a monograph published by the (Am. Soc'y for Personnel Admin., 606 North Washington St. Alexandria, Va 22314) (1984); *"Performing Job Analysis and Making Reasonable Accommodations, In the* MAINSTREAM, Jan.–Feb. 1989, at 3–5; and "Making Sense Out of Essential Function," IN THE MAINSTREAM, Sept.–Oct. 1990, at 11–12.
30. *See* Proctor, *Practical Steps Toward Employing More Persons With Disabilities*, IN THE MAINSTREAM, Jan.–Feb. 1990, at 9–10.
31. Americans with Disabilities Act, §102(b)(6), 42 U.S.C. §12112 (West 1991).
32. *Id.* at §102(b)(7), 42 U.S.C. §12112 (West 1991).
33. The United States Office of Personnel Management, 1900 E Street, NW, Washington, DC 20415, has conducted a number of studies on timed tests and other testing methods applied to disabled and nondisabled individuals. For additional information, see various issues of *Public Personnel Management Journal* and the Blindness and Vision Impairments entry in Part II of this book. For two good articles, see M. Nester, *Employment Testing for Handicapped Persons*, PUB. PERSONNEL MGMT. J., Winter 1984, at 417–437; and S. SHERMAN & N. ROBINSON, ABILITY TESTING OF HANDICAPPED PEOPLE: DILEMMA FOR GOVERNMENT, SCIENCE, AND THE PUBLIC (Nat'l Acad. Press 1982).
34. The Job Matching Checksheet is adapted from an excellent monograph, Bragman and Cole, *Job-Match: A Process for Interviewing and Hiring Qualified Handicapped Individuals* (Soc'y for Human Resource Mgmt., 606 North Washington St., Alexandria, VA 22314, phone (703) 548-3440).

Chapter 5

Making Accommodations for Disabled Employees

The Americans with Disabilities Act (ADA) requires employers to make: "reasonable accommodations to the known physical or mental limitations of an otherwise qualified individual with a disability who is an applicant or employee, unless . . . (the employer) can demonstrate that the accommodation would impose an undue hardship on the operation of the business . . . ."[1]

This chapter will discuss the limited legal guidance given under the law and regulations regarding what constitutes a reasonable accommodation, followed by examples of accommodations and practical advice on making reasonable accommodations.

The Ground Rules

The language of the ADA quoted above indicates four important points:

1. The duty to make accommodations does not arise until an employer knows of a person's disability.
2. The duty to accommodate applies both to job applicants and current employees.
3. Only reasonable accommodations must be made. The ADA itself lists several examples of accommodations that *may* be appropriate:
   (A) making existing facilities used by employees readily accessible to and usable by individuals with disabilities, and

(B) job restructuring, part-time or modified work schedules, reassignment to a vacant position, acquisition or
modification of equipment or devices, appropriate
adjustment or modifications of examinations, training
materials or policies, the provision of qualified readers or
interpreters, and other similar accommodations. . . .[2]
This list of accommodations in the ADA provides examples
only, and not a complete list of accommodations.

4. Accommodations that impose undue hardships on employers do not have to be made. However, the ADA and the
regulations of the Equal Employment Opportunity Commission (EEOC) give only general guidance as to what is
reasonable and what is an undue hardship. The ADA states
that "undue hardship means an action requiring significant
difficulty or expense."[3] Following the language of the ADA,
EEOC regulations state that the following factors should be
considered in determining if there is an undue hardship:

   (i) The nature and net cost of the accommodations needed
   under this part, taking into consideration the availability of tax credits and deductions, and/or outside
   funding;

   (ii) The overall financial resources of the facility or facilities
   involved in the provision of the reasonable accommodation, the number of persons employed at such facility,
   and the effect on expenses and resources;

   (iii) The overall financial resources of the covered entity,
   the overall size of the business of the covered entity
   with respect to number of its employees, and the
   number, type and location of its facilities;

   (iv) The type of operation or operations of the covered
   entity, including the composition, structure and functions of the workforce of such entity, and the geographic separateness and administrative or fiscal relationship of the facility or facilities in question to the
   covered entity; and

   (v) The impact of the accommodation upon the operation
   of the facility, including the impact on the ability of
   other employees to perform their duties and the impact
   on the facility's ability to conduct business.[4]

There is little guidance as to how these factors will be applied to
real-life fact situations. Congress explicitly rejected an amendment

that would have established a limit on accommodations based upon a dollar amount.[5] Instead, the ADA requires a case-by-case analysis based upon the general factors listed above.

Past Case Decisions and Law

The ADA's reasonable accommodation requirement and undue hardship definition generally follow that of the Rehabilitation Act of 1973,[6] and especially the regulations issued under section 504 of the Rehabilitation Act.[7] Some cases decided under the Rehabilitation Act and similar state laws give guidance in distinguishing a reasonable accommodation verses one that creates an undue hardship.

In *Wallace v. Veterans Administration,*[8] a hospital refused to hire a registered nurse because she was a recovering drug abuser and RNs normally handle controlled drugs. The court, however, found that only 2 percent of the nurse's time would be spent handling drugs, and that the hospital could make a reasonable accommodation by providing for some minor job duty switching with other nurses so that the applicant did not have to handle drugs.

Another failure of a government agency to reasonably accommodate an employee's disability occurred when the United States Army failed to allow a typist/clerk to mix typing and filing.[9] The employee had undergone cancer surgery and prolonged sitting caused pain. On two occasions, she passed out and had to be taken to the hospital. Because there was an abundance of both typing and filing needed in the office in which the employee worked, allowing the employee to do both caused no hardship.

Reasonable Accommodations Not Provided

In the following cases, courts found requested or available accommodations to be reasonable. Therefore, an employer's refusal to provide such an accommodation was a violation of law.

Standardized Test

A job applicant with dyslexia was unable to pass a standardized, written examination that would qualify him for a position as a heavy equipment operator. The employer's only attempted accommodation was a request to the testing service that the examination be given orally. When the request was denied, the applicant was not hired. The court said the employer must find a method to test the actual qualifications of the applicant.[10]

Easy to Accomplish

An employee with severe back pain resulting from an accident requested reduced work time, a wooden, straight back chair, and the use of an elevator located in the building. The employer refused the requests.[11] The court found that the governmental employer could have granted all of these accommodations at minimal expense without undue hardship.

Must Seek Alternatives

In a case under Michigan law similar to the ADA, the court held that a fire department could not automatically discharge a fire fighter for violation of the department's grooming code because of the fire fighter's refusal to shave.[12] The employee had pseudo-folliculitis, a genetic disease that causes skin infections and scaring, making it difficult to safely shave. Although the grooming code was safety related—to allow air masks to seal with the face—the court found the employer should look into alternatives such as adaptive devices or other methods of protection from smoke.

An Iowa court found an employer had illegally discharged a cafeteria worker after she had an epileptic seizure at work.[13] The employee spent most of her time in nondangerous work such as cleaning tables, serving food, and operating a cash register. Only on rare occasions did she operate the grill, use the meat slicer, or work with the deep-fat fryer. The court reasoned the employer could easily accommodate her epilepsy by refraining from assigning her the more dangerous work.

In another Iowa case, the court held that an employee who lost his driver's license due to a disability had suggested a reasonable accommodation when he said he would personally "hire" his wife to drive him to work locations in his own car.[14]

In a federal case in Iowa, a well-qualified applicant for a teaching position with a governmental agency was not interviewed when the agency discovered that the applicant's disability prevented him from driving a school bus. In finding a violation of the Rehabilitation Act,[15] the court noted three reasonable accommodations. First, the agency could have asked the local school district to transport students, rather than using the teacher supplied by the agency. Second, it could have considered using one of three other teachers who were available to drive the bus. Third, it could have hired a part-time bus driver.

How Far Must an Employer Go?

The extent of legally mandated reasonable accommodations are illustrated by a case where an employee was denied the position of time and attendance clerk at a United States Post Office because he was deaf.[16] The job description stated that a time and attendance clerk must collect and keep records of the time each employee works, the times absent from work, and the reasons for absences. Furthermore, the clerk must explain rules involving leave and pay matters, maintain assignment cards, and make studies concerning time worked. The court found all of the following ideas to be reasonable accommodations that would allow the deaf employee to successfully perform the job:

1. Allowing one of the three other clerks to answer phones.
2. Use of laminated cards containing phrases the employee would use frequently.
3. Prepared lists of terms and questions frequently encountered by the clerk, to allow people to point to the topic they wish to discuss and thereby make lipreading easier.
4. Elementary training of other employees to make them aware of common mistakes in dealing with deaf people.
5. Training the few employees who often come into contact with the clerk in basic sign language or finger spelling. This training can be done in about one hour.
6. Expanding the use of the TTY keyboard for the hearing impaired that was already available in the post office.

Accommodations Found to Create Undue Hardship

Undue hardship may be found when the suggested accommodation is financially too expensive, would fundamentally alter the nature of the job, or would unduly disrupt the workplace. Some accommodations that have been found to create an undue hardship under laws similar to the ADA are illustrated by the following cases.

Unreasonable Requests

In *Treadwell v. Alexander*,[17] an applicant for a park technician's position with the Corps of Engineers who had a nervous
condition and heart problems was denied a job. He claimed discrimination because the employer refused to reallocate duties so that the
applicant could avoid walking over rough terrain, handling disor-
derly park visitors, and operating a boat alone. The court decided
these accommodations did not have to be offered because they
involved releasing the applicant from the essential duties of the job.
Because the agency employed only three other persons at the work
site, it would be impossible to reallocate the job duties. Instead, a
second employee would have to be hired to do the applicant's job—
an undue burden on the employer.

In another case involving the Corps of Engineers, the court
found that an employee with bipolar, manic-depressive illness who
requested a job assignment in Saudi Arabia required an accommodation that would create an undue hardship.[18] The location of the
job was in a city that did not have a physician-staffed hospital. The
nearest fully staffed hospital was several hours away. The employee
contended that the Corps should allow his physician to write up a
step-by-step procedure for handling incidents of euphoria or
depression and provide for transportation to an Army hospital in
Germany. The court stated that the suggested accommodations
were both ineffective and an undue hardship.

Unworkable Accommodations

A case under Maine law similar to the ADA upheld a paper
company's refusal to hire an applicant with back problems and a
50-pound limit on lifting.[19] The entry level job, called a "spare,"
required employees to rotate around the plant to replace absent
workers. Much of the work involved heavy lifting, including rolling
spools of paper that weighed from 900 pounds to 5 tons. The court
decided job restructuring would create an undue hardship since it
would exempt the employee from doing tasks that were essential to
the job.

In a case under West Virginia law similar to the ADA, the court
found undue hardship and upheld a hospital's decision to refuse to
restructure a job by allowing a cleaning person with a back injury to
do only "high cleaning."[20] The employee requested that she be
teamed with another cleaning person. She could do the "high

cleaning" that did not require bending or stooping, while the other employee would do the "low cleaning." The court said that an employer is not required to create a new job category as an accommodation. However, a 1991 Minnesota decision[21] found that a nursing home should restructure a housekeeper's job to allow a stroke victim to return to work. The court decided that teaming the stroke victim with another housekeeper would solve the problem of the stroke victim's inability to remember which rooms she had cleaned.

A 1991 decision under the Federal Rehabilitation Act found that a city had exceeded its duty to offer reasonable accommodations when it attempted to modify the essential duties of the job, transfer the individual to another job, and even considered creating a new job category for a building inspector with Parkinson's disease.[22] The inspector's condition made it impossible to climb around unfinished buildings, a task that involved 50 percent of working time and was the key to inspecting buildings. To accommodate the inspector, the city considered splitting the job in half, keeping the individual in the office and another inspector doing the outside work. The split of responsibilities did not work, however, because the inside work was useful only if done by the person who physically inspected buildings. The city considered transferring the individual to another job, but no other job positions were available. It even considered creating a new job category, but budget restraints prevented this. The court made two points in response to the individual's claim that the city should have considered a part-time job. First, the law does not require the creation of a new job position—full-time or part-time—as an accommodation. Second, the requested accommodation still would not permit the individual to do inspections.

Need Not Ignore Safety and Efficiency

A postal employee with achondroplastic dwarfism who was four-feet, five-inches tall with disproportionately short arms applied for a promotion to a distribution clerk's position that involved reaching over specially designed boxes to sort the mail.[23] The employee claimed the provision of a stool would be a reasonable accommodation that would allow him to do the work. The postal service refused to provide the stool because it would substantially interfere with other employees' movements, would have to be constantly moved by the individual as he went down the rows of boxes (thus slowing the work), and it would be dangerous because the employee's short arms would necessitate leaning over the boxes, causing a substantial risk of falling. The court agreed with the postal service that the requested accommodation was not reasonable.

Drawing the Line

Some accommodations involving major expenses may be determined to be reasonable. However, they will not be required if they are not effective. Two past cases under the Rehabilitation Act illustrate this balancing.

In *Nelson v. Thornburgh,*[24] three blind employees whose positions required interviewing applicants for financial aid and completing substantial amounts of paper work asked their agency to pay readers to assist them with the paperwork. The employees had originally paid readers from their personal funds and could successfully perform all their job duties with readers. The court discussed four possible accommodations:

1. Converting all forms to braille.
2. Printing the 1,000-page agency rules manual in braille at a cost of approximately $34,000.
3. Purchase of machines that scan and read aloud written materials. At the time accommodations were requested the cost would have been $7,700 per machine, plus a maintenance contract of $700 per year (currently such machines may be found at lower prices).
4. Paying the employees' readers, as they requested, by using employees who would do clerical work part-time and read for the blind employees part-time at a cost of about $6,000 per year per blind employee.

In light of the agency's administrative budget of $300 million dollars and the practicality of employing readers/clerks, the court found that *any* of the four alternatives would be a reasonable accommodation.

A different result involving the same federal agency occurred in *Arneson v. Heckler.*[25] An employee with duties similar to the workers in the previous case asked for a reader or another claims administrator to aid him. The cost of a full-time reader would be from $15,738 to $25,343, plus benefits, depending upon the grade level of the person hired. A second claims administrator would cost from $26,261 to $34,135. A private office was also requested. The employee's disability, apraxia, is a condition affecting the brain that results in varying symptoms. In the employee's case, the disease made it difficult to understand written or oral language.

The court found the requests to be unreasonable. The private office would not help overcome the employee's impairment. Providing a reader would also be ineffective since the employee had difficulty in understanding orally stated information to the same extent as written material. Hiring another claims administrator was found to be unreasonable because it would require the hiring of another person to do the work the employee was hired to do. Reasonable accommodations allow the employee to accomplish the essential tasks of the job, and do not require substituting another person to do those tasks for the disabled employee.

EEOC Guidance

The EEOC has issued an interpretive guidance that, while not legally binding, offers some guidelines.[26] The EEOC guidance contains three types of accommodations: those required to ensure equal opportunity in the application process; those that enable employees with disabilities to perform the essential functions of the job; and those that enable disabled employees to enjoy equal benefits and privileges of employment enjoyed by other employees.[27]

EEOC guidance provides examples of possible accommodations including permitting the use of paid sick leave or providing additional unpaid leave for medical treatment, making employer-provided transportation accessible, providing personal assistants such as a page turner or travel attendant, and providing reserved handicapped parking spaces.[28]

Other accommodations discussed in the interpretive guidance include accessibility, job restructuring, and job reassignment. Accommodations to consider in making the physical premises accessible should include both those that will allow an employee to perform the essential tasks of the job, and those that give access to nonwork areas such as company cafeterias or lounges.[29]

Job restructuring is a reasonable accommodation if it reallocates nonessential or marginal job duties. For example, an employer may have two jobs, each of which entails the performance of a number of marginal functions. When an employer hires a disabled employee who can perform some, but not all, of the marginal functions, the employer may reallocate the functions so the other employee performs those functions the disabled employee is unable to perform.[30]

The EEOC states that an employer is not required to reallocate essential functions. For example, suppose a security guard position requires the employee to inspect identification cards. An employer would not have to provide a blind security guard with an assistant to look at identification cards. In effect, this would require the assistant to perform the guard's basic job.[31]

Reassignment to a vacant position may be a reasonable accommodation for a current employee with a disability. The EEOC warns, however, that such reassignment is reasonable only if accommodations in the employee's current job cannot be made. Although reassignment to a less favorable job will be closely examined, it is a reasonable accommodation if all other accommodations fail, even if the employee must take a pay cut as a result of the reassignment. Promotion as a reasonable accommodation is not required.[32]

Undue Hardship

The EEOC makes it clear that undue hardship is not limited to financial cost. Undue hardship may also be shown if the suggested accommodation is unreasonably disruptive to the workplace or fundamentally alters the operation of the business.[33] For example, turning up the lights in a nightclub or restaurant to accommodate a visually impaired employee who cannot see in dim light is an undue hardship if the ambience of the nightclub or restaurant is destroyed. Increasing the heat in a building to accommodate a disabled employee is unreasonable if it makes the facility unduly hot for other employees or customers. However, an employer cannot show undue hardship if the disruption to its employees is the result of employees' fears or prejudices toward the disabled individual and not the result of the disruption caused by the accommodation.[34]

Although the EEOC regulations cited earlier in this chapter state that costs to an individual job site may be considered when judging undue hardship, EEOC interpretive guidance indicates that the financial resources of the entire business will be the key consideration regarding cost. The only example given by the EEOC limiting cost considerations to a local facility's financial resources is in the case of a franchise where the franchisee only pays an annual franchise fee—in effect, an independent business.[35]

In judging the financial burden of making accommodations to determine whether they create an undue burden, only the net cost to the employer should be considered.[36] In many cases a state rehabilitation agency, a public interest group such as the Braille

Institute, or the employee, will pay part or all of the cost of the accommodation. For example, in 47 placements of visually impaired workers arranged by the Sensory Aids Foundation of Palo Alto, California, the employer paid for the accommodation device in only 14 cases and shared the cost in 3 other cases. In 27 cases a state vocational rehabilitation agency or public interest group paid the cost, while in another 3 cases the employee provided the accommodation device.[37]

Decisions about a reasonable accommodation, like decisions about whether a suggested accommodation creates an undue hardship, must be made on a case-by-case basis. What is an undue hardship to one employer at a specific time may not be an undue hardship to other employers, or even the same employer at a different time.[38]

Undue hardship cannot be determined by comparing the expense of the accommodation to the disabled person's pay. The cost becomes an undue burden only if it is unreasonable in relation to the employer's financial resources, following the rules given earlier in this chapter.[39]

Other EEOC Guidelines

Several additional subjects are covered in the EEOC's interpretive guidance.

1. An employer may not compel a disabled individual to accept an accommodation. However, if a reasonable accommodation is refused and this refusal results in the individual being unable to meet reasonable performance standards, the individual is not a qualified worker, and thus is not entitled to protection under the ADA.[40]
2. Employers are not required to provide personal items as an accommodation. Accordingly, employers normally would not be obligated to provide a prosthetic limb, wheelchair, or eyeglasses. Nor will employers be required to provide hot plates, refrigerators, or other items of personal convenience, unless they are supplied to nondisabled workers. However, nothing in this paragraph prohibits an employer from voluntarily supplying such items. And if the items are specifically designed for on-the-job use (such as eyeglasses designed to be used in reading a computer monitor), they may be required as a reasonable accommodation.[41]

3. The term "supported employment" has been used to describe various forms of assistance to help severely disabled individuals to gain employment. Often it has included the allowance of a job coach to help train the employee during the first weeks of employment. The terms "supported employment" and "reasonable accommodations" are not synonymous. However, many types of supported employment may qualify as a reasonable accommodation. Each type should be examined on a case-by-case basis applying the usual rules concerning what is reasonable and what is an undue hardship.[42]

4. Accommodations that result in violation of federal laws or regulations, usually in the health and safety areas, are not reasonable accommodations, and therefore need not be provided.[43]

5. Although the ADA prohibits discrimination against individuals because of their association with people who are disabled, an employee is not entitled to an accommodation needed to care for a disabled person.[44] For example, an employee's husband has Parkinson's disease. The employee asks for a flexible work schedule so she can go home in the middle of the day to tend to her husband. The ADA does not require the employer to grant such an accommodation. Reasonable accommodations are required if necessary to adjust for a worker's disability, not the disability of an employee's spouse, family member, or other person.

The EEOC's interpretive guidance illustrates the process of making reasonable accommodations by giving the following example of the process that should be followed:

Suppose a Sack Handler position requires that the employee pick up fifty-pound sacks and carry them from the company loading dock to the storage room, and that a sack handler who is disabled by a back impairment requests a reasonable accommodation. Upon receiving the request, the employer analyzes the sack handler job and determines that the essential function and purpose of the job is not the requirement that the job holder physically lift and carry the sacks, but the requirement that the job holder cause the sacks to move from the loading dock to the storage room.

The employer then meets with the sack handler to ascertain precisely the barrier posed by the individual's specific disability to the performance of the job's essential function of relocating the sacks. At this meeting the employer learns that the individual can, in fact, lift the sacks to waist level, but is prevented by his or her disability from carrying the sacks from the loading dock to the storage room. The employer and the individual agree that any of a number of potential accommodations, such as the provision of a dolly, hand truck, or cart, could enable the individual to transport the sacks he or she has lifted.

Upon further consideration, however, it is determined that the provision of a cart is not a feasible effective option. No carts are currently available at the company, and those that can be purchased by the company are the wrong shape to hold many of the bulky and irregularly shaped sacks that must be moved. Both the dolly and the hand truck, on the other hand, appear to be effective options. Both are readily available to the company, and either will enable the individual to relocate the sacks he or she has lifted. The sack handler indicates his or her preference for the dolly. In consideration of this expressed preference, and because the employer feels that the dolly will allow the individual to move more sacks at a time and so be more efficient than would a hand truck, the employer ultimately provides the sack handler with a dolly in fulfillment of the obligation to make (a) reasonable accommodation.[45]

PRACTICAL TIPS

Complying With the Legal Rules of Accommodation

1. Examine the need for an accommodation for job applicants and employees when you first learn of the disability.
2. Determine possible accommodations on a case-by-case examination of the facts.
3. Do not offer accommodations that change the essential nature of the job or are unduly disruptive to the work process.
4. Do not offer accommodations that are ineffective.
5. When examining the costs of possible accommodations consider only the net cost to the company.
6. Normally, calculate the cost of the accommodation in relation to the financial resources of the entire company.

Making Accommodations

As shown by the preceding material, the bad news to employers concerning accommodations is that the legal standards that distinguish a reasonable accommodation from an undue hardship are not clearly defined. The good news is that making accommodations is often inexpensive.

After a 1981 survey on the employment of disabled people, the DuPont Company concluded that "[t]he cost of most accommodations is nominal."[46] In 1988, the Job Accommodation Network disclosed that of the thousands of accommodations it had recommended since 1984, 31 percent involved no cost to the employer, 19 percent cost under $50, another 19 percent cost from $50 to $500, another 19 percent cost from $500 to $1,000, and 12 percent cost from $1,000 to $5,000.[47] An earlier Business Roundtable study found that one-half of all accommodations require no cost,[48] while a major Department of Labor study found 51.1 percent entailed no cost.[49]

Low-Cost and No-Cost Accommodations

Many examples of low-cost or no-cost accommodations are listed under the various medical condition entries in Part II. The following are other examples of accommodations actually implemented after consultation with the Job Accommodation Network.[50]

- A secretary in a secondary school who used a wheelchair could not use the furniture in the office because the desk height was too low for the wheelchair to fit into it. The desk height was raised with scrap wood blocks with holes bored into them for the desk legs to fit at a cost of the janitor's time spent boring holes in the blocks and placing them under the desk.
- A plant worker with a hearing impairment was able to use a telephone amplifier designed to work in conjunction with hearing aids, allowing him to retain his job and not be transferred to a lower paying job, at a cost of $23.95.
- A clerk with limited use of her hands was provided with a "lazy Susan" file holder for her desk at a cost of $85. This file holder prevented her from having to reach across the desk and allowed her to remain at work.
- An individual with the use of only one hand needed to be able to use a camera as part of his job. A waist pod (like that used in carrying flags) allowed him to use a camera and keep his job at a cost of $50.
- A seamstress diagnosed as having carpal tunnel syndrome due to repetitive wrist motion purchased a pair of spring-loaded ergonomically designed scissors at a cost of $18.
- A receptionist who was blind was provided a light probe that allowed her to determine which lines on a telephone were ringing, on hold, or in use at a cost of $45.

- An individual with an eye disorder in which glare on the computer screen caused increased fatigue purchased an anti-glare screen at a cost of $39.
- A light was installed at the door of a company to alert the security guard of an approaching employee who used a wheelchair and needed assistance in opening the door at a cost of $50.
- A one-handed person working in a food service position was able to perform all the tasks of her position except opening cans. A one-handed can opener was purchased at a cost of $35.
- A groundskeeper who had recovered from a stroke had limited use of one arm, yet remained able to rake grass by the use of a detachable extension arm on the rake that allowed him to grasp the handle and control the rake with one hand at a cost of $19.80.
- An individual with dyslexia working as a police officer had trouble filling out forms at the end of the day. Providing him with a tape recorder and allowing a secretary to type his reports allowed him to continue working at a cost of $39, plus the secretary's time.
- A medical technician who was deaf needed a timer that had an indicator light in order to perform laboratory tests at a cost of $26.95.

Being Creative

Often the most difficult part of making an accommodation is developing an inventive method to allow employees to do their jobs. Examples of creative accommodations are listed below.[51]

- A potato inspector was required to core out bad spots in potatoes with a potato corer. Carpal tunnel syndrome drastically reduced his ability to perform the task. An adapted potato corer mounted on a table allowed him to continue working at a cost of less than $33.
- A housekeeper in a motel who had restrictions on bending needed to inspect under the beds as she cleaned rooms. A mirror on an extended wand and a reacher device was provided at a cost of $11.
- A fast-food worker on the burger line who was mentally retarded was unable to read the orders that came on a com-

puter tape. The individual could match letters. Therefore, all the individual bins of food were labeled exactly like the computer tape at no cost. For example, ketchup was labeled "Ketch" on the bin, exactly like it was on the computer tape.

More Expensive Accommodations

Some accommodations are more expensive. However, state rehabilitation agencies or other groups may pay part or all of the cost. The following list contains examples of more expensive accommodations.[52]

- A visually impaired insurance agent required an $8,200 voice-synthesized IBM computer. A state rehabilitation agency paid the entire cost.
- A new, legally blind paralegal required a Kurzwell Reading machine that at the time cost $12,000 (current price is lower). A state agency paid $4,000 and the employee used social security disability insurance money to fund the remaining cost.
- A blind applicant for a programmer position with a major bank needed a $7,912 Opticon scanner and voice synthesizer, plus a light probe. Half the cost was paid by a state rehabilitation agency, while the other half was paid by the Braille Institute.
- A blind secretary for a governmental unit needed a $6,050 computer system for word processing. Forty percent of the cost was paid by the individual, 10 percent by a state agency, and 50 percent by a public interest group. This funding arrangement allowed her to keep her $25,000 plus senior secretary's position.

Partial or full funding of accommodation devices by state rehabilitation agencies is most likely when hiring new employees. Funding by insurance companies is more likely when attempting to return current employees to their jobs. Paying for an accommodation device may save the insurance company money by halting continued disability or workers' compensation insurance payments. In both types of cases, private foundation or public interest group money may be available, particularly to smaller businesses. Some private agencies are listed under various medical conditions covered in Part II.

Not all accommodations are cost-free, inexpensive, or funded by outside sources. For example, a Prab Voice Command I package useful for office workers with severely impaired physical functions listed for $49,500 in 1989. It includes a Zenith computer, special monitor, voice-controlled keyboard, robotic arm, Hewlett-Packard LaserJet printer, telephone system, and specially designed work center. The workstation includes a cubical that is designed for wheelchair use, an adjustable height desk, and even space for a refrigerator and microwave oven. A basic version called the Voice Command II System listing for $21,900 excludes the robotic arm, laser printer, and special furniture. Other illustrations of more expensive acccommodations are given in Part II under the heading, Spinal Cord Injury and Wheelchair Users. Many companies have adaptive equipment and accommodation devices for sale. A partial list of companies appears in Appendix III.

Tax Credits and Government Aid

In addition to possible partial or full funding of accommodation devices by state vocational rehabilitation agencies or others, federally funded aid and tax credits may help pay the costs of needed job accommodations.

Small Business Tax Credit

The Omnibus Budget Reconciliation Act of 1990 provides a tax credit for small businesses that incur expenses in complying with the ADA.[53] An eligible small business is one that in the preceding tax year either had gross receipts of one million dollars or less, or had 30 or fewer employees. The satisfaction of either test qualifies a company. For example, a company with 25 employees with gross receipts of five million dollars would qualify because it meets the latter of the two tests.

The amount of the tax credit for any one year is fifty percent of the cost of accommodations that exceed $250 but do not exceed $10,250. For example, if a company spends $8,250 on accommodations in a tax year, it may apply $4,000 against its federal tax liability (50 percent of cost after subtracting the $250 deductible).

Expenses that qualify for the tax credit include amounts paid for:

1. Removing architectural, communication, or transportation barriers that prevent a business from being accessible and usable by individuals with disabilities—customers, clients, or employees
2. Providing qualified interpreters for those with hearing impairments, or qualified readers, taped texts, or other accommodations for visually impaired people
3. Acquiring or modifying equipment or other devices as a reasonable accommodation for disabled workers
4. Other reasonable expenditures to accommodate disabled employees or better serve disabled customers and clients.

The tax credit may be used for expenses incurred in modifying a current structure to make it more accessible, but it cannot be used if the expense is incurred during construction of new facilities.

Tax Deduction—Large and Small Businesses

For taxable years beginning on or after January 1, 1991, any business can declare as an expense, rather than a capital account that must be capitalized, up to $15,000 per year spent in removing architectural barriers for the benefit of disabled or elderly persons.[54]

The Job Training Partnership Act

The Job Training Partnership Act (JTPA)[55] is best known for the practical and financial aid it provides for hiring and training economically disadvantaged people. However, its provisions also apply to some physically and mentally disabled people. The JTPA allows an employer to enter into a contract with an On-the-Job-Training (OJT) agency and receive reimbursement for the job training expenses and up to 50 percent of the first six-months wages of eligible employees. Additionally, the OJT agency often provides assistance in recruiting, hiring, counseling, and other support services.[56]

Targeted Job Tax Credit

The Targeted Job Tax Credit (TJTC)[57] may be available when hiring disabled individuals referred by a state vocational rehabilitation agency, supplemental security income recipients, or others who meet certain low-income tests. A company may take a credit against its federal taxes of up to 40 percent of the first $6,000 of an eligible individual's pay for the first year of employment. In recent years, this law has been extended by Congress on a year-to-year basis.[58]

The Process of Determining Reasonable Accommodations

Employers should follow the basic procedures covered in Chapter 4, "Determining if a Disabled Person is Qualified," in recruiting, testing, and matching disabled job applicants with the proper jobs. EEOC regulations provide that "[t]o determine the appropriate reasonable accommodations it may be necessary . . . to initiate an informal, interactive process with the qualified individual with a disability."[59] A practical process of determining accommodations that comply with EEOC regulations may be accomplished by taking the following steps:

Step 1. Encourage newly hired and current employees to voluntarily disclose physical or mental disabilities and request accommodations, if needed. Chapter 8, "Company Policies and Forms," contains example forms for voluntary disclosure and Chapter 10, "Managing Disabilities," presents a suggested disability management program. It is normally to the company's advantage to make reasonable accommodations to allow new and older workers to perform to their maximum abilities, rather than hiding their disabilities. However, do not require disclosure of disabilities, and do not ask about the cause of the disability or the person's general medical history.

Step 2. When a job applicant or current employee discloses a disability or the employer otherwise learns of the disability (for instance, when it is obvious), ask the individual if an accommodation might be needed. If the answer is no, do not persist in raising the issue. Simply treat the individual as you would any other applicant or employee—maintain the same standards.

Step 3. If the answer is yes or possibly yes, use the job matching process described in Chapter 4, "Determining if a Disabled Person is Qualified," to analyze the essential functions of the job compared to the individual's physical and mental capabilities.

Step 4. Consult the individual about specific limitations. Do not assume disabled people cannot perform certain job functions.

Some disabled people have unique and inventive ways of performing tasks that nondisabled people would never dream possible.

Step 5. Ask the individual for accommodation ideas. Often the disabled person is the best source of information concerning practical, inexpensive modifications. If the individual's suggestions appear to be reasonable and effective, adopt them. If the suggestions are unreasonable or more costly than other effective methods, the employer does not have to comply with them.

Step 6. If the problem is not fully solved in Step 5, gather additional ideas. In addition to ideas presented in Part II listed under various physical and mental condition entries, some major sources of ideas on accommodations include:

1. The Job Accommodation Network (JAN). Phone: (800) 526-7234 (in West Virginia, phone: (800) 526-4698, in Canada phone: (800) 526-2262). JAN is a service of the President's Committee on the Employment of People With Disabilities and is funded by corporate and foundation grants. It offers free advice and ideas for accommodation. JAN offers very practical accommodation ideas using a data base of over 20,000 successful accommodations reported by various companies, many of them leaders in the employment of disabled persons such as DuPont, IBM, McDonalds, Marriott Corporation, and Sears.
2. The IBM National Support Center for Persons With Disabilities. Phone: (800) 426-2133. This IBM-funded nonprofit agency has information on thousands of computer hardware and software accommodation devices. The information is cost-free.
3. ABLEDATA. Phone: (800) 344-5405 (in Connecticut, phone: (203) 667-5405). Funded by the United States Department of Education's National Institute on Disability and Rehabilitation Research Office, ABLEDATA has a data base of over 17,000 disability and accommodation-related products from over 2,000 companies. Upon being informed of the type of product or accommodation needed, ABLEDATA will send a list of product names and suppliers. There are approximately three product entries per page, and up to eight pages will be furnished free of charge. Lists that exceed eight pages will cost from $10 to $35. It is also possible to conduct your own search of the data base by

computer modem for a subscription price. For information about the subscription service, contact BRS Information Technologies at (800) 345-4BRS.

4. Architectural and Transportation Barriers Compliance Board. Phone: (800) 872-2253. The Board is a governmental agency that can supply legal and practical information on physical accessibility of worksites.

5. The National Rehabilitation Information Center. Phone: (800) 34-NARIC. The Center is a federal agency with an extensive data base of rehabilitation information. It will not recommend specific accommodation devices, but it can supply an annotated bibliography of articles on various subjects such as workstations, computers, and other areas for research and reading. The cost is $10 for up to 100 references.

6. Phonic Ear. Phone: (800) 227-0735 (in California, (800) 772-3374). Although a private supplier of communications equipment, Phonic Ear publishes a book, *The Many Faces of Funding*, that explains possible sources of outside funding for accommodation devices. The book costs $45, including monthly newsletters. A yearly subscription to the newsletters only costs $8.

7. Rehabilitation Engineering Center. Phone: (202) 955-5822. The center offers a variety of booklets and articles on technological accommodation devices.

8. Trace Research and Development Center on Communication, Control and Computer Access for Handicapped Individuals. Phone: (608) 262-6966. The center has a variety of articles and studies on the fields of communication, control, and computer access.

Never Assume Accommodation is Impossible

No matter how severe an individual's disability appears, accommodations probably exist to allow the person to function effectively in the job market. A story told by three experts in vocational rehabilitation appearing in the *Journal of Rehabilitation*[60] illustrates how time, patience, and cooperation between employers and rehabilitation people can overcome serious obstacles.

The story involved a 31-year old machinist at an air tool manufacturing plant who suffered a severe stroke that left him unable to speak or walk, and with minimal use of his right arm and leg. While he could feed himself with his left hand, he needed assistance in all other activities. During his weeks in the hospital it appeared as if he would never work again. However, the following events occurred in the man's progress in the indicated months after the stroke:

Month 1: Patient transferred from a hospital to a rehabilitation facility for intense physical therapy.

Month 2: Individual discharged from rehabilitation facility to home, but therapy as an outpatient was continued twice a week.

Month 6: He had gained the ability to walk with a quad cane and speak words (but not sentences), plus understand simple conversations.

Month 13: After persistent statements by the man that he intended to return to his job, his rehabilitation team consisting of a physical therapist, an occupational therapist, a vocational counselor, and a speech pathologist, visited the individual's former work site. The employer expressed a strong desire to help return the worker to employment with the company.

Months 13-18: Armed with the knowledge of the type of job duties and physical functions required at the employer's workplace, the occupational therapist worked with the man to improve physical job skills. A simulated work program was begun in which the stroke victim "worked" a four-hour shift once a week.

Month 18: The rehabilitation team met with the employer to explain the man's physical status. He was still unable to speak complete sentences, had serious problems with physical stamina, and continued to have limitations on the use of his right arm. The rehabilitation team and the employer agreed that he was not able to return to operating a Blanchard grinder, the machine he worked on before the stroke. However, it was determined that he could oper- ate another machine, a profilator, if a button designed to be pushed with a finger was replaced with a large palm button. The employer agreed to start him on a four-hour per day shift, gradually increasing to a full day shift.

Months 18 to 24: The returning employee was warmly wel- comed back by other employees. At first his rate of work was quite slow. The palm button caused problems, so it was replaced with a foot-controlled switch. As the months passed, the employee's rate of production improved substantially.

Month 24: The employer decided that the disabled employee had recovered sufficiently to be transferred to work on the machine he had operated before his stroke. Although he again started at a low rate of production, he gradually increased his endurance and skill to the point where he met all production requirements. He is now a fully capable and loyal employee.

ADDITIONAL PRACTICAL TIPS

Accommodating Disabilities

1. Do not assume all disabled individuals need accommodations. Many do not.
2. Do not think in terms of groups such as all blind individuals or all wheelchair users. Each disabled person has different needs and often requires different accommodations.
3. Never make arrangements for accommodations without discussing them with the disabled person.
4. Feel free to ask the disabled person for advice regarding reasonable accommodations.
5. Do not assume that technical devices, particularly expensive ones, are needed. Think first in terms of low-cost or cost-free methods of restructuring the job or the workplace.
6. Distinguish between devices needed for general living such as wheelchairs, eyeglasses, hearing aids, and devices needed to perform a job such as a raised desk, voice synthesizer, or flashing telephone ringer. The disabled individual is responsible for obtaining general living aids. The employer is only required to consider accommodations and devices that allow disabled people to perform their jobs.
7. Approach the problem of providing accommodations in a constructive, problem-solving manner. Provision of reasonable accommodations is not only a duty, but a way to allow qualified people to perform effectively for the benefit of the employer.
8. Do not reinvent the wheel by trying to use only your personal knowledge in making accommodations. Contact sources such as JAN to find out what others have found to be reasonable answers.
9. Obtain the input of workers and supervisors regarding possible accommodations (without identifying the disabled individual to co-workers). Often those closest to the job may have the most practical ideas.

10. Where two or more alternative, reasonable, effective accommodations are discovered, consider allowing the employee to choose the accommodation desired. However, if all alternatives are effective and there are significant variations in cost, consider choosing the least costly alternative.

11. Create a centralized fund to pay any accommodation costs, rather than taking it out of the budget of the department where the individual will work.

12. Remember that the requirement of reasonable accommodation does not allow for poor performance or low productivity. Accommodations should be limited to methods that make the disabled individual an effective worker.

NOTES

1. Americans with Disabilities Act §102(b)(5)(A), 42 U.S.C.A. §12112 (West, 1991).
2. Americans with Disabilities Act, §101(9), 42 U.S.C.A. §12111 (West, 1991).
3. *Id.* at §101(10), 42 U.S.C.A. §12111 (West, 1991).
4. EEOC Regulations on the Americans with Disabilities Act, 56 Fed. Reg. 35,736 (1991) (to be codified at 29 C.F.R. §1630.2(p)).
5. H.R. REP. No. 485, 101st Cong., 1st Sess. pt. 3, at 41 (1990). The amendment would have limited accommodation costs to no more than 10 percent of the employee's annual salary.
6. 29 U.S.C.A. §701.
7. 34 C.F.R. §104.
8. 683 F. Supp. 758, 46 FEP Cases 1012 (D. Kan. 1988).
9. Harrison v. Marsh, 691 F. Supp. 1223, 46 FEP Cases 971 (W.D. Mo. 1988).
10. Stutts v. Freeman, 694 F.2d 666 (11th Cir. 1983).
11. Perez v. Philadelphia Hous. Auth., 677 F. Supp. 357 (E.D. Pa. 1987).
12. Shelby Township Fire Dep't v. Shields, 320 N.W.2d 306, 33 FEP Cases 650 (1982).
13. Foods, Inc. v. Iowa Civil Rights Comm, 318 N.W.2d 162, 39 FEP Cases 132 (Iowa 1982).
14. Halsey v. Coca-Cola Bottling Co., 410 N.W.2d 250, 48 FEP Cases 1585 (Iowa Ct. App. 1987).
15. Fitzgerald v. Green Valley Area Educ. Agency, 589 F. Supp. 1130, 39 FEP Cases 899 (S.D. Iowa 1984).
16. Davis v. Frank, 711 F. Supp. 447, 50 FEP Cases 1188 (N.D. Ill. 1989).
17. 707 F.2d 473, 32 FEP Cases 62 (11th Cir. 1983).
18. Gardner v. Morris, 752 F.2d 1271, 36 FEP Cases 1272 (8th Cir. 1985).
19. Plourde v. Scott Paper, 522 A.2d 1257, 48 FEP Cases 1452 (Me. 1989).
20. Coffman v. W. Va. Bd. of Regents, 386 S.E.2d (W. Va. 1988).
21. LaMott v. Apple Valley Health Care Center, No. C5-90-1436 (Minn. Ct. App. January 29, 1991) cited in BNA Policy and Practice Series, *Fair Employment Practices*, February 28, 1991.
22. Chiari v. League City, 920 F.2d 311 (5th Cir. 1991).
23. Dexler v. Tisch, 660 F. Supp. 1418, 43 FEP Cases 1662 (D. Conn. 1987).
24. 567 F. Supp. 369, 32 FEP Cases (E.D. Pa. 1983), *aff'd,* 732 F.2d 146, 34 FEP Cases 835 (3d Cir. 1984), *cert. denied,* 469 U.S. 1188, 36 FEP Cases 1264 (1985).

25. 879 F.2d 393, 50 FEP Cases 451 (E.D. Mo. 1990).
26. Interpretive Guidance on Section I of the ADA, 56 Fed. Reg. 35,739-35,753 (1991) [hereinafter Interpretive Guidance].
27. *Id.* at 35,744.
28. *Id.*
29. *Id.*
30. *Id.*
31. *Id.*
32. *Id.*
33. *Id.*
34. *Id.* at 35,752.
35. *Id.* at 35,745.
36. *Id.*
37. Sensory Aids Foundation Study, 399 Sherman Ave., Palo Alto, CA 94306.
38. Interpretive Guidance, *supra* note 26, at 35,752.
39. *Id.*
40. *Id.* at 35,749.
41. *Id.* at 35,749.
42. *Id.* at 35,752.
43. *Id.*
44. *Id.* at 35,747.
45. *Id.* at 35,747.
46. DUPONT, EQUAL TO THE TASK, 1981 SURVEY OF EMPLOYMENT OF THE HANDI-CAPPED 17–18 (1982).
47. IN THE MAINSTREAM July-Aug. 1988, Min. Report #4.
48. Arthur Anderson & Co., COST OF GOVERNMENTAL REGULATION STUDY FOR THE BUSINESS ROUNDTABLE, (1979).
49. BERKELEY PLANNING ASSOCS. FOR THE U.S. DEP'T OF LABOR, EMPLOYMENT STANDARDS ADMIN. A STUDY OF ACCOMMODATIONS PROVIDED TO HANDI-CAPPED EMPLOYEES BY FEDERAL CONTRACTORS, VOL. 1, STUDY FINDINGS 20 (1982).
50. JOB ACCOMMODATION NETWORK, TYPICAL JOB ACCOMMODATIONS. (Available from the President's Committee on the Employment of People With Disabilities, 1111 20th St., NW, Washington, DC 20036).
51. *Id.*
52. SENSORY AIDS FOUNDATION, *supra* note 37.
53. See I.R.S. Code §44.
54. See I.R.S. Code §190.
55. 29 U.S.C. §§1501 et. seq.
56. Additional information concerning the JTPA may be obtained from section 205 of BNA Policy and Practice Series, *Personnel Management,* or from the National Alliance of Business, 1015 15th St., NW, Washington, DC 20005. Local agencies may be listed in the phone book under the heading of the Alliance for Business and Training.
57. See I.R.S. Code §51.
58. Additional information concerning the law may be obtained from section 205 of BNA Policy and Practice Series, Personnel Management, or from the Internal Revenue Service (ask for IRS Publication 906, Jobs and Research Credits).
59. EEOC Regulations on the Americans with Disabilities Act, 56 Fed. Reg. 35,736 (1991) (to be codified at 29 C.F.R. §1630.2(o)(iii)(2)).
60. Raderstorf, Hein & Jencsen. *A Young Stroke Patient with Severe Aphasia Returns to Work: A Team Approach,* JOURNAL OF REHABILITATION, Jan.–Mar. 1984, at 23–26.

Chapter 6

Risk of Future Injury: Epilepsy, Diabetes, and Bad Backs

Some of the most perplexing problems employers face in dealing with disabled job applicants and employees involve situations where the individual's disability appears to increase the chance of an accident or future health problems. Employers are often concerned about the risk of future injury in cases of epilepsy, diabetes, or back problems. These problems will be discussed in this chapter. Risk of future injury can also be an issue when individuals have AIDS or other infectious diseases, alcohol or drug problems, or are obese. These problems will be discussed in Chapter 7, "AIDS, Infectious Diseases, Drug and Alcohol Problems, and Weight Problems."

Risk of Future Injury

If an employer hires or retains a person whose disability causes an on-the-job accident or job-related sickness, future claims may result in higher workers' compensation insurance costs. On- or off-the-job injuries and sicknesses may lead to increased costs in providing health and disability insurance coverage. Injury to co-workers may also increase workers' compensation costs, and injury caused to outsiders such as customers or clients can result in large liability lawsuits. A customer or other outsider may even bring a negligent hiring lawsuit against an employer who placed an employee in a dangerous job without adequate examination of the employee's qualifications to perform the work safely.

On the other hand, denying employment to persons with disabilities because they might cause accidents or have more frequent health insurance claims is employment discrimination based upon the person's disability. Cases during the past decade decided under the Rehabilitation Act of 1973 and state handicapped laws with provisions similar to the Americans with Disabilities Act (ADA) reveal that governmental agencies and courts tend to emphasize the rights of disabled people.

Fears and Concerns Not Enough

The United States Supreme Court's *School Board of Nassau County v. Arline*[1] decision clearly establishes that the employer's decision to deny a job to a person who may pose a risk of future injury to others must be based upon a *reasonable medical judgment* about the risks involved. The decision must not be based upon irrational fears and reflective reactions to actual or perceived handicaps.

Reasonable Probability

An entire line of legal decisions not only supports this view, but goes further by requiring that there be more than just a possibility of future injury or disability to the employee or other individuals. For example, a United States Court of Appeals case, *Mantolete v. Bolger*,[2] summarized the law concerning risk of future injury by stating that an employer cannot deny an individual a job merely because of an *elevated* risk of injury. Instead, an employer may legally deny a disabled person a job only if the employer can prove the employment of the individual creates a reasonable *probability* of *substantial* harm.

Mantolete had applied for a United States Postal Service job as a machine distribution clerk; a job that required using a Multi Purpose Letter Sorter Machine (LSM). She passed the written employment test. However, the Postal Service refused to hire her because its physician recommended she not be placed in a position that required driving or working with machines with moving parts because of her epilepsy. Mantolete then sued for handicapped discrimination under the Rehabilitation Act.

The lower court found that she was not qualified to work on an LSM because she suffered from grand mal (major) seizures and partial complex (more minor) seizures. The court determined that the flashing lights on the LSM could increase the chance of seizures and Mantolete could be seriously injured if she had a seizure while working on the machine. However, the evidence showed that Mantolete averaged only one daytime grand mal seizure per year during her first few years of epilepsy, and during the past several years had suffered no daytime seizures. During more than a decade of operating various machines with moving parts in her previous employment with the Motorola Company, she had suffered only three seizures while at work, none of which caused any injury or other problems, even though some of the machines had flashing lights and rhythmic movements.

Mantolete's physician testified that her potential for having a seizure at work was extremely small and the chance of her being injured as a result of a seizure while at work was even more remote. He further stated that her epilepsy was in complete control. In finding unlawful discrimination against Mantolete, the court announced several important rules:

1. Rather than making blanket rules that exclude whole classes of disabled people from certain jobs, employers should look to each individual's work history and medical history.
2. The deciding question is whether the individual presents a reasonable probability of substantial harm. An elevated risk of harm is not sufficient.
3. A finding of a reasonable probability of substantial harm requires the gathering of a considerable amount of information by the employer.
4. Employers must evaluate both the probability and the severity of potential harm. For example, a high probability of events that cause little or no harm should not be a basis to reject a person. Also, a small possibility of great harm should not be enough. An employer can reject the individual only if there is a reasonable probability of severe injury.
5. While the plaintiff in a discrimination lawsuit bears the burden of proving he or she is qualified to perform the job, with or without reasonable accommodations, it is the defendant's (employer's) burden to prove the plaintiff cannot do the job without a substantial risk of future harm.
6. A good-faith belief by the employer that an individual cannot safely perform a job is not a sufficient defense. The good-faith belief must be based upon reasonable medical evidence.
7. Employers cannot rely upon a single physician's opinion. In this case the employer followed the medical judgment of its

physician only. However, this reliance was insufficient to overcome a finding of discrimination.

Physician's Judgment

Two other legal decisions help illustrate that an employer cannot safely rely upon the medical judgment of a company physician or a physician to whom the company referred a job applicant or employee. The first case, under Wisconsin law similar to the ADA, involved an employee's bad back, while the other interprets the Federal Rehabilitation Act as applied to an individual with diabetes.

In the Wisconsin case, *Bucyrus-Erie Company v. Wisconsin Department of Industry, Labor & Human Relations,*[3] a 23-year-old applicant for a welder's position was otherwise qualified for the job. However, the company physician recommended against hiring him because a preemployment physical examination disclosed three congenital back defects. The medical reasons for not hiring the individual appeared strong.

The company physician, a board-eligible internist, consulted with a radiologist who examined the applicant's back X-rays and concluded that he had an incomplete fusion of the first sacral vertebra, spondylolisthesis of the fifth lumbar vertebra, and an abnormal angulation of one of the corresponding joints between the last lumbar and first sacral vertebra. Although people with spondylolisthesis generally do not have problems early in life, the company physician noted that those who perform heavy work throughout their lives have a substantial chance of developing back difficulties. Furthermore, the physician concluded that the applicant's spondylolisthesis might lead to spondyloysis, a disintegration or dissolution of the vertebra—a serious condition. Because company welders work in cramped quarters in unusual positions, climb ladders, lift and carry up to 60 pounds of cable, and use a 10-pound welding stick and a 20-pound chipping hammer, the physician concluded the applicant should not be hired.

However, the applicant's physician testified in court that the applicant had no history of back injury, back pain, or leg pain, and that while the X-rays showed a possibility of spondylolisthesis, he had no current back defect. Furthermore, the applicant had previously worked, without problems, in a job that required lifting items weighing up to 70 pounds. After being rejected for the job, he passed a preemployment physical exam at another welding company where he worked without any physical problems.

In ruling that the company illegally discriminated under the state handicapped employment law, the court stated the following:

> It is important that each case be individually evaluated and decided. . . . Further, we do not believe that it can reasonably be held that an employer has not discriminated because it categorically relies upon the opinion of the company doctor, important as his expert and medical opinion may be. . . .
>
> [I]f the evidence shows that the applicant has a present ability to physically accomplish the tasks that make up the job duties, the employer must establish to a reasonable probability that because of the complainant's physical condition, employment in the position sought would be hazardous to the health or safety of the complainant or to other employees or frequenters of the place of employment. However, in the instant case . . . [the company] has not proved such facts. . . .[4]

The court found a lack of proof of a substantial risk of serious injury because the company physician was unable to say when back problems such as spondylolisthesis would develop. Nor could the physician state the percentage of people with similar X-ray results who actually develop back problems. As a result, there was no proof of a *probability* that spondylolysis would occur.

An interesting difference of opinion among physicians became the focus of a United States Court of Appeals case under the Rehabilitation Act. In *Bentivegna v. United States Department of Labor*,[5] the city of Los Angeles refused to retain Bentivegna when a posthiring physical examination report disclosed he had uncontrolled diabetes. His blood sugar tests showed various levels at different times, including a six-hour blood sugar reading of 190 and a fasting blood sugar reading of 226. The city's physician stated that proof of controlled diabetes is shown only by a series of blood sugar readings over a period of months at around 150. The physician also stated that "diabetics who are not under good control, i.e., those with high blood sugar levels, are more prone to get serious infections from relatively minor injuries, they heal less rapidly than others, and they are more likely to have long-term health problems causing absenteeism and shorter careers."[6] Despite the physician's testimony, the court found that the city illegally discriminated when it denied Bentivegna a job as a building repairer.

The decision in favor of the employee was based upon several factors, including the following:

1. A memo from an expert medical doctor stated that most diabetics with levels up to 175 are considered reasonably

well controlled and "blood sugars of less than 250–300 usually cause *no detectable disability symptoms*".[7] The memo continued, "The long term dangers to Mr. Bentivegna with sugars at (his) level, as with all diabetics, are unclear, the short term dangers at those levels are minimal."[8]

2. Two doctors who worked for the city testified that there is little evidence that future health problems are more serious for those with high blood sugar, as compared with lower blood sugar levels.

3. There was no evidence that Bentivegna would be safer over time if he managed to lower his blood sugar.

4. While all the physicians agreed that lower blood sugar readings are better than higher ones, the evidence that Bentivegna's blood sugar readings were high did not prove a substantial increase in the risk of future, serious health problems.

The court concluded that "allowing remote concerns to legitimize discrimination against the handicapped would violate the effectiveness of the . . . [Rehabilitation] Act."[9]

The discussion later in this chapter concerning epilepsy and diabetes includes other examples of dealing with the risk of future injury, as do many of the cases in Chapter 7, "AIDS, Infectious Diseases, Drug and Alcohol Problems, and Weight Problems." Some additional risk of future injury cases include the following:

Loss of Adrenal Glands No Threat

A state court upheld the finding of the New York Human Rights Commission that a school district discriminated on the basis of an applicant's disability when it refused to hire a school bus driver who had both adrenal glands removed and was taking daily medication for hormone replacement.[10] The commission's decision was based upon extensive medical testimony showing the bus driver posed no threat of injury to schoolchildren or others.

Employers Sometimes Win

In a case decided under West Virginia law,[11] the court found that an employer did not violate the law by denying a coal mining job to a woman with psoriasis. The preemployment physical examination disclosed active lesions on the woman's lower legs, leading the physician to determine that crawling on her hands and knees in a damp mine would seriously aggravate the applicant's medical condition. The uncontroverted testimony of the physician was that 50 percent of those with psoriasis develop what is known as Koebner phenomenon, caused by trauma to unaffected parts of the body resulting in the spread of psoriasis—just the type of trauma occurring to hands, elbows, and knees when crawling in coal mines.

Another example of an employer successfully defending a lawsuit by proving a risk of future injury is a case covered in Chapter 5, "Making Accommodations for Disabled Employees," where a postal service applicant with achondroplastic dwarfism was denied employment.[12] The court found the applicant's short stature would require him to stand on a stool while leaning over a machine with dangerous, moving parts. This created a substantial risk of falling and suffering severe injury.

Flunking Test Is Not Enough

An employee requesting promotion to a railway job requiring the ability to distinguish colors was rejected when he was unable to pass one of three color tests.[13] The medical director of the railroad contended that safety required train operators to pass all three tests. However, a court found illegal discrimination because other doctors testified that passage of the two tests was sufficient to prove ability to recognize red, green, and white colors. Also, the applicant had taken a field test that showed he could recognize signs and signals used by the railroad.

PRACTICAL TIPS

Dealing With the Risk of Future Injury

1. Do not make blanket rules that exclude all persons with specific disabilities from certain jobs.
2. Examine each situation based on the particular facts of the individual and the job.
3. Be sure generally accepted medical opinion proves the individual's disability will create a substantial risk of serious injury or death if hired or promoted into the job in question.
4. Be sure company physicians are informed of the law: there must be a *substantial risk of serious future injury* before a job may be denied.

5. Be sure company physicians understand their personal medical opinion is less important than the generally acceptable medical opinion.

6. Be sure all physicians analyzing an applicant's medical condition understand the exact physical duties of the job. If disputes arise with the applicant's personal physician, be sure the personal physician has a realistic understanding of the job duties.

7. Encourage company physicians to consult with the applicant's personal physicians and other doctors before making a final decision to disqualify a person because of a disability.

8. If an applicant is denied a job because of a disability, fully explain the problem to the applicant. If the applicant's physician has rendered a judgment of fitness for the job, also contact the physician and explain the decision to reject the applicant.

Epilepsy

Epilepsy precipitates the single largest category of lawsuits under the Rehabilitation Act of 1973 and state laws with definitions of disabilities similar to the ADA. The reasons for this distinction are simple. A large number of persons have epilepsy—an estimated 2,135,000 in the United States. Most people with epilepsy have no work restrictions. However, the stereotypes and false assumptions about epilepsy are numerous.

Myths About Epilepsy

For centuries, epilepsy has been linked to insanity and violence. In the Dark Ages epileptics were social outcasts, and well into the nineteenth century many were locked up in insane asylums. Until 1965 several states prohibited epileptics from marrying, while five states still have laws authorizing involuntary sterilization. As late as 1975, *Black's Law Dictionary* defined epilepsy as a disease "of deterioration, the brain being gradually more and more deranged in its functions in the intervals of attack, and the memory and intellectual powers in general becoming more enfeebled, leading to a greatly impaired state of mental efficiency, or to dementia, or a condition bordering on imbecility."[14] In recent years, several lawyers have attempted to use epilepsy as a defense in charges of violent crime, creating more negative publicity. In addition, many middle-aged and older persons can remember seeing a person with epilepsy have an epileptic "fit," a sometimes wild and frightening event.

Facts About Epilepsy

Despite the scientific progress of the twentieth century, medical experts still do not know what causes epilepsy. However, it is known that it is not a disease, but rather a spectrum of symptoms that range from a momentary loss of concentration and staring into space, sometimes called a petit mal seizure, to the alarming acts of falling, losing consciousness, and the jerking convulsions of a grand mal seizure.

Epilepsy may be the result of a birth defect, childhood illness, head injury, or infection, among other causes. Medication can prevent seizures in many people and lessen the frequency and severity of seizures in almost all other cases. Most people with epilepsy will never have an on-the-job seizure, and all states allow people with epilepsy to obtain driver's licenses, under varying conditions. Almost all individuals with epilepsy are qualified to work. The major handicap they face is not physical or mental, but rather is the result of society's fear and misunderstanding of their medical condition. See the material listed under the Epilepsy entry in Part II for additional information.

Epilepsy and Employment Law

The legal decision that best summarizes the typical legal approach to epilepsy and employment discrimination is a case that was decided under the New Jersey handicapped employment law, *Jansen v. Food Circus Supermarkets.*[15] Jansen was a meat cutter employed by Food Circus, a company with an excellent affirmative action program for hiring disabled, disadvantaged, and retarded employees. One day while Jansen was cutting meat with a large steak knife he suffered an epileptic seizure. He stopped cutting and stood staring into space. After a co-worker removed the knife from his hands, he sat down, said "this is it, it's all over," and then walked out of the room. A few minutes later he was found in the restroom in a dazed condition, unable to remember what happened. Shortly thereafter, he returned to normal. However, he could not recall what happened.

Jansen was sent home and instructed not to return to work until he obtained a doctor's authorization. Four days later he returned with a note from his personal physician stating that his seizures "have been under full control on medication," and that the doctor had increased his medication to prevent future seizures. For two days Jansen performed his duties without incident. However, fellow workers told management they did not want to work around him because they feared for their safety.

Food Circus arranged for a medical examination of Jansen by a company-selected psychiatrist who reported that while he found no psychopathology in Jansen, he thought meat cutting jobs to be risky and dangerous for epileptics. A company-selected neurosurgeon completed a thorough physical examination and reported his belief that patients such as Jansen "need to be protected, as well as other people, from the effects of such seizures," and therefore, "any occupational activity in which the patient might injure himself or others, were he to have a seizure, should be avoided."[16] Upon receiving these reports, Food Circus terminated Jansen's employment.

In determining that Food Circus acted illegally, the New Jersey Supreme Court stated:

> In deciding whether the nature and extent of an employee's handicap reasonably precludes job performance, an employer may consider whether the handicapped person can do his or her work without posing a serious threat of injury to the health and safety of himself or herself or other employees.
>
> The appropriate test is not whether the employee suffers from epilepsy or whether he or she may experience a seizure on the job, but whether the continued employment of the employee in his or her present position poses a reasonable probability of substantial harm.
>
> [T]he assumption that every epileptic who suffers a seizure is a danger to himself or to others reflects the prejudice that the Law seeks to prevent. . . . Food Circus must prove, not assume, that Jansen was dangerous.
>
> [T]he failure of Food Circus's medical experts to distinguish between the risk of a seizure and that of harm to others rendered their reports deficient. Furthermore, . . . [one doctor's] report reflects a failure to make an individualized assessment of the probability that Jansen's handicap would pose a risk of harm to Jansen or others.
>
> An employer cannot rely on a deficient report to support its decision to fire a handicapped worker. . . . Food Circus should have ascertained from its experts whether another seizure was probable or just possible. The employer should also have ascertained the probability that the employee would cause serious harm to himself or co-employees if he suffered another seizure.[17]

Additional Epilepsy Cases

Upon learning that a railroad employee had a long history of epileptic convulsive seizures, a company physician recommended the employee not be allowed to work around moving machinery, trains, turntables, or stationary engines with exposed shafts or gears. The physician also recommended that he not be allowed to work alone. Because the employee's job required working in all these conditions, his employer discharged him. The Maine Supreme Judicial Court concluded that the "mere discovery that the Plaintiff had a history of epileptic seizures did not constitute a sufficient individualized assessment of the health or safety risk posed by his continued employment."[18]

The court posed the following questions that should be examined to assess the risk of future injury: What if the seizures were always nocturnal? What if the seizures were preceded by warning signs (technically called "auras")? How reliable are the auras? Did the employee ever have on-the-job seizures? Did any injuries result?[19] The court also found that the fact that railroads are common carriers and subject to virtually unlimited liability for personal injuries does not mean that the company is "entitled to employ only the healthiest and least accident-prone segments of society."[20]

Automatic Application of Rules

In another railroad case, one of the company's rules provided that any welder with epilepsy could not return to the job as long as he or she had epilepsy.[21] A worker who acquired epilepsy as a result of being injured in an automobile accident suffered two major seizures, about three months apart, but suffered no more seizures after being placed on medication. In compliance with the company rule, he was discharged. Welders had to use equipment that weighed up to 230 pounds, be able to drive a "high rail" truck, work far removed from medical assistance, and work around switching areas. The Supreme Court of Wisconsin upheld a finding that the company's rule was unreasonable because it discharged the individual without first finding a reasonable probability of serious future harm. Medical testimony showed that the worker had suffered no seizures since being placed on medication, had never had an on-the-job seizure, and that 70 to 90 percent of all people with epilepsy who are placed on medication do not suffer future seizures.

Safety is Still Important

Two physicians, one a neurologist with extensive experience, gave a job applicant preemployment physical examination and found him to be unable to work in the job for which he applied because of his epilepsy. The job involved custom "job shop" man-ufacturing, using machines that performed high-speed grinding, boring, and cutting. Safety guards were not possible due to the customized job-to-job changes required in specialty steel manufac-turing. Although the applicant's physician testified he was qualified to do "ordinary factory work," the court held that the company had not violated the law by refusing to hire the applicant.[22] The com-pany physician was an expert in occupational medicine who had examined the workplace, as well as the applicant, to determine safety. All the physicians agreed that the applicant had no early warning signs of seizures, such as an aura. The applicant's seizures often resulted in complete loss of consciousness, and the applicant's own doctor stated that he was safe to work in "ordinary factory jobs," not specialized and dangerous work.

Employee Must Be Unsafe

In a 1989 West Virginia case,[23] a Shoney's Restaurant manager discharged a salad bar attendant after she suffered a seizure at work early one morning before the restaurant opened. The court found a violation of law even though the employee had an average of four to six seizures per month and fellow employees testified that one seizure caused her to fall to the floor. The court ruled the discharge illegal because most seizures were preceded by an aura that allowed her to sit down before they occurred. Furthermore, she had never injured herself or others, she had never dropped any food or other items, she had missed no work because of seizures, and the restau-rant fired her without first determining if her seizures would lead to any serious harm to herself or others.

Hazardous Job

The United States Navy rejected an applicant for a criminal investigator's position because he had epilepsy. The job includes the use of firearms, participation in lengthy day and night surveillance, investigation of sabotage and subversive activities, interrogation and apprehension of criminal suspects, and the operation of motor vehicles. The position is classified by the Office of Personnel Man-agement as hazardous, requiring freedom from seizures for at least two years. During training the applicant suffered a seizure, result-ing in his termination. The court found no violation of law.[24] The hazardous nature of the job required employees to be free from on-the-job seizures. Furthermore, the applicant would continue to experience seizures without medication and he was negligent in taking his medication.

Past Record Important

A hospital refused to hire an applicant for a position as a respiratory therapist because of a hospital rule disqualifying anyone with epilepsy from jobs that involved direct patient care. The Colorado Court of Appeals found the rule to be in violation of the state handicapped employment law.[25] The applicant had worked as a respiratory therapist for eight years for several different hospitals, treating thousands of patients, without any problems. Her epilepsy had never affected her work, and expert witnesses testified that the chances of her having a seizure were 1 in 1,000.

Employer Has Burden of Proof

An applicant for a position that required climbing ladders and operating an overhead crane to pour molten metal with a temperature of 3,240 degrees was rejected because of his epilepsy.[26] Company policy prohibited workers with any of 19 medical conditions, including epilepsy, from obtaining the job. The applicant had experienced three major seizures in his life, the last occurring seven years earlier during a traumatic divorce proceeding. The company physician—who had never inspected the workplace—stated that every epileptic was unsuited for the job. However, the applicant had worked in a similar metal-smeltering job for another company without problems. The applicant's physician testified that the worker always experienced an aura before any seizure. In overturning a trial court's summary judgment for the employer, the court noted that expert testimony showed that 90 percent of all people with epilepsy could perform the job without creating a safety hazard, and blanket rules disqualifying all people with certain medical conditions are not valid unless the employer can prove *all* or *substantially all* people with the medical condition could not safely perform the job.

Medical Assumptions Dangerous

A boilermaker mechanic was assigned to a job doing repair work in Florida Power & Light Company's Turkey Point nuclear power plant. The job required medical clearance and the use of a respirator while working within the containment shell of the reactor. The mechanic was examined by a nonmedical employee who took his blood pressure, pulse, height, and weight, and asked several standard health-related questions. In response to one question, the mechanic stated he had been diagnosed with epilepsy several years ago, was taking medication, and had never suffered a seizure. Based solely on the employee's statement, the company doctor, an occupational physician with 30 year's experience, disqualified the employee from working where a respirator or buddy system was required for safety.

The court found that the decision was unreasonable and illegal for several reasons: the physician did not make an individualized determination that the mechanic created an unreasonable risk of injury; the physician did not even examine the mechanic, but rather disqualified him based only on his response to a standardized question; and the company physician did not contact the employee's doctor, even though he was in the same town.[27] The court stated that the decision to disqualify the mechanic must "reflect a well-informed judgment grounded in a careful and open-minded weighing of the risks and alternatives, and must avoid" simple conclusions based upon "reflective reactions."[28]

Cannot Rely Solely Upon a Physician

PPG Industries refused to hire a person with epilepsy as a production laborer based upon the recommendations of a physician to whom the job applicant had been referred by the company. In an administrative hearing and appeal under the Rehabilitation Act, it was determined that the company violated the law by relying solely upon the physician's report. The appellate opinion stated that the employer "did not fulfill their duty to gather all relevant information about . . . (the job applicant's) work history and medical history and independently assess both the probability and severity of potential injury."[29] Neither the employer nor the employer's physician had checked in any detail with the job applicant's physician. The applicant had been free of seizures for almost two years, leading to the conclusion that his seizures were under control.

PRACTICAL TIPS
Dealing With Epilepsy

1. Do not use blanket rules disqualifying all people with epilepsy except in the very rare cases where it can be proven that *all* people with epilepsy cannot safely perform the job.

2. Do not make employment decisions based upon co-workers' fears and prejudices. If a person with epilepsy can safely perform, but co-workers are worried about safety, educate the co-workers rather than discriminating against the person with a disability.

3. Refuse to hire or retain a person with epilepsy only if you can prove the condition creates a substantial risk of serious future harm to the individual or others. If either the risk or extent of injury is low, the person should not be denied a job.

4. Base employment decisions upon generally acceptable medical evidence.

5. Remember that even physicians are subject to the old biases and prejudices concerning epilepsy. Be sure that any company physician is making a judgment based upon the facts of the case and sound medical opinion.

6. Be sure that any company physician knows the workplace and its risks, as well as the medical facts.

7. Because our fears and prejudices concerning epilepsy are so ingrained, think twice about any adverse employment decisions resulting from a person's epilepsy.

Diabetes

A decision as to whether a person with diabetes is qualified for a particular job depends on the type of diabetes, the methods used to control the diabetes, whether control methods have been effective, and the exact duties of the job. Although there are exceptions based upon the facts of each case, there are some general rules that may be applied.

Non-insulin-dependent diabetics who control their blood sugar levels solely by diet or orally ingested pills are medically qualified for almost all types of jobs, including those that are hazardous. Non-insulin-dependent diabetics typically have type II diabetes, sometimes called adult-onset diabetes because the condition is usually first diagnosed when the individual is an adult.

Insulin-dependent diabetics who have achieved good control of their blood sugar levels also are qualified for most types of jobs, including hazardous work. However, occupations that involve irregular hours, missed meals, and unusual, out-of-the-way locations might not be suitable. Diabetics with very poorly controlled blood sugar levels may be disqualified from many jobs, especially those involving hazardous activities.

Physician Opinions Vary

As the *Bentivegna*[30] case covered earlier in this chapter shows, employers need to be careful to refrain from automatically accepting the opinion of one physician as to what constitutes poorly controlled and potentially dangerous blood sugar levels. In *Bentivegna*, the employer's physician defined well-controlled blood sugar as a series of blood sugars over three or four months at about 150 or below. However, the court accepted the opinion of the job applicant's physician that levels up to 175 show good control and levels as high as 300 "usually cause *no detectable disability* or symptoms."[31]

Exception to the Blanket Rule Prohibition

In some specialized types of jobs, the courts may uphold a general prohibition of insulin-dependent diabetics. *Davis v. Meese*[32] was such a case. An FBI clerical worker was invited to apply for a position as a special agent. He met all job requirements except one. It was discovered that he was an insulin-dependent diabetic, and under the rules of the FBI he was disqualified from the special agent job. The FBI hires people with all types of diabetes for most jobs, and allows the employment of special agents who have diabetes controlled by diet or pills. However, the FBI rules disqualify special agents and investigative agents who have insulin-dependent diabetes.

The court stated that "[a]lthough blanket exclusions are generally unacceptable, legitimate physical requirements are proper . . . [i]f the requirements are directly connected with and substantially promote legitimate safety and job performance concerns. . . ."[33] The court then discussed the dangers of insulin-dependent diabetics experiencing a hypoglycemic condition in the context of the position of a special agent for the FBI:

A hypoglycemic condition can occur very suddenly and unexpectedly and can be either mild or severe. Among the recognized effects of a hypoglycemic occurrence are sweating, feeling of hunger, pounding of the heart, fatigue, tremors, anxiety, mental confusion, and in several occurrences, the inability to function without assistance, loss of consciousness, seizures and even death.

Every insulin-dependent diabetic is constantly at risk of a hypoglycemic occurrence even under fully controlled conditions. Fully controlled conditions exist when the scheduling of meals and diet and the amount of physical exertion are regular and pre-planned, and the amount, type and timing of insulin injections can be predetermined.

History and testing, such as an insulin infusion test, are helpful in predicting the probability that an individual will suffer a severe hypoglycemic occurrence, but there is presently no test that can reliably predict whether, when and under what precise circumstances an individual will have a severe hypoglycemic occurrence.[34]

Because the job duties of a special agent frequently involve extended surveillance, extreme physical exertion, missed meals, and long and irregular hours while armed and dealing with criminals and other dangerous people, the court held that the FBI's disqualification was not a violation of the Rehabilitation Act because the decision is based upon the safety and health of the diabetic person, co-workers, and members of the general public.

Insulin-Dependent Diabetes Insufficient Reason for Denial

An applicant for a school bus driving job was denied employment because he failed to obtain a driver's license endorsement to drive school buses as required by state law due to his insulindependent diabetes. The court found this denial to be illegal discrimination under the Rehabilitation Act because the applicant was refused the job solely because of his diabetes.[35] The applicant's diabetes had never required hospitalization, never caused him to miss work, and the examining physician's conclusion was that the applicant could safely drive a school bus. An interesting aspect of the case is the fact that one agency of state government denied the license, but another, the school district, was found responsible for employment discrimination.

The Best Defense

The city of New York successfully defended a case where it had refused to hire a person with diabetes for work as a sanitary worker.[36] The applicant's blood sugar readings over a three-year period ranged from 195 to 390. The high readings appeared to be the result of the applicant's refusal to take steps to learn how to control his diabetes. He had several on-the-job hypoglycemic reactions during his previous employment with the United States Postal Service, although the reactions caused no serious problems. The court found that his personal condition rendered him unqualified because the job involved driving garbage trucks, using mechanical sweepers and snowplows, and operating various pieces of heavy equipment under all types of weather conditions. It is important to note that the court also placed weight on the fact that the city did not automatically disqualify all insulin-dependent diabetes, but rather decided each case on its own merits.

Past Record Important

Over a period of several years, the employer of a warehouse worker with diabetes made several attempts to accommodate his disability. However, the employee suffered several hypoglycemic reactions at work in which he lost all control, becoming so violent that he required physical restraint (a very unusual reaction). Consequently, he was discharged. The court stated that "[i]n order to be able to perform work, a handicapped individual must possess the ability to perform the job safely and efficiently with reasonable accommodation. . . ."[37] Such uncontrolled outbursts in a warehouse requiring the use of fork lifts, open moving belts, and electric powered saws made the employee unsafe to himself and to others. The court took special note that he was not fired when the company learned he had diabetes, but only after repeated episodes of violence and unsafe acts.

Irregular Hours and Stress

United Airlines' rules prohibit insulin-dependent diabetics from working in ramp service jobs because the duties involved major flight delays, unscheduled overtime, delayed meals, and unusual stress during bad weather conditions. A United States Department of Labor administrative law judge ruled the job restriction was legitimately and directly related to reasonable health and safety concerns involving essential job functions.[38]

PRACTICAL TIPS

Dealing With Diabetes

1. Avoid blanket rules that disqualify all diabetics from a particular job.
2. Do not refuse to hire a person with diabetes simply based upon the fact that the person has an increased risk of developing future medical problems.
3. As a general rule, do not disqualify from employment, regardless of the job hazards, any non-insulin-dependent per-

son who achieves control of his or her blood sugar by diet or pills alone.

4. Limit job denials to insulin-dependent diabetics only if the particular individual's record of diabetes proves a safety risk.

5. Do not necessarily depend upon one physician's opinion as to whether a person's diabetes is not in control and will create a future risk of harm.

6. Explain to any physicians whose recommendations the company may follow that the law does not allow disqualification unless it can be objectively proven that the person's condition causes a specific and substantial risk of harm to the person with diabetes or other individuals. Physicians may know medicine, but most do not know the law.

7. Think twice before deciding to deny a job to any diabetic individual who is making a good-faith effort to control his or her blood sugar. However, you need not be as concerned about the legal liability of denying jobs to people who are negligent in taking personal responsibility for controlling their own blood sugar levels.

Bad Backs

Most legal problems concerning bad backs occur when an employer-provided physical examination includes a back X-ray that discloses some deformity or disease. Lawsuits occur when the physician makes a notation of a back problem on the report to the employer or recommends against employment of the individual. Based upon that recommendation, the company—without further consideration—refuses to hire the job applicant, or if already employed, discharges the person.

Difficulty of Determining Facts

The legal principles concerning rejection of employment based upon back problems are the same as applied to epilepsy and diabetes. However, factual issues concerning back problems are more difficult. Back problems constitute the single largest category of occupational accidents and workers' compensation claims. X-ray examinations may disclose physical deformities causing current problems and even possible future problems. However, many people with bad backs show no physical manifestation of the problem in an X-ray. And disagreements among physicians concerning the risk of future injury to a person whose X-ray shows a deformity appear to vary even more than in cases involving epilepsy and diabetes.

Some Risk of Future Injury Not Enough

One of the better examples of the problems that arise with bad backs is illustrated by a decision of the New York Court of Appeals, *State Division of Human Rights v. City of New York.*[39] The applicant, Granelle, applied for a position as a police officer and passed the written test and a physical agility examination. His preemployment physical examination included an X-ray that disclosed he had a spinal condition known as spondylolisthesis. New York Police Department rules automatically disqualified applicants with this condition.

Granelle did not even know he had a back problem until he was told the results of the medical examination. He suffered no pain or other problems even though he had an employment history of 10 years in which he worked in the heavy construction industry and frequently lifted up to 150 pounds. He had pulled a back muscle several years earlier, but missed no work as a result. Granelle's physician agreed that he had spondylolisthesis. However, the physician stated the condition exists in approximately 10 percent of the general population and Granelle "would have no difficulty in performing the duties required of a New York City Police Officer."[40]

A City of New York physician explained that spondylolisthesis is a congenital widening of two vertebrae that is probably caused by a defect in the neural arch. While in the early stages there may be no problems, the physician believed there was a strong likelihood of low back disability developing in the future. However, the physician also stated there were no reliable statistics regarding the likelihood of future problems, and some people with spondylolisthesis will never develop any medical problems. Despite the lack of reliable studies, the physician concluded that there was a 25 to 50 percent increased probability of low back disability occurring in people who suffer this defect.

An independent orthopedist also confirmed Granelle's spondylolisthesis diagnosis and stated that he had "a statistically higher probability of symptoms developing compared to a similar person with normal back X-rays."[41] Although he declined to make a specific prediction, he thought that performing police functions would tend to aggravate the condition.

Nevertheless, the court upheld a state agency's finding of unlawful discrimination. Explaining its decision, the court stated that the law requires an "individualized standard" by which the employer must demonstrate that the disability is such that would "prevent the complainant from performing in a reasonable manner the activities involved in the job or occupation sought."[42] The court noted that the employer agreed Granelle was presently qualified to act as a police officer and was rejected only because of a "reasonable expectation that he will be unfit to perform the duties of a police officer some time in the future."[43] His present physical ability to perform the functions of the job was established by passing the physical agility test. The court stated:

> [the] record is barren of any satisfactory medical evidence to support a reasonable expectation that Granelle, in light of his particular medical history and present condition, will become unfit to reasonably perform the duties of a policemen in the future. Employment may not be denied based upon speculation and mere possibilities, especially when such determination is premised solely on the fact of an applicant's inclusion in a class of persons with a particular disability rather than upon an individualized assessment of the specific individual.[44]

Proof of Substantial Risk of Harm Vital

In *Frank v. American Freight Systems*,[45] the employer denied a truck driving job to Frank because of a company rule disqualifying from employment anyone with one of 16 specific back problems. Frank, 49 years of age, had injured his back some 20 years earlier and had undergone a laminectomy and fusion surgery for one of the 16 specific disqualifying conditions. Since that time he had worked as a truck driver and engaged in heavy lifting without problems.

Although the court criticized the company's blanket rule that automatically disqualified applicants with certain back problems, it found that an individualized assessment of Frank's back showed a substantial risk of future injury. The job in question required the loading and unloading of boxed meat weighing up to 150 pounds. The company physician's evaluation of Frank's past medical history and X-rays led him to estimate the likelihood of future injury and disability to be "greater than fifty percent, possibly greater than seventy-five percent."[46] Additionally, an American Academy of Orthopedic Surgeons' report showed that a combination of heavy lifting and the vibrations from riding in a truck presents an increased risk of back injury for truck drivers.

Possibly the key fact in the case was that Frank offered no medical witnesses to dispute the facts given above, leading the court to conclude:

> Even assuming Frank is presently having no problems with driving or lifting, as he contends, there still is a substantial likelihood that he will suffer symptoms in the future under the stress of driving and lifting.

> [W]e believe American Freight is justified in looking ahead to the situation, which the medical evidence shows to be probable, in which Frank will not be able to do the job.[47]

Additional Back Problem Cases

A woman who applied for a job as a cement truck driver had back injuries that had required surgery nine years earlier. Based upon this fact and a physical examination, the company physician concluded that her back could cause problems sometime in the future. Therefore, she was not hired. The Office of Federal Contract Compliance Programs, which enforces the Rehabilitation Act as applied to federal contractors, ruled that the company had violated the law.[48] It was determined that no more than a tenuous prediction of future injury was made, and there was no imminent risk that she would suffer back problems.[49]

Consistency Required

A railroad company's rule prohibited the hiring of new job applicants until they had six trouble-free years following back surgery. A job applicant who was denied employment under the company rule successfully sued the railroad by showing that current employees with back surgery were sometimes allowed to return to work in less than six years.[50] The court concluded the company's actions in judging the fitness of current employees on an individualized basis proved that a blanket rule against hiring job applicants was unnecessary and unreasonable.

Two Close Cases

A split decision of the Indiana Supreme Court (with strongly stated dissenting opinions), interpreting state law that is somewhat different from the ADA, found a company had not violated the law by refusing to hire a five-foot, one-inch, 124-pound woman whom the company physician found to be unfit for heavy work due to a congenital spinal defect (sacralization). The job duties included climbing and lifting from 50 to 120 pounds above dangerous power lines, sometimes during stormy weather. The court believed the company was reasonable in concluding the applicant could not safely perform the work.[51]

Another split decision with a strong dissent based upon a state handicapped law found that a custodian who injured her back while at work could be discharged.[52] The custodian requested light work and submitted a letter from her physician stating she should not lift more than 10 to 15 pounds. She was transferred from garbage collection to general cleaning work, but continued to have problems. Additional medical exams showed she could not do work that required bending. Her new position required bending almost one-half of work time. After failing to locate another position for the woman, the employer discharged her. The court found that her current back problem prevented her from performing the essential duties of the job, and, therefore, she was not qualified. The dissent argued that the employer could have made accommodations (see Chapter 5, "Making Accommodation for Disabled Employees," for a discussion of accommodations).

Transportation Companies

Companies subject to Department of Transportation (DOT) regulations for truck drivers have an absolute defense to a charge of discrimination if they are simply complying with required physical examinations and hiring standards under the regulations. Transportation companies can go beyond the requirements of the DOT regulations and apply stricter standards concerning bad backs. However, standards that are stricter than DOT regulations must comply with the law as covered in this section.[53]

Cannot Base Decisions Solely on X-rays

A Department of Labor administrative law judge (ALJ) found a violation of the Rehabilitation Act when a company used X-rays as the sole method of determining whether job applicants were physically qualified to work.[54] The ALJ found that the company's sole reliance on X-rays failed to take into account an individual's actual medical history and capability to perform the job in question, even though the X-ray examination was performed by a well-qualified physician.

Employer's Burden of Proof

The case of *E.E. Black, Ltd. v. Marshall*,[55] determined that a blanket rule against hiring carpenters with bad backs is a violation of the Rehabilitation Act. The court said that the employer must be able to prove one of three things to deny a job to a person with back problems who is currently able to perform the job duties: a high degree of risk of future injury, a reasonable risk of serious injury, or an imminent risk of injury.[56]

PRACTICAL TIPS

Dealing With Bad Backs

1. Do not have blanket rules disqualifying all people with specified back problems.
2. Be sure any employer-provided physician is informed that all judgments must be on a case-by-case basis, taking into account the individual person and the physical duties of the job in question.
3. Remember that most physicians, even those who specialize in occupational medicine, do not know the physical duties of various jobs.
4. Consider providing the physician with a job description or written summary of the physical duties of the job in question each time you refer a job applicant or employee for a physical examination. Even better, give the physician a video tape showing a worker performing the job.
5. Be sure all employer-provided physicians are informed that the disqualification of a person must be based upon a provable, substantial (meaning probable) risk of future injury or disability.
6. Encourage physicians to be as specific as possible in any negative recommendation. For example, encourage them to estimate a percentage chance of future injury, or use words, if true, such as "probable," "probability," and "substantial risk."
7. If a physician's statement recommends against the employment of an individual, discuss the problem with the physician before denying the job to an individual. A discussion should help insure that the physician knows the legal rules, and that the employer understands the physician's conclusions.

8. If the disqualified individual disagrees with the decision against hiring or retaining, inform the person that he or she may submit reports or letters from personal physicians.

9. If a disqualified person submits letters, reports, or recommendations from physicians tending to show the person can work, contact these physicians to make sure they understand the physical requirements of the job. If such contact changes their medical opinions, obtain a letter or memo documenting the change.

10. If company and personal physicians continue to disagree, the employer should make the final decision on hiring or retaining the worker, following the principles of law explained in this chapter.

Summary

In dealing with job applicants and employees whose medical conditions create a risk of future injury—whether due to epilepsy, diabetes, back problems, or other disabilities—the rights of employers are balanced against the rights of the individual. However, the ADA, Rehabilitation Act, most state handicapped employment laws, and most courts upset the balance somewhat by tending to favor the individual.

Before an employer can safely deny a job to a disabled person because of a risk of future injury, there must be proof that the individual's specific condition creates a substantial risk of future injury. Blanket rules, speculation, and personal beliefs are insufficient. Nor can an employer rely upon only one physician's recommendations. The employer must prove that under generally acceptable medical opinion, employment of the person will almost certainly lead to serious injury or death.

Notes

1. 480 U.S. 273, 43 FEP Cases 81 (1987).
2. 767 F.2d 1416, 38 FEP Cases 1081 (9th Cir. 1985).
3. 90 Wis. 2d 408, 280 N.W.2d 142, 22 FEP Cases 563 (1979).
4. *Id.*, 280 N.W.2d at 150.
5. 694 F.2d 619, 30 FEP Cases 875 (9th Cir. 1982).
6. *Id.*, 694 F.2d at 622.
7. *Id.*, 694 F.2d at 620.
8. *Id.*
9. *Id.*, 694 F.2d at 623.

10. New York State Div. of Human Rights v. LeRoy Cent. School Dist., 485 N.Y.S.2d 907, 107 A.2d 153 (N.Y. App. Div. 1985).
11. Ranger Fuel v. W. Va. Human Rights Comm'n, 376 S.E.2d 154 (W. Va. 1988).
12. Dexler v. Tisch, 660 F. Supp. 1418, 43 FEP Cases 1662 (1987).
13. Quinn v. S. Pac. Transp. Co., 711 P.2d 139 (Or. 1985).
14. Pollak, *The Epilepsy Defense*, ATLANTIC, May 1984, at 20.
15. 541 A.2d 682, 52 FEP Cases 1632 (1988).
16. *Id.*, 541 A.2d at 685–86.
17. *Id.* at 687–90.
18. Higgins v. Maine Cent. R.R., 471 A.2d 288 (Me. 1984).
19. *Id.* at 291.
20. *Id.* at 292.
21. Chicago & Northwestern R.R. v. Wisconsin Labor & Indus. Review Comm'n, 297 N.W.2d 819 (Wis. 1980).
22. Lewis v. Remmele Eng'g, 314 N.W.2d 1, 29 FEP Cases 576 (Minn. 1981).
23. Davidson v. Shoney's Big Boy Restaurant, 380 S.E. (2d) 232 (W.Va. 1989).
24. Pineiro v. Lehman, 653 F. Supp. 483, 43 FEP Cases 65 (D.P.R. 1987).
25. Silverstein v. Sisters of Charity, 43 Colo. App. 446, 614 P.2d 891, 21 FEP Cases 1077 (1979).
26. Rose v. Hanna Mining Co., 616 P.2d 1229 (Wash. 1980).
27. Kelly v. Bechtel Power Corp., 633 F. Supp. 927, 47 FEP Cases 83 (S.D. Fla. 1986).
28. *Id.*, 633 F. Supp. 927 at 934.
29. OFCCP v. PPG Indus., No. 86-OFC-9 (Jan. 9, 1989).
30. 694 F.2d 619, 30 FEP Cases 875 (9th Cir. 1982).
31. *Id.* at 620 (emphasis in original).
32. 692 F. Supp. 505, 47 FEP Cases 828 (E.D. Pa. 1988).
33. *Id.*, 692 F. Supp. at 517.
34. *Id.*, 692 F. Supp. at 515.
35. Jackson v. Maine, 544 A.2d 291, 47 FEP Cases 395 (Me. 1988).
36. Serrapica v. City of New York, 708 F. Supp. 64 (S.D.N.Y. 1989).
37. Pannell v. Wanke Panel Co., 618 F. Supp. 41, at 43; 26 FEP Cases 1849 (D. Or. 1985).
38. OFCCP v. United Airlines, No. 86-OFC-12 (Feb. 3, 1989).
39. 510 N.E.2d 799 (N.Y. 1987).
40. *Id.*, at 800.
41. *Id.*, at 801.
42. *Id.*, at 802.
43. *Id.*, at 802.
44. *Id.*, at 802.
45. 398 N.W.2d 797, 48 FEP Cases 1573 (Iowa 1987).
46. *Id.*, 398 N.W.2d at 801.
47. *Id.* at 802.
48. Dep't of Labor v. Tex. Indus., 47 FEP Cases 18 (OFCCP 1988).
49. An unfortunate, but interesting fact concerning this case, is that it took 11 years to decide. Ultimately the office's decision included an order for back pay for the entire 11 years, in addition to an order to hire the job applicant.
50. Me. Human Rights Comm'n v. Canadian Pac. R.R., 458 A.2d 1225, 31 FEP Cases 1028 (Me. 1983).

51. Ind. Civil Rights Comm'n v. S. Ind. Gas & Elec. Co., 553 N.E.2d 840 (Ind. 1990).
52. Coffman v. W.Va. Bd. of Regents, 386 S.E. (2d) 1 (W.Va. 1988).
53. OFCCP v. Yellow Freight Sys., No. 79-OFCCP-7 (Aug. 26, 1988).
54. OFCCP v. Tex. Generating Co., No. 85-OFC-13 (Mar. 2, 1988).
55. 479 F. Supp. 1088 (D. Haw. 1980).
56. *See* Chapter 3, "Determining Who is Disabled," for additional discussion of *E.E. Black*.

Chapter 7

AIDS, Infectious Diseases, Drug and Alcohol Problems, and Weight Problems

Changes in the law created by the Americans with Disabilities Act (ADA), as well as changes in society, may cause special problems in dealing with job applicants and employees with Acquired Immune Deficiency Syndrome (AIDS), other infectious diseases, drug and alcohol problems, and weight problems.

AIDS

Although the percentage rate of growth of AIDS cases has slowed, the total number of people infected with the HIV virus and AIDS will continue to increase. It is estimated that people treated for AIDS and HIV infections will rise from 250,000 in 1992 to 600,000 in 1996.[1] AIDS has spread from limited high risk groups such as drug abusers, homosexuals, and hemophilia patients to the general public. During the early stages of the AIDS crisis, infected people usually became too sick to work almost immediately after being infected and died a short time later. Today, many with the infection are able to work for months or years, with reasonable accommodations.

Understanding the Infection

When a person is ill with AIDS the individual is in the final stage of a series of health problems. AIDS is only one of three related conditions:

1. Infection with the HIV virus. Infection occurs from exchanges of bodily fluids in both heterosexual and homosexual sexual acts, an exchange of blood from one person to another, or from mother to unborn child. An infected person may have no physical or mental symptoms of AIDS, and some infected persons will not develop any future AIDS problems. However, anyone infected with the HIV virus can infect sexual partners, unborn children, or other people by an exchange of blood. Tests exist to determine if one has the HIV virus infection. However, they are not effective during the first few weeks of an infection, and employers have no basis to use these tests, for reasons to be explained in this chapter.

2. AIDS Related Complex (ARC). People with ARC test positive for the HIV virus and have developed physical symptoms such as loss of appetite, weight loss, fever, night sweats, skin rashes, diarrhea, lack of resistance to infection, or swollen lymph nodes. However, these manifestations of the disease are not as serious or life threatening as AIDS, and they are common symptoms of other diseases. A medical diagnosis of ARC is the only method to distinguish ARC from other health problems. People with ARC may or may not progress to the more serious form of the infection.

3. AIDS. Only a qualified health professional may diagnose AIDS. However, associated symptoms may include a persistent cough and fever, shortness of breath, and multiple purplish blotches and bumps on the skin. Although the virus is the same in each individual, symptoms vary from person to person. The main danger of AIDS is that it causes the body's immune system to deteriorate, thus making the person vulnerable to diseases such as pneumonia and skin cancer.

Infection Not Spread Easily

Medical experts agree that the HIV virus, ARC, and AIDS are *not* spread by:

- Casual or business-related contacts
- Coughing or sneezing
- Swimming pools or hot tubs
- Sharing food or food implements
- Sharing telephones, linens, doorknobs, etc.
- Sharing toilets, wash basins, soap, or showers

- Tears or saliva
- Pets or insects
- Giving blood or receiving injections administered by qualified medical personnel

Infection Is a Legal Disability

People with the HIV virus—even those with no current physical symptoms—as well as those with ARC or AIDS, are legally disabled under the ADA, the Rehabilitation Act of 1973, and most state handicapped employment laws. Following the precepts of the United States Supreme Court decision in *School Board of Nassau County v. Arline*[2] (see Chapter 3, "Determining Who is Disabled") and the opinion of the Surgeon General of the United States, the Department of Justice issued a memorandum[3] stating that people with the HIV virus, ARC, or AIDS are legally disabled. Shortly, thereafter, the United States Department of Labor issued a notice[4] following the same conclusions as applied to federal contractors subject to section 503 of the Rehabilitation Act. Since 1988, every relevant court decision interpreting the Rehabilitation Act has held that AIDS-related infections are legal disabilities.

There is no doubt that HIV virus infections, ARC, and AIDS are disabilities under the ADA. The ADA's definition of a disabled person exactly matches that of the Rehabilitation Act. Also, congressional committee reports in the Senate and House of Representatives make it clear that Congress intended the Rehabilitation Act and regulations issued under that law to apply to the ADA (see Chapter 3, "Determining Who is Disabled"). Even a proposed amendment allowing HIV-infected food service workers to be transferred to other duties was defeated in Congress.

Job applicants and employees infected with the HIV virus, ARC, or AIDS must be treated the same as other individuals with a disability. If they are otherwise qualified to perform relevant job duties, with or without reasonable accommodations, they must be treated the same as nondisabled people.

The Legal Rules—A Case Example

A 1990 United States District Court case, *Cain v. Hyatt*,[5] interpreting Pennsylvania regulations identical to the regulations issued under the Rehabilitation Act of 1973 and the ADA, illustrates a number of practical and legal issues in dealing with AIDS.

The Facts of the Case

In the lawsuit, Clarence Cain alleged that Hyatt Legal Services violated the Pennsylvania Human Relations Act by removing him as regional partner of Hyatt's Philadelphia office because he contracted AIDS. In 1986 Cain, a graduate of the University of Virginia Law School with 10 years experience, was hired by Hyatt under its "Fast Track Regional Partner Program." After some training and brief work in a regional office, Cain was promoted to regional partner on November 24, 1986.

Within six months his relationship with his superiors at Hyatt began to deteriorate. Cain stated he did not like the "sales" component of his job, nor did he like to review the managing attorneys under his supervision. Even though he had been reprimanded for unsatisfactory processing of client complaints, Cain's salary was increased to the highest of any regional partner on May 28, 1987.

Cain was briefly hospitalized in June and returned to work more vocally dissatisfied than ever. At a national Hyatt Legal Services meeting, he loudly voiced derogatory comments about the firm and its senior partners. He was later reprimanded for his statements. An additional reprimand was given on July 6 that noted Cain's disinterest in executing his duties. Cain replied that he was "not a cheerleader."[6]

Cain entered the hospital July 13 because of pneumonia, and three days later he was told that he had AIDS. Cain asked his superior to talk to his doctor. The physician informed Cain's boss that Cain did in fact have AIDS, however, he could not make any prediction of the future course of the disease. The doctor stated that Cain would likely be able to return to work by mid-August. He also stated that many AIDS patients die in a year or two after diagnosis.

Within a week after Cain's hospitalization, the executives of Hyatt Legal Services decided to discharge him. Although Cain's physician had stated that Cain would be able to return to work and that no one could predict the future course of the ailment, the executives felt apprehensive about working with a person with AIDS and thought other employees of Hyatt would feel the same. To replace Cain, they induced another attorney, Fisher, to delay his planned move to Denver and accept the position for one year. Fisher had Cain's desk cleaned because he did not want to touch any items associated with Cain. Cain learned he had been fired on August 2.

On August 3, Cain was told that because he had AIDS and because of his past conduct, "under no circumstances" would he be allowed to return to his former job.[7] He was told he could accept a $12,000 severance package or take a staff attorney's job in Hyatt's Falls Church, Virginia, office. Cain became hysterical and ordered Hyatt's executive out of his house. On August 5, 1987, Cain was placed on medical leave and removed from the payroll.

Cain's health improved markedly by the end of August. His physician decided he was physically ready to return to his old job. A second physician stated that Cain was medically able to continue in his former position until June 13, 1988, when he contracted a bronchial infection. After that date he was unable to work due to health problems.

On June 29, 1988, after Cain filed a handicapped discrimination complaint with the Pennsylvania Human Relations Commission, Hyatt offered to remit to Cain full back pay and fringe benefits, as well as reinstating him to a position comparable to the job he had before the AIDS diagnosis. Cain refused the offer and filed a lawsuit.

The Court's Decision

The court found AIDS to be a handicap, for two reasons: First, "both the underlying viral condition and the symptomology of AIDS give rise to physical impairments that substantially limit one's abilities to engage in major life activities;" and second, "societal prejudices deem persons with AIDS as having such an impairment."[8] Explaining these conclusions, the court stated:

> HIV-seropositivity, AIDS-related complex (ARC), and AIDS form a spectrum of related conditions. There is a time lapse, often of several years, between exposure to HIV and the onset of symptoms generally identified with ARC or AIDS, and it presently is unclear how many HIV-infected persons eventually will develop AIDS. . . . Today, AIDS is incurable and fatal.
>
> [E]ven if it were asymptomatic, the plaintiff's HIV infection constitutes a substantial physical limitation upon major life activities. HIV, which disables white blood cells, including lymphocytes, "creates a physiological disorder of the hemic (blood) and lymphatic system. Because of the risk of transmission, an HIV carrier cannot procreate "without endangering the lives of both the offspring and other parent. . . . [T]his significant injury to the reproductive system impedes a major life activity (citations omitted).
>
> [E]xcluding healthcare professionals who perform invasive procedures, AIDS cannot be transmitted through workplace exposure.

Yet, despite authoritative medical evidence to the contrary, fully one-third of the American population believes "AIDS is as contagious, or more contagious, than the common cold," and "few aspects of a handicap give rise to the same level of public fear and misapprehension as contagiousness."

[AIDS] mythology has fomented not only private judgments about carriers of the virus. It has spawned calls for punitive, oppressive official action against them "in every public forum and institution in this society, in virtually every context imaginable." . . . Thus, to conclude that persons with AIDS are stigmatized is an understatement; they are widely stereotyped as indelibly miasmic, untouchable, physically and morally polluted.

These and other related prejudices substantially curtail the major life activities of AIDS victims.[9]

In finding that Cain's AIDS was not a job-related disqualification, the opinion stated:

The Court cannot agree that . . . Cain's handicap was job related under the circumstances.

[F]rom September 1987 until June 1988 the plaintiff's illness in fact would not have impaired his ability to function as regional partner. The pertinent inquiry therefore is whether Cain's heightened risk of future symptomatic job-related disability, as understood when the termination decision was made, warranted the action. The Court finds it did not.[10]

The opinion stated that the law does not

allow an employer's qualms, well-founded or not, concerning the future performance of an employee or applicant who is presently able to discharge the functions of the position to justify adverse employment action, unless the safety of that person or others was implicated.

[That] the defendants made absolutely no effort to accommodate the plaintiff's disability is patently obvious. They terminated him as regional partner within one week of his having informed them that he had AIDS. They did not consult either Cain or his treating physician regarding what, if any, alterations would be necessary to allow Cain to resume his employment.

[T]he defendants were obliged to permit the plaintiff to exhaust his sick and vacation days and then, if necessary, place him on a medical leave of absence until he could return to his former job or until the situation posed an undue hardship on Hyatt.

. . . Cain's disability was not job related on any notable respect from September 1987 to June 1988. He therefore would not have required any cognizable accommodation at all during that period. Nor can the Court grant credence to the claim that because the plaintiff faced a shortened career span his tenure would have disrupted the continuity of leadership in the Philadelphia region. At the time Hyatt replaced Cain with Fisher, Fisher's express commitment to the region was for no more than one year.[11]

The court held that the offer of a staff attorney's job in the Falls Church office was not a reasonable accommodation because it involved a demotion from regional partner, as well as requiring legal work with clients, rather than the managerial position of regional partner.

In response to Hyatt's argument that it removed Cain from his position due to the fears of other employees in the Philadelphia office, the court stated the following:

> [T]he asserted reticence or unwillingness of coworkers and clients to associate with an AIDS victim who is without any contagious opportunistic infection does not convert a handicap into a job-related one. The "unreasonable and unfounded fears of coemployees is not an exception to an employer's obligation not to discriminate against a handicapped person. Under Title VII [of the Civil Rights Act of 1964], (c)ustomer preference has repeatedly been rejected as a justification for discrimination against women. . . . It is similarly . . . forbidden . . . to refuse on racial grounds to hire someone because your customers or clientele do not like his race (citations omitted). The rationale for this rule is wholly applicable to the . . . [handicapped discrimination law].[12]

In response to Hyatt's argument that at least part of the decision to discharge Cain was because of dissatisfaction with his actions and attitudes before he was hospitalized, the court stated:

> [W]hen the evidence reveals that both legal and illegal considerations lay behind the employment action, see *Price Waterhouse v. Hopkins,* 490 U.S. 228, 109 S.Ct. 1775, 1790, 104 L.Ed.2d (1989), and the plaintiff demonstrates that the impermissible consideration was a "motivating" . . . or "substantial" . . . factor in the adverse employment decision, the employer may prevail only if it proves by a preponderance of the evidence that it would have taken the same action with the illegitimate motive removed from the calculus. . . . There is no question that the defendants would not have removed Cain as regional partner in July if he had not contracted AIDS.[13]

The Court Award

The court awarded back pay plus interest from July 28, 1987, to June 13, 1988, the date when Cain became incapacitated, a total of $42,888.18. In addition, the court awarded $65,000 for Cain's mental anguish and humiliation, and $50,000 in punitive damages, for a grand total of $157,888.18. Punitive damages were awarded upon the court's finding that Hyatt's conduct was not merely inexcusably insensitive and illegal, but also outrageous.[14]

Possible Defenses to a Charge of AIDS Discrimination

Reasons advanced for refusing to hire or retain people with an HIV infection, ARC, or AIDS, and the legal effectiveness of such reasons, include:

Risk of Infection to Others

Because the infection is not transmitted by events that occur in the workplace, this is an ineffective defense to a charge of discrimination under almost all fact situations. Even in health care settings, the risk of transmission is very small. A 1988 study of 1200 doctors, nurses, and hospital workers who were accidentally exposed to HIV infected blood over a five year period, found only four people who subsequently tested positive for the HIV virus.[15]

The employer's case is not strengthened by the fact that an employee works in close contact with young children. In *Chalk v. United States District Court*,[16] the trial court had refused a preliminary injunction to keep a school district from excluding a public school teacher from the classroom. Although the trial court found that AIDS is a disability, it also found there was not enough evidence present to completely rule out the risk of infection that might be present if the teacher continued to work with children.

In reversing the trial court's denial of an injunction, the United States Court of Appeals for the Ninth Circuit relied on more than 100 journal articles submitted by the plaintiff showing that the risk of transmitting the HIV virus through casual contact was insignificant. The court concluded that the Supreme Court's reasoning in the *Arline* case dictates that an employee be excluded from the workplace only if the employer can prove a significant risk of communicating the infectious disease to others.

Inability to Commit to Long-Term Employment

Employers may hesitate in hiring employees with AIDS or related medical conditions when the job involves extensive or expensive training, or a commitment to a project that will last a number of months or years. It seems unreasonable for an employer to hire or retain a person who may have excessive future absenteeism because of health problems, or may not even live long enough to finish the training or the project. One federal case tends to support employers who face this position. A 1987 case[17] found reasonable a Department of State's policy of testing foreign service employees for HIV infection and denying overseas posting for those testing positive. The court stated that HIV-infected employees are not qualified for overseas posting because of the long terms of such postings.

. However, the weight of court decisions appear to agree with the principles of *Cain,* refusing to allow speculation concerning future health problems or death to be used to discriminate against people who are currently able to perform their duties of employment. *Shawn v Legs Diamond,*[18] a 1989 New York case not only adopted this approach, but also upheld an award of punitive damages. When the producers of a Broadway show, Legs Diamond, discovered their choreographer had tested positive for the HIV virus, they demanded that the choreographer and his physician give a guarantee that he would be able to continue working until the opening of the show. Because neither could give such a guarantee, the choreographer was fired even though he was currently able to work. The court found that the firing not only constituted illegal handicapped discrimination, but also was outrageous.

Excessive Costs of Health or Other Benefits

It is unlikely that a court will allow the excessive costs of benefits as a justification for discrimination. There are no known cases that have allowed such a defense. Discharge or discrimination against employees with the HIV infection will not only violate the ADA, but also the Employee Retirement Income Security Act (ERISA) which states:

> [I]t shall be unlawful for any person to discharge, fine, suspend, expel, discipline or otherwise discriminate against a participant or beneficiary for exercising any right to which he is entitled under the provisions of an employee benefit plan. . . .[19]

If the cost of providing fringe benefit protection such as health, life, or disability insurance for new employees is too high, the employer and insurance provider may use a preexisting conditions clause that denies coverage for any health problems that existed before employment began. Normal health underwriting principles are expressly allowed under the ADA. However, any exclusions for preexisting medical conditions must be applied to all new employees, not just those who appear to be disabled or ill.

Co-Worker or Customer Fear of AIDS

As covered in *Cain*, the courts are consistent in ruling that employment discrimination cannot be based upon customer or co-worker fears and prejudices.

Unqualified Individual

If the job applicant or current employee is not able to perform the essential duties of the job, with or without reasonable accommodations, the employer is not obligated to employ the person, even if the lack of qualification is caused by ARC or AIDS. For example, excessive absenteeism or poor performance caused by the opportunistic infections resulting from ARC or AIDS may be justification for discharge of an employee. A job applicant who is currently ill and unable to successfully perform the duties of the job is similarly unqualified and need not be hired. See Chapter 4, "Determining if a Disabled Person is Qualified," for the general rules concerning qualified versus unqualified workers.

Reasonable Accommodations

The ADA's reasonable accommodations requirement may include the granting of a reasonable amount of sick leave (as in *Cain*, discussed above), temporary part-time work status, changes in job duties, or other accommodations (see Chapter 5, "Making Accommodations for Disabled Employees," and Part II).

Other reasonable accommodations include actions to protect the safety of the employee with ARC or AIDS, and to protect fellow workers from infection. To accommodate the ARC- or AIDS-infected employee, reasonable steps should be taken to avoid on-the-job exposure to the opportunistic infections that may cause illness or death to the employee whose immune system is impaired. These steps include provision of a face mask to avoid airborne viruses, installation of clean filters in the air ducts, or even isolation of the employee, if necessary, and if reasonable both to the employee and the employer.

Because the only known method of on-the-job transmission of the HIV infection is through blood exchanges from an infected person to another, there is a slight risk of infection where two or more employees work closely in jobs that may cause cuts or bleeding. A reasonable accommodation to allow the infected worker to keep working without danger of infecting others is to provide gloves to protect against inadvertent blood transfers.

Other possible accommodations may include granting requests for job transfers, even if there is a general freeze on job relocations; providing home work stations for employees; allowing time off for medical treatment; and expanded medical coverage for experimental drugs such as AZT. See the AIDS entry in part II for additional ideas.

Employee Education

The single most important step in handling HIV infections, ARC, or AIDS is an education program for company managers and employees. Discrimination against infected applicants and employees will occur unless both managers and employees understand the facts about AIDS. Surveys show that as little as 18 percent of medium and large size businesses have AIDS policies that include the education of employees.[20] Speakers at a BNA conference, "AIDS Action Plans,"[21] recommended that companies establish policies on AIDS with education as the keystone. A company policy prohibiting discrimination on the basis of HIV infection, ARC, or AIDS should be distributed immediately before an educational program for managers and supervisors, followed shortly thereafter by educational programs for employees. Employee education programs should include qualified, outside medical experts. Outside experts should help convince the participants that the information given is valid. Training sessions should be followed by additional educational efforts such as notes in company newsletters, distribution of booklets on AIDS, and training for employee counselors and safety personnel.

The AIDS entry in Part II provides some sources of information for AIDS training. In addition, the American Red Cross has developed a training program for businesses that is offered for a very low fee. Contact the local chapter of the Red Cross for information.

AIDS Testing

Employers normally have no reason to test new or current employees for AIDS. AIDS tests actually test for the presence of the HIV virus. Many people with the HIV virus will not develop AIDS or suffer from AIDS-related complications until months or years later. Since the condition is a protected disability and the presence of the HIV infection does not disqualify a person from work, it is useless to test for it.

Several other reasons argue against testing:

1. Governmental employers may violate the right of privacy guarantees implied under the United States Constitution.[22] For example, the Nebraska Human Services Agency was found to have violated the unreasonable search and seizure protection of the Fourth Amendment to the United States Constitution by requiring all employees who work with retarded clients to undergo AIDS and Hepatitis B tests.[23] Testing of a hospital's patient care workers, however, may be valid.[24] Although the Constitution does not apply to private employers,[25] some state constitutions with similar provisions do.

2. Many states have prohibited or limited the right of employers to test for AIDS or use the test results in employment decisions.[26]

3. Test results are not always accurate. In addition to mistakes in the lab, the HIV infection may not be detected by a test during the first few weeks after exposure to the virus.

4. There is the danger of a large invasion of privacy lawsuit if test results are accidentally disclosed.

Handling Employees with AIDS

Regardless of how an employer learns that an employee has tested positive for the HIV infection, or has ARC or AIDS, confidentiality is the first priority. The ADA, many state laws, and the threat of private lawsuits make breaches of confidentiality very dangerous. Upon learning of an employee's AIDS-related condition, employers should do the following:

1. Establish a process for assuring confidentiality by which no more officials than necessary learn of the condition. Typical persons who might be informed should be limited to a member of the human relations department, company physician (if any), and the employee's supervisor, if accommodations are needed. All written records should be kept in a secure file separate from the employee's personnel file.

2. Schedule a meeting between a member of the human relations department and the employee to explain company fringe benefits such as health insurance coverage and sick

leave. Do *not* attempt to limit or change preexisting fringe benefits upon learning of the AIDs infection. This is a violation of the ADA and the Employee Retirement Income Security Act (ERISA).[27]

3. Discuss any needed accommodations such as sick leave time, release time to see a physician or receive medical treatments, or changes in work duties. Inform the employee that he or she will be treated just like any other employee, after reasonable accommodations are made. Therefore, excessive absenteeism or poor work performance may be a reason for suspension or discharge.

4. Obtain the employee's written consent to allow the employee's physician to disclose medical information to the company to be used in making accommodations or judging ability to work. Reserve the right to have the employee examined by a company physician.

Developing a Company AIDS Policy

Some experts believe that companies should not have a corporate policy on AIDS, preferring instead to have a general policy on infectious and catastrophic illnesses. However, AIDS is subject to so many misunderstandings and prejudices that a specific policy is desirable. The following is a sample written policy based in large part on separate policies developed by the San Francisco Chamber of Commerce and the Bank of America.[28]

Policy on AIDS and AIDS Related Conditions in the Workplace

_____ Company recognizes that Acquired Immune Deficiency Syndrome (AIDS) and its related conditions such as ARC (Aid Related Complex), or positive testing for the HIV virus pose substantial and serious issues in the workplace. We also recognize that any sensible and humane response to the AIDS epidemic must be based upon accurate information, not irrational fear, prejudice, and discrimination.

Based on the overwhelming weight of medical and scientific evidence, including statements from the United States Public Health Service, Centers for Disease Control, and others, there is no evidence that the AIDS virus is transmitted in ordinary social or business settings or occupations. Therefore, it is the policy of _____ Company to hire and retain employees who are currently qualified to work, with or without reasonable accommodations, regardless of whether they have an HIV infection, ARC, AIDS, or an AIDS-related disease. It is also company policy that upon request, these employees be furnished reasonable accommodations.

Policy. It is _____ Company policy that in dealing with individual job applicants and employees with AIDS, AIDS-related medical conditions, or other life-threatening illnesses, the Company and its agents will:

1. Offer applicants and employees the right to work so long as they are able to satisfactorily perform their jobs, and as long as the best medical evidence indicates their continued employment does not present a health or safety risk to themselves or others.
2. Treat all medical information obtained from employees or others as strictly confidential. Confidentiality of medical records should comply with all existing legal, medical, and ethical management practices.
3. Treat all individuals with compassion and understanding.
4. Offer reasonable accommodations.
5. Be sensitive to the needs of critically ill colleagues, and to recognize that the continued employment of people with life-threatening illnesses may be a vital concern for the ill person, both medically and emotionally.
6. Recognize that in regard to the life-threatening disease of AIDS and its related conditions, a person carrying the AIDS virus is not a threat to co-workers because AIDS is not spread by common contact or workplace activities. For this reason, AIDS or AIDS antibody testing shall not be required of any employee.
7. Engage in educational programs to remove the irrational fear that AIDS invokes. Educational programs for employees and managers shall begin immediately and shall cover all relevant aspects of the AIDS problem.

Guidelines. When dealing with situations involving employees with AIDS-related conditions or other life-threatening medical conditions, managers should:

1. Remember that an employee's health record is confidential. All reasonable precautions shall be taken to protect such information.
2. Contact the (personnel, human relations department, or other office) if you believe that you or another employee

need information about AIDS or related health problems.

3. Contact the (personnel, human relations department, or other office) if you have any concern about the possible contagious nature of an employee's medical condition.

4. If warranted, make reasonable accommodations for an employee's illness, consistent with the business needs of your unit of the company. If desired, contact the (personnel, human relations department, or other office) for advice concerning possible accommodations.

5. If a job transfer is requested by an infected employee, make a reasonable attempt to comply with the request.

6. Be sensitive and responsive to co-worker fears. If needed, contact the (personnel, human relations department, or other office) for additional employee education or training.

7. Be sensitive to the fact that continued employment may sometimes be therapeutically important in the remission or recovery process. Continued employment may even aid in prolonging the employee's life.

8. If co-workers continue to refuse to work with HIV- or AIDS-infected workers, even after additional education and counseling is given, begin progressive disciplinary steps. The refusal to work should be treated just as any other refusal to work.

PRACTICAL TIPS

Dealing With AIDS

1. Treat people with AIDS, ARC or the HIV virus the same as anyone with a serious, life-threatening illness.

2. Base employment policies and decisions on scientific truths, not rumor or stereotypes.

3. Educate top management and enlist their strong support for education and a corporate policy on AIDS.

4. Immediately develop and give to all managers and employers an informational program on AIDS in the workplace. Do not wait until the next employee has AIDS.

5. Issue a corporate policy explaining AIDS and the lack of risk in the workplace, a strong management statement against discrimination on the basis of AIDS, and penalties employees will face if they discriminate.

6. Assure that all AIDS reports, test results, and other related materials concerning an individual be kept strictly confidential.

7. Do not require HIV or AIDS medical screening of applicants or employees.

8. Ensure that all managers and supervisors know it is company policy to offer people with AIDS-related conditions reasonable accommodations in order to allow them to work as long as possible.

9. If after repeated attempts at education an employee refuses to work with a person with AIDS-related conditions, either transfer or discharge that person. Do not transfer, layoff, or discharge the person with AIDS, ARC, or HIV virus (unless he or she can no longer perform the essential tasks of the job).

Other Infectious Diseases

Many infectious and communicable diseases such as the flu may not be legal disabilities because of their temporary nature. Others such as AIDS, tuberculosis (TB), and certain forms of hepatitis do substantially limit a major life activity and will be considered disabilities under the ADA.

Regardless of whether classified as a disability, companies need to increase their activities in monitoring and controlling workplace exposure to infectious diseases, for several reasons:

1. **The increase in number of adults contracting communicable diseases.** Because of a lack of childhood exposure to epidemics that give future immunity, more adults risk infection than in the past. For example, there has been an increase in recent years of adult-onset mumps. While mumps in children may cause only minor problems, it can be very serious for adults.

2. **The increase in the number of people with suppressed immune systems.** This condition results not only in an increased chance of being infected, but also in a greatly increased chance of serious complications because the body cannot effectively fight the infections. Included in this category are persons who have had organ transplant surgery, chemotherapy for cancer, and AIDS. Many other medical conditions and drug treatments also decrease the body's immune defenses, including diabetes, lymphoma, Hodgkin's disease, leukemia, and steroid drugs (which are used to treat a variety of medical problems).

3. **The legal liability to customers or families of workers.** Although workers who are infected on the job are limited to workers'

compensation benefits, lawsuits may be filed by family members and by customers who catch an infection from the employee.

4. High absenteeism when epidemics occur. Reducing the spread of contagious disease may limit the number of sick days taken by workers.

Dealing with Communicable Disease

Employees with immune system deficiencies are legally disabled and entitled to reasonable accommodations. The following guidelines may be useful when dealing with communicable diseases.[29]

1. Categorize and Understand Communicable Diseases. Each infectious disease should be examined to determine if it is communicable in the employer's workplace, the probability of infection, and the severity of the disease. For example, AIDS ranks low (extremely low in the workplace) in probability of infection, but high in severity of the disease. However, influenza ranks high in probability of infection (a single sneeze can spread it), but lower in severity. As a general rule, the following diseases, among others, may be found to be transmittable in the workplace with a high enough degree of infectiousness and severity to warrant action:

  a. influenza—high probability of infection, and dangerous to certain persons such as those with suppressed immune systems
  b. infectious mononucleosis—high probabilty of infection, although the symptoms are not severe except in people with a suppressed immune system
  c. hepatitis A—high probability of infection, although symptoms not severe in most people
  d. hepatitis B, non-A or non-B hepatitis—lower probability of infection, but more severe symptoms than hepatitis A, and more common in health care institutions, as compared to other institutions
  e. staphylococcal (staph) infections—high probability of infection in health care institutions, lower in other employment settings, with mild to severe symptoms
  f. tuberculosis—low probability of infection, moderate symptoms that can be long lasting, or severe complications to HIV-infected people and some others

2. **Identify employees at risk.** The company should attempt to identify employees who are at an increased risk of infection, and employees who may pass along the infection to a family member who is in a high risk group. These people include those with suppressed immune systems and pregnant women, as well as those who have not been immunized against diseases such as measles and mumps.

3. **Take steps to protect at-risk employees.** Depending upon the seriousness of the risk to employees or their family members, steps that may be taken include the following:
   a. Temporary job transfers to separate the employee with a suppressed immune system or a family member with a suppressed immune system from employees with communicable diseases, if possible.
   b. Use of a mask to avoid airborne transfers of germs.
   c. Liberal sick leave for infectious employees to avoid exposing other employees.
   d. Added cleaning or sterilization procedures.[30]

PRACTICAL TIPS
Dealing With Infectious Diseases

1. Temporary infectious diseases such as influenza need not be treated as legal disabilities. However, chronic ones such as AIDS, most types of hepatitis, and tuberculosis are disabilities under the ADA.
2. Do not discriminate against or restrict employees with infectious diseases that are not transmitted in the workplace. In most workplaces, this category would include people with HIV infection, AIDS, tuberculosis, and hepatitis B.
3. Provide workplace accommodations for employees with suppressed immune systems such as those undergoing chemotherapy, those with the HIV infection or AIDS, and those with certain types of cancer.
4. Consider protecting immune suppressed workers by liberal sick leave policies for contagious co-workers, temporary job reassignments, or even face masks or protective clothing.

Drug and Alcohol Problems

The ADA treats employee use of illegal drugs differently from use of alcohol. It excludes from the definition of a legally disabled person anyone "who is currently engaging in the illegal use of drugs."[31] This rule is absolute. A person currently using illegal drugs has no legal protection under the ADA.

However, an employer may take action against an employee using alcohol, only if there is unsatisfactory work performance, or if the employee drinks on the job in violation of company rules. The ADA's alcohol rule states that an employer "may hold an employee . . . who is an alcoholic to the same qualification standards for employment or job performance and behavior that such entity holds other employees, even if any unsatisfactory performance or behavior is related to the . . . alcoholism of such employee."[32] . . . . Employers are allowed to take disciplinary action, including discharge, against employees under the influence of drugs or alcohol while at work. Stricter alcohol consumption rules may be required if a company is subject to the regulations of the Nuclear Regulatory Commission, Department of Transportation, or Department of Defense.

Illegal Drugs

Drug testing of job applicants and employees is permitted under the ADA, as is compliance with the Drug Free Workplace Act of 1988.[33] Employers may fire or refuse to hire any person who tests positive on a drug screening test. However, general principles of law and fairness should be followed by asking for information concerning legal drug use and by giving a second drug test to individuals who test positive but deny they have taken drugs. The ADA, Drug Free Workplace Act, and state laws do not require employers to discipline or discharge employees if they test positive for drugs. Companies remain free to set their own policy.

The major legal problem that may be encountered in dealing with job applicants and employees who test positive for illegal drugs is the ADA's provision that a legally disabled person includes an individual who

(I) has successfully completed a supervised drug rehabilitation program and is no longer engaging in the illegal use of drugs, or has otherwise been rehabilitated successfully and is no longer engaging in such use;

(II) is participating in a supervised rehabilitation program and is no longer engaging in such use;

(III) is erroneously regarded as engaging in such use, but is not engaging in such use.[34]

The Rehabilitation Act of 1973 is also amended by the ADA to include the language quoted above.[35]

The provision that former users of illegal drugs are protected from discrimination as legally disabled persons raises several questions. What evidence is acceptable to prove that a person who has taken illegal drugs is no longer doing so? How long does an individual have to refrain from the illegal use of drugs to be considered one who is not currently using drugs? In what type of rehabilitation program, if any, must a past drug user participate in order to receive the protection of the ADA? How can an employer prove an individual is still a current user of illegal drugs? The ADA, congressional committee reports, and regulations of the EEOC answer most of these questions with the following guidelines:

1. The key issue is whether an individual currently uses illegal drugs. When an employer has a suspicion that an individual's claim of being currently drug free is untrue, drug testing should be conducted. If illegal substances are detected, the employer can assume current use even though some illegal substances are detected days or weeks after use. The ADA states that "it shall not be a violation of this Act for a covered entity to adopt and administer reasonable policies and procedures, including but not limited to drug testing, designed to ensure an individual is no longer engaging in such use."[36]

2. If the drug test is positive, confirm it with a second, more sophisticated test. Failure to do so may create legal liability because the ADA offers legal protection to those who are erroneously regarded as engaging in illegal drug use.[37] Failure to confirm positive drug tests has already created liability under some state laws, including New York.[38]

3. Periodic follow-up drug tests to ensure continued abstinence from illegal drugs are permissible if reasonable in total number, frequency, and procedure.

4. If a former illegal drug user claims to be currently drug free, treat the person as one with a legal disability unless drug testing or other specific evidence proves the individual is using drugs.

5. Do not distinguish among former drug users on the basis of whether they have entered a drug rehabilitation program, finished such a program, or stopped using drugs on their

own. Again, the key is whether they currently use drugs, not how they stopped using drugs.

6. Treat as a legally protected person any individual who is involved in a drug rehabilitation program even if such a person is taking legally administered treatment drugs such as in a methadone maintenance program.

7. Do not discriminate against or treat differently any employee who is taking legally prescribed drugs, unless there is proof that the drug's side effects make the person unqualified to effectively and safely perform current job duties.

8. Do not test for any drugs except those illegal drugs listed in schedules I through V of section 202 of the Controlled Substances Act.[39] Compliance with these schedules is especially important when giving drug screening tests to job applicants. As the only exception to the ADA's prohibition of medical testing before a conditional job offer is extended, congressional committee reports emphasized that drug tests should not disclose legal prescription drugs prescribed for treatment of a person's disability.[40] For example, it is a violation of the law to test for the drug dilantin, a drug that is prescribed for people with epilepsy.

9. Do not deny employee benefits such as health or life insurance coverage simply because of an individual's current or past drug use. Although employers may take disciplinary steps against current illegal drug users, up to and including discharge, they cannot deny non-drug-related benefits to employees who are retained.

10. Employers subject to Department of Transportation, Nuclear Regulatory Agency, or Department of Defense rules should check the agency regulations for additional drug-related requirements.[41] Most states also have laws or regulations concerning drug testing, employee usage, and company drug policies.[42]

Alcohol Problems

The provisions of the ADA and the ADA amendment to the Rehabilitation Act concerning alcohol abuse state that an employer "may hold . . . an alcoholic to the same qualification standards for employment or job performance and behavior that such entity holds other employees, even if any unsatisfactory performance or behavior is related to the . . . alcoholism of such employee."[43] However, an employer may discipline or discharge employees who are intoxicated while at work or who bring liquor into the workplace.[44] Before taking action, employers should adopt company policies on alcohol and inform the employees of those policies.

Apparently, the only alcohol users entitled to legal protection under the ADA are alcoholics. This terminology is used to describe individuals in the ADA[45] and the amendment to the Rehabilitation Act.[46] This approach is also illustrated by a case decided under Pennsylvania law similar to the ADA.[47] Columbia Gas Company fired Small, a meter reader, after it learned that she had been arrested for drunken driving. The two supervisors who made the decision did not know that she was an alcoholic and they had not observed any of the warning signs of alcoholism such as excessive absenteeism, physical appearance, or the smell of liquor on her breath. Their stated reason for discharge was the fact that she had violated a criminal law and that meter readers must be trusted since they enter people's homes. The court held that there was no proof that the company knew the employee was an alcoholic, and therefore it could not have discriminated on the basis of her alcoholism.

Direct Threat to Health & Safety

Under the ADA, employers can impose a qualification standard that "an individual shall not pose a direct threat to the health and safety of other individuals in the workplace."[48] This provision can be used to transfer, suspend, or discharge employees whose alcohol use creates a danger in the workplace, whether they are alcoholics or simply intoxicated. For example, in *Butler v. Thornburgh,*[49] a 1990 case, the court upheld the discharge of an FBI special agent who had caused repeated problems as the result of his frequent intoxication. In addition to being in a position to carry guns and sometimes being involved in highly dangerous activities, the agent had lost his car several times because of his intoxication, and he had engaged in two or more fights while drinking. Based on these facts, the court found the agent to be unqualified. Similar reasoning may be applied to police officers, nuclear power plant employees, and others with safety-sensitive jobs.

Handling Alcoholic Employees

Although the ADA states that alcoholics may be held to the same job standards as nonalcoholics, alcoholism is a legal disability.

Therefore, an employee should not be disqualified solely on the basis of alcoholism, as a medical condition. However, if reasonable accommodations are provided and the worker still cannot adequately perform the job, or creates a safety problem to others, the employee may be disciplined, suspended, or discharged.

The ADA requires that employers treat alcoholism as they do other diseases or health problems. If an employer has a policy of granting sick leave for employees who need medical treatment, the same sick leave policy should cover treatment for alcoholism. If an employer allows work-time flexibility for a cancer patient to have radiation treatments, the same flexibility should be extended to alcoholics needing to attend rehabilitation counseling.

Different treatment can be a violation of law. For example, discrimination based upon disability was shown in an Ohio case where an alcoholic employee was fired as soon as he told his employer about his condition.[50] Performance evaluations showed the employee had received consistently high ratings. Thus, no poor job performance could be proven. The court took particular notice of the fact that the employer had recently granted three to four weeks sick leave for an employee to receive treatment for phlebitis, while another worker received a month's sick leave to recover from a heart attack. Not granting a reasonable amount of sick leave for alcoholism treatment was discriminatory.

An employer's duty to accommodate will end when the alcoholic employee refuses reasonable accommodations. For example, the Federal Aviation Administration was found to have acted properly in the following situation.[51] The FAA gave an alcoholic employee several leaves of absence to undergo alcoholic treatment programs that did not work. After many warnings, she was told she would be fired unless she entered and completed another program. She failed to show up to her first appointment with the treating physician and later told her supervisor that it would be ridiculous for her to try another program. In upholding her discharge from employment, the court noted that the FAA had made an extensive attempt to accommodate her condition by offering several leaves of absence, and that it would be an undue hardship on the FAA to continue to accommodate her after she had notified them she did not intend to remain in the rehabilitation program.

Federal Employees

Alcoholic federal employees have extra protection under the law because of two factors. First, the Comprehensive Alcohol Abuse and Alcoholism Prevention, Treatment, and Rehabilitation Act of 1970[52] establishes a complex series of steps that must be followed in counseling, treatment, warnings, and other procedures before a federal employee may be discharged.

Second, the ADA's amendment to the Rehabilitation Act,[53] stating that alcoholics are not considered disabled if their current use of alcohol keeps them from performing their jobs or creates a health or safety danger, amends only section 503, applicable to federal contractors, and section 504, applicable to those who receive federal aid. It does not apply to the federal government under section 501.[54]

A case illustrating the lengths that the federal government must go to accommodate an alcoholic employee was decided in 1989.[55] On November 4, 1988, an admitted alcoholic was dismissed after a 23-year career in HUD's Office of Finance and Accounting. In September 1985, she received a reprimand for her poor job performance due to alcohol that cited numerous instances of absences and falling asleep on the job. She was directed to see the agency employee counseling director. After receiving counseling, she voluntarily entered a rehabilitation program. In January 1986, she received 120 hours of sick leave to attend an in-house alcohol abuse program. After her return to work, she suffered a relapse that resulted in a large number of absences. When she did come to work, she was often drunk.

On April 26, 1986, a notice of proposed termination of employment as of June 20 was given to the employee. However, on June 20, the termination notice was extended, giving her nine more months, during which she was to get treatment. She spent a month in an in-house treatment center in July. During the next year she attended HUD's employee assistance program for treatment of alcoholism. However, another relapse occurred in September, 1987, resulting in a number of days lost from work. After a five-day suspension from work during which no improvement was noted, she was discharged on November 4, 1987.

Almost any reasonable person would argue that the employee was given reasonable accommodation for her alcoholism. However, the court issued a preliminary injunction restoring her job position. The court explained:

> [O]nce an employee has shown evidence that her handicap can be accommodated, the burden of persuasion is on the agency to show that it cannot accommodate the employee.

In this case the agency has not met its burden. Ms. McElrath has demonstrated that treatment is available and that she is willing to pursue that treatment. I am persuaded, based upon expert testimony as well as the plaintiff's own testimony, that there is some likelihood that Ms. McElrath will recover.

It is clear that accommodating Ms. McElrath will not unduly burden the agency. It is a fact that the agency did not even consider the possibility of having the employee take leave-without-pay while she underwent a treatment program.[56]

PRACTICAL TIPS

Dealing With Drug & Alcohol Problems

1. The ADA does not restrict employers' ability to discipline or discharge employees who come to work with alcohol or illegal drugs, or who are under the influence of such substances while at work.

2. Drug testing, before or after a conditional offer of employment, is permitted.

3. Positive drug test findings should be confirmed by a second test before detrimental action is taken.

4. Past drug abusers who currently are not using illegal drugs are considered legally disabled. Therefore, do not discriminate on the basis of past use.

5. Do not discriminate against an individual solely because of alcoholism. Take action only if an employee's attendance or work performance is poor, or if the employee creates safety problems.

6. Discipline or discharge of nonalcoholic employees for alcohol-related acts may be permissible. However, these actions are dangerous because the individual may later argue and prove alcoholism.

7. Alcoholic employees are entitled to a reasonable accommodation, just as other disabled employees.

8. If an alcoholic employee refuses a reasonable accommodation such as rehabilitation services, nonfederal employers may discharge the worker.

9. Federal agencies must be aware of the stricter rules concerning accommodation and rehabilitation applicable to federal employers.

10. Always check possible additional rules involving drug and alcohol problems. These include regulations under the Department of Transportation, Nuclear Regulatory Commission, and Department of Defense for defense contractors.

11. Always check state law. Many states add rules concerning disability discrimination, drug testing, and related matters.

Obesity

Obesity has not been declared a legal disability under the Rehabilitation Act of 1973, nor is it specifically listed in the ADA. To the contrary, in a 1984 case brought under the Rehabilitation Act, a man who was denied employment as a flight attendant because he exceeded the company's maximum weight for his height, was found not to be disabled because his excessive weight was the result of voluntary body building activities.[57] However, employers should be aware of the possibility that an obese person may win a discrimination lawsuit under the ADA or state laws.

Two state court decisions applying state handicapped employment laws have held that obesity may be a disability. A 1989 Oregon Court of Appeals decision,[58] applying a definition of disability identical to the ADA and the Rehabilitation Act, stated that an obese person may be protected against discrimination in two types of situations. First, if the excess weight substantially limits a major life activity. Second, if people treat an obese person as if the individual has a disability.

An older, more famous case, *New York State Division of Human Rights v. Xerox*,[59] was based on a charge of handicapped discrimination under New York law. Catherine McDermott was denied a systems consultant position with Xerox after the company physician found that her weight of 249 pounds on a five-foot, six-inch frame was medically obese—about 100 pounds too heavy. Under state law provisions written somewhat differently from the Rehabilitation Act and the ADA, the court found illegal discrimination based upon a disability. Because McDermott was otherwise qualified for the job and because there was no proof she could not perform the job, Xerox was found to be in violation of the New York Human Rights Act.

There is no reason why these state court decisions cannot be extended to the ADA. It is clearly arguable that extremely obese people either suffer a physical impairment that may substantially limit one or more major activities, or if not truly disabled, are considered by many to be impaired. Because the ADA protects those who have physical or mental impairments, a past record of impairment, or are considered by others to be impaired, it should cover obese individuals who otherwise meet the ADA's requirements for protection.

PRACTICAL TIPS

Dealing With Obese People

1. To be legally safe, now and in the future, treat obesity as a disability.
2. Base employment decisions on ability, not size or appearance.
3. Employ obese people if they are qualified, with or without a reasonable accommodation.
4. Do not deny employment because of a risk of increased health claims (see Chapter 6, "Risk of Future Injury: Epilepsy, Diabetes, and Bad Backs," for additional information on this subject).

Notes

1. Harris, *The New Economics of AIDS*, U.S. NEWS & WORLD REP. Aug. 13, 1990, at 56.
2. 480 U.S. 273, 43 FEP Cases 81 (1987).
3. Justice Department Memorandum on the Applicability of Section 504 of the 1973 Rehabilitation Act to HIV-Infected Persons, September 27, 1988, Daily Lab. Report (BNA), D-1, Oct. 7, 1988.
4. Acquired Immune Deficiency Syndrome (AIDS) and Related Conditions as Protected Handicaps Under Section 503 of the Rehabilitation Act of 1973, Office of Federal Contract Compliance Programs, Number FCCM Notice/Ch 6, December 23, 1988.
5. 734 F. Supp. 671, 50 FEP Cases 195 (E.D. Pa. 1990).
6. *Id.*, 734 F. Supp. at 674.
7. *Id.*, 734 F. Supp. at 676.
8. *Id.*, 734 F. Supp. at 678.
9. *Id.*, 734 F. Supp. at 679–680.
10. *Id.*, 734 F. Supp. at 681.
11. *Id.*, 734 F. Supp. at 683–684.
12. *Id.*, 734 F. Supp. at 681.
13. *Id.*, 734 F. Supp. at 685.
14. *Id.*, 734 F. Supp. at 686.
15. Bishop, *Very Few Workers Exposed to AIDS Showed Infection*, Wall St. J., September 26, 1988, p. B6.
16. 840 F.2d 701, 46 FEP Cases 279 (9th Cir. 1988).
17. AFGE Local 1812 v. Dep't of State, 662 F. Supp. 50, 43 FEP Cases 955 (D.D.C. 1987).
18. *Shawn v. Legs Diamond* L.P., 51 EPD §39,381 (N.Y. 1989).
19. 29 U.S.C.A. §1140 (1985 & Supp. 1989).

20. "AIDS: A Plan for Confronting Problems in the Workforce," BNA Policy and Practice Series, *Fair Employment Practices* April 27, 1989, p. 51.
21. *Id.*
22. *See* Rendell-Baker v. Kohn, 457 U.S. 830 (1982) : Jackson v. Metro. Edison, 419 U.S. 345 (1974).
23. Glover v. E. Neb. Community Office, 867 F.2d 461, 49 (8th Cir. 1989).
24. Leckelt v. Bd. of Comm'rs of Hosp. Dist. No. 1, 714 F. Supp. 1377 (E.D. La. 1989).
25. *See* Jackson v. Metropolitan Edison Co., 419 U.S. 345 (1974); and Rendell-Baker v. Kohn, 457 U.S. 830 (1982).
26. BNA Policy and Practice Series: *Personnel Management*, 247:143.
27. 29 U.S.C.A. §1140.
28. *See* AIDS IN THE WORKPLACE: RESOURCE MANUAL (3d ed., BNA Special Report 1989).
29. This material is taken, in part, from Richards & Rathbun, *A Careful Balancing of Rights: Communicable-Disease Plan Must Confront Increasing Problems of the Workplace*, PREVENTIVE L. REP. June 1989, at 19–22.
30. Additional information on medical testing and the collection of health information is given in Chapter 2, "Major Changes to Conform to the Law," under the "Hiring Process" subheading, as well as in Chapter 4, "Determining if a Disabled Person is Qualified," and Chapter 5, "Making Accommodations for Disabled Employees." For a complete discussion of medical screening in employment, see M. ROTHSTEIN, MEDICAL SCREENING AND THE EMPLOYEE HEALTH COST CRISIS (Washington: BNA Books 1989).
31. Americans with Disabilities Act §104, 42 U.S.C.A. §12114 (West, 1991).
32. *Id.*
33. 41 U.S.C. §701 et seq.
34. Americans with Disabilities Act §104, 42 U.S.C.A. §12114.
35. *Id.* at 512, 42 U.S.C.A. §12211.
36. *Id.* at §104, 42 U.S.C.A. §12114.
37. *Id.* at §511, 42 U.S.C.A. §12211.
38. Olsen, *Legal and Practical Considerations in Developing a Substance Abuse Program*, THE LAB. LAW. Fall 1990, at 876.
39. 21 U.S.C. §812.
40. *See* HOUSE COMM. ON RULES REPORT ON THE AMERICANS WITH DISABILITIES ACT, H.R. REP NO. 488, 101st Cong., 2d Sess.
41. *See* BNA Policy and Practice Series, *Personnel Management*, 247:401 et seq.
42. *Id.* at 581.
43. Americans with Disabilities Act §104, 42 U.S.C.A. §12114.
44. *Id.*
45. *Id.*
46. *Id.* at §512, 42 U.S.C. §12211.
47. Small v. Columbia Gas of Pa., 525 A2d 424, (Pa. 1987).
48. Americans with Disabilities Act §103, 42 U.S.C.A. §12113.
49. 900 F.2d 186 (5th Cir. 1990).
50. Hazlett v. Martin Chevrolet, 496 N.E.2d 478, 51 FEP Cases 1588 (Oh. 1986).
51. LeMere v. Burnley, 683 F. Supp. 275, 46 FEP Cases 845 (D.D.C. 1988).
52. 42 U.S.C. §290dd-1(d).
53. Americans with Disabilities Act §512, 42 U.S.C.A. §12211.
54. *Id.*

55. McElrath v. Kemp, 714 F. Supp. 23, 49 FEP Cases 908 (D.D.C. 1989).
56. *Id.*, 714 F. Supp. at 26.
57. Tudyman v. United Airlines, 608 F. Supp. 739, 38 FEP Cases (C.D. Cal. 1984).
58. Oregon State Correctional Inst. v. Bureau of Lab. & Indus., 780 P2d 743 (Or. 1989).
59. 491 N.Y. S.2d 106, 37 FEP Cases 1389 (1985).

Chapter 8

Company Policies and Forms

Effective hiring and retention of employees with disabilities, as well as maximizing the performance of employees with physical or mental health problems, cannot be accomplished solely by good intentions. Success in dealing with disabled job applicants and employees, as well as avoiding lawsuits, can be achieved only by the adoption and enforcement of effective company policies and procedures.

Traditionally, only larger businesses have adopted formal, written employee policies and procedures. However, companies of all sizes should take the time and effort to develop policies and procedures to be used in dealing with job applicants and employees with disabilities. Without effective policies and procedures, the risk of accidentally causing a successful disability discrimination lawsuit increases.

This chapter contains suggested policy statements and forms that may be used in dealing with job applicants and employees who may be disabled. However, affirmative action policies required of federal contractors by the Rehabilitation Act of 1973 are not included.[1]

Company Policies and Forms

Company policy statements and forms covered in this chapter that appear consistent with the Americans with Disabilities Act (ADA) include the following:

1. Company Policy Statement on Hiring, Accommodating, and Retaining Disabled Employees—a complete general company policy.

2. Company Policy Statement Regarding Disabled Job Applicants and Employees—An alternative, briefly stated company policy statement.
3. Sample letter or statement by a company CEO concerning disabled job applicants and employees.
4. Sample union contract clauses to cover employee disability problems.
5. Suggested job position announcement or advertisement language.
6. Sample Job Application Form for compliance with the ADA, state handicapped laws, and general equal employment principles.
7. Job Applicant and Employee Consent Form for a Physical Examination.
8. Sample Applicant and Employee Consent Form for Drug Use Screening.
9. Voluntary Disclosure of Disability and Request for Accommodations Form.

Although it is feasible to revise a company's equal employment policy statement to reflect the requirements of the ADA, a separate policy statement is desirable. Such a statement helps demonstrate the company's commitment to the idea of hiring, accommodating, and retaining disabled workers. It also allows the policy to be written with more specific reference to disabled people.

Distribution of the longer form (the first form presented below) can be an educational device as well as a company policy.

1. SAMPLE COMPANY POLICY—LONG FORM

Company Policy on Hiring, Accommodating, and Retaining Disabled Employees

Introduction

Equal employment opportunities for disabled persons is the policy of _____ Company, not only because it is required by law, but also because it is fair and it helps the company attract and retain good employees. Therefore, we are committed to take action to employ and advance in employment qualified disabled individuals. We are also committed to eliminating artificial impediments to the employment and advancement of disabled workers by striving to remove barriers to employment, whether physical, social, or arising from misconceptions concerning the abilities of disabled persons.

This commitment includes engaging in outreach programs to find qualified, disabled persons, and conducting company activities while recruiting, interviewing, hiring, training, and evaluating individuals so that each disabled person's abilities are recognized, and reasonable accommodations are provided that allow disabled employees to perform at their maximum potential.

All managers and supervisors are expected to become familiar with the provisions of this policy and other company policies and procedures concerning disabled workers, and to discuss these concepts with employees under their supervision. Annual performance evaluations of managers and supervisors shall include an examination of each person's commitment and action in helping the company implement the goals of this policy.

Policy Statement

Our company policy to increase equal employment opportunities to disabled individuals is as follows:

1. Recruit, hire, train, place, and promote qualified individuals without regard to their physical or mental disabilities.
2. Take positive steps to attract, hire, and retain qualified employees with disabilities.
3. Work with disabled job applicants and employees to find reasonable accommodations to each individual's disability so each person can be an effective, valued employee.
4. Base all employment decisions, (including, but not limited to, hiring, job placement, performance evaluations, merit pay, job transfer, and promotion) upon each individual's performance, after reasonable accommodations have been made.
5. Treat each person as an individual and refrain from acting upon stereotypes concerning disabled people's limitations or work restrictions.
6. Comply with the letter and spirit of all federal and state laws concerning the employment of disabled persons, including the Americans with Disabilities Act and applicable state handicapped laws.

7. Investigate and take appropriate action concerning complaints of discrimination made by disabled job applicants or employees, complaints of a failure to make reasonable job accommodations, or any other complaints that, if true, violate the spirit of this policy or any relevant law.
8. Cooperate with governmental agencies investigating complaints of discrimination filed by disabled individuals or groups.

Disabled Job Applicants and Employees

For employment purposes, a disabled person is one who has a physical or mental impairment that substantially limits one or more major life activities, any person who has a past history of such an impairment, or any person who is treated as if he or she has such an impairment. All individuals with nontemporary physical and mental problems that may cause work problems are legally disabled. This definition includes people who are paralyzed, blind, deaf, or have other noticeable disabilities. It also includes people with diabetes, heart problems, bad backs, or other less serious or nonobvious problems. Additional examples of people who are disabled include recovering alcoholics, recovering drug abusers, individuals with mental problems, and individuals with AIDS or the HIV virus.

Job applicants and employees should be considered to be disabled if

1. There is an obvious physical or mental condition that is likely to cause problems in obtaining a job or doing the work involved.
2. The job applicant or employee claims a disability or a medical condition that qualifies as a disability.
3. Information concerning the job applicant or employee's disability otherwise comes to the company's attention.

In the cases of (2) and (3), the company physician or medical staff may be asked to confirm or deny the individual's disabled status, state any necessary work restrictions, and suggest reasonable accommodations, if appropriate.

Voluntary Self-Identification of Disabilities

Many job applicants and employees actively hide their physical or mental problems because of fear that such information will be used against them. However, we encourage job applicants and employees to voluntarily identify themselves as disabled if they have any work restrictions or need for accommodations. No discrimination will be allowed against those who identify their disabilities. Instead, the information given shall be used to consider, and if appropriate, implement reasonable work accommodations. Only through reasonable accommodations can the company aid each individual and maximize productivity.

Medical Examinations

Nothing in this policy statement shall prevent the company from requiring physical or mental health examinations by qualified physicians, or from collecting medical information on an individual after a job applicant is tentatively hired or later during an individual's term of employment. However, no disabled applicant or employee shall be singled out for medical testing, unless his or her job performance is unsatisfactory, and there is probable cause to believe a physical or mental impairment may be the cause of the poor performance. In all other cases, all employees must be treated the same.

Confidentiality

All information collected concerning employee health and disabilities shall be kept in a secured place of storage, separate from the employee personnel records. This information shall be disclosed only on a "need to know" basis. Distribution of medical information will be limited to individuals who need the data for purposes of job placement and making reasonable accommodations; managers and supervisors, if needed for effective supervision; health or safety professionals who may be called upon to provide medical attention; and proper government officials investigating compliance with various disability discrimination laws.

Reasonable Accommodations

The company is committed to making reasonable accommodations for the known physical and mental disabilities of qualified job applicants and employees. All managers and supervisors are expected to cooperate with company officials and with the disabled person to devise changes in work procedures, equipment, or other aspects of a job position so that a disabled person may successfully perform the major duties of the job. While the disabled person should be included in the decision-making process, the final decision as to reasonable accommodations shall be made by the appropriate company officials, not the employee.

With the exception of minor accommodations that successfully offer a solution to a disabled employee's work problem, all accommodation decisions shall be made only after consultation with the (personnel department, human resources manager, or other appropriate office or person). Minor accommodations are those that are cost free or involve an expense of less than ($250 or other desired monetary amount).

Education and Training

_____ Company is committed to providing orientation and training to newly hired and newly disabled employees with physical or mental impairments. We are also committed to providing appropriate training and education concerning disabled workers to line and staff managers, supervisors, and other employees.

The (personnel, human relations, or other appropriate office), in cooperation with managers and supervisors, is responsible for conducting orientation and training of disabled employees. It shall also be the duty of the (personnel, human relations, or other appropriate office) to develop and institute a training program for managers and supervisors (and employees, if the company desires) in compliance with the requirements of the Americans with Disabilities Act, state handicapped employment laws, and other relevant laws. This training should include methods that may be used to increase the number of disabled employees, and effectively accommodate the disabilities of all employees. The (personnel, human relations, or other appropriate department) shall periodically revise and distribute additional training materials.

Duties of Line Managers and Supervisors

Managers and supervisors are responsible for the following:

1. Taking appropriate action to institute reasonable job accommodations that are needed for any obvious or self-identified disability of an employee under their supervision.

2. Working with the (medical department, personnel office, human relations department, or other appropriate office) and any disabled person to devise reasonable accommodations
3. Implementing reasonable accommodations
4. Complying with medical or work restrictions imposed by the (company physician, medical staff, human relations department, or other appropriate office)
5. Consulting with the (medical department, human relations department, or other appropriate office) to learn any health and safety requirements necessary to protect any disabled person under their supervision, including emergency procedures
6. Monitoring the success of the disabled employee and working with the employee and others so that desired modifications and accommodations can be instituted, as needed
7. Reviewing the company policy and any additional information concerning disabled workers distributed by the company, and conducting a formal review of company disability policies at least once per year
8. Giving a yearly update to employees under their supervision concerning the company disability policy, and inviting current employees to self-identify any disability so that the manager or supervisor, alone or in conjunction with appropriate staff members, may make reasonable accommodations to improve employee's work performance

Conclusion

Questions concerning this policy, complaints of discrimination, and requests for information concerning reasonable accommodations shall be made to the (human resources department, personnel manager, or other appropriate office or official).

2. SAMPLE COMPANY POLICY—SHORT FORM

Company Policy Statement Regarding Disabled Job Applicants and Employees

The policy of _____ company is to hire and advance in employment, qualified disabled individuals.

No individual shall be discriminated against on the basis of a mental or physical impairment. All employment decisions shall be based only upon an objective determination of each person's job qualifications and job performance.

We are committed to a program of positive action to assure equal employment opportunities for qualified disabled individuals by offering reasonable accommodations for the known physical and mental disabilities of each individual in order to maximize the individual's abilities.

The company will take appropriate action to cure any reasonable complaint concerning discrimination based upon disability, and to cooperate with all governmental investigations regarding compliance with local, state, and federal laws concerning the employment of disabled workers.

Managers and supervisors are expected to become familiar with the requirements of our company and the law regarding the employment of disabled people. They are also expected to cooperate in making reasonable accommodations for disabled workers.

Any questions concerning the implementation of this policy should be directed to the (human relations department, personnel manager, or other appropriate office or officer).

Company policies are seldom effective without strong support from top management. To insure that all employees are convinced of top management's support for a company policy concerning the hiring, accommodation, and advancement of disabled individuals, the chief executive officer should issue a personal statement for distribution to all employees. The statement should also be given to all new employees and redistributed every two years to all employees. The following is a sample CEO statement.

3. SAMPLE CEO LETTER

I believe that equal employment is essential to the success of our company. It is our company policy, and my personal goal, that each job applicant and employee be treated as an individual, without discrimination based upon arbitrary factors such as race, sex, or disability.

I believe our company must

1. Encourage individuals with physical or mental disabilities to apply for employment.

2. Take direct action to attract and hire qualified disabled employees.
3. Make reasonable accommodations for the known disabilities of job applicants and employees.
4. Encourage current and new employees to identify themselves as disabled so that reasonable accommodations may be made to aid the company and the employee.
5. Comply with all local, state, and federal laws concerning the employment of disabled persons.
6. Cooperate with governmental agencies investigating any complaints under employment discrimination laws for disabled people.
7. Emphasize the abilities of employees, rather than any disabilities or limitations; and
8. Insure that the maximum opportunity to excel is given to each individual, regardless of any mental or physical impairment.

I expect all employees at every level of our company to join me in opening our workplace to all qualified workers. I urge any employee with a physical or mental condition that causes any problem with their effectiveness at work to identify yourself so that accommodations may be made to allow you to more fully realize your potential.

A sustained effort to attract, hire, and accommodate disabled workers is an investment in people that can help our company grow and prosper. Not only does it provide economic benefits, but it is the fair thing to do. Like myself, I am sure that you want to be proud of your company. Effective action and results to open our company to all qualified workers and to help all individuals achieve their work goals by emphasizing each person's abilities and by accommodating any disabilities, can give us reason to be proud.

(signed) _____
Chief Executive Officer

Because the ADA applies to employers and unions, new contracts between management and unions should provide standards for dealing with disabled job applicants and employees. The following sample contract language has been developed by the International Association of Machinists and Aerospace Workers Union.[2]

4. SAMPLE UNION CONTRACT LANGUAGE

1. NONDISCRIMINATION. The employer shall not discriminate against any employees covered by this agreement on the basis of disability, race, gender, religious belief, sexual preference, or national origin.

2. JOB RETENTION. Both parties to this agreement will work cooperatively to retain in employment a worker who becomes disabled on or off the job. Both parties also agree to work together to facilitate the individual's return to work as soon as possible.

3. REASONABLE ACCOMMODATION. It will be the policy of (name of employer) to make reasonable accommodations for the known limitations of a worker who has a disability. Such accommodations may include, but are not limited to, such things as workstation modification; making building facilities, such as rest rooms, cafeterias or other facilities accessible; adaptation of tools and equipment, work schedules, and travel/transportation adjustment. The employee with a disability who is affected will be consulted on an accommodation. Any accommodation made will assure that the work will be performed safely.

4. RETRAINING AND/OR TRANSFER OF EMPLOYEE. It shall be the policy of (name of employer) that if an employee injured on or off the job is unable to return to his or her present job, the employer and the union will work together to make every effort to place the worker in another position for which he or she is qualified or can be qualified through training or accommodation.

5. PROMOTION. It will be the policy of (name of employer) that promotions will be based on the ability to do the job and merit. This policy will apply to all employees, including those who have disabilities. Disability alone shall not be grounds for excluding a candidate from consideration.

6. JOINT LABOR-MANAGEMENT COMMITTEE ON WORKERS WITH DISABILITIES. In order to enhance the productivity of workers with disabilities and provide an opportunity for their full participation in employment-related and employer-sponsored activities, a joint Labor-Management Committee on Workers with Disabilities shall be established. The Committee's functions will be to keep track of problems and recommend solutions as well as to review company policies and programs, and recommend any necessary changes.

Although not required under the provisions of the ADA, job announcements, letters to employment agencies, and newspaper advertisements for new employees should state the company's desire to consider disabled people. Several alternatives for doing this are given below.

5. SUGGESTED JOB POSITION ANNOUNCEMENTS AND ADVERTISEMENTS

If already in current use, consider retention of these statements:

"Equal Opportunity Employer,"
"Affirmative Action/Equal Opportunity Employer,"
"AA/EOE."

If "Equal Opportunity Employer. Women & Minorities Encouraged to Apply," is currently used, change to:

"Equal Opportunity Employer. Women, Minorities, and Disabled Persons Encouraged to Apply."

If "EOE, M/F" is currently used, consider:

"EOE, M/F/D."

The best statement, if not a governmental agency, recipient of federal funds, or a federal contractor subject to affirmative action, is:

Equal Opportunity Employer
Women, Minorities, and Disabled People Encouraged to Apply

If subject to affirmative action as a federal contractor or recipient of federal aid, use:

AA/EOE
Women, Minorities, and Disabled People Encouraged to Apply

The following is a job application form that meets the requirements of the ADA and other federal equal employment laws, as well as most state equal employment laws.[3]

6. SAMPLE JOB APPLICATION FORM
for Compliance with ADA and Other Employment Laws

APPLICATION FOR EMPLOYMENT

Acme Company
123 Elm Street
Anytown, Homestate 00000

Acme Company is an equal employment opportunity employer dedicated to a policy of nondiscrimination in employment upon any basis, including race, color, creed, religion, age, sex, national origin, ancestry, sexual orientation, marital status, military status, or the presence of any physical or mental medical condition or disability. In reading and answering the following questions, please keep in mind that none of the questions are intended to imply any limitations, illegal preferences, or discrimination based upon any non-job-related information.

This application will be given complete consideration, but its receipt does not imply that the applicant will be employed. <u>Optional:</u> Acme Company arranges for a surety bond for each employee, at the company's expense. Unless your background will pass scrutiny by a surety company (not related to the factors listed in the previous paragraph such as race or sex), it will be difficult or impossible to secure a surety bond, and the company will be unable to offer employment.

POSITION(S) APPLIED FOR: _____

Type of Work Desired: _____ Full Time   _____ Part Time   _____ Temporary

Date Available to Start Work: _____

PERSONAL DATA

Name _____ Social Security Number _____

Current Address: _____
Street Address or Box Number   City   State   Zip

Permanent Address: _____
(Leave Blank if the Same as Your Current Address)

Daytime Phone at Which You Can be Reached: (_____) _____
Area Code

Evening Phone at Which You Can be Reached: (_____) _____
Area Code

GENERAL INFORMATION

1. Have you ever applied for a job with this company in the past?   ___ Yes   ___ No
If yes, please give the date of application and the position for which you applied. State your name at that time, if different from present name.

2. Have you ever been employed by this company in the past?   ___ Yes   ___ No
If yes, please give dates of employment, position(s) held, and state your name while employed, if different from present name.

3. If hired, will you be able to work during the normal days and hours required   ___ Yes   ___ No
for the position(s) for which you are applying? If no, please explain:

4. Do you have any commitments to another employer that might affect your
   employment with our company?   ___ Yes   ___ No
   If, yes, please explain:

5. If hired, can your furnish proof that you are 18 years of age, or if under 18,
   do you have a permit to work?   ___ Yes   ___ No
   If no, please explain:

6. If hired, can you furnish proof that you are eligible to work in the United
   States? (If unsure of the documents needed to prove eligibility to work in
   the U.S., we will be happy to explain the legal requirements).   ___ Yes   ___ No
   If no, please explain:

7. Are you capable of satisfactorily performing the job(s) for which you are
   applying?   ___ Yes   ___ No
   If no please explain:

8. Do you have any experience from your military service that would be
   relevant to the job(s) for which you are applying?   ___ Yes   ___ No
   If yes, please explain:

9. Do you have any language abilities (such as reading or speaking a foreign
   language) that might help you perform the job(s) for which you are applying?   ___ Yes   ___ No
   If yes, please explain:

10. Have you been convicted of a felony, or released from prison in the past 10
    years? Note: A yes answer does not automatically disqualify you from
    employment since the nature of the offense, date, and type of job for which
    you are applying will be considered.   ___ Yes   ___ No
    If yes, please explain:

11. Are you charged with an unresolved criminal charge (have you been
    charged with a crime that has not yet resulted in a plea of guilty, court
    trial, or a dropping of the charge)? Note: a yes answer will not automati-
    cally disqualify you from employment.   ___ Yes   ___ No
    If yes, please explain fully:

12. Special Questions. Answer the questions in the following box <u>only if checked,</u> therefore indicating the question(s) are relevant to the job for which you are applying.

☐ a. Are you willing and physically able to travel to out-of-town locations, including overnight trips? If no, please explain: _____ Yes _____ No

☐ b. Do you have a valid driver's license? _____ Yes _____ No

☐ c. During the past seven years, have you ever been denied a driver's license, or convicted of a moving traffic offense, including, but not limited to, driving while intoxicated or reckless driving? If yes, please explain: _____ Yes _____ No

☐ d. Are you willing to undergo a physical examination by a physician, to prove you are physically able to perform the tasks of the job for which you have applied? _____ Yes _____ No

☐ e. Do you have all the licenses and professional certification listed in the job announcement, job advertisement, or job description, or that are necessary to perform the job(s) for which you are applying? If no, please explain: _____ Yes _____ No

☐ f. Do you know of any reasons that might make it difficult for the company to obtain a surety bond insuring your honesty? If yes, please explain: _____ Yes _____ No

☐ g. Example Skills Area Questions

Typing Speed (Corrected Words Per Minute) _____

Stenographic Speed (Words Per Minute) _____

Can you transcribe machine dictation? _____ Yes _____ No

List the business machines, computers, and word processors you can operate:

☐ h. Example Questions Where Job Involves Manual Labor
(For purposes of illustration, assume the job requires lifting 50 lb. sacks)

Are you physically able to lift 50 lb. sacks on a continued, hour-by-hour, day-by-day, basis? _____ Yes _____ No

If the answer to the preceding questions is Yes, do you agree to take a test, at your own risk of injury, to prove your ability? And do you agree that the test will be conducted without any legal liability upon the company for any injuries which might result? _____ Yes _____ No

☐ i. Example Question Where the Job Involves Extra Trust (bank teller, bellboy, etc.)

Have you ever been convicted, pled guilty, or pled "no contest" to any criminal offense involving dishonesty or a breach of trust, including, but not limited to, theft, fraud, passing bad checks, credit card fraud, forgery, or other crime? If you were charged, but the charges were dropped or you were acquitted, answer "No." Note: A yes answer does not automatically disqualify you from employment since the nature of the offense and date will be considered. If yes, please explain: _____ Yes _____ No

13. EMPLOYMENT HISTORY

PRESENT & FORMER EMPLOYERS (List Most Recent First)		
MAY WE CONTACT YOUR PRESENT EMPLOYER? ___ Yes ___ No		

Company Name	Job Title & Duties
Address	
	Dates of Employment From To
City, State, Zip	Reason for Leaving
Supervisor (and phone number, if known)	Your Name When Employed, If Different From Present Name
Company Name	Job Title & Duties
Address	
	Dates of Employment From To
City, State, Zip	Reason for Leaving
Supervisor (and phone number, if known)	Your Name When Employed, If Different From Present Name
Company Name	Job Title & Duties
Address	
	Dates of Employment From To
City, State, Zip	Reason for Leaving
Supervisor (and phone number, if known)	Your Name When Employed, If Different From Present Name
Company Name	Job Title & Duties
Address	
	Dates of Employment From To
City, State, Zip	Reason for Leaving
Supervisor (and phone number, if known)	Your Name When Employed, If Different From Present Name

Company Name	Job Title & Duties
Address	
	Dates of Employment From To
City, State, Zip	Reason for Leaving
Supervisor (and phone number, if known)	Your Name When Employed, If Different From Present Name

Please Account for Any Time You Were Not Employed After Leaving School in the Past Ten Years
(You need not list any unemployment periods of one month or less)

    Time Period(s)   Reason(s) for Unemployment

IF YOU WERE UNABLE TO LIST ALL PAST JOBS OR PERIODS OF UNEMPLOYMENT ON THIS FORM,
PLEASE ATTACH ADDITIONAL INFORMATION ON A BLANK SHEET OF PAPER.

14. EDUCATIONAL DATA

SCHOOLS ATTENDED	NAME OF SCHOOL AND LOCATION	DID YOU GRADUATE? YES NO	DEGREE/ DIPLOMA/ CERTIFICATE?	GRADE POINT AVERAGE	MAJOR COURSE OF STUDY
HIGH SCHOOL	CIRCLE HIGHEST GRADE COMPLETED 1 2 3 4 5 6 7 8 9 10 11 12		DO NOT ANSWER		DO NOT ANSWER
TECHNICAL, VOCATIONAL, BUSINESS OR MILITARY TRAINING					
COLLEGE OR UNIVERSITY					
GRADUATE SCHOOL					
PROFESSIONAL SEMINARS					

ADDITIONAL JOB-RELATED SEMINARS, SHORT COURSES, WORKSHOPS, OR OTHER EDUCATIONAL EXPERIENCES:

14. REFERENCES   LIST THREE INDIVIDUALS WHO ARE NOT FORMER EMPLOYEES OR RELATIVES

NAME	ADDRESS	CITY, STATE, ZIP	PHONE NUMBER	OCCUPATION

16. OTHER JOB-RELATED EXPERIENCE. Some people gain job-related experience in positions other than as an employee. For instance, an accountant may gain experience as a treasurer of a civic or school organization, or a manager may gain experience while working on civic projects, or in school organizations, or in PTA activities. Please list and describe any paid or unpaid activities, honors, experience, or training that might aid you in performing the job(s) for which you have applied, and have not been listed previously in this application. (You may omit any activities, honors, memberships or other items that tend to identify your race, sex, national origin, age, disability or other personal traits that you prefer not to disclose.)

17. Please add any additional information (except that which identifies your race, sex, age, religion, national origin, disability or other non-job-related personal information) that you think may be relevant to a decision to hire you.

IMPORTANT

Please Read Carefully and Initial Each Paragraph Before Signing

By my signature and initials placed below, I promise that the information provided in this employment application (and accompanying resume, if any) is true and complete, and I understand that any false information or significant omissions may disqualify me from further consideration for employment, and may be justification for my dismissal from employment, if discovered at a later date. I agree to immediately notify the company if I should be convicted of a felony, or any crime involving dishonesty or a breach of trust while my job application is pending, or during my period of employment, if hired.

_____ Initials

I authorize the investigation of all statements contained in this application (and accompanying resume, if any). I also authorize the company to contact my present employer (unless otherwise noted in this application form), past employers, and listed references. I understand that the company may request an investigative consumer report from a consumer reporting agency that includes information as to my character, general reputation, personal characteristics, and mode of living. I understand that the investigative consumer report may involve personal interviews with my neighbors, friends, relatives, former employers, schools, and others. I also understand that under the Federal Fair Credit Reporting Act I have the right to make a written request to the company, within a reasonable time, for the disclosure of the name and address of the consumer reporting agency so that I may obtain a complete disclosure of the nature and scope of the investigation.

_____ Initials

I authorize any person, school, current employer (except as previously noted), past employer(s), and organizations named in this application form (and accompanying resume, if any) to provide the company with relevant information and opinion that may be useful to the company in making a hiring decision, and I release such persons and organizations from any legal liability in making such statements.

_____ Initials

I give permission for a complete physical examination, including a drug screening exam and x-rays, and I consent to the release to the company of any and all medical information, as may be deemed necessary by the company in judging my capability to do the work for which I am applying.

_____ Initials

I understand that if my employment is terminated by the company for dishonesty, breach of trust, or any criminal acts the authorities may be notified and I may be criminally prosecuted. I also understand that, if hired, I may not hold other employment, nor engage in sales, investments or other activities that create a conflict of interest with my position with this company.

_____ Initials

I understand that this application does not, by itself, create a contract of employment. I understand and agree that, if hired, MY EMPLOYMENT IS FOR NO DEFINITE PERIOD OF TIME, and may, regardless of the date of payment of my wages or salary, BE TERMINATED AT ANY TIME. I understand that NO PERSON IS AUTHORIZED TO CHANGE ANY OF THE TERMS MENTIONED IN THIS EMPLOYMENT APPLICATION FORM.

_____ Initials

Date _____   Signed: _____

THIS APPLICATION FOR EMPLOYMENT WILL REMAIN ACTIVE FOR _____ WEEKS

AFFIRMATIVE ACTION FORM

Employers with a $2,500 federal government contract must take affirmative action to employ and advance qualified disabled persons. Most states also have laws on handicapped employment. Employers with a contract of $10,000 or more with the federal government must take affirmative action to hire disabled veterans and Vietnam Era veterans.

These companies may wish to add the following special box to their employment application forms:

SPECIAL NOTICE TO DISABLED VETERANS, VIETNAM ERA VETERANS AND INDIVIDUALS WITH PHYSICAL OR MENTAL HANDICAPS

Government contractors are subject to Section 402 of the Vietnam Veterans Readjustment Act of 1974 that requires contractors to take affirmative action to employ and advance in employment qualified disabled veterans and veterans of the Vietnam Era; and Section 503 of the Rehabilitation Act, as amended, requires government contractors to take affirmative action to employ and advance in employment qualified disabled individuals.

If you are a disabled veteran, a Vietnam Era Veteran, or have a physical or mental disability **YOU ARE INVITED TO VOLUNTEER** this information. The purpose is to provide information concerning proper placement and appropriate accommodations to enable you to perform the job(s) for which you have applied in a proper and safe manner. This information will be kept confidential. **FAILURE TO SUPPLY THIS INFORMATION WILL <u>NOT</u> JEOPARDIZE OR ADVERSELY AFFECT ANY CONSIDERATION YOU MAY RECEIVE FOR EMPLOYMENT, OR LATER ADVANCEMENT IN EMPLOYMENT.**

If you desire, check the appropriate category(ies) and sign below:

____ DISABLED PERSON ____ DISABLED VETERAN ____ VIETNAM ERA VETERAN

Signed _____

TEAR-OFF FORM

Employers with 50 or more employees, and federal contracts of $50,000 or more per year must take affirmative action to remove any inequities in their labor force, if the employer is deficient in utilizing the services of any covered minority or females. These employers must adopt affirmative action programs that may require accumulating statistics regarding the race, sex, national origin, and disabilities of job applicants and employees.

The following form should be used **only** by companies that require data under an affirmative action program. **THIS FORM MAY BE USED <u>ONLY</u> IF ON A TEAR-OFF SHEET THAT IS SEPARATED FROM THE EMPLOYMENT APPLICA- TION FORM BEFORE IT IS SEEN BY ANY PERSON OR PERSONS MAKING THE HIRING DECISION.** It must be kept in a separate file and used for statistical purposes only.

APPLICANT DATA RECORD

Applicants are considered for all positions, and employees are treated during their employment, without regard to their **race, color, creed, religion, sex, national origin, age, marital status, sexual orientation, military status, or any non-job-related disability or medical condition.**

As an employer taking affirmative action to insure the removal of any possible past discrimination, and to help comply with governmental record-keeping requirements, we would appreciate your completing this form in this box. However, **COMPLETION OF THIS BOX IS STRICTLY VOLUNTARY. This data will be physically separated from the remainder of your job application before the application is considered for possible employment. This information will be kept in a confidential file, WITHOUT YOUR NAME ON IT, SEPARATE FROM YOUR APPLICATION FOR EMPLOYMENT.**

Date: _____ Position(s) Applied For: _____

How Were You Referred to Our Company? ___ Saw Newspaper Advertisement ___ A Private Employment Agency ___ A Relative or Friend Employed by This Company ___ Other: Explain:

PERSONAL TRAITS: Check One: ___ Male   ___ Female
Check One: ___ White   ___ Black   ___ Hispanic   ___ Asian/Pacific Islander
___ American Indian/Alaskan Native

Check Any That Apply: ___ Vietnam Era Veteran ___ Disabled Veteran ___ Disabled Person

---

FORM FOR NEWLY HIRED EMPLOYEES

Employers are required to examine the documents of all newly hired employees, complete an Employment Eligibility (I-9) Form, and retain it. This must be done <u>after hiring, but within three days of the beginning of the employee's work</u> (on the same day as beginning of work if the job is to last less than three days). Additional information that has traditionally been asked on employment application forms may be asked at this time without the danger of a lawsuit based upon a claim of discrimination in hiring. These items of information may include the person to be notified in case of an emergency, accommodations needed for religious observances or disabilities, or information about the new employee's age, sex, spouse, children or other dependents, and other items, if needed for the administration of insurance or pension plans, or other valid reasons. Some example questions are as follows:

EMPLOYEE INFORMATION FORM

Your answers to the following questions can help the company provide you with employee fringe benefits, meet your special needs, and help insure that all legal and ethical standards are met. No person is authorized to use the answers given to make employment decisions, including hiring, pay, promotion, discharge, or to otherwise discriminate. The information given on this form will remain confidential.

1. Name _____ Social Security Number _____

2. Age _____ Birthdate _____ Sex _____

3. Name, address and phone number of the person to be contacted in case of a personal emergency:

Name _____ Phone Number (___)
                                              Area Code

Address _____

4. Please list the names, ages, and type of relationship of your spouse and all dependents:

<u>Name</u>   <u>Age</u>   <u>Relationship</u> (Wife, Child, etc.)

5. Do you need any accommodations for your religion or religious activities?
   If Yes, please explain: ___ Yes   ___ No

6. Do you need any special accommodations for any physical or mental
   disability? If Yes, please explain: ___ Yes   ___ No

7. Do you need any special accommodations or leave time for National Guard
   or Military Reserve duties?   ___ Yes   ___ No

Companies who give all entering employees in each job classification a medical or physical examination, can add to the job application form:

> IF YOU ARE HIRED, A MEDICAL EXAMINATION WILL BE REQUIRED BEFORE YOU START WORK. IF THE EXAMINATION DISCLOSES MEDICAL CONDITIONS THAT PREVENT YOU FROM SUCCESSFULLY PERFORMING THE ESSENTIAL FUNCTIONS OF THE JOB, THE COMPANY WILL ATTEMPT TO MAKE ACCOMMODATIONS TO ALLOW YOU TO WORK. IF NO REASONABLE ACCOMMODATIONS CAN BE FOUND, OR THEY CAUSE AN UNDUE HARDSHIP ON THE COMPANY, THE TENTATIVE OFFER OF EMPLOYMENT WILL BE WITHDRAWN.

This statement, preferably in bold letters, may be added just before the signature line for the job applicant.

Since the ADA prohibits asking job applicants about physical or mental impairments, but allows questions about an applicant's ability to perform the job, Question 12 on the sample application form can be adapted to fit the specific jobs offered by an individual company. The major functions of various jobs may be listed under Question 12 and individualized for each different job. For example, Question 12b asks if the applicant has a valid driver's license. This question should be checked if the job involves driving. If the job involves lifting, then a lifting question similar to Question 12h can be checked. Additional job-related questions may be added by each employer as necessary. However, be sure all checked questions involve a major job duty of the position for which the individual applicant has applied.

Although the sample application form contains a consent form for a medical examination and release of medical information, some companies may prefer to have a separate consent form. The following is an example of such a consent form:

7. SAMPLE CONSENT FOR PHYSICAL OR MENTAL EXAMINATION

Job Applicant and Employee
CONSENT FORM FOR A PHYSICAL EXAMINATION

I, _____, hereby consent to a physical or mental examination by a qualified physician at company expense. I also consent to periodic physical or mental examinations at company expense if conducted in furtherance of the company wellness plan or similar programs, or if reasonable questions as to my ability to safely and effectively perform my job arise. Furthermore, I authorize the examining physician to release the examination results and provide medical opinions as to my physical or mental ability to perform my job (or the job for which I have applied) to _____ company or its authorized representatives.

AGREED TO: _____ DATE _____
           (Signature)

REFUSED: _____ DATE _____
           (Signature)

REASON FOR REFUSAL:

The ADA does not prohibit pre- or postemployment drug tests. A sample release form follows.

8. SAMPLE RELEASE FORM FOR DRUG-USE SCREENING

Job Applicant and Employee
CONSENT FORM FOR DRUG SCREENING

I, _____, hereby consent for the __(name of company)__ and its authorized representatives to collect blood, urine, saliva, or hair samples from me and to conduct any necessary tests to determine the presence or use of drugs or controlled substances. Furthermore, I give my consent for the release of the results of such test and related medical opinion to the __(name of company)__ or its authorized representatives. I understand that if I refuse to consent, I may be refused employment, or if already employed, subject to disciplinary action, including discharge from employment.

AGREED TO: _____ DATE _____
           (Signature)

LIST OR EXPLAIN ANY PRESCRIPTION OR NON-PRESCRIPTION DRUGS YOU HAVE RECENTLY TAKEN:

REFUSED: _____ DATE: _____
           (Signature)

REASON FOR REFUSAL:

Although the ADA prevents prehiring questions about the applicant's disability, it is permissible for the applicant to volunteer information about a disability. Additionally, the earlier an employer learns of a disability the more time is available to consider any necessary accommodations.

Although some employers who use voluntary identification forms list a large number of medical problems and have the employee check any that are applicable, it may be better to explain to the employee or job applicant what constitutes a disability, but not limit the form to specified disabilities. The following is a form complying with this concept:

9. VOLUNTARY DISCLOSURE OF DISABILITY AND REQUEST FOR ACCOMMODATION

Voluntary Disclosure of Disability and Request for Accommodations

_____company policy, as well as the law, prohibits the company from asking job applicants about possible disabilities or giving a health questionnaire or examination until after employees are tentatively hired. Whether a job applicant or employee, you may desire to VOLUNTARILY disclose physical or mental health conditions and ask for reasonable accommodations so the company may consider possible changes and accommodations that allow you to work at your full potential.

If you desire to do so, please complete this form and return it with the job application form. Your answers will be used only in considering reasonable accommodations. Information given on this form, or the failure to complete this form, will not be used to discriminate or otherwise subject you to unfair treatment. The information will remain strictly confidential. Disclosure will be made only to those people necessary to aid in determining and implementing reasonable accommodations.

The company is strongly committed to taking all reasonable steps to ensure that all qualified applicants be hired and all qualified employees be allowed to work to their fullest potential, despite any physical or mental problem.

For the purposes of this form, a potential disability appropriate for disclosure is any physical or mental condition that does, or may, create any degree of difficulty in performing your job. This may include obvious disabilities such as being paralyzed or blind; nonobvious impairments such as epilepsy, diabetes, or heart problems; mental problems such as depression and eating disorders; learning problems such as dyslexia; and less serious conditions such as obesity or the early stages of arthritis. Also included as impairments are AIDS, the HIV infection, or other contagious diseases; persistent back problems; past or current alcoholism; past drug addiction; and other medical conditions.

Name _____
Job Position(s) Applied For or Held _____
Type of Disability (for example, diabetes, mental disease, amputated arm, cancer, high blood pressure)

_____

Description of Physical or Mental Impairment (for example, unable to walk, cannot do heavy lifting, sensitive to heat, legally blind)

_____
_____

Suggested Accommodations (for example, ramp over stairs, amplifier for telephone, flexible work schedule)

_____
_____

The company will consider your suggestions and attempt to make reasonable accommodations. However, the final decision regarding what accommodations are reasonable and desirable remain in the sole discretion of the company.

Signed _____

Date _____

The interpretive guidance issued by the Equal Employment Opportunity Commission (EEOC) specifically allows federal contractors taking affirmative action under the Rehabilitation Act to ask job applicants to self-identify themselves as disabled and to ask for reasonable accommodations.[4] Other employers should use the preceding voluntary disclosure form only with newly hired and current employees.

Notes

1. For more information on affirmative action, *see* BNA's Policy and Practice Series, *Fair Employment Practices*, 403:499 and 421:201.
2. Pati & Stubblefield, *The Disabled are Able to Work*, PERSONNEL J. Dec. 1990, at 30, 33.
3. Modified from materials appearing in Frierson, *Dangerous violations of employment law found in almost all applications*, and Frierson's *"Safe" Job Application Forms*. PREVENTIVE L. REP. Dec. 1988, at 3–27.
4. EEOC Interpretive Guidance on Section I of the Americans with Disabilities Act, 56 Fed. Reg. 35,750 (1991).

Chapter 9

Legal Enforcement Procedures

The Americans with Disabilities Act (ADA) adopts the enforcement procedures of Title VII of the Civil Rights Act of 1964, as amended,[1] and is enforced by private lawsuits or the Equal Employment Opportunity Commission (EEOC). The ADA enforcement rules vary from Title VII in two areas only. First, in a Title VII case, defendants may raise as a defense the fact they were complying with a written interpretation or opinion of the EEOC. The ADA does not provide such a defense. Second, under Title VII elected officials' personal staffs are not protected against discrimination. However, these employees are covered by the ADA.

Coverage of the ADA

The following are employers subject to the ADA's employment law section:

1. Effective July 26, 1992: Any person or organization engaged in an industry affecting interstate commerce that has 25 or more employees, and all employment agencies, labor organizations, joint labor-management committees, and state and local governmental agencies.
2. Effective July 26, 1994: Any person or organization engaged in an industry affecting interstate commerce that has 15 or more employees.[2] As a general rule, all businesses affect interstate commerce.

To determine the number of employees, count all full-time and part-time employees,[3] including managers, officers, and professional employees. However, sole proprietors, managing partners,

197

and nonworking directors or shareholders of a corporation are not counted. If the employer has the requisite number for each working day for 20 or more weeks in the current or previous year, the ADA and Title VII apply.[4]

Not Subject to the Law

The ADA does not apply to:

1. The federal government or its wholly owned or controlled agencies. However, section 501 of the Rehabilitation Act with similar rules applies to the federal government.[5]
2. Indian tribes.[6]
3. A bona fide private membership club that is not a labor organization, if the club is exempt from taxation under section 501(c) of the Internal Revenue Code of 1986.[7] However, a tax exempt club may be subject to the law if it is not truly a private membership club. For example, in 1991 the tax exempt University Club of Chicago was found to be subject to equal employment laws because nonmember "guests" were given full member privileges and the organization had "no meaningful limitation for admitting new members" other than a requirement that a new member be 21 years of age and a graduate of a university.[8] The court found that the club was not really "private" since it was open to such a large number of people.

Religious Organizations

Although not exempt from the employment law section of the ADA, the law does state that a religious corporation, association, educational institution, or society may give preference in employment to individuals of the entity's particular religion. Furthermore, these organizations may require all job applicants and employees to conform to their religion's general beliefs and tenets.[9] Religious organizations are completely exempt from the public accommodations section of the ADA.

Enforcement Procedures

Procedures used to enforce the ADA are the same as those used under Title VII of the Civil Rights Act of 1964 and are governed by

EEOC regulations.[10] Although private lawsuits are allowed, an aggrieved party must first properly file a charge with the EEOC and allow time for the agency to act upon the charge.

Filing Charges

Any person who believes he or she has been harmed by an employment practice in violation of Section I of the ADA may file a charge, or authorize another person or organization to file a charge. Charges filed on one or more employees' behalf by unions, civil rights organizations, or other groups are accepted.

A charge must be in writing and identify the name and address of the person who alleges harm, the name and address of the person or organization who allegedly violated the law, a statement of the facts, whether a complaint has been filed with a local or state agency, and the number of workers employed by the alleged wrongdoer, if known. The charge may be filed on an EEOC charge form, or any other written method, including an informal letter. The EEOC is very liberal in accepting charges. If some of the information listed above is not included, the EEOC will allow the filing and ask for additional information. Charges may be made in person or by mail at the EEOC headquarters in Washington or any field office. Charges may also be filed by any commissioner of the EEOC.

In areas of the country that are not under the jurisdiction of a state or local fair employment practices (FEP) agency certified by the EEOC to receive charges, the complainant must file charges with the EEOC within 180 days of the alleged violation of the ADA.

In other areas of the country where a local or state FEP agency (formerly called a "706 Agency") exists, the FEP agency must first be given a chance to act upon the complaint. This requirement may be met by filing the charge with the FEP agency, giving them 60 days to act, and then filing with the EEOC within 300 days of the alleged violation of law. Alternatively, the complainant may file directly with the EEOC, who then forwards the complaint to the FEP agency. In either case, the first filing must be done within 240 days so that the FEP agency will have 60 days to consider it and still be within the 300-day overall filing limit.

A person or organization filing a charge on behalf of another individual can request that the EEOC keep the identity of the individual confidential, as long as it is feasible to do so.

EEOC Action

The EEOC must notify the employer and other parties who are charged with possible violation of the law within 10 days of receiving the charge. After notification, the EEOC is authorized to investigate, but is not required to do so. The EEOC can subpoena documents, hold hearings, compel testimony, or conduct informal investigations. The duty of the EEOC is to attempt to obtain a settlement to any charges it finds to be valid.

If a voluntary settlement of the charge is not reached, the EEOC may file a lawsuit. If the EEOC decides not to sue, it must provide the charging party with a "right to sue letter." The letter may state that the EEOC found that no reasonable cause exists to believe the ADA has been violated, or that reasonable cause is found, but the agency is surrendering the right to sue to the individual(s) who filed the charge. Legally, it makes little difference which form of right to sue letter is given because both permit a subsequent, private lawsuit.

Lawsuits

To file a lawsuit, a complainant must receive a right to sue letter and file a lawsuit within 90 days of receipt of the letter in a United States District Court.

Normally, the complaint filed with the district court may not include added complaints of actions not included in the charge to the EEOC, nor can it add new parties as defendants. However, exceptions are made when the new complaints closely relate to the original charge, or the new party is closely related to the alleged wrongdoer and would have been aware of the original EEOC charge.

Court trials of Title VII and ADA lawsuits follow the general procedural rules of federal courts. Class action lawsuits may be filed pursuant to Rule 23 of the Federal Rules of Civil Procedure. Most trial and appellate procedures are the same as in other similar federal district court cases.

In many cases a jury trial is not available. However, the Civil Rights Act of 1991 amended the ADA and Title VII to allow a jury trial when compensatory or punitive damages are claimed because of alleged intentional discrimination.[11] It is expected that plaintiffs' attorneys will add claims of intentional discrimination to cases of disparate impact (unintentional discrimination) in order to obtain jury trials. Juries tend to be more sympathetic toward disabled individuals than judges.

Typical ADA Charges and Defenses

The list below summarizes some typical charges that may be filed with FEP agencies, the EEOC, and the federal courts, along with possible defenses that might be successfully raised by the employer.

1. *Charge:* Refusal to hire, promote, or retain a disabled person who is qualified for the job.

Defenses: Several general defenses are possible: (1) Prove the individual did not meet minimum qualifications based upon essential job tasks, even after reasonable accommodations were considered. Show that the criteria used in making a decision was based upon job-related standards that were based upon business necessity. A preexisting, written job description is helpful in showing the required qualifications, but it is not conclusive. (2) Show that the person selected for the job is more qualified than the disabled person, even after reasonable accommodations are considered. (3) Prove that neither the employer nor its agents knew the individual was disabled. An employer cannot illegally discriminate in violation of the ADA unless there is knowledge of a disability. (4) Prove that the employer's actions complied with a federal law or regulation, such as safety requirements issued by the Department of Transportation or the Nuclear Regulatory Commission.[12]

2. *Charge:* The hiring or promotion of a less qualified person over a more qualified disabled person.

Defense: Prove the disabled person is less qualified than the person selected, or not qualified at all, after consideration of reasonable accommodations.[13]

3. *Charge:* Discrimination in hiring, pay, promotion, or other aspect of employment because of the individual's inability to perform nonessential job tasks.

Defense: Prove the job task is an integral part of the essential duties of the job. Show that deletion of the task changes the nature of job and produces a poorer final result, or lower productivity.[14] See

Chapter 4, "Determining if a Disabled Person is Qualified," for more information.

4. *Charge:* Failure to consider or provide reasonable accommodations for a disabled person.

Defenses: Show that the possible accommodations would create an undue hardship on the employer, or that they would not allow the disabled person to effectively perform the essential duties of the job.[15] See Chapter 5, "Making Accommodations for Disabled Employees," for more information.

5. *Charge:* Employment discrimination based upon a stereotypical, biased, or false belief that the individual's disability will create a health or safety problem.

Defense: Produce expert medical evidence showing a substantial likelihood of serious future injury or harm to the employee, co-workers, or customers.[16] See Chapter 6, "Risk of Future Injury: Epilepsy, Diabetes, and Bad Backs," and Chapter 7, "AIDS, Infectious Diseases, Drug and Alcohol Problems, and Weight Problems," for additional information.

6. *Charge:* Discrimination in hiring, job assignment, discharge, or other employment benefit because a person has AIDS, the HIV virus, or related medical problems.

Defense: Prove that the employer's actions were not based upon the presence of AIDS or related medical conditions. Alternatively, prove the individual's medical condition created a health or safety risk to fellow workers or customers. The latter usually cannot be proven, even in the cases of food service workers or elementary school teachers. However, it may be possible to prove it in some health care jobs.[17]

7. *Charge:* Discrimination in pay or other job benefits based upon an individual's disability.

Defense: Show that similar nondisabled employees are treated the same as the disabled employee. In the alternative, prove that employer(s) to which the disabled individual is compared are different in seniority, job skills, relevant and job-related education, or other nondiscriminatory factors.[18]

8. *Charge:* Segregating disabled workers or otherwise limiting or classifying them in a way that adversely affects their opportunity or status based upon their disability.

Defense: Usually none. Different rates of pay, separate seniority lists, or separate physical facilities or workplaces based upon disability are illegal. However, an employer may limit a disabled person to one section of the facility if the other sections are physically inaccessible and structural changes improving access constitute an undue hardship.[19]

9. *Charge:* Discrimination in employer-provided health or life insurance.

Defense: Limitation or exclusion of insurance coverage was based upon normal insurance industry methods of classifying risks, including preexisting conditions exclusions. The key to a successful defense is to show that the benefits were the same for all employees in the complainant's job category. It is not necessary to show that all medical conditions are covered equally.[20] See Chapter 1, "A Summary of the Law," for more information concerning fringe benefits.

10. *Charge:* Employment discrimination is based upon an individual's association with disabled people.

Defense: Offer evidence showing the claim is not true—that any different treatment was based upon other, nondiscriminatory reasons, such as poor work performance. Alternatively, prove the employer did not even know of the individual's association with disabled people.

11. *Charge:* Employment discrimination is based upon an individual's record of past disability.

Defense: Offer evidence showing the claim to be untrue. Prove that all adverse employment decisions were based upon other factors such as lack of qualifications, poor work performance, or excessive absenteeism. In the alternative, prove that the employer was unaware of any past disability.

12. *Charge:* Employment discrimination is based upon the employer's perception that an individual was disabled.

Defense: Offer evidence showing the claim to be untrue. Justify all adverse employment decisions on other factors such as lack of qualifications, poor performance, or excessive absenteeism. Alternatively, prove that the person or persons making the adverse employment decision did not know or believe the individual was disabled.

13. *Charge:* The employer is responsible for discrimination or other ADA violations committed by a union, employment agency, independent contractor, provider of fringe benefits, organization providing training or apprenticeship program, or other third party.

Defense: Prove that the employer has no contractual relationship with the third party, thus the employee had no way to control third-party discrimination against the job applicant or employee.[21]

14. *Charge:* Job qualification requirements or employment tests were used that screen out or tend to screen out qualified, disabled people.

Defense: The standards and tests adequately measure essential job skills that are consistent with business necessity, and reasonable accommodations were provided to allow the individual to show qualifications.[22]

15. *Charge:* A qualified, disabled job applicant was unable to successfully interview for a job or take qualifying examinations because of physical barriers or inability to take the tests.

Defense: Very limited. Show that the job applicant never attempted to qualify for the job. Alternatively, prove that the applicant who failed a qualifying examination because an impairment caused difficulty in taking the exam did not ask for any accommodation. All employment tests and other selection criteria must be administered in the most effective manner to insure disabled people are not screened out.[23] See Chapter 2, "Major Changes to Conform to the Law," for additional information.

16. *Charge:* Employer asked about health, disability, past or present medical problems, or other health-related questions before a tentative hiring decision was made.

Defense: Show that the questions were related solely to illegal drug use. Prove that the questions asked related solely to the applicant's ability to perform the essential duties of the job and did not ask about physical or mental impairments.[24] See Chapter 2, "Major Changes to Conform to the Law," for more information.

17. *Charge:* Employer asked health questions or required a physical examination after a tentative offer of employment was given and the information was used in a way that was detrimental to a disabled individual.

Defenses: The questions or physical examination were required of all employees, regardless of disabilities; any resulting decisions that adversely affected a disabled person were based upon proof that the person could not effectively and safely perform the essential tasks of the job involved; and the information was kept confidential. Alternatively, show that the health questions or medical tests were part of a voluntary employee health program; or prove that the information was gathered solely to determine a current employee's ability to perform essential job tasks.[25]

18. *Charge:* Medical or disability-related information obtained by the employer became known to other persons.

Defense: The employer made reasonable attempts to keep the health, medical, or disability information confidential, and: (a) the information was stored in a secured file separate from employee personnel files, (b) it was released only to managers and supervisors who need to be informed of any work restriction or are involved in making reasonable accommodations, workers' compensation officials, or to government officials investigating compliance with the ADA.[26]

19. *Charge:* Job applicant or employee was subject to unfavorable treatment in retaliation for opposing practices made illegal under the ADA, filing a charge, testifying, or cooperating with any investigation of a possible ADA violation.

Defense: Prove that the action by the employer that was detrimental to a job applicant or employee was based upon other, valid reasons such as lack of qualifications, excessive absenteeism, or violation of company rules.[27]

20. *Charge:* Employer did not meet the posting requirements of the ADA.

Defense: Show that the current "Consolidated EEO Poster" that includes information on the ADA was posted at each job site in a location where job applicants and employees would be expected to see it. If available, use a poster printed in large print and braille in order to prove it was accessible to all disabled applicants, including those with vision problems.[28]

21. *Charge:* A job applicant or employee was discriminated against because of past drug use.

Defenses: Show claim is untrue by proving current drug use (offer drug test or other proof), or show that the different treatment was not based upon past drug use. For example, show that the employee was fired for valid reasons such as poor work quality, fighting, or excessive absenteeism.[29] See Chapter 7, "AIDS, Infectious Diseases, Drug and Alcohol Problems, and Weight Problems," for additional information.

22. *Charge:* Employer discriminated against job applicant or employee because of the individual's alcoholism.

Defenses: Prove that the employee was drunk on the job, drank or possessed alcohol on the job in violation of company rules, or that he or she had poor work performance (whether caused by alcohol use or not). Alternatively, prove that the individual is not disabled because he or she is not an alcoholic and was not considered to be an alcoholic. In the alternative, prove that the actions taken conformed with federal regulations issued by the Departments of Defense or Transportation or the Nuclear Regulatory Commission.[30] See Chapter 7, "AIDS, Infectious Diseases, Drug and Alcohol Problems, and Weight Problems," for an additional discussion of alcohol and drugs.

23. *Charge:* Lack of physical accessibility of work areas, cafeterias, rest rooms, and other areas employees are expected to use.

Defense: Cost of making changes is an undue burden on the employer if building was not completed after January 26, 1993, or undergone major renovation since January 26, 1992. If built or renovated after these dates, the only defense would be compliance with building accessibility regulations issued by the United States Attorney General.[31] See Chapter 2, "Major Changes to Conform to the Law," for additional explanation.

24. *Charge:* Lack of physical accessibility for customers and clients.

Defense: The building was constructed before January 26, 1993, or renovated before January 26, 1992, and necessary changes were not readily achievable (not minor costs). If the building was constructed for first occupancy after January 26, 1993, or major modifications were begun after January 26, 1992, the only defense is compliance with the regulations of the United States Attorney General.[32]

25. *Charge:* Intentional discrimination justifying compensatory and punitive damages because of a failure to provide an accommodation for a disabled employee.

Defense: The disabled person did not inform the employer of a need for accommodation; or if informed, the employer made a good faith effort, in consultation with the disabled person, to provide a reasonable accommodation that would not involve an undue hardship on the company.[33]

Special Title VII and ADA Procedural Rules

Although Title VII and ADA lawsuits follow most of the procedural rules of federal courts, a few special rules exist in employment discrimination lawsuits. Among these are the following principles:

1. Upon application to the court by the complainant, the court may appoint an attorney and authorize commencement of the lawsuit without fees, costs, or security deposit.[34]
2. Normally, company affirmative action plans are not subject to discovery and presentation in a lawsuit because they often have self-disclosed derogatory information. Public policy dictates that employers be free to critically examine their own past discrimination when devising affirmative action plans.[35]
3. A previous arbitration decision may not preclude an employment discrimination lawsuit in federal court.[36]
4. A state agency's adjudication of a claim cannot preclude a federal lawsuit.[37]
5. A state court decision on the same facts applying substantially similar law will bar a subsequent federal court claim.[38]
6. An informed and intelligent release of claims in exchange for some consideration that is part of a settlement of a charge of discrimination will bar a subsequent, private lawsuit.[39] However, it does not prohibit a lawsuit by the EEOC.
7. A release signed before any charges are filed (such as at time of discharge from employment) is against public policy and will not be effective.[40]

Remedies

The remedies available for a violation of the ADA follow those that are available under Title VII of the Civil Rights Act of 1964, as amended,[41] with one exception. Violations of the physical accessibility requirements when making major modifications to structures or when building new commercial facilities may result in a lawsuit by an individual or the United States Attorney General for a court order requiring compliance with the law. A lawsuit by the Attorney General can also seek civil penalties of up to $50,000 for a first violation of ADA accessibility standards and up to $100,000 for subsequent violations.[42]

Federal courts may order any combination of the following remedies for violations of Title VII and the employment section of the ADA:[43]

1. Reinstatement or an order to hire.
2. Back pay, but for no longer than two years prior to the filing of the charge, and interim earnings or amounts that could be earned with reasonable diligence shall be deducted.
3. An order of promotion, transfer, or other equitable remedy that will place the individual in the position he or she would have been, if the law had not been not violated.
4. In rare cases, front pay (lost future earnings) may be awarded. Front pay is awarded only if it is unreasonable to order reinstatement or hiring because of the animosity among the parties.
5. Interest on awarded back pay.
6. Reasonable attorneys' fees, expert witness fees, and costs.
7. In appropriate cases of systematic discrimination, an order of affirmative action requiring the employer to establish outreach programs to increase the hiring and promotion of disabled people.

In disparate impact cases only the remedies and damages listed above may be obtained under the ADA and Title VII. Disparate impact cases are those involving unintentional discrimination such as a company rule adopted for nondiscriminatory reasons that results in different treatment based upon disability, race, color, religion, sex, or national origin. For example, a company rule that requires all warehouse workers to have the ability to lift 100 pounds would be illegal disability discrimination as applied to an individual who has lost a leg, if the requirement is not a job necessity. It would not be a necessity if the job duties rarely require lifting up to 100 pounds, or an accommodation such as minor job duty switching with other employees or a mechanical lifter may be obtained without an undue hardship on the employer. However, it would be an unintentional violation (disparate impact) because the 100 pound rule appeared to be a reasonable rule that was not intended to discriminate against disabled people.

The Civil Rights Act of 1991 allows a limited amount of compensatory and punitive damages in cases of disparate treatment, which is intentional discrimination under the ADA, section 501 of the Rehabilitation Act of 1973 applicable to the federal government as an employer, or Title VII.[44] Compensatory damages may include claims for past or "future pecuniary losses, emotional pain, suffering, inconvenience, mental anguish, loss of enjoyment of life, and other nonpecuniary losses."[45] The traditional equal employment remedies of back pay, interest on back pay, and other specific remedies under Title VII are not considered to be compensatory damages. Punitive damages may be awarded if the jury finds the intentional acts to be malicious or with reckless indifference to the individual's equal employment rights.[46] An example of actions that might be found to justify both compensatory and punitive damages would be where an employer fires an employee as soon as it is learned he or she has AIDS, or where an employer asks for health or medical information, or requires a physical exam of all job applicants.

Compensatory and punitive damages cannot exceed the following amounts, except for past pecuniary losses such as medical bills:

- $50,000, if the defendant employs 15 to 100 employees.
- $100,000, if the defendant employs 101-200 employees.
- $200,000, if the defendant employs 200-500 employees.
- $300,000, if the defendant employs over 500 employees.[47]

Relation of ADA, Rehabilitation Act of 1973 and State Handicapped Employment Laws

Employers' violations of the ADA may also violate the Rehabilitation Act of 1973 (applicable to companies with federal contracts of $2,500 or more and recipients of federal aid), and state handicapped discrimination laws. Because federal contractors cannot be sued by individuals under the Rehabilitation Act, the only added danger of a Rehabilitation Act violation is an investigation by the Office of Federal Contract Compliance Programs of the Department of Labor and possible loss of government contracts. However, state laws may be used to substantially increase the damages a private plaintiff may collect in an ADA lawsuit.

Pendent Jurisdiction

Claims alleging a violation of the ADA that are filed in federal court may also add claims of state law violations under certain circumstances. The exercise of authority over additional state claims is called pendent jurisdiction. The United States Supreme Court has created a two-part test for federal courts to determine if both federal and state claims should be heard.[48] As applied to a possible violation of the ADA, the test requires the court to ask:

1. Does the court have power over the state law claims? The answer is "yes" if:
   a. there is a federal claim sufficient to confer subject matter jurisdiction on the court (the ADA);
   b. the state and federal claims are derived from a common nucleus of operative fact (disability discrimination); and
   c. the plaintiff's claims are those that would ordinarily be tried in one judicial proceeding (ADA and similar state handicapped law).
2. Should the court, in its discretion, entertain the state causes of action? The answer is "yes" if judicial economy, convenience, and fairness to the parties are present.

This test should be satisfied in most lawsuits that combine actions based on the ADA and state handicapped laws. Many state handicapped laws allow for added damages. For example, the New Jersey Law Against Discrimination specifically allows "[a]ll remedies available in common law tort actions. . . ."[49] Therefore, pain and suffering, emotional distress, and punitive damages may be requested in addition to the federal remedies. Oregon law provides "compensation for emotional distress and/or impaired personal dignity;"[50] while Tennessee's law provides for damages for "humiliation and embarrassment."[51] Most other state handicapped discrimination laws provide types of damage claims not currently allowed under the ADA. However, the exact types of damages provided vary from state to state.

Notes

1. 42 U.S.C.A. §2000e.
2. Americans with Disabilities Act §101, 42 U.S.C.A. §12111 (West 1991).
3. Court decisions are split on the inclusion of part-time employees. See Thurber v. Jack Reilly's Inc., 717 F.2d 633 (1st Cir. 1983) for a decision counting part-timers, and Zimmerman v. N. Am. Signal, 704 F.2d 347 (7th Cir. 1983) for a case excluding part-time employees.
4. Supra, note 2.
5. 29 U.S.C.A. §791.
6. Americans with Disabilities Act §101, 42 U.S.C.A. §12111 (West 1991).
7. *Id.*
8. EEOC v. University Club of Chicago, 736 F. Supp. 985 (E.D. Ill. 1991). See BNA Policy and Practice Series, *Fair Employment Practices*, Vol. 27, No. 10, May 23, 1991, p. 55.
9. Americans with Disabilities Act §103(c), 42 U.S.C.A. §12113 (1991).
10. EEOC Title VII and ADA Procedural Regulations, 29 C.F.R. Part 1601, *amended by* 56 Fed. Reg. 45, effective April 8, 1991.

11. Civil Rights Act of 1991, 42 U.S.C. 1981A(c) (1991).
12. Americans with Disabilities Act, §§101(8), 103(a), 42 U.S.C.A. §§12111, 12113; EEOC Regulations under the Americans with Disabilities Act, 56 Fed. Reg. 35,738 (1991) (to be codified at 29 C.F.R. §1630.15(e)).
13. *Id.*
14. *Id.*
15. Americans with Disabilities Act §101(10), 42 U.S.C §12111.
16. *Id.* at §103(b), 42 U.S.C.A. §12113 (West, 1991); 56 Fed. Reg. 35,736 (1991) (to be codified at 29 C.F.R. §1630.2(r)).
17. *Id.* at §103(B), 42 U.S.C.A. §12113 (West 1991).
18. *Id.* at §102(a) and (b), 42 U.S.C.A. §12112 (West 1991).
19. *Id.* at §102(6), 42 U.S.C.A. §12112 (West 1991).
20. *Id.* at §501(c), 42 U.S.C.A. §12201 (West 1991).
21. *Id.* at §102(b)(2), 42 U.S.C.A. §12112 (West 1991).
22. *Id.* at §102(b)(6), 42 U.S.C.A. §12112 (West 1991).
23. *Id.* at §102(b)(7), 42 U.S.C.A. §12112 (West 1991).
24. *Id.* at §102(c), 42 U.S.C.A. §§12112, 12210 (West 1991).
25. *Id.* at §101(c), 42 U.S.C.A. §12112 (West 1991).
26. *Id.* at §102(c)(3)(B), 42 U.S.C.A. §12112 (West 1991).
27. *Id.* at §503, 42 U.S.C.A. §12203 (West 1991).
28. *Id.* at §105, 42 U.S.C.A. §12115 (West 1991). Section 711(b) of Title VII of the Civil Rights Act of 1964 imposes a fine of $100 for each separate offense of nonposting. In addition, some courts have extended the statute of limitations for filing charges to include the time period an employer did not display the poster. Vance v. Whirlpool Corp., 716 F.2d 1010 (4th Cir. 1983).
29. Americans with Disabilities Act, §104, 42 U.S.C.A. §12114 (West 1991).
30. *Id.*
31. Americans with Disabilities Act §§(8), (9) & (10), 42 U.S.C.A. §12111.
32. *Id.*, Title III, 42 U.S.C.A. §§12181 et. seq. (West 1991).
33. Civil Rights Act of 1991, 42 U.S.C. 1981A(a)(3).
34. 42 U.S.C. §2000c.
35. Jamison v. Storer Broadcasting Co., 511 F. Supp. 1286 (E.D. Mich. 1981), *aff'd in part*, 830 F.2d 194, 45 FEP Cases 300 (6th Cir. 1987); O'Conner v. Chrysler Corp., 86 F.R.D. 211 (D. Mass. 1980); Webb v. Westinghouse Elec. Corp., 81 F.R.D. 431 (E.D. Pa. 1978).
36. Alexander v. GardenerDenver Co., 415 U.S. 36 (1974); Barrentine v. Arkansas-Best Freight Sys., 450 U.S. 728 (1981); McDonald v. City of West Branch, 466 U.S. 284 (1984). *But see* Gilmer v. Interstate/Johnson Lane Corp., 59 USLW 4407, 55 FEP Cases (1991) where the Supreme Court held that an arbitration decision concerning the discharge of a securities broker could not be tried in court under the Age Discrimination in Employment Act because the broker had signed an arbitration agreement when he registered as a securities broker, as required by employer. However, this ruling may apply only to instances where a party has signed an arbitration agreement separate from the basic employment contract, because section 1 of the Federal Arbitration Act states that the law does not apply to "contracts of employment. . . ." 9 U.S.C. §1.
37. Univ. of Tenn. v. Elliott, 478 U.S. 788, 41 FEP Cases 177 (1986).
38. Kremer v. Chem. Constr. Corp., 456 U.S. 461 (1982).
39. M. PLAYER, EMPLOYMENT DISCRIMINATION LAW, §5.84 (West 1988).

40. *Id.* (citing Rogers v. General Elec. Co., 781 F.2d 452, 39 FEP Cases 1581 (5th Cir. 1986); Pilon v. Univ. of Minn., 710 F.2d 466, 32 FEP Cases 508 (8th Cir. 1983)).
41. 42 U.S.C. §2000e.
42. Americans with Disabilities Act §308(b)(2), 42 U.S.C.A. §12188 (West 1991).
43. 42 U.S.C. §2000e.
44. Civil Rights Act of 1991, 42 U.S.C. 1981A(2) (1991).
45. *Id.*, 42 U.S.C. 1981A(b) (1991)
46. *Id.*
47. *Id.*
48. United Mine Workers v. Gibbs, 383 U.S. 715 (1966).
49. BNA Policy and Practice Series, *Fair Employment Practices*, 455:2614–5.
50. *See* BNA Policy and Practices, *Fair Employment Practices*, 457:679.
51. TENN. CODE ANN. §4-21-306.

Chapter 10

Managing Disabilities

When studying equal employment laws—especially the Americans with Disabilities Act (ADA)—there is a tendency to concentrate on the hiring process. What questions may be asked of job applicants? When can medical examinations be given? What accommodations must be given to new employees? More often, however, employers must deal with employees who become disabled after employment begins.

Most illnesses such as cancer, diabetes, stroke, AIDS, and mental illness occur when a person is an adult. In addition, a majority of disabling accidents occur after individuals enter the labor force. For example, a work unit with only four workers who are 30 years of age and healthy can expect a 98.1 percent chance that one or more will have a disability causing three months or more lost time from work before the employees reach retirement age.[1]

The process of effectively dealing with employees who become disabled is referred to as "disability management." Disability management means using services, people, and materials to (1) minimize the impact and cost of disability to the employer and employee, and (2) encourage return to work for employees with disabilities.[2] It focuses on effective, quick action to rehabilitate, accommodate, and return disabled employees to work. An effective program will result in lower workers' compensation costs, decreased disability payments, legal compliance with the ADA, reduced job turnover costs, and better employees.

Major financial benefits to employers may result. For example, Sprague Electric Company of Concord, New Hampshire, reduced its average disability absence rate by 50 percent. At one company location with 1,200 employees, Sprague's disability management program reduced annual workers' compensation costs from

$350,000 to $40,000 in just 2 years. It reduced the rate of days lost per injury from 6.5 days to 1.0 day.[3] Federal Express experienced similar benefits. Its disability management program saved the company $4 million in the first year of operation.[4]

A survey of 181 U.S. companies conducted by the Institute for Rehabilitation and Disability Management found that while almost all of the companies had established procedures to process disability claims, only 16 percent had established a specific return to work program, and only 13 percent coordinated return to work activities with state vocational rehabilitation agencies or used financial incentives to encourage a quick return to work.[5] The limited number of effective disability management programs that do exist tend to be in large companies. However, all companies, regardless of size, can benefit from a good program. Although different procedures are necessary, depending upon the type and size of the business, some common elements of an effective program include the following:

1. Strong support from top management
2. A commitment to return injured or ill employees to work as rapidly as possible
3. An analysis of company policies and procedures, including fringe benefits, to insure they are consistent with the goal of rapid and effective return to work
4. The institution of a company wellness or safety program to prevent disabilities
5. Education of employees concerning company health and disability plans
6. Early identification of employee health problems and disabilities
7. Coverage of on-the-job and off-the-job injuries and illnesses
8. Establishment of a disability management team that is given the information and authority necessary to take effective action
9. Commitment to be flexible in returning employees to work and making necessary accommodations

Case Examples

Examples of companies that have successfully instituted a disability management program include the following:

Alcoa[6]

In the early 1980s, Alcoa found that sickness and accident expenses had become its second largest employee benefit cost. The average number of days lost from work where Alcoa was paying disability benefits varied greatly from one location to another—from 6.3 days to 19.8 days. The company began an absenteeism management program that included the following:

1. Extensive communication to employees, supervisors, and local physicians concerning the costs of excessive absenteeism
2. Gaining support from supervisors to place employees with temporary medical restrictions
3. Development of a team at each plant consisting of the plant physician, nurse, benefits administrator, and industrial relations supervisor, which meets once a week to analyze and act upon employee absences
4. Adoption of a policy by which supervisors and company physicians make early contact with absent employees
5. Establishment of a procedure to contact employees' personal physicians to discuss an early return to work

In 1981, the costs of Alcoa's sickness and accident benefits totaled $7.7 million, or $369.14 per hourly employee. By 1986, these costs dropped to $5.2 million, or $311.99 per worker. Over a four-year period, Alcoa estimates a savings of $17 million, including indirect costs.

Weyerhaeuser[7]

Before 1982, Weyerhaeuser's workers' compensation department functioned like those in most large companies. Claims were paid from a self-insurance fund at the company headquarters. Supervisors had little to do with claims, and no incentive to keep costs down.

In 1984, the company changed procedures so that workers' compensation costs were charged to the local departments. Each manager was given a summary of every claim filed by employees in their departments, plus a periodic, clearly stated, financial summary of the department's workers' compensation costs. In addition, Weyerhaeuser required that each counselor or other service provided furnished by outside vendors in the rehabilitation field be interviewed and trained by company staff. One person at each company location was made responsible for becoming knowledgeable about the local medical community, maintaining employee motivation to return to work, tracking claims, and identifying possible jobs and accommodations for returning workers.

Supervisors and managers were strongly encouraged to allow light or part-time return to work, where possible. In one plant, by arrangement with a local company that provided a company sawmill with security guards, employees who were unable to do heavy labor were given first choice in obtaining security guard positions. This program allows Weyerhaeuser to cease workers' compensation disability payments, while permitting the employee to return to gainful employment and providing the security company with guards who are familiar with the facilities to be guarded. Weyerhaeuser's workers' compensation payments declined from $26.1 million in 1984 to $16.5 in 1988.

Polaroid[8]

Polaroid developed a program to offer psychological counseling to employees in 1960. The counseling department has five full-time and seven intern psychologists who provide on-site counseling for any employee who asks for counseling services. There is no restriction on how often an employee can ask for help, but the company does try to avoid counseling family members. The counseling department also offers substance abuse control and other educational programs for employees.

Polaroid officials state that the company saves five dollars for every one dollar invested in the program, not including substantial savings in decreased absenteeism and reduced job turnover. They also estimate a productivity gain of 10 percent for those employees who have been counseled.

Burlington Northern Railroad[9]

The railroad company created over two dozen teams consisting of a medical doctor, rehabilitation counselor, and internal benefits claims agent. In each individual case, the employee's immediate supervisor was added. The major goal was to expedite each disabled employee's return to work. In order to reach this goal, teams were given the authority to make recommendations on everything from medical and mental treatment to formal job training. Over a 21-

month period, the number of employees unable to return to work because of disability was cut by 50 percent and the number of lost workdays was reduced by 3,000.

Lawrence Livermore National Laboratory[10]

When an employee absence occurs due to medical reasons, the laboratory's return-to-work coordinator contacts the employee as soon as is medically reasonable to explain the laboratory's benefits, offer help in dealing with the problems caused by the disability, and show the laboratory's intent to return the employee to work. The coordinator encourages the worker to contact his or her supervisor periodically. As the employee's condition improves, a plan of action for return to work is formulated. Where possible, the employee's personal physician is given a description of the employee's work tasks and is interviewed concerning the employee's prognosis.

The coordinator is authorized to suggest accommodations, including part-time work, home work, and job reassignment. For example, when a 45-year-old electrician suffered a heart attack and applied for disability retirement benefits, the laboratory's coordinator arranged for placement of the employee as an inspector and advisor for an independent contractor working with the laboratory. The employee, who knew that he was physically unable to return to his old job, was pleased to be employed and earning the same salary as in his old job. The company saved approximately $200,000 in disability retirement benefits.

Principles of an Effective Program

The principles a company should employ in establishing a disability management program, as given below, are adapted in large part from *The Disability Management Sourcebook*, an excellent guide published by the Washington Business Group on Health and the Institute for Rehabilitation and Disability Management. For additional information or copies of the sourcebook, write the organization at 229½ Pennsylvania Avenue SE, Washington, D.C. 20003, or phone (202) 408-9320.

Principle 1: Obtain support for disability management from all levels of the company. In addition to obtaining early, strong commitment from top management, educate middle management, line supervisors, and employees regarding the overall benefits of reducing disability leave time.

Principle 2: Develop a case management capability. Small companies may assign case management to a single individual, usually a personnel manager, other officer, or a full- or part-time nurse or physician. Larger companies may desire a team approach. Teams are often comprised of a representative of the human relations department, a vocational rehabilitation expert, a medical expert, and a supervisor. At Xerox, such teams include an internist with a staff of three nurses, one of whom acts as a rehabilitation coordinator working with the personnel department.[11] Honeywell uses a team that includes the employee whose disability is at issue, a benefits administrator, a union representative, and the employee's supervisor.[12] Some large companies vest authority in one person. For example, the Gillette Company gives the medical director the final authority to make decisions. However, the physician has a staff of 20 assistants.[13]

Principle 3: Intervene early. The disability manager or coordinator should contact disabled employees as soon as practical. FMC Corporation of Chicago contacts its employees within 24 hours of accidents.[14] To accomplish early intervention, procedures must be established to notify the individual responsible for contacting disabled employees of absences. Intervention before a disability causes absences is even better. It can help avoid or minimize later absences or, at a minimum, give more time to plan a return to work. Surveying health insurance claim forms and encouraging supervisors to report employees with problems may provide the notice required for action before absences occur.

Principle 4: Make the intervention positive. A key benefit of early intervention can be increased employee morale and desire to return to work; but only if it is handled in a positive manner. When contacting disabled employees, emphasize the company's personal interest in helping the individual recover from the disability, and explain all applicable fringe benefits.

Principle 5: Establish a return to work date. As early as possible after consultation with the employee and his or her physician, set a date for returning to work. Never leave the date open, because the employee will have no goal to reach, and the open-endedness may help create an attitude of disability. If the date set becomes impracticable, it can be changed.

Principle 6: Create modified or light duty jobs to allow early return to work. In making the transition from sick leave to a full schedule of work, Sprague Electric brings disabled employees back to work for as little as four hours per week.[15] Honeywell will return an employee receiving workers' compensation to almost any type of work at any number of hours per week.[16]

Principle 7: Encourage supervisors and managers to help with return to work programs and accommodations. Modified or light duty schedules, part-time work, special accommodations, and other methods to reduce employee disability costs will not succeed without the immediate supervisor's cooperation. There are three effective methods to achieve cooperation. First, educate supervisors as to the financial, legal, and personal benefits of helping disabled employees. Second, make cooperation in obtaining a return to work and accommodating disabled employees a factor in supervisors' performance evaluations. Third, and possibly most effective, charge the costs of workers' compensation, disability pay, and other company disability costs to supervisors' budgets, but assess the costs of accommodation or early, limited return to work to a central budget.

Principle 8: Study disability benefits and change, as needed. Insure that the total benefits package makes it more profitable for a disabled employee to quickly return to work, rather than extend the time of disability.

Principle 9: Choose medical and rehabilitation experts who are aggressive in treating disabilities. Identify local physicians, physical therapists, and other rehabilitation specialists who keep current with the new trend toward positive, aggressive treatment.

Principle 10: Educate local doctors. Disabled individuals' personal physicians play a key role in effecting a quick, but medically safe return to work. Most physicians know little about workplaces or the demands of nonmedical jobs. Often they are too conservative and do not give the patient permission to return to work quickly enough. Other times they may give return to work permission too early because of a lack of knowledge of the physical duties the job requires. A disability coordinator should contact the personal physician early in the employee's disability, explaining the duties of the job, possible temporary and part-time work assignments, and feasible accommodation ideas. Sprague Electric invites physicians to visit the workplace, or videotapes a worker performing the job(s) in question to show to the doctor.

Principle 11: Involve the disabled person in the planning of accommodation and return to work. This involvement is important to ensure that the employee accepts the program as something that offers personal benefit. No one likes to be told what to do.

Principle 12: If applicable, involve unions in the establishment and operation of a disability management program. The program is not only an employee issue suitable for discussion, or even collective bargaining; it is also a program requiring flexibility such as part-time work and temporary job assignments—just the type of issues that can cause labor problems. Effective cooperation cannot be achieved unless the union is involved at each stage of the development and implementation of the program.

Principle 13: Give the disability manager or team authority to provide accommodations, modified work schedules, or job transfers. Maximize the authority of a disability manager or team to provide accommodations and minimize time delays and administrative hassles. Quick action is effective action.

Principle 14: Use company employee assistance programs. Companies with established employee assistance programs (EAPs) can expand them to include working with disabled employees. Most established EAPs deal with personal problems such as alcoholism, drug abuse, and emotional difficulties. Expanding EAPs to cover physical and mental disabilities may be a reasonable method to comply with the law and reduce disability costs. However, if a company EAP has gained a reputation of dealing with "problem" workers, applying EAPs to physical and mental disabilities may send the wrong message to supervisors and employees.

Principle 15: Creatively consider job outplacement, if necessary. If a disabled employee cannot return to any job at the company, placing the individual in a job at another company can still save workers' compensation and disability expenses. Attempt a placement with subcontractors (such as Weyerhaeuser did in placing employees with their security company), or contact vendors who do business with the company such as travel agents, office supply companies, janitorial service companies, and printing companies.

Principle 16: Remember job applicants. The same disability manager or team that gains expertise by dealing with disabled employees should be called upon to assist in determining accommodations and job assignments for disabled job applicants or new employees. Furthermore, accommodation devices, changed job duties, and permanent changes in work times provided to returning disabled employees, but not to similar job applicants and new employees, is strong evidence of illegal discrimination under the ADA and state laws. By the same token, accommodations given to job applicants or new employees in an attempt to comply with the ADA, but not similarly offered to returning disabled employees can be evidence of illegal discrimination. Consistency is the key.

Principle 17: Insure confidentiality. The ADA requires that all employee medical and health information be strictly confidential and be maintained in files separate from employee personnel files. Employers should not only follow the law, but also should assure employees of confidentiality. Employee concerns about confidentiality can ruin an otherwise good program.

Choosing Disability Management Vendors

Outside suppliers offer a number of disability management information systems—using written materials or computer programs—and over 3,000 firms now offer rehabilitative services such as physical therapy, job hardening (therapy designed to return each worker to a specific job), and return to work programs. Companies should consider the following questions when contemplating purchase of a disability management information system.[17]

1. How much does it cost, including software, hardware, training, maintenance, and ongoing support?
2. How long has the system been in use? What other companies have bought the system? Check with these companies.
3. How many cases can be managed on the system?
4. Are hardware and software compatible with the company's current computers and information systems?
5. What safeguards exist to insure confidentiality of files?

Factors to consider when selecting firms to provide rehabilitative services should include the following, as adapted by the author from a list developed by John Hancock Mutual Life Insurance Company:[18]

1. Professional and educational background of provider
2. Length of time provider has been in business and location(s) of firm

3. List of clients (talk to some)
4. Size of average caseload per professional employee
5. Time typically spent on each case and usual response time between initial client assessment and notice to insurance company and employer
6. Frequency of provider contact with employer and relevant insurance companies
7. Criteria for selecting professional employees, including professional certification and licensing of staff
8. Whether the firm has sufficient professional liability insurance
9. Type(s) of vocational testing offered
10. Range of services available
11. How the firm facilitates rapid return to work, including the average time it takes to place clients back at work
12. Whether there are job placement specialists on the staff

PRACTICAL TIPS
Small Business

Smaller businesses that cannot afford to have medical and rehabilitation experts on their staff should consider the following steps.[19]

1. The personnel director or other appropriate officer of the company should visit the disabled employee as soon as practical to demonstrate concern and encourage an early return to work.
2. Always try to return the worker to his or her old job, even if accommodations or flexible work time is required. This minimizes the complications to the disabled employee and maximizes the company's advantage of having a trained employee.
3. Use community resources. State or local rehabilitation agencies and support groups may aid in a successful return to work with little or no expense to the business.
4. Ask your workers' compensation, health, or disability insurance company for resources or payments for rehabilitative services or necessary accommodations. See Chapter 5, "Making Accommodations for Disabled Employees," for more sources that are low-cost or free.
5. Make a special effort to educate the disabled person's physician regarding the requirements of the job and possible changes and accommodations.

Education and Training

Companies may adopt formal policies and procedures concerning the employment of disabled people, as well as providing training concerning the ADA and other laws, and still not comply with the letter and spirit of these laws. Effective compliance—reducing the number of discrimination claims—occurs only if employees at all levels of a business learn to accept disabled people as qualified workers. As Paul Meyer of the David Taylor Research Center of the United States Navy stated:

> You can have all the money in the world (to make accommodations) and it would not change the (employment) numbers (of persons with disabilities). The number one factor is fear. Most able-bodied people will avoid working alongside someone who is disabled. The number one thing we need to do is provide (managers and supervisors) with training—through seminars, through summer internships—anything that will make able-bodied people more comfortable around persons with disabilities.[20]

A thumbnail sketch of some of the educational efforts of two large companies that are leaders in dealing with disabilities, illustrates what can be done.

AT&T

The company's employee magazine, *FOCUS*, frequently carries articles detailing the accomplishments of employees with disabilities or explaining company services offered to disabled employees and the community at large. The Corporate Education and Training Division offers seminars to supervisors and employees concerning disability issues. Disability issues are included as parts of more general seminars, as well as the focus of separate seminars. Emphasis is placed on attitudes toward disabled persons, rather than technical legal compliance.

A strong corporate policy statement on disabilities signed by the chairman and CEO is distributed. The company employs about 40 job accommodation specialists who receive periodic updates on laws, technical advice, and accommodations. In addition, the specialists are sent to various seminars and conferences. AT&T also engages in extensive public service activities, including support of the Job Accommodation Network, Mainstream, Inc., and the Special Olympics.[21]

IBM

IBM has developed one of the most extensive sets of disability education and training materials in the United States. Although some seminars and written materials cover the legal and technical aspects of dealing with disabled people, most concentrate on sensitivity toward and understanding of disabled people. One full-color booklet, entitled *Challenged,* personalizes individual disabled employees by the use of excellent photographs and descriptions of the individuals. An annual publication, *An Ongoing Commitment,* does an equally effective job of showing the company's current activities, both internal and external, in dealing with social and employment issues, including disability programs. IBM also has developed fact sheets on dealing with employee disabilities, manuals for use by supervisors, and other handbooks. The company established the IBM National Support Center for Persons With Disabilities to provide free information for employers and the public about possible accommodation for disabled workers (See Chapter 5, "Making Accommodations for Disabled Employees," for more information).

Recently, IBM has begun to move from an emphasis on disability education as a separate issue, toward incorporating it into a broader coverage of handling diversity. Increasingly, the company intends to engage in sensitivity training that emphasizes individual differences in employees, including differences resulting from individuals' race, sex, marital status, age, economic and social background, and disabilities, among other factors. This new emphasis should help incorporate disabled people into the mainstream, rather than treating them as a separate class of people.[22]

Educational Materials

The Bureau of National Affairs has an excellent training program entitled *Breakthrough,* on dealing with hiring, supervising, and accommodating disabled individuals in a legal and sensitive manner.[23]

Summary

Recruiting, hiring, and accommodating disabled individuals is good business, for both legal and nonlegal reasons.

1. **The Americans With Disabilities Act (ADA) may cause an explosion of litigation.** Courts will tend to be sympathetic to disabled plaintiffs. As Gerald Maatman of America's largest law firm, Baker & McKenzie, put it, "No jury is going to want to rule against someone in a wheelchair when they're up against the big corporation."[24]

2. **There are emerging labor market shortages.** Employment openings are expected to rise 19 percent from 1989 to 2000.[25] However, the low birth rate from 1965 to 1980 has resulted in only 1.5 million new workers entering the workplace at a time when the estimated need for new workers is between 2 and 3 million.[26] In addition, physical abilities are becoming less important as the economy shifts to more service and information oriented sectors. The Department of Labor reports that during the 1990s, professional and managerial jobs will experience an increase of 6.7 million, while operative and labor jobs will grow by only 450,000.[27] Extending employment opportunities to disabled people may prove an important method of finding new, qualified workers.

3. **The number of disabled people of working age is increasing.** Over the past 25 years, the number of severely disabled people between the ages of 17 and 44 increased 178 percent.[28] Resulting from medical advances that save lives but leave people disabled, a comparable increase in disabilities among people aged 45 to 65 is probable. Also, as the baby boom generation moves into middle age, the number of older workers, who are more likely to have disabilities, will increase significantly—up to 46 million American workers 45 years of age or older by the year 2000.[29]

4. **Most disabled workers become disabled while employed, leading to the rapidly increasing costs of workers' compensation, medical insurance, and disability pay.** Companies taking an active role in managing and accommodating worker disabilities can substantially reduce the business costs of disability.

5. **There is a large pool of qualified, disabled individuals who desire to work.** A 1986 Louis Harris and Associates poll found that 66 percent of disabled people are of working age, and 66 percent of this group are not working, although 67 percent say they want to work.[30]

All major laws and regulations applicable to businesses create problems in compliance and extra costs. This increase in cost is especially true during the first few years of enforcement. The ADA is no different from other laws in this respect. However, while compliance with some laws is a win-lose proposition—individuals or society-at-large gain benefits at the expense of business—compliance with the ADA is a win-win-win situation.

1. Disabled people win by gaining a better chance for productive employment.
2. Society wins because of reduced social security disability or other government aid payments and a corresponding increase in the number of employed taxpayers.
3. Business wins by finding a new source of qualified employees in these times of a shrinking labor force.

Notes

1. PSI International. Sick Pay. Will You Make the Right Decision? (The Guardian Health Insurance Co., 1987).
2. SCHWARTZ, WATSON, GALVIN & LIPOFF, THE DISABILITY MANAGEMENT SOURCEBOOK (1989).
3. *Injured Workers: Cost-Cutting Rehabilitation Option*, BNA Policy and Practice Series, Bulletin to Management, Oct. 15, 1987.
4. Lucas, *Putting a Lid on Disability Costs*, MGMT. SOLUTIONS, April 1987, at 17.
5. *Id.* at 18.
6. *Id.* at 28.
7. *Id.* at 41.
8. *Id.* at 32.
9. *Id.* at 17–18.
10. *Return to work—Checkpoints Along the Rehabilitation Trail*, OCCUPATIONAL HAZARDS, Jan. 1984, at 43–44.
11. *Managing Disability in the Workplace*, The New York Business Group on Health, (1987).
12. *Id.*
13. *Id.*
14. Watson, *Disability Management*, PERSONNEL ADMIN. (Feb. 1989) at 72–74.
15. BNA Policy and Series, *Bulletin to Management*, (Oct. 15, 1991).
16. *Supra* note 14.
17. Lucas, *supra* note 4, at 30.
18. "Employment-Based Disability Management Programs, *REHAB BRIEF: Bringing Research into Effective Focus*, National Institute on Disability and Rehabilitation Research, Vol. XI, No. 6 (1988), p. 4.
19. *Supra* note 10.
20. Untitled article, IN THE MAINSTREAM, Jan.–Feb. 1990, at 1.
21. For additional information, contact David Swain, Division Manager, Management Resources Center and Affirmative Action Center, AT&T, 100 Southgate Pkwy. Morristown, N.J. 07962, Phone (201) 898-8000.
22. For additional information, contact J.A. Honeck, Program Manager, EO Communications, IBM, 2000 Purchase St. Purchase, N.Y. 10577, Phone (914) 697-7556.

23. *Breakthrough* may be previewed, rented, or purchased from BNA Communications, Inc., 9439 Key West Ave., Rockville, Md. 20850; Phone (800) 233-6067, in Maryland phone (301) 948-0540.
24. BNA *Fair Employment Practices Newsletter*, February 14, 1991.
25. *In the Mainstream*, Min. Report #6, May–June 1989, Mainstream, Inc., Washington, D.C.
26. Carbine, Schwartz & Watson, Disability Intervention and Cost Management Strategies for the 1990s 3 (July 1989) (Washington Business Group on Health & Institute for Rehabilitation and Disability Management Report on the Second Annual National Disability Management Conference) [hereinafter Carbine].
27. *Supra* note 24.
28. SCHWARTZ, WATSON, GALVIN & LIPOFF, THE DISABILITY MANAGEMENT SOURCEBOOK 7 (1989).
29. "Special Issues in Disability Management," *REHAB BRIEF, Bringing Research into Effective Focus*, Vol. XIII, No. 7 (1991).
30. Carbine, *supra* note 25.

Part II

Accommodating Specific Disabilities

Accommodating Specific Disabilities

Although each disabled worker has different medical symptoms and accommodation needs, the following materials (arranged alphabetically by name of disease or condition) may help in understanding an individual's condition, as well as offer ideas for possible accommodations. Most medical conditions are followed by a listing of additional sources of information. In addition, the following sources of information may be useful in accommodating all types of disabilities:

Job Accommodation Network
P.O. Box 468
Morgantown, WV 26505
(800) JAN-PCEH (526-7234)
Assists employers by giving advice to solve specific accommodation problems. This is normally the most practical source of information for employers.

ABLEDATA
Adaptive Equipment Center
Newington Children's Hospital
181 East Center Street
Newington, CT 06111
(800) 344-5405 or (203) 667-5405
Supplies lists of accommodation devices and possible vendors. Since the organization cannot test all devices, it does not guarantee the effectiveness of all recommended devices.

Mainstream, Inc.
3 Bethesda Metro Center
Suite 830
Bethesda, MD 20814
(301) 654-2400

Provides information on accommodating disabled workers, conducts seminars, sells a manual on corporate training to accommodate disabled workers, and issues a monthly newsletter.

The National Rehabilitation Information Center
8455 Colesville Road, Suite 935
Silver Spring, MD 20910
(800) 34-NARIC
A rehabilitation information center with an extensive data base, newsletter, and other information concerning rehabilitation and accommodation. A reference list of articles and books may be provided concerning specific disabilities.

In Part II, Kunz & Finkel *The American Medical Association Family Medical Guide*, (Random House, 1987), was used to gain general background knowledge of various medical conditions. Physicians on the staff of the James H. Quillen College of Medicine, East Tennessee State University, checked the descriptions of diseases and health conditions for medical accuracy. However, the author is solely responsible for any mistakes.

A listing of a medical condition in Part II does not guarantee it is a disability as defined in the Americans with Disabilities Act or other laws. Costs given for tools, equipment and accommodation prices are taken from various 1990-1991 catalogs (see Appendix III for names and addresses of suppliers). The actual price paid will vary, depending upon the supplier and other factors.

ADDISON'S DISEASE

The Problem. Addison's disease occurs when the adrenal glands gradually decrease the production of steroid hormones. It may cause loss of appetite and weight, weakness, gastrointestinal problems, and a striking darkening of the skin. A related condition, Cushing's syndrome, occurs when there are too many steroid hormones in the body, either from taking steroids (for instance, in the treatment of arthritis) or as a result of overproduction by the adrenal glands. Physical symptoms include weight gain, fattening of the face and area around the shoulders, weakness, and spotty skin.

Treatment and Accommodation. Both Addison's disease and Cushing's syndrome may be classified as disabilities because patients must permanently take medication. However, little or no accommodation is needed. Temporary sick leave may be required immediately after diagnosis for medical treatment. Thereafter, workers should be capable of performing the same work they performed before the medical problem arose.

AIDS

The Problem. Acquired Immune Deficiency Syndrome (AIDS) is a blood-borne viral disease with an incubation period that appears to range from six months to ten years. The first stage of AIDS is an infection with the Human Immunodeficiency Virus (HIV). Most people with the HIV infection will eventually contract AIDS or AIDS-Related Complex (ARC), a somewhat less serious complication than AIDS. All persons with HIV infection may transmit it to noninfected people.

AIDS is not currently curable, and it is expected that almost all people with AIDS will die. However, those infected with AIDS do not die from it. AIDS attacks the body's immune system, leading to a major decrease in the body's ability to fight off infections. Most AIDS patients die from a specialized type of pneumonia, a cancer of the blood vessel walls, or other opportunistic infectious diseases.

Although the HIV infection, and therefore AIDS, is an infectious disease, experts agree that it is not transmitted in ordinary social and work situations, but rather by the following:

1. Sexual intercourse where bodily fluids such as semen, vaginal secretions, or blood are transmitted from an HIV positive partner to a noninfected partner.
2. Direct transfer of blood; which may occur when intravenous drug users share injection needles, or medical personnel accidentally stick themselves with a needle that was used on a patient with the HIV infection.
3. Transfer from a mother to an unborn child.
4. In the past, receiving blood transfusions. However, blood is now tested for the HIV virus before transfusion and the risk of transmitting HIV has been greatly reduced. Furthermore, no person has ever contracted AIDS as a result of donating his or her own blood.

The HIV virus cannot be contracted from using the same toilets used by people with AIDS, ARC, or HIV infection. Nor can a food handler with the HIV infection or AIDS transmit it to people who eat the food. Studies of 500 families who shared kitchen and bathroom facilities with HIV infected people and AIDS patients proved a total lack of transferability in normal relations. Not one family member became infected.

Although medical laboratories have found a small amount of the HIV virus in the tears, urine, and saliva of AIDS patients, no case of transmission by these routes has ever been found. The tiny amounts in these bodily fluids is probably one reason. The HIV virus is not transmitted by touching, coughing, or sneezing. Except for health care and emergency personnel and patients, there is no documented case of a co-worker or customer contracting HIV infection from an infected employee.

Accommodations. People who contract the HIV infection, ARC, or AIDS need accommodations in four areas:

1. Education about HIV infection and AIDS to relieve unfounded fears of co-workers
2. Flexible leave time to medically treat the symptoms of ARC or AIDS
3. The right to continue working as long as they are physically and mentally capable of performing their work
4. Access to medical, rehabilitative, and disability leave on the same basis as other employees who develop life-threatening diseases

The first, and possibly the key step in accommodating HIV-infected workers is the education of management, supervisors, and co-workers of the facts about HIV infection and AIDS. Employer surveys conducted between 1988 and 1990 find that a majority of companies had no AIDS education program, nor any company policy on AIDS. Other surveys show that employees appear to know that AIDS cannot be transferred through casual contact. However, many of these same people state they are afraid of working beside a person suspected of having AIDS. Other surveys confirm the disparity between knowledge and feelings by showing that people understand the facts, but they still have irrational fears about eating with a person who has AIDS, or sharing bathrooms, cafeterias, and employee break rooms.

Because the ADA prohibits informing co-workers of a person's disability, AIDS education should be a general program without reference to any one person. Even if the education program is first adopted in response to learning of a job applicant or employee who has AIDS, workers should not be told the reason for the program. Simply present a general educational program on AIDS, HIV infection, and related matters.

A successful company education program should include the following considerations:

1. If still possible, conduct the program before the workplace has its first HIV-infected employee or AIDS case.
2. Train managers and supervisors first so they can assist in the education of workers.
3. Combine the talents of the company human relations or personnel department staff with a recognized expert in conducting brief employee education programs. A medical doctor explaining the minimum risks of HIV infection and AIDS in the workplace will be more effective than simply using in-house people.
4. Follow up the original training with updates, brochures, or other written materials.

An alternative method of education is to contact outside people to conduct the training. All 3,000 local Red Cross chapters offer training to an employer's work force at nominal cost. Additional information may be obtained from companies or trade unions that have been the leaders in the field of employee education on AIDS, including the Bank of America, Levi Strauss, Wells Fargo, Syntex Corporation of Palo Alto, California, General Motors, and the AFL-CIO.

Typical accommodations offered to a job applicant or employee should include reasonable time off to receive medical treatment, enforcement of the education and nondiscrimination policies of the company, and allowing the worker to continue working as long as the employee is able to successfully perform the job. However, as with any other medical problem, an employer does not have to accept poor performance or excessive absenteeism, even if caused by the medical problem. With some sensitivity and compassion, hold HIV-infected and AIDS workers to the same standards as other workers.

Sources of Information Used in This Section:

BNA Special Report, *AIDS IN THE WORKPLACE* (3d ed.), Bureau of National Affairs, Inc., 9435 Key West Avenue, Rockville, MD 20850, phone (800) 373-1033.

BNA Policy and Practice Series, *Personnel Management* (Vol. II) 247:143, Bureau of National Affairs, Washington, DC 20037.

"Dealing with AIDS," BNA Policy and Practice Series, Fair Employment Practices, Bureau of National Affairs, Washington, DC 20037 (Apr. 26, 1990), p. 53.

"An AIDS Policy that Works," BNA Policy and Practice Series, Fair Employment Practices, Bureau of National Affairs, Washington, DC 20037 (Dec. 7, 1989).

"No Time Like Now for AIDS Education," BNA Policy and Practice Series, Bulletin to Management, Bureau of National Affairs, Washington, DC 20037 (Apr. 28, 1988), pp. 129–30.

"How Employers are Responding to AIDS in the Workplace," BNA Policy and Practice Series, Fair Employment Practices Newsletter, (Feb. 18, 1988), p. 21.

Coping with AIDS, Alcohol, Drug Abuse and Mental Health Administration, National Institutes for Health, Rockville, MD 20857.

A Businesslike Approach to AIDS, U.S. NEWS & WORLD REPORT (April 2, 1990), p. 44.

Other General Sources of Information: *(See also pp. 231–32)*

Consulting Program
AIDS Foundation
P.O. Box 6182
San Francisco, CA 94101
    Discusses strategies and resources to help keep AIDS patients at work and reduce lawsuits.

AIDS Hotline
Centers for Disease Control
Recorded Message: (800) 342-2437
Individual Questions: (800) 447-2437

American Foundation for AIDS Research
1515 Broadway, Suite 3601
New York, NY 10036
    Publishes *AIDS Education: A Business Guide* and other guidelines.

ALCOHOL AND DRUG ABUSE

The Problem. Although drug abuse has become a serious problem in industry, alcohol causes more economic loss. Both drug abuse and alcohol addictions may cause excessive absenteeism, poor performance, safety dangers, and even employee theft. In a survey of white-collar and professional workers, only 4 percent admitted to using drugs during the workday, but 54 percent reported they consumed alcohol during working hours.

Identifying Alcohol and Drug Abusers. Drug tests are legal in most states, and are permitted under the ADA. However, drug tests are not infallible, thus a positive result should be confirmed with a follow-up test. Even then, it is almost impossible to determine if the person took drugs on or off the job. Tests for alcohol check for the current presence of alcohol and will not indicate the presence of alcohol consumed days earlier.

Supervisors should be trained to detect alcoholism problems. Common symptoms include bloodshot eyes, bloated or flushed face, tremors in the hands, increased restlessness or irritability (especially in the morning), extra long lunch hours, mood swings, increased absenteeism (particularly on Mondays), and increased tardiness at work. However, one or more of these factors may be symptoms of other diseases.

Supervisors should also be taught to recognize the symptoms of drug abuse. For cocaine and crack abuse, these symptoms include overactivity, unusual nervousness, and dilation of the pupils. Marijuana use tends to cause the user to become dreamy and unproductive and have bloodshot eyes. Unusual antics or speech, comparable to alcohol intoxication, sometimes results from the use of marijuana.

Rehabilitation. Although employers have the legal right to discharge an employee who is an illegal drug user or an alcoholic whose work is affected, successful treatment and return to work should be attempted in most cases. This approach demonstrates the company's loyalty to its employees, avoids the loss of a possibly good employee, and avoids the costs of hiring and training a replacement worker.

The following is a recommended outline of steps that may be taken once an employee is determined to have alcohol or drug problems:

1. Use "Constructive Confrontation." The supervisor meets with the employee and clearly outlines the employee's defi-

ciencies in job performance and interviews the employee as to the cause. This confrontation should be combined with an explanation of any company-provided employee assistance program (see Chapter 8, "Company Policies and Forms"), health benefits, counseling, or other relevant company services. Any current company drug or alcohol rehabilitation policy should also be outlined as part of the overall services offered to employees. However, the main emphasis of the meeting should remain on job performance. The supervisor should write a note concerning the time and content of the meeting and have it placed in the employee's medical or personnel file. If the note indicates alcoholism or past drug use, it should be placed only in the employee's confidential health file, separate from the personnel file (see Chapter 2, "Major Changes to Conform to the Law," concerning confidentiality of medical information).

2. Should the employee's job performance continue to deteriorate, the supervisor should have a second meeting with the employee. In this meeting, the supervisor should again outline the employee's performance deficiencies. The worker should be calmly and clearly told of the consequences he or she faces, including termination from employment. Any health or benefit plans, counseling, leave time for rehabilitation, or other benefits should be fully explained and the employee should be strongly encouraged to control his or her own problems with help from the listed company services, or other services. The supervisor should place a memorandum summarizing what was said and giving the date of the conference in the employee's file. Although not necessary, it might be helpful to have the employee sign the memorandum.

3. If no improvement in performance and no apparent action by the employee to get counseling or take other remedial actions occurs, a third meeting with the supervisor, personnel manager, and employee should be held. The rehabilitative sources should also be explained. If drug or alcohol abuse still appears to be the problem, the employee should be given a document to sign such as the following sample:

I, __(name of employee)__ , agree that I have been warned three times concerning my poor work performance caused, at least in part, by my use of <u>name of substance(s)</u>. I also agree that during each warning I was informed of various company and noncompany rehabilitation programs, leaves of absence, and other benefits.

I agree to enter a rehabilitation program for <u>(name of substance problem)</u> by <u>(date—earlier the better)</u>, complete the program, and remain <u>(drug, alcohol), or drug and alcohol)</u> free in the future.

I agree that <u>(name of employer)</u> may immediately discharge me from employment if I fail to observe any of the conditions listed in the previous paragraph. I agree that <u>(name of employer)</u> has a right to conduct drug or alcohol screening tests on me at anytime without notice.

In return for the company's decision not to discharge me at this time, I agree that I will not file any lawsuit, arbitration claim, or other legal action if I am discharged for violating any of the promises made in the second paragraph above.

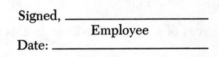

Signed, _____
                         Employee
Date: _____

See your attorney in order to revise this memorandum to conform to any local or state law requirements.

Accommodations. In addition to directing employees to obtain help and providing necessary leaves of absence, employers should take several steps to aid the employee in returning to work after rehabilitation.

1. Reduce the chance of a relapse by open communication. Managers should learn and explain to supervisors the types of conditions that often cause a person to revert to drug or alcohol abuse. The employee should also be reminded of any company programs that aid recovering addicts and abusers.
2. On the employee's first day back at work, the supervisor should clearly describe all job performance expectations. To individualize the warning signs of resumed abuse, the employee should be asked to explain any warning signs of future problems that were told to the employee during the rehabilitation program.
3. Supervisors should be aware of a common warning sign of a relapse where an employee pushes too hard and tries to be a super-employee.

4. While continuing to require good job performance, supervisors should attempt to reduce the stress on the employee. Stress may result from the employee's lack of knowledge about the extent of his or her authority, a lack of clear performance standards, inadequate communication, or from being treated as a number or machine, rather than a person.

5. Closely supervise the worker (without being too obvious). Complement as well as criticize.

6. If productivity declines again because of suspected drug or alcohol abuse, repeat some or all of the steps given above under the **Rehabilitation** heading, including drug testing and possible discharge.

See Chapter 7, "AIDS, Infectious Diseases, Drug and Alcohol Problems, and Weight Problems," for a legal discussion of drug and alcohol problems.

Sources of Information Used in this Section:

How Employers Can Help Ensure the Recovery of Chemically Dependent Employees, BNAC Communicator 5, Bureau of National Affairs, Inc., Washington, DC 20037.

Keeping Disabled People In Your Place: Focus on Individuals Who Abuse Alcohol and Drugs, Mainstream, Inc., 3 Bethesda Metro Center, Suite 830, Bethesda, MD 20814, phone (301) 654-2400.

Hunsaker and Pavett, *Drug Abuse in the Brokerage Industry*, Personnel 54–58 (July 1988), pp. 54–58.

Other General Sources of Information: *(See also pp. 231–32)*

BNA Books
1250 23rd St., NW
Washington, DC 20037-1165
(800) 372-1033
    BNA Books has a number of books on alcohol and drug abuse, including *Drug Testing in the Workplace* and *Substance Abuse and Employee Rehabilitation*.

National Clearinghouse for Alcohol Information
P.O. Box 2345
Rockville, MD 20852

National Institute of Drug Abuse
Alcohol, Drug Abuse and Mental Health Administration
5600 Fishers Lane
Rockville, MD 20857
(301) 443-6500

ALLERGIES AND ASTHMA

The Problem. Almost 60 million Americans suffer from allergies. Most allergies are not severe enough to be legal disabilities. However, some severe cases will meet the ADA's definition of a physical impairment, and some are actually caused by the exposure of individuals to certain substances in the workplace. Severe allergies can result in serious medical conditions, including death.

Allergies are caused by an overreaction of the body's immune system to some normal substance such as pollen or animal fur, or workplace substances such as glues or chemicals. The effects are usually limited to upper respiratory inflammation, skin rashes, hives, and itching. However, even these can become disabling if severe and long lasting.

A chronic and often serious condition triggered by allergies is asthma. Asthma creates periodic attacks of wheezing and difficulty in breathing. These attacks are a result of a partial constriction of the windpipe caused by a constriction of the muscles of the windpipe and a partial blockage caused by mucus. Although more common in children, 2 to 3 percent of adults suffer from this condition.

Treatment and Accommodation. Allergies may be treated with antihistamines, a series of desensitizing injections, or avoidance of the substance causing the allergy.

If employees are unable to schedule medical tests and their weekly desensitizing injections during nonworking hours, employers should consider giving reasonable time off.

For employees who develop allergies after coming to work or after a job reassignment, employers should help the employee experiment to determine if on-the-job exposure is the problem. Temporary job transfers to different areas of the workplace might help identify the substance causing the allergy. Temporary changes in substances used in the workplace, such as inks, paper, and fabrics, may also identify the cause.

Employers' actions to accommodate allergies should be a starting point for the accommodation of asthma. However, employers should do even more. In most cases, an employee with asthma needs a location that is as dust free and smoke free as possible. To achieve this environment, air conditioning vents should be examined and cleaned, the filters should be frequently cleaned or replaced, and no smoking should be allowed. Also, remove any moldy items such as old plants and avoid using any kind of aerosol sprays. Fumes from gasoline, ammonia, and other substances may also cause problems.

In the case of an acute attack of asthma on the job, a supervisor or co-worker should be available to get the employee's asthma drugs or inhaling apparatus from his or her desk or locker. If a co-worker is to provide this service it is safer under the law to have the employee with asthma ask the co-worker. This will insure that the company does not violate any of the confidentiality requirements of the ADA.

During an asthma attack, the person should be made comfortable (usually sitting up, arms on desk or table, with fresh air or oxygen), and only one person should stay with the asthmatic. If the prescribed medicine or inhaling device does not stop the attack, the employee should be taken to the emergency room of the nearest hospital.

Sources of Information Used in This Section:

Teaching Patients to Manage Acute Asthma, Nursing 77–82 (April 1983).

Other Sources of Information: See Pages 231–32.

AMPUTATION

The Problem. The effects of amputations vary greatly, depending upon the type of amputation and the age of the amputee. An arm amputation causes a decrease in manual dexterity, while a leg amputation may cause mobility problems. Amputations of both arms, or both legs, obviously cause more problems than the amputation of one extremity. Adults find it much more difficult to adjust to an amputation than do young children.

Most amputees can be fitted with a prosthesis. Although a modern prosthesis may have some amazing features, it will never be as effective in function as the original limb. Modern prosthesis will allow people to engage in almost any type of work. However, the use of a prosthesis can cause some work-related problems.

One common problem of amputees that use a prosthesis is perspiration at the stump of the amputated arm or leg. The moisture interferes with the suction used to attach the prosthesis, as well as causing possible fungal, bacterial, and viral infections.

Many people with single-leg amputations find that prolonged standing can be more difficult than walking. Others find bending, stooping, or kneeling to be difficult.

A common problem of amputations that is not obvious to non-amputees is that of loss of feeling or sensation. For example, a person whose leg is replaced by a prosthesis will have difficulty in driving a shift vehicle because they cannot "feel" the clutch. More difficulties in loss of sensation occur in an upper-limb amputation. While the manual operation of the prosthesis may be excellent, many manual tasks are completed by feel as much as by sight. For example, a nurse uses feeling more than sight to determine the location of a vein for giving an injection. A factory worker soldering circuit boards will feel the solder to see if it is complete.

Accommodations. Do not assume that a missing limb disqualifies a person from any job (other than those few that may be prohibited by governmental regulations). Once the disability has been disclosed, talk with the individual to determine what limitations, if any, are imposed on job-related functions.

Two accommodations are available where heat or stress on the job causes perspiration on the stump. The obvious, nontechnical method is to cool the work area or reduce stressful situations. A more high-tech method is the use of a process called "iontophoresis" where an electrical current is passed through the skin, causing a reduction in sweating at the site of the treatment. In the past this could only be done in a hospital. However, General Medical Co. (1935 Armacost Ave., Los Angeles, CA 90025) produces a kit that can be used at home or work that has been favorably reviewed in several medical journals. The Drionic (trademarked name) device costs $125. It can lead to greatly reduced perspiration within several weeks of self-treatment.

Usually the only accommodation needed for prolonged standing is a stool that the employee can partially rest upon while standing so as to not place all body weight on one leg. Jobs that require employees to kneel or bend may be accommodated by the purchase of a grab bar or reacher that allows one to pick up or adjust floor-level items while standing. Most sell for $30 or less.

An example of a technical accommodation for a person who has an upper extremity amputated is a $60 foot-controlled pedal that may be attached to a computer or word processor so that a person can type or enter data with only one good hand.

Sources of Information Used in This Section:

Gething, Leonard, and O'Loughlin, *Person to Person: Community Awareness of Disability*, Brookes Publishing Company, Baltimore, MD (1989), pp. 1–11.

Akins, Meisenheiner and Dobson, *Efficacy of the Drionic Unit in the Treatment of Hyperhidrosis*, Journal of the American Academy of Dermatology (Apr. 1987), pp. 828–832.

Elgart and Fuchs, *Tapwater Iontophoresis in the Treatment of Hyperhidrosis*, International Journal of Dermatology (Apr. 1987), pp. 194–97.

Other General Sources of Information: *(See also pp. 231–32)*

National Rehabilitation Association
633 South Washington Street
Alexandria, VA 22315
(703) 836-0850
    Assists employers by giving advice and conducting seminars on accommodating disabilities.

AMYOTROPHIC LATERAL SCLEROSIS: See Nerve Disease

ANEMIA

    The Problem. Anemia results from a decrease in either hemoglobin or red blood cells. Anemia may be a temporary or permanent medical condition. If temporary, it may not rise to the level of a legal disability. Anemia may also be a side effect of another medical problem such as arthritis, hepatitis, or tuberculosis, and thus not a separate disability. Serious and more permanent conditions such as sickle cell anemia, thalassemia, or hemolytic congenital anemia are legal disabilities that may require accommodations.
    Sickle cell anemia meets the legal definition of a disability under federal law and is specifically listed as a disability under some state handicapped employment laws. About 40,000 Americans have this inherited disease, largely limited to blacks and those descended from persons who lived in some parts of Italy, Greece, Arabia, and

India. Symptoms include extreme fatigue, weakness, fainting, breathlessness, and heart palpitations, depending on the degree of anemia. It can also cause severe pain in the bones or abdomen and help cause blood clots in the lungs, kidney, brain, or other organs. Abnormal bone growth and severe infections may also develop.

There is no cure for sickle cell anemia, but symptoms can be treated. Episodes of pain can be treated with painkillers and I.V. fluids, but this often requires hospitalization. In the past, few adults with sickle cell anemia would be in the work force due to the extremely serious complications of the disease and a high death rate at young ages. Today's treatments allow more adults with sickle cell anemia to work, and many now live to middle or older age.

Sickle cell anemia should be distinguished from sickle cell trait. Persons with sickle cell trait normally inherited it from only one parent and no impairment results. More than 2,000,000 people have the trait. Sickle cell anemia occurs when both parents had the sickle cell trait.

The medical conditions known as Thalassemia and Hemoglobin C are similar to sickle cell anemia, but the symptoms are usually less serious. As with sickle cell anemia, one may have a Thalassemia or Hemoglobin C trait rather than the disease itself. The trait does not cause medical problems.

Accommodation. Employees with general anemia due to loss of blood, underlying illness, or an iron deficiency normally require no accommodation beyond a temporary period of rest and chance to receive medical treatment. Blood transfusions may be necessary in severe cases.

Accommodations for employees with sickle cell anemia and related diseases may require a good deal of flexibility. The disease creates random episodes of pain—especially in the abdomen and legs—and damage to various organs, including the lungs, kidneys, gallbladder, legs, and almost any other part of the body.

Flexibility in granting absences from work for medical treatment may be the most frequent accommodation needed by an employee with sickle cell anemia. Other possible accommodations include the following:

1. Modifying job duties to avoid cold temperatures or providing heaters or other equipment. It appears that some of the random occurrences of pain and severe symptoms may be brought on by exposure to cold temperatures.

2. Providing rubber mats or carpeting to reduce the shock to the legs when walking on hard surfaces. This may reduce the risk of leg ulcers, one of the major complications of sickle cell anemia. Some people also find that wearing shoes with rubber heels aids in preventing leg problems.
3. Avoiding infectious diseases. People with sickle cell anemia are at a high risk of developing serious complications if they contract infections. See Chapter 7, "AIDS, Infectious Diseases, Drug and Alcohol Problems, and Weight Problems," for more on infectious diseases.
4. Avoiding flying in unpressurized airplanes or working at elevations of over 6,000 feet. If it is not possible to avoid these situations, the employee should obtain medical permission and instructions as to minimizing the harmful effects of high altitude.

Sources of Information Used in This Section:

Paul Heller, *Sickle Cell Anemia: Questions Most Often Asked*, Consultant (March 1982), pp. 249–265.

Sickle Cell Anemia, The Merck Manual (15th ed. 1987), pp. 1120–21.

Fact Sheet on Sickle Cell Anemia and *Fact Sheet on Hemoglobin C*, published by the National Association for Sickle Cell Disease, Inc., Suite 360, 4221 Wilshire Blvd., Los Angeles, CA 90010, phone (800) 421-8453.

Other Sources of Information: See Pages 231–32.

ANEURYSMS: See Heart and Circulatory Problems.

ANGINA: See Heart and Circulatory Problems.

ANXIETY: See Mental Illness or Disease.

ARTERIAL EMBOLISM: See Heart and Circulatory Problems.

ARTHRITIS

   The Problem: Ranked as the nation's primary crippler, nearly 40 million Americans have arthritis. The term arthritis actually includes over 100 afflictions that account for over 27 million lost workdays annually. Symptoms can range from minor swelling and pain to total disability.

The two major types of arthritis are rheumatoid arthritis and osteoarthritis. Rheumatoid arthritis may begin at any age. However, most people are between the ages of 20 and 50 when symptoms first appear. It may cause a mild inflammation of one or several joints, resulting in minor pain and swelling, or it may be a general attack that becomes so severe that a total disability results. Although arthritis is a progressive disease, it may subside or even disappear. Unfortunately, the more typical course of action is a progression whereby joints become increasingly swollen and painful, often with muscular weakness. Osteoarthritis is usually a manifestation of aging. The joints of the fingers, knees, shoulders, or spine become swollen, stiff, and painful. The progression of the symptoms is gradual in some people, rapid in others.

Other types of arthritis include rheumatoid arthritis of the spine (sometimes called Marie-Strumpell's disease or rheumatoid spondylitis), gout, and arthritis due to rheumatic fever, infection, or a physical injury. Related medical problems include nonarticular rheumatism, fibrositis, lumbago, bursitis, tendinitis, tenosynovitis, systemic lupus erythematosus (SLE), and psychogenic rheumatism.

Treatment and Accommodation. Early detection and continuous medical supervision is essential to control the extreme symptoms of arthritis.

Nontechnical accommodations may include allowing an employee to mix heavy activities such as lifting objects with lighter ones such as taking inventory or filling out forms. Allowing an employee to plan his or her own workday may be helpful and should be considered if it does not disrupt required business activities. Some workers with arthritis prefer to come to work early, or stay late, in order to take extended rest periods during the day.

Some examples of technical accommodations include:

- Cutting knife with plastic-coated handle that can be bent to the shape of a person's hand. Cost: $6.75.
- Gripping device to open bottles. Cost: $11.95.
- Rubber door knob extender that allows leverage to turn the knob without clasping it. Cost: $4.50.
- Diskette holder that makes it easier to insert and remove diskettes from a computer. Cost: $8.95.

- Mobile stand that allows one to rest in a standing position. Cost: $85.95.
- Pneumatic chair lifter to aid in rising from a chair. Cost: $250.
- Wrist supporter or hand splint. Cost: $10–25.
- Phone handle allowing a person to hold the phone without grasping it. Cost: $6.75.
- Device used in writing with pen or pencil without grasping it. Cost: $19.95.
- Pen and pencil grips: $2.66 for a set of three.
- Wheeled walker with basket. Cost: $295.

Additional office or workplace modifications may include the provision of a small electric heater if the employee finds the workplace temperature to be cool, thus aggravating stiffness and pain. Employees who sit in office chairs may need a chair that is appropriate to the person's body size, thus giving full support.

See **SPINAL CORD INJURY AND WHEELCHAIR USERS** for additional examples of accommodations for those who have trouble grasping or handling things.

Sources of Information Used in This Section:

Putting Disabled People in Your Place: Focus on Individuals with Arthritis, Mainstream, Inc., 3 Bethesda Metro Center, Suite 830, Bethesda, MD 20814, phone (301) 654-2400.

Living with Arthritis, Health (Feb. 1982), pp. 42–44.

You Can Fight Arthritis—And Win, Reader's Digest (March 1985), pp. 103–106.

Living With Arthritis, Newsweek (March 20, 1989), pp. 64–70.

How to Cope With Arthritis, Consumers' Research (March 1984), pp. 16–19.

Other General Sources of Information: *(See also pp. 231–32)*

Arthritis Foundation
3400 Peachtree Rd., NE
Suite 1101
Atlanta, GA 30326
(404) 266-0795

ASTHMA: See Allergies.

ATHEROSCLEROSIS: See Heart and Circulatory Problems.

BACK PROBLEMS

The Problem. About 80 percent of Americans will experience back pain that can range from a dull, annoying ache to complete agony. After headaches, it is the most common ailment in the United States. Backaches are the leading cause of disability for people under 45 years of age, as well as the leading cause of workers' compensation claims. Total costs in lost time from work, medical treatments, and other expenses are estimated to be 20 billion dollars or more per year.

There are many possible causes of back problems, including physical injuries, arthritis, pregnancy, infections, general wear and tear, excessive strain or incorrect lifting procedures, excessive sitting, poor posture, and obesity. In many cases the cause is what experts call nonspecific—no provable cause.

The terminology used to describe back problems is confusing and contradictory. For example, many people say they have a slipped disc. However, the term "slipped disc" is inaccurate (the correct term is "bulging disc") and only around 5 to 10 percent of back problems involve this condition. Because of this confusion, descriptive terms are not very useful.

Eighty to 90 percent of back problems result from stresses and strains on the muscles and ligaments that support the spine. These problems most often occur to people between the ages of 17 and 45. Most commonly, they result from prolonged sitting without effective back support or poor sitting posture, or from bending and twisting while lifting or by lifting loads that are beyond the strength of the individual. Many of the remaining backaches result from more serious problems such as spinal or brain tumors, osteoporosis, and rheumatoid arthritis.

Several aspects of back problems create special problems for employers. As explained in Chapter 6, "Risk of Future Injury: Epilepsy, Diabetes, and Bad Backs," employers cannot refuse to hire individuals with an increased risk of back problems unless it can be proven there is a *probability* of *substantial* future injury. Furthermore, because the first onset of a back problem tends to occur during a person's adult years, many employers will experience back problems only after they are already employed.

Adding to employer difficulties is the fact that traditional medical procedures have relied upon the individual's description of pain to determine if there is a medical problem. This may result in fake back problem claims in some cases. In many other cases the individual does experience pain. However, individuals' tolerance for pain varies considerably; thus any medical diagnosis may depend more on the individual's tolerance than the actual medical condition of the back.

Few true remedies exist for back pain. Surgery may help only in 1 to 2 percent of cases. Although some physicians order complete bed rest, it may not alleviate the problem. Chiropractic manipulation, acupuncture, or the wearing of a corset or cast may temporarily reduce pain and discomfort, but seldom cure the problem. Weight loss and proper exercises may be the most effective cure. However, individuals often fail to detect any immediate improvement and therefore quit their diet or exercise program.

The longer an employee is absent from work or under work restrictions because of back pain the more likely the problem will get worse. The likelihood of developing an attitude of disability is great.

Accommodations. The best accommodation for employees with back pain is the adoption of a procedure that most quickly returns the employee to unrestricted employment in their original job. The key elements in a quick return to full duty include a method to validly determine the extent of back injury, a program that encourages rapid recovery, and a way to make a valid determination of the person's physical progress. The introduction of new methods and medical machines makes this possible in most cases. A procedure to use in handling back pain should be as follows:

1. Immediately contact any employee who is absent or has reduced work duties because of back problems. Inform the employee of the company's personal concern and a commitment to effectuate a quick return to health and work (see Chapter 10, "Managing Disabilities," for more on corporate disability management programs).
2. Select (or have preselected) a physician or rehabilitative facility who specializes in back problems and has a reputation of taking aggressive action in treatment, as well as having the proper equipment. The key piece of equipment is a low-back machine that can determine if a problem is

faked, determine the type and extent of the problem, and can be used in measuring rehabilitative progress.

Because the low-back machines cost $45,000 or more, many physicians and rehabilitation facilities may not have them. To determine if they do, ask if they have the B-200 that is manufactured by Isotechnologies, Inc., of Hillsborough, North Carolina, or a similar machine produced by the Cybex division of the Lumen Company, in Ronkonkoma, New York. Since the *Wall Street Journal* publicized these companies in a 1989 article, additional manufacturers may have appeared.

3. Have the employee tested on the low-back machine as soon as possible to determine the extent of disability and course of treatment. Encourage the physician to institute a very specific, "fast-track" rehabilitation program.
4. Be sure the rehabilitation facility constantly monitors the employee's progress. One of the advantages of the newer low-back machines is that they can measure the results of exercise or other rehabilitative measure and offer feedback to the individual so they are less likely to give up.
5. In conjunction with the rehabilitative experts, plan for the earliest return to work that is physically safe. If the employee cannot yet return to his or her old job, or return to full-time work, try to arrange a temporary job reassignment or part-time work.

Aggressive but fair action is not only a reasonable accommodation for the employee, but it also aids employers. If done properly, it can save substantial amounts of workers' compensation and health insurance benefits, and be used as evidence in workers' compensation lawsuits.

Other Accommodations. Some suggestions that may be appropriate in specific cases include:

- Training employees in correct lifting procedures.
- Small, manually-operated lifter and pallet cart. Cost: $81.
- Hydraulic lifter. Cost: $828.
- Collapsible floor crane for lifting and swinging up to 1500 pounds. Cost: $511.50.
- Lumbar support belt designed to reduce the chance of back sprains. Normally used only with physician's consent. Cost: $9.50 to $23.95.

- Inflatable lumbar support belt. Should be used only with physician's consent. Cost: $49.85.
- Angled foot rest to give more back support to typists, word processors, and others. Cost: $29.
- Ergonomically designed chair. Cost: From $250 to $2,390.
- Wooden bead back and seat rest for office chairs or car seats. Cost: $10 to $50.
- Portable plastic seat device to give more support to spine. Cost: $39.50.
- YMCA six-week back exercise program. Cost: Approximately $60.
- Balans chair (the type with a knee rest and no back). Cost: $300.

Sources of Information Used in This Section:

Zamula, *Back Talk: Advice for Suffering Spines*, FDA Consumer (Apr./May 1989), pp. 28–35.

Willis, *Back Pain: Ubiquitous, Controversial*, FDA Consumer (Nov. 1983), pp. 5–7.

Low Back Pain Gives Up Some Secrets, Wall Street Journal (Sept. 1989) (reprint).

Fletcher, *Watch Costs of Early Rehabilitation: Study*, Business Insurance (Feb. 27, 1989).

Moretz, *How to Prevent Back Injuries*, Occupational Hazards (July 1987).

Scandura, *Good Ways to Stop a Bad Back*, Working Woman (Feb. 1988), pp. 112–115.

Hofmann, *Employers Play Key Role in Rehabilitation*, Business Insurance (Sept. 28, 1987), pp. 22–23.

Your Aching Back—What Doctors Can Do About It, U.S. News & World Report (Oct. 17, 1983), pp. 85–86.

Pekkanen, *I am Joe's Aching Back*, Readers Digest (Nov. 1989), pp. 131–136.

An Epidemic of Back Pain, MACLEAN'S (Apr. 7, 1986), pp. 36–39.

Willens, *Help for Your Aching Back*, Money (March 1987), pp. 129–136.

Other Sources of Information: See Pages 231–32.

BELL'S PALSY: See Nerve Disease.

BLINDNESS AND VISION IMPAIRMENTS

The Problem. The terms "blind" and "blindness" are loosely used. Fourteen million Americans have visual impairments, defined as an inability to read regular-size print, even with glasses. Eight hundred thousand people are legally blind; however, 90 percent have some residual vision. Only 80,000 Americans are totally blind. In this section, reference to blindness or blind people describes people who are totally blind or have extremely limited sight. Reference to vision impairments or visually impaired people describes people with serious vision impairments who are able to see shapes, furniture, and faces, but not written words or details.

Recruiting. There are a large number of qualified blind and visually impaired people who are potential employees. Studies show that of working-age people with serious vision problems, 70 percent are unemployed or underemployed. The studies also show that their major barrier to employment is uninformed employer opinion, not their visual problems.

Interviews with personnel managers at six large companies in the Midwest indicated that four of the six managers thought blind workers present a safely problem, while all six reported that dealing with blind people made them uncomfortable. Other surveys show a common belief that blind and visually impaired people have higher than average absence rates, as well as being late more often than other workers because of transportation problems. And most of all, employers often believe a blind or visually impaired person cannot work on an assembly line, be a secretary, or take other positions where sight is thought to be important. The experience of DuPont and IBM, two leaders in hiring disabled persons, contradicts these opinions.

DuPont found visually impaired workers to be better than average in safety and nearly average in attendance and on-time arrival. IBM found blind and visually impaired workers to be as good or better than average in all employment settings. They have successfully employed numerous people with serious vision problems.

Potential employees who are blind or visually impaired may be located by contacting the state vocational rehabilitation agency or Job Opportunities for the Blind (1800 Johnson Street, Baltimore, MD 21230, phone: (800) 638-7518 or (301) 659-9314). A state vocational rehabilitation agency may provide job training at no cost to the employer and may finance adaptive equipment needed for job accommodations (see Chapter 5, "Making Accommodations for Disabled Employees," for examples of the aid outside agencies may give).

Interviewing. When interviewing a blind or almost blind job applicant the following ideas may be useful:

1. Walk to the applicant, introducing yourself by name, and shake hands. You will need to initiate the handshake by reaching down for the person's hand.
2. Ask if the applicant desires assistance in traveling across the room. *Never* give assistance without asking first.
3. If assistance is desired, let the applicant take your arm. *Never* grab the applicant's arm or shoulder. As you walk, let the applicant hold your arm and walk slightly behind you. Identify any obstacles in the person's path and guide their arm to the back of any chair in which the applicant will sit, while at the same time telling the applicant whether the chair has arms or not.
4. If the job applicant does not desire physical assistance, give directions to the appropriate chair or location, describe obstacles, and tell the person how many steps it is to the location.
5. If the person has a guide dog, do *not* pet it. In fact, there is no need to refer to it except in rare cases, such as working in a restaurant's kitchen, where the use of a dog may require special accommodations.
6. Talk to the person in a normal voice unless you know he or she has a hearing problem. Too often sighted people act as if blind people are hard of hearing.
7. Do not worry about using terms such as "you see my point?" or "I looked at it," or even "he was blind to the fact. . . ." Blind people use these terms just the same as sighted people.

8. If there is written material, such as a job description, either read it to the applicant or have the applicant take the written material home to look it over using their normal adaptive devices (see, it is O.K. to have them "look" it over).

9. If you normally give job applicants a tour of the office or working areas, do so with blind or visually impaired applicants. As you tour, simply describe the things around you.

10. Be sure to tell the applicant when you are leaving the room.

11. You may, and should, discuss the applicant's visual problem as it refers to their ability to do the job for which they have applied. A failure to discuss a job applicant's blindness in a job interview will probably give the impression you are not seriously considering hiring the applicant. However, before discussing the applicant's visual problems, talk with the applicant in the same way you normally start an interview, such as engaging in social small talk, describing the job, or discussing the applicant's qualifications.

12. Do *not* assume the applicant cannot perform certain types of jobs. Blind people are lawyers, physicians, computer programmers, auto mechanics, engineers, secretaries, retail managers, and custodians. Almost any job can be performed with the correct accommodations.

13. Do *not* ask how the employee will get to work. Unless travel is part of the job description, it is none of your business. Studies show visually impaired workers make their own arrangements and seldom cause any problems to the employer.

14. Discuss needed job accommodations with the applicant. Often the applicant knows exactly what is needed, and sometimes the applicant already has the proper equipment, such as a tape recorder or braille reader. The applicant may also be familiar with sources of funding for accommodation devices.

15. Show your willingness to consider different accommodations. If no accommodation is obvious, tell the applicant you need a little time to check out some accommodation ideas. Arrange for a second interview or later phone conversation after you have had time to investigate possible accommodations.

Testing. Between one third and one half of visually impaired people have sufficient vision to read written tests if they have a magnifier or the test is given in large print. However, some visually impaired people have a limited visual field that slows the reading process. Others cannot read written tests. When an employer knows of an applicant's visual impairment, the applicant should be asked in advance what type of accommodation is needed to take tests.

Employers should also inform applicants of the testing date and place and that they may use note-taking equipment such as a slate and stylus, braille writer, tape recorder, or other device for visually impaired people. For tests involving mathematical calculations, the applicants should be told they can use the Cranmer abacus, arithmetic-type slate, or other computation aid. If these aids are used, the notes, calculations, and other materials should be given to the test administrator or destroyed after the test ends.

Four types of media are possible when giving written tests to visually impaired job applicants: large print, braille (Grade 2), cassette tape, or live reader. In smaller businesses, a cassette tape or live reader may be the only reasonable accommodations. However, do not assume these methods are preferred by applicants. The U.S. Office of Personnel Management found that when offered large print or braille copy, two thirds of visually impaired applicants choose the hard copy rather than a cassette tape or live reader.

Compared to sighted people taking a written test, all the methods listed above are inherently slow. Therefore, timed tests are usually inappropriate. However, as a rule of thumb, the multiples of time needed by visually impaired people as compared to sighted people taking a written test are shown in the following display:

TYPE OF TEST	LARGE PRINT	FORMAT USED BRAILLE	CASSETTE TAPE	READER
Comprehension of Written Material	2.0	3.0	2.3	2.6
Choosing Answer From List of Letters	3.4	4.1	5.0	3.9
Mathematical	5.0	7.1	6.9	7.6

Because of the length of time the test might take, rest breaks should be provided.

If the test is read aloud, the reader should do the following:

1. Read the entire test, preferably aloud, in advance of giving it to the applicant.

2. Read each question and each choice as clearly as possible. Give special emphasis to words that are printed in capitals, italics, or bold print—and tell the applicant which are given emphasis.
3. In multiple choice questions, be sure to give equal emphasis to each response. If the applicant chooses a response before all possibilities are read, ask if the applicant wants to hear the remaining choices.
4. If the applicant does not respond for a considerable time after reading the question, ask if it should be read again.
5. If the applicant wants to skip a question, be sure to mark it so you can come back to it at the end of the test.
6. Spell any word upon the request of the applicant. Spell out words that sound alike. Example: capitol and capital.
7. Avoid any discussion with the applicant when giving a test.

Applicants should be allowed to use the method of answering that is most convenient: oral, written, or braille writer. If a braille writer is used, the answers can be dictated by the applicant at the end of the test.

Accommodation Ideas. Fortunately, there are many technical devices to aid blind or visually impaired workers, and many are inexpensive. Real-life examples of accommodations for blind employees, published by the American Foundation for the Blind, include the following, as summarized by the author:

1. A blind machinist for Rugby Hydraulics of Rugby, North Dakota, has a job that involves machining parts for hydraulic cylinders. Permitted tolerances allowed are about the thickness of a human hair. The accommodation necessary for her to perform: a braille micrometer to measure the diameter of metal shafts. The current cost of a braille micrometer is $150 to $250, depending upon the type needed.
2. A blind electrical engineer for a phone company has performed well for many years. In addition to receiving excellent performance evaluations, he redesigned a piece of equipment that saved his company a substantial amount of money. The accommodation necessary for him to perform: a braille terminal for his computer. Such terminals can be purchased for less than $500.
3. A DuPont employee who lost his sight because of an optic nerve tumor was away from work only four months while he recovered from an operation. He returned to his job as a

computer programmer after receiving government-provided job training. The accommodation provided by the company: a voice synthesizer for his computer to allow it to "talk." The current cost of a computer voice synthesizer runs from under $500 to about $1,200.

Other examples of technical devices that may be used to accommodate blind employees include:

- Safety saw guide for blind carpenters. Cost: Less than $25.
- Talking calculator. Cost: Under $40.
- Telephone that stores 100 names and 200 phone numbers and will automatically dial the number(s) upon a spoken command and the name of person to be called. Cost: Under $200.
- Computer printer that simultaneously prints in braille and regular print. Cost: $900.
- Portable, pocket-size speech synthesizer for a blind person to carry and attach to various computers. Cost: $150.
- Complete computer system including printer and software that allows a blind person to do anything on a computer that a sighted person can do, including scanning and reading all types of written documents, using the Word Perfect word processing program and sending and receiving fax messages. Cost: $9,000 to $14,000.
- Computer voice commands that work with most popular word processing programs. Cost: $240.
- Voice recognition system that allows one to convert spoken commands into 64 different computer commands. Cost: $150.
- Braille printer for computer. Cost: $995.
- Talking lap computer with Braille command system. Cost: $2795. As an add-on to current computer, $1450.
- The Kurzweil Reading Machine that converts printed words into braille or synthesized speech. In 1976 it cost about $50,000 and could read about 78 words per minute, if the words were perfectly written. By 1988 the cost had decreased to $12,000 and the machine could read 350 words per minute, including carbons, newspapers, and poor photocopies. By 1991 the price dropped to under $8,000 for a handheld unit, while the most expensive unit remained at almost $12,000. The price should continue to drop as quality improves.
- Tape measure that talks. Cost: Under $100.
- Braille pocket folding tape measure. Cost: $13.

- Talking wristwatch. Cost: $85.
- Talking smoke alarm that produces a loud noise, followed by prerecorded verbal instructions. Cost: $55.
- Money identifier that allows customers to insert bills into a small machine that checks to see that the bills are not counterfeit and signals the employee as to their denominations. Cost: Under $900.
- Talking cash register. Cost: $2,590.
- Various talking measuring tools. Cost: $100 to $400.
- Talking tachometer. Cost: $450.
- Device to attach to any electrically-driven visual meters such as test equipment, automotive testing equipment, or electronic dials. Cost: $225. For a version that can be attached to four different visual meters, add $100.

Examples of technical devices for employees with serious vision problems who are not totally blind include:

- Illuminated magnifiers. Cost: From $20 to $50.
- Magni-focuser that is worn in a method similar to a headband. Cost: Under $20.
- Combination lamp and magnifying glass. Cost: $35.
- Enlarged, easy-to-read numbers that fit over a touchtone phone. Cost: Under $13.
- Large print display processors added to desktop computers to allow magnification from 2 to 16 times normal-size print. Cost: From $150 to $2,500, depending upon brand and features desired. An optical scanner that reads books, reports, or papers can be added. Cost: $500 to $800.
- Portable print enlarger with handheld scanner to enlarge any written work. Cost: $950 to $1785.
- Electric typewriter that types double-size letters. Cost: $325.

Two important nontechnical accommodations that are vital to the successful employment of visually impaired and blind employees are job orientation and the education of supervisors and co-workers.

A blind or visually impaired person needs extra time and assistance in becoming oriented to the workplace. The new employee should be shown around the office, sales floor, assembly line, or other place of work. Everything should be described in detail. The person should be walked through the premises so that he or she can learn how to walk in and out of the workplace, get to the restroom, and otherwise move about the workplace. The location of tools, office supplies, and similar items should be explained, and the employee should be encouraged to touch each of the items to allow a physical illustration of their locations.

Once the employee begins work, supplies and equipment the blind employee must use, including filing cabinets, tape dispensers, tools, and phones, should not be moved from one place to another unless necessary. If moved, inform the employee.

Co-workers should be introduced one at a time with a short conversation so that the new employee can learn to associate each co-worker's name and voice.

Supervisors and co-workers should be informed of the new employee's needs and qualifications before the employee begins work. Cooperation will be much easier if all those who will work with the employee know and understand the situation in advance. Simply throwing a blind or visually impaired employee into a work situation may cause resentment, especially if those working around the employee are asked to help the employee. However, if the vision problem is not obvious, co-workers should not be informed of the disability until after the visually impaired person has voluntarily disclosed the problem to them.

One method of employee education is to have employees simulate blindness for an hour or so while on the job. Blindfold employees (one at a time—having all do this at the same time can be dangerous), and let them attempt to perform their normal duties. If this procedure is inappropriate for co-workers, at least have employees in the personnel or human relations department, as well as supervisors who might deal with blind and visually impaired applicants, try it. This should be done as a general educational activity unrelated to any specific visually disabled person.

Supervisors and employees need to learn many of the methods of dealing with a blind or visually impaired person mentioned under the subsection on interviewing.

If the visual problem is obvious or the disabled person has voluntarily disclosed the disability, encourage co-workers to engage in job-swapping when they notice certain tasks that cause difficulty for the visually impaired worker. Supervisors can help by suggesting minor exchanges of duties. For example, an office supervisor might suggest that a sighted worker obtain needed supplies for a blind worker in exchange for the blind worker answering phone calls.

Some helpful physical accommodations in the workplace may include the use of tactile (raised) or braille lettering on files, bins, and storage containers. Raised edges on desks and tables to prevent items from falling to the floor and railings on staircases may also be helpful. The employee may be able to give other helpful suggestions, especially after he or she has performed the job for a week or two and experienced specific problems in the workplace. Additional information about physical accessibility is given in Chapter 2, "Major Changes to Conform to the Law."

Sources of Information Used in This Section:

A Good Employee is Capable, Conscientious & Productive and *Creating Careers for Blind People: Rehabilitation and Technology*, American Foundation for the Blind, 15 West 16th Street, New York, NY 10011, phone (800) 232-5463. Contact their National Consultant on Employment at the same address, phone (212) 620-2000.

Have You Considered. . . . ?, Job Opportunities for the Blind (JOB), 1800 Johnson Street, Baltimore, MD 21230, phone (800) 638-7518 or (301) 659-9314.

Putting Disabled People in Your Place: Focus on Blind and Vision-Impaired Individuals, Mainstream, Inc., 3 Bethesda Metro Center, Suite 830, Bethesda, MD 20814, phone (301) 654-2400.

Nester, *Employment Testing for Handicapped Persons*, Public Personnel Management Journal (Winter 1884), pp. 419–424.

Suggestions for the Examiner: Testing Applicants with Vision Impairments, In the Mainstream (July-Aug. 1988) (MIN. Report #5).

Other General Sources of Information: *(See also pp. 231–32)*

National Association for Visually Handicapped
22 West 21st Street-6th Floor
New York, NY 10010
(212) 899-3141

IBM National Support Center for Persons With Disabilities
P.O. Box 2150

Atlanta, GA 30055
(800) 426-2133

Provides information on computers, software, and technical devices to accommodate blind or visually impaired workers. The majority of recommended products are not sold by IBM.

BLOOD CLOTS. See Heart and Circulatory Problems.

BRAIN INJURY

The Problem: Almost one million Americans suffer from the effects of brain injuries. Over 400,000 new injuries serious enough to require hospitalization occur each year. A majority are caused by automobile accidents in which young males are most likely to be involved.

Two major types of brain injuries occur. Penetrating injuries are caused by a bullet or sharp object that actually pierces the skull and enters the brain. This type of injury often causes problems that last for years. A study by the Veterans Administration of people who had completed medical treatment and no longer had any medically recognized symptoms of brain injury found that 80 percent still had constant headaches.

The second type, closed head injuries, are more common and are caused by collision between the head and some object. Obviously, some closed head injuries are minor, while others are serious. Outcomes vary in type, intensity, and length of disability.

Symptoms can vary greatly, including loss of muscle control, epilepsy, personality changes, deafness, and facial tics.

Rehabilitation and Return to Work. Because each case is different, it is impossible to predict when, or even if, a person with a serious brain injury can return to work. Statistically, a National Institute of Neurological and Communicative Disorders and Stroke study found that of those experiencing a severe brain injury, 50 percent showed good recovery after three months, while another 30 percent showed considerable improvement. A study by the University of Virginia Medical Center found that a surprising number of people with seemingly minor head injuries were unable to work for several months.

Persons with severe brain injuries who are most likely to return to work are younger employees who are employed in technical or managerial positions. Employees over 45 years of age, particularly blue-collar workers, are the most unlikely to return to work.

A frequent problem encountered by people with serious head injuries is difficulty with thought processes and short-term memory. The employee may have a problem in understanding and remembering verbal instructions or other spoken information. Possible related problems include inflexibility of thought and occasional poor judgment. Many of these problems will not be recognized by the employee until after returning to work. While these problems may be permanent, most are temporary.

Professional and managerial employees are most likely to return to work after a serious brain injury. Difficulty encountered in return to work is created because the abilities most affected by a brain injury—memory and thought processes—relate directly to the requirements of the job. Because of this, lawyers, accountants, managers, and other professional employees may have serious problems during their first few weeks back at work. A lawyer may be unable to follow lengthy arguments, an insurance agent may have problems comprehending a list of conditions, and an accountant may have problems with mathematical calculations. The inability to do these things often causes irritability, fatigue, anxiety, and depression.

Accommodation Ideas. Upon return to work or entry into a new job after a serious brain injury, the employee's supervisor should be informed of the medical problem and asked to comply with the following steps for accommodation of the brain-injured person:

1. Try to use a balanced approach in encouraging good performance. While poor performance should not be ignored simply because the employee has a medical problem, the employee should not be constantly criticized or pushed to do better. Quietly offer criticism and suggestions, and let the employee know the supervisor understands some of the employee's problems and cares about the employee as a person.
2. Consider the amount of work given to the employee, the rate at which the employee will have to work, and the complexity of the work. Remember that the employee will have problems in processing information quickly, and often has a short-term memory loss.
3. Establish a daily routine for the first few weeks whereby the employee does the same, simple-as-possible tasks each day.

4. If possible, use visual cues to augment spoken language. This is one situation in which a picture actually may be worth a thousand words. For professionals, try to convey information in writing. If major oral instructions or information are given, try to follow it up with a written memo.

5. Minimize confusion in the employee's immediate work area. Loud noise, people constantly coming and going, and other disruptions should be avoided if at all possible. Some people recovering from brain injuries even have problems with messy offices or plaid wallpaper.

6. Ideally, a brief explanation to co-workers concerning the employee's condition and need for accommodation should be given. Co-workers can then be enlisted in aiding the brain-injured worker by doing such things as being quiet or remaining low key when around the employee, at least for the first few weeks. However, informing co-workers of an employee's disability is not provided for in the Americans With Disabilities Act. It should be reasonably safe, however, to arrange such accommodations if the employee has agreed to disclosure of the disability in order to make arrangements with co-workers.

7. If the brain-injured employee is new to the job, a written job analysis or videotape of the duties may help the worker understand the job duties.

Other possible accommodations include furnishing the employee with a pocket computer to do simple tasks of calculation or recall, supplying printed forms such as appointment books or priority lists so everything can be written down, and rearranging the employee's work schedule. For example, if the brain-injured person is a professional person who is scheduled to see various people throughout the day, such as a lawyer or manager might do, arrange appointments with 10- to 15-minute breaks between them to allow the employee to write lists of what transpired during the last appointment or what should be covered in the next appointment.

Additional possible accommodations, depending upon their cost, availability, and reasonableness, are to give the employee a permanent or temporary private office, make minor adjustments to the employee's work schedule so that rush hour traffic may be avoided, transfer the employee to a quieter area or to a job involving more routine, structured work, or similar adjustments. Be creative. Even accommodations that cost money or cause some difficulties to the company may be worth it in order to retain a good employee. Some examples of accommodations under the section entitled **SPINAL CORD INJURY AND WHEELCHAIR USERS** may also be useful where brain injuries are involved.

Because some employees will not recognize their work problems until after they return to work, be prepared for a request for a second leave of absence, as well as anger caused by frustration with the job. Apathy and depression are also quite common. The employer, personnel office, or supervisor should watch for signs of these problems and consider a referral to mental health professionals.

A relatively new concept used in accommodating brain-injured employees when they first return to work is to use a "job coach." The job coach is an individual assigned to plan accommodations and work with the brain-injured worker, the supervisor, and if necessary, co-workers. The job coach can be a member of the company's human relations staff or a part-time outside consultant trained in vocational rehabilitation. The job coach analyzes the job and breaks it down into components that may easily be accomplished by a returning employee, or taught and accomplished by a new employee. The job coach is then responsible for obtaining the cooperation of management, supervisors, and necessary fellow workers in order to make the accommodations work. The coach advises the employee, helps in early training or retraining, and periodically checks to see that the entry or re-entry to the job is progressing on schedule. Local rehabilitative agencies may furnish job coaches.

Accommodations for brain-injured employees may be a difficult task. However, most of the difficulties involve little in the way of technical devices and costly equipment. The most important aspects of a successful accommodation that may help lead to the employee's full recovery is understanding and making practical adjustments in the work environment.

Sources of Information Used in This Section:

The Office of Scientific and Health Reports of the National Institute of Neurological & Communicative Disorders and Strokes
Building 31, Room 8A06
National Institutes of Health
Bethesda, MD 20205
(301) 496-5751
A pamphlet entitled *Head Injury* was used and is available.

Mainstream, Inc.
3 Bethesda Metro Center, Suite 830
Bethesda, MD 20814
(301) 654-2400
    Publishes *In the Mainstream.* The January-February 1990
issue, pp. 11–12, was used in this section.

Other General Sources of Information: *(See also pp. 231–32)*

National Head Injury Foundation
280 Singletary Lane
Framingham, MA 01701
(617) 879-7473

The National Easter Seal Society
2023 West Ogden Ave.
Chicago, IL 60612
(800) 221-6827 or (312) 243-8400

American Speech-Language-Hearing Association
10801 Rockville Pike
Rockville, MD 20852
(800) 638-8255 or (301) 897-5700

National Institute of Handicapped Research
U.S. Department of Education
Mail Stop 2305
Washington, DC 20202

Clearinghouse on the Handicapped
U.S. Department of Education
400 Maryland Ave, SW
Room 3119, Switzer Building
Washington, DC 20202

BRAIN TUMOR: See Cancer.

BUERGER'S DISEASE: See Heart and Circulatory Problems.

CANCER

    The Problem. There are over five million Americans alive
today who have had cancer. About 70 million Americans will be

treated for cancer during their lifetime. Approximately 80 percent of employed people will return to work after a diagnosis of cancer. However, up to 84 percent of these workers report job problems, and 25 percent report discrimination against them based upon their cancer. The types of discrimination, listed from the most frequent to the least frequent, are denial of new employment, termination from work, transfers to less favorable jobs, demotion or lack of promotion, refusal to accommodate, and adverse fringe benefit changes.

Many who have undergone treatment for cancer are cured of the disease and should not be treated differently than any other worker. However, because they have a past history of a disability, they are protected under the Americans With Disabilities Act.

The groups at greatest risk of employment discrimination based upon cancer are young people with no job experience and those with physically noticeable cancer results. Many who have had cancer report more problems with co-workers than with management or the human relations department.

The physical effects of cancer, mortality, type of treatments, and length of absence from work vary greatly depending upon the type, location, and date of diagnosis. A study by Vincent Mor of Brown University of patients in Rhode Island who had been diagnosed with lung, breast, and colorectal cancer showed that within two months of the original diagnosis 76 percent of blue collar employees and 87 percent of white collar employees were back at work.

Some major types of cancer are as follows:

Skin Cancer: Skin cancers are caused by excessive exposure to the sun or occupational exposures to substances such as arsenic, radium, coal tar, and creosote. About 600,000 new cases are diagnosed each year. With early detection, most skin cancers are curable. However, malignant melanoma skin cancer can involve a spread of the cancer to other parts of the body, and the five-year survival rate is only a little over 80 percent. Skin cancers may be treated with surgery or radiation therapy. Tissue destruction may be treated by the application of heat or by freezing.

Breast Cancer: About 150,900 new cases of breast cancer are diagnosed each year. When caught early it is seldom fatal. Treatment varies from a simple removal of the tumor to a radical mastectomy (removal of the breast and nearby lymph nodes), plus radiation and chemotherapy treatments.

Colon-Rectum Cancer: About 155,000 new cases are diagnosed each year. Surgery is the primary treatment. The cancerous parts of the digestive system are removed by a resection (cutting out the diseased part and sewing the unaffected parts back together), or an ileostomy or colostomy (creating an artificial exit for the intestine). Additional information is given in the section on **DIGESTIVE DISEASES.** Surgery may be followed by radiation treatments or chemotherapy, or both.

Lung Cancer: About 157,000 new cases of lung cancer are diagnosed each year in the United States. Smoking is not the only cause of lung cancer; occupational exposures, especially to asbestos, can cause lung cancer and increase the chance of smokers contracting the disease. Lung cancer may be treated by surgery, radiation, or chemotherapy, or by a combination of these treatments. The survival rate is usually low, although the chance of survival can range up to 37 percent for certain types of lung cancer that are diagnosed in an early stage.

Leukemia: Only about 25,000 new cases are diagnosed each year. Contrary to the public belief that this is a childhood disease, 90 percent of the new cases of chronic leukemia are diagnosed in adults. Chronic leukemia may be controlled for several years with oral medications. Leukemia can be caused by occupational exposure to radiation, benzene, or other chemicals. Survival rates for acute leukemia have increased dramatically in the past two decades. However, it still remains at less than 50 percent. Most cases are treated by chemotherapy, but bone-marrow transplants and other new procedures increasingly are being used.

Brain Tumors: Brain tumors can be malignant (cancer) or benign. The effect of the tumor varies, depending primarily upon the size and location, or whether it is malignant or benign. Tumors can alter emotional moods and cause a person to act in a manner that is sometimes diagnosed as mental illness, rather than a tumor. Early symptoms may include dizziness and lack of coordination. Other symptoms include persistent headaches, visual complaints, weakness, and in some cases, seizures. About 15,600 new cases of brain cancer are diagnosed each year.

Oral Cancer: Almost 30,500 new cases of oral cancer are found each year in the United States. The cases include cancer of the lips, mouth, tongue, throat, or larynx. Treatment is usually by surgery or radiation, or a combination of the two. Surgery can often result in a noticeable disfigurement or a laryngectomy (removal of the larynx) causing major speech difficulties or complete loss of the ability to speak.

Uterine Cancer: Approximately 46,500 new cases are diagnosed each year, consisting of about 13,500 cases of cancer of the cervix, while the remaining are cancers of the endometrium (the lining of the uterus).

Rehabilitation and Return to Work. Although each case differs, there are also general similarities in rehabilitation and return to work based upon the type of cancer. Many people diagnosed with skin cancer will be absent from work for a very short period of time, if at all. However, other treatments may require an extended absence or, more frequently, several short periods of absence for radiation, chemotherapy, or follow-up evaluations.

Employee absences from work due to breast cancer range from just a few days to several months, followed by occasional short absences for radiation treatment or chemotherapy. The mortality rate for colon-rectum cancer has improved greatly in recent years. However, employees will typically have to miss greater periods of work to recover from surgery, as compared to many skin and breast cancer cases.

Leukemia victims and those with brain tumors are returning to work in increasing numbers. Both may require periodic leaves from work for further treatment; however, such leaves are usually brief for chronic leukemia. Acute leukemia treatment may require an employment leave of two to six months for treatment.

Accommodation Ideas. Workers with cancer should be encouraged to return to work as soon as possible, with their physician's consent. Whether a returning employee or a newly hired employee, the employer should cooperate with the employee's physician. If feasible, another physician (such as a company physician in larger corporations) should also be consulted to determine the date of starting work and necessary accommodations. After informing the physician as to the nature and demands of the job involved, the employee's physician and company physician should be asked the following questions:

1. When and under what conditions can the worker return to work? Part-time? Full-time?
2. What physical limitations will the employee have?
3. What accommodations can help?
4. Will there be future absences for treatment?

5. What side effects of any medication or treatment will the worker have?
6. What other health professionals, such as rehabilitation specialists, might be helpful in aiding a successful return to work?

After learning the medical diagnosis and the physicians' answers to the above questions, a team effort consisting of a representative from the human relations office, medical support personnel (a doctor, rehabilitation specialist, or other expert), the employee, and the employee's supervisor may be used to work out the details of a return to work and reasonable accommodations. Consultation with a local or state chapter of the American Cancer Society may also be useful. State vocational rehabilitation agencies and local private rehabilitation agencies may also serve as a source of information concerning accommodations.

Because a major temporary physical problem of cancer victims is weakness and excessive fatigue, a temporary change of job duties may be appropriate. Sometimes this is all that is required. In other cases, only a flexible work schedule is needed.

Employees with cancer require few technical devices or physical accommodations (unless the cancer resulted in amputation or other procedure that results in a major physiological change). However, some necessary accommodations that have been given include a bullhorn so a foreman with cancer of the throat could communicate in an outdoor construction project, equipment to help lift heavy loads, or adequate ventilation and dust control for workers with throat and voice problems.

A major problem some workers with cancer report is co-worker attitudes and actions. A survey conducted by F.L. Feldman for the American Cancer Society found that 10 percent of employees returning to work after a diagnosis of cancer faced outright hostility and mimicry by co-workers, especially if cancer of the head or neck was involved since these cancers (or surgeries) are physically obvious. For example, during an American Cancer Society workshop one participant recounted the story of a governmental employee who returned to work after a laryngectomy. The employee was accommodated by the moving of smokers away from the employee's desk and the provision of humidification equipment. Everything went well the first three days, but by the fourth day the employee broke down crying and was ready to quit. She found that each time she left her desk other employees sprayed the area with Lysol spray because they were desperately afraid of "catching" her disease.

Frequently people with cancer find no overt, open discrimination, but rather isolation caused by other workers physically avoiding them. In addition to the belief of some co-workers that cancer is contagious, even more people feel uncomfortable dealing with cancer victims. Because supervisor and co-worker cooperation is the key to integrating the employees into a job, education is vital.

Employer silence may even be taken as support for discrimination against cancer victims. Unfortunately the ADA prohibits employers from informing co-workers of an individual's disability. Therefore, cancer education of employees should not be given where direct reference to an individual cancer patient is made. However, nothing in the law says an employer cannot give general cancer education at the same time an individual with cancer is hired or returned to a job.

A brief meeting or seminar conducted by management, with a representative of the medical community or the American Cancer Society, may be helpful. If this is not possible, pamphlets or other written materials should be distributed, along with a company policy statement supporting the employment and accommodation of persons who have cancer. Pamphlets and other materials may be obtained from the American Cancer Society.

Many people who have been treated for cancer are cured and need no accommodations. However, where accommodations are needed, even temporarily, they should be decided upon after consultation with the disabled person, a supervisor, and medical or rehabilitative experts.

Informing co-workers of a new or returning employee who has been diagnosed or treated for cancer can be helpful in enlisting their aid in making accommodations and stopping unfounded rumors. However, because the ADA does not provide for telling co-workers about an employee's disability, employers are thus faced with two alternatives concerning informing co-workers. First, let the new or returning employee tell co-workers of the problem, possibly followed by management enlisting co-worker aid. Second, with the permission of the disabled person, ignore the legal provisions and inform co-workers, asking for their help. Employees who may resent and even fear an employee who has had cancer may be quite helpful if they are fully informed and asked to help.

Sources of Information Used in This Section:

Putting Disabled People in Your Place: Focus on Individuals with Cancer Histories, Mainstream, Inc., 3 Bethesda Metro Center, Suite 830, Bethesda, MD 20814, phone (301) 654-2400.

Proceedings of the Workshop on Employment, Insurance and Cancer, 1987, American Cancer Society. Contact your local or state American Cancer Society chapter, or American Cancer Society, 777 Third Ave., New York, NY 10017, or call (800) ACS-2345.

Brain Tumors: Hope Through Research, Office of Scientific & Health Reports, National Institute of Neurological & Communicative Disorders & Strokes, National Institutes of Health, Bethesda, MD 20205.

Other General Sources of Information: *(See also pp. 231–32)*

The American Cancer Society has a large number of booklets, books, tapes, and video cassettes on various cancer topics. Ask for the *Program Materials List, Service and Rehabilitation* for a complete list of available materials. See the address given above.

CARPAL TUNNEL SYNDROME: See Repetitive Motion Injury.

CEREBRAL HEMORRHAGE: See Heart and Circulatory Problems.

CEREBRAL PALSY: See Nerve Disease.

CERVICAL OSTEO-ARTHRITIS: See Arthritis.

CIRCULATORY PROBLEMS: See Heart and Circulatory Problems.

COLOSTOMY: See Digestive Diseases.

CORONARY HEART DISEASE: See Heart and Circulatory Problems.

CROHN'S DISEASE: See Digestive Diseases.

CUMULATIVE TRAUMA DISORDERS: See Repetitive Motion Injury.

CUSHING'S SYNDROME: See Addison's Disease.

DEAFNESS AND HEARING IMPAIRMENTS

The Problem. Estimates of the number of hearing impaired people in the United States range from 15 to 21 million. The number of totally deaf individuals is thought to be anywhere from 350 thousand to 2 million. There are four types of hearing loss: conductive, sensorineural, mixed, and central.

Conductive hearing losses are caused by diseases or obstructions in the middle or outer ear. This condition often is not severe and can be aided by the use of a hearing aid, medicine, or surgery. Conductive hearing loss usually causes a similar reduction of hearing at all frequencies.

Sensorineural hearing losses result from damage to the sensory hair cells of the inner ear or the nerves connected to the inner ear. This may cause a person to have difficulty hearing certain frequencies of sound, but not others. Or sound may be heard, but it is severely distorted. The problem may be so severe that hearing aids will not be effective. Certain types of noises, e.g., from selected motors, air conditioners, and machinery, may be especially irritating.

Mixed hearing losses occur in the outer, middle, and inner ear, combining the problems discussed above.

A central hearing loss results from damage or impairment of the central nervous system, either in the pathways to the brain or in the brain itself. This type of disorder is the most likely to cause total deafness, often from birth.

There are numerous causes of deafness. About 50 percent of the cases of total deafness are probably caused by genetic factors, thus an inherited condition. Other causes of deafness include accidents, illness, side effects of taking legal drugs, Rubella or other viruses, problems in delivery at birth, tumors, and exposure to loud noises. There is absolutely no connection between intelligence and hearing ability. However, people who have been deaf from birth or from an early age may be less knowledgeable than their hearing peers due to problems in language, speech, and education.

As with other disabilities, the practical effect of a hearing loss varies greatly from person to person, depending upon the type of hearing loss, severity of loss, educational opportunities, and other factors. However, the largest differences are based upon the time of the hearing loss. Prelingual deafness, occuring at birth or before learning to speak, usually causes the most severe problems. Prelingual deaf people may be unable to speak. Those that do speak often produce unusual sounds or variations in the loudness of their speech. Since they have not heard speech from others, they cannot adequately speak themselves.

Many people with prelingual deafness do not read and write as quickly and competently as similar people without a hearing loss.

Since deaf persons have often communicated visually and thought more in terms of visual signs, rather than words, their reading and writing may be different. For example, sign language has its own vocabulary, grammar, and syntax, so a prelingual deaf person may write letters and reports that conform to sign language, but violate general principles of good English. Sign language is actually another language, just like a foreign language, so it is understandable that some deaf people have difficulty in reading and writing in English.

Sign language, officially "American Sign Language" (ASL), is only one type of communication used by those with profound hearing loss. Some use "fingerspelling," which is somewhat like writing in the air with one's fingers. Most deaf people who became deaf later in life can speak, and many deaf people use a combination of speech or even "pidgin" speech, ASL, fingerspelling, and other gestures.

The most common misconception about deaf people's communication skills is that they can "lip read." While many deaf people can lip read or speech read to some degree, their ability varies widely and lip reading is difficult, even for the best lip readers. Only about 30 percent of English sounds are visibly apparent (shown by movement of the mouth), and 50 percent of these lip movements are identical when saying different words. For example, the words "kite," "height," and "night" produce the same physical movements of the lips. The extent of the ability to lip read has no correlation to intelligence. Some people are just naturally better at it than others, just as some people are naturally better at sports than others.

Many deaf people use a variety of communication aids, including lip reading, signing, and written notes. It is best to ask the individual which types of communication he or she uses.

Accommodation Ideas. Reasonable accommodations must start in the hiring process. Job application forms should not have complicated instructions (remember that English is sometimes like a foreign language), but if they do, a person should be available to help the hearing-impaired person fill out the form.

Companies desiring to find qualified hearing-impaired and deaf job applicants, especially for technical, professional, and managerial positions, can contact the Placement Office, Gallaudet University, 800 Florida Avenue, NE, Washington, DC 20002, or the National Technical Institute for the Deaf, Rochester Institute of Technology, 1 Lomb Memorial Drive, Rochester, NY 14623. Most states have state-sponsored schools for the deaf that often graduate people who are potential applicants for clerical, blue collar, and other job positions.

Interviewing. If an interviewer knows an applicant is hearing impaired, special arrangements should be made. Often the job applicant will volunteer the fact of his or her hearing impairment, or there may be an indication of it, such as a job application form stating that the applicant is fluent in American Sign Language. If possible, write the applicant and ask what accommodations are needed in an interview.

One of the most requested accommodations is to have a sign language interpreter available. Often the applicant brings an interpreter, but if not, the company should provide one. To find a qualified sign language interpreter, contact your local vocational rehabilitation agency, or The National Registry of Interpreters for the Deaf, Inc., 814 Thayer Avenue, Silver Spring, MD 20910, phone: (301) 588-2406.

If an interpreter is used during the job interview, do not speak to the interpreter. Communicate directly with the applicant, keeping eye contact. Do not ask any questions of the interpreter, especially as to the job qualifications of the applicant. Have the applicant sit directly in front of you, and be sure that there is no window or bright lights behind you. If possible, have the light source behind the applicant so that it is directed toward your face, making your face easy to see. Speak in a normal fashion, not loudly.

Do not place anything in your mouth while talking, and be sure your hands stay away from your face. Be animated in your speaking with normal facial expressions, hand gestures, and body language. If you must stop the interview to answer the phone or respond to a knock on the door, explain to the applicant what you are doing. Don't just pick up the phone or get up from your seat. If no interpreter is present, closely watch the applicant's face and expressions to determine if you are being understood. If not, repeat your statements. If this does not work, use paper and pencil.

If you have problems in understanding the applicant's speech, give yourself some time to become adjusted to it by asking some general, open-ended questions of minor importance so that you can listen and learn the speech. For example, ask about the weather, yesterday's ball game, or other general "ice-breakers." Be sure to refrain from asking about how they became deaf, the extent of their general problems of deafness, their age, their family, or other issues that might later be used to show discrimination based upon disability, age, race, or other illegal factors.

If you continue to have problems in understanding important statements, such as information about the applicant's training or qualifications, ask the applicant to repeat the information. Don't be embarrassed. You need this information in order to give the applicant a fair chance for the job. The applicant is accustomed to being asked to repeat things.

Testing. Hearing-impaired applicants may need extra help or modifications in completing any tests. Even written tests may be difficult for prelingual deaf applicants due to their problems with the English language.

Applicants with hearing impairments or deafness occurring during their teenage or adult years should have no problems with written exams. However, verbal exams and verbal instructions for written exams may need to be written. Prelingual deaf applicants should be asked if they will need extra time to complete an exam, or if they prefer to have verbal or written tests translated into sign language.

Accommodations. If the applicant is hired for a job that requires training, the accommodations listed above, such as light sources and interpreters, should be continued into the training sessions. Additionally, the new employee should be given extra time and assistance in reading written training materials.

Accommodations on the job may consist of a combination of technical devices and common sense changes in procedure. The most overlooked accommodation is the provision of information. Hearing employees gain informal, but essential job information from interaction with other employees and workplace gossip. Employees learn who to see if they need to get effective action on certain problems, who to be nice to, who to avoid, what the "real" company rules are, how to obtain a promotion, and many other things by way of informal oral talks.

Deaf and seriously hearing-impaired employees often fail to obtain this information. For the good of the employer and the employee, a way must be found to communicate this information to hearing-impaired employees.

One method may be to assign a nonhearing impaired employee as a "mentor" to keep the hearing-impaired person aware of informal communications. The key personal attribute of a mentor must be a willingness to help. Therefore, a human relations department staff member or a supervisor should look for volunteers within the organization. If the hearing-impaired employee uses American Sign Language, the company might consider paying for a brief training period in sign language for the mentor. Also, while mentoring should be voluntary, the company may reward the mentor by favorable performance evaluations, pay, or other benefits.

Another inexpensive method of allowing the hearing-impaired person to work better with co-workers and receive important information is to give a brief explanation of the person's hearing problem and provide some simple training for the co-workers. However, this may safely be in conformance with the Americans with Disabilities Act only after the hearing-impaired person has informed co-workers of the disability.

After the hearing-impaired employee has disclosed his or her hearing problem to co-workers, the employees who will work with the hearing-impaired person should be instructed in oral communications by informing them of the guidelines given above for interviewing a hearing-impaired applicant, i.e., talking directly to the person, using gestures, avoiding back lighting, etc. In addition, co-workers should be advised to keep written communications short and simple and to use drawings where helpful, but to never assume the hearing-impaired person wants to communicate only in writing. Hearing-impaired employees should always be asked about their preferred manner of communication.

New accommodation devices for the hearing impaired are being developed at a rapid rate. One may expect that within a few years reasonably priced computer devices that transcribe spoken words into printed words will be available. This will be especially useful for hearing-impaired white collar and professional employees. Some courts are now using computer-aided transcription (CAT) systems that allow the court reporter's transcription to be converted into text that instantaneously appears on a computer screen, plus be saved and printed as a hard copy. Companies who transcribe committee meetings or other programs should consider adding a CAT system if a hearing-impaired person is to attend.

Many severely hearing-impaired persons can now use a wireless FM system whereby the speakers are given a small unit to pick up their voices. The speech is then amplified and sent to a hearing-impaired person's receiver. This system can be used in almost any setting—in meetings, seminars, offices, and on factory floors.

Some other devices that are currently available include Easy Talk, an IBM compatible computer that functions as a regular typewriter in addition to having voice output that allows the hearing impaired to type and the hearing person to listen. The Kurzweil Reading Machine described in the section **BLINDNESS AND**

VISUAL IMPAIRMENTS converts print into braille or synthesized speech.

Safety is one of the most important areas of accommodation for deaf people and others with severe hearing loss. Fire and smoke alarms that have a visual signal such as a flashing bright red light can be purchased for as little as $35. A less efficient alternative is to assign another employee the responsibility of communicating the fire, smoke, or other alarm to each hearing-impaired employee.

Hearing-impaired employees should work in locations where there is good lighting so that they can do partial lip reading. Deaf employees who use sign language can be greatly aided by the training of their immediate co-workers in American Sign Language. The basics of sign language can be learned in just a few hours, so the expense to the company is minimal. A federal agency accommodated a prelingual deaf distribution clerk who was constantly asked the same questions by other employees by providing six small question signs the hearing employees could use to state their questions, and 12 preprinted cards the deaf employee could use in answering.

Over 100,000 TDDs (telecommunication devices for the deaf) are in use today, and companies may both accommodate hearing-impaired employees and offer better service to hearing-impaired customers by furnishing TDDs. Older models were called teletypewriters, or TTYs. A TDD or TTY allows the deaf person to type out a telephone message. In the past it could be used only if the person on the other end of the phone call also had a TDD or TTY to receive the printed message. The Americans with Disabilities Act has changed this restriction by requiring telephone companies to provide relay services whereby a deaf person can use a TDD or type in an outgoing message that is converted by the phone company into a form that may be heard by the recipient of the phone call. Conversely, voice communications to a deaf recipient are relayed from voice to TDD. Therefore, deaf people, as well as those who cannot speak, may use phones in roughly the same manner as people without these disabilities. TDDs and TTYs cost from $150 to over $1,000, depending upon the brand and the number of options added such as a printer or memory.

Although relay services will be available for customers and clients calling a business, a hearing-impaired employee in a professional office, retail store, or service business with a TDD may still increase the company's business since it will allow direct contact by any one of the over 100,000 deaf customers who currently use a

TDD. With prices for TDDs falling and a potential market of millions of deaf and hearing-impaired people, companies may even find it profitable to have a TDD operated by a hearing employee if a deaf employee is not available. Companies who have TDDs should obtain a TDD phone book and have their TDD number listed in it, as well as on company literature and local phone books. The national *Telecommunications for the Deaf, Inc. Directory* may be ordered from Telecommunications for the Deaf, Inc., 814 Thayer Avenue, Silver Spring, MD 20910, phone TDD (301) 589-3006 or voice (301) 589-3786.

Additional devices for the deaf include:

- Flashing lights as a "door bell" or signal for customer service, or placed on doors to warn that someone is approaching from the other side. Cost: $50.
- A vibrator that senses if a person has entered the room, or any room in the building. Cost: $399.
- Telephone flasher that signals when the phone rings. Cost: $24.
- Flashing alarm clock to remind employees of appointments. Cost: $37.

Other accommodation devices are available for employees who are hard of hearing, but not deaf, such as:

- Portable telephone amplifier. Cost: $29.
- Trendline II amplified telephone. Cost: $69.
- High-intensity telephone ringer. Cost: $40.
- Extra volume doorbell. Cost: $24.

Sources of Information Used in This Section:

Deafness: A Fact Sheet, Reasonable Accommodation in the Selection and Employment of the Deaf, and *The Barrier of Deafness,* National Information Center on Deafness, Gallaudet University, 800 Florida Avenue, NE, Washington, DC 20002. Additional publications also available.

Telecommunications Devices for the Deaf: A Guide to Selection, Ordering and Installation, U.S. Architectural and Transportation Barriers Compliance Board, 330 C Street, SW, Room 1010, Washington, DC 20202, phone (TDD or voice) (202) 472-2700.

Putting Disabled People in Your Place: Focus on Deaf and Hard-of-Hearing Individuals, Mainstream, Inc., 3 Bethesda Metro Center, Suite 830, Bethesda, MD 20814, phone (301) 654-2400.

Nester, *Employment Testing for Handicapped Persons*, Public Personnel Management Journal 424–31 (Winter, 1984).

Other General Sources of Information: *(See also pp. 231–32)*

National Institute for the Deaf
Rochester Institute of Technology
Division of Public Affairs, Dept C
One Lamb Memorial Drive
P.O. Box 9887
Rochester, NY 14623
(716) 475-6824
   A Catalog of Educational Print Materials, A Catalog of Captioned Educational Videotapes, and other publications are available.

Alexander Graham Bell Association for the Deaf, Inc.
3417 Volta Place, NW
Washington, DC 20007
(202) 337-5220
   Disseminates various types of information on deafness.

American Deafness and Rehabilitation Association
P.O. Box 55369
Little Rock, AR 72225
(501) 375-6643
   Information concerning services, research, and legislation.

Better Hearing Institute
P.O. Box 1840
Washington, DC 20013
(800) EAR-WELL or (703) 642-0580
   Provides general information about deafness, including amplification assistance.

Deafness and Communicative Disorders Branch
Rehabilitation Services Administration
Office of Special Education & Rehabilitation Services
Department of Education, Room 3316

330 C Street, SW
Washington, DC 20202
(202) 732-1401 or TDD (202) 732-1298
Provides information on rehabilitation services and technical assistance.

National Association of the Deaf
814 Thayer Avenue
Silver Spring, MD 20910
(301) 587-1788
The largest deaf persons membership organization, it can supply addresses of state chapters and general information concerning deafness.

IBM National Support Center for Persons With Disabilities
P.O. Box 2150
Atlanta, GA 30055
(800) 426-2133
Provides information on technical devices to accommodate disabled employees, the large majority of which are not IBM products.

DEPRESSION: See Mental Illness or Disease.

DIABETES

The Problem. Eleven million Americans have diabetes, and half of these people do not even know it. Diabetes is the seventh largest cause of death in the United States and can lead to other medical problems such as eye, kidney, and foot disease, especially if not treated.

Diabetes is a defect in the body's ability to use food for energy, resulting in high blood glucose levels. Five percent of diabetics have Type I diabetes, usually the most serious kind. In the past, Type I diabetes has also been referred to as juvenile or insulin-dependent diabetes. Ninety-five percent have Type II diabetes, previously called adult diabetes or non-insulin-dependent diabetes. However, some Type II diabetics must take insulin injections.

Type I diabetes requires the person to follow a strict diet and take daily insulin injections for his or her entire life. Many Type II diabetics can be treated by diet, exercise, or an oral medication, or a combination of these.

Insulin-dependent diabetics may occasionally have a reaction to insulin injections because the insulin has decreased their blood sugar (glucose level) too low. This is called insulin shock or hypoglycemia. Occasionally, Type II diabetics may also have this reaction, particularly if they have recently adjusted their oral medication or are taking insulin injections. Major contributing factors causing hypoglycemia are irregular meal times or working hours, or increased activity or exercise without a corresponding reduction in insulin dosage or oral medication. Sometimes these factors can be offset by an adjustment of the person's insulin injection schedule.

Hypoglycemia causes weakness, shakiness, and even fainting or loss of consciousness in rare cases. Eating or drinking something with sugar will usually cure the problems within a few minutes. However, any person who loses consciousness should be immediately transported to a hospital. Do not attempt to give sugar if the person is unconscious.

Most diabetic individuals, even insulin-dependent ones, are able to regulate their blood sugars without any work site problems by taking their medication or injecting their insulin at home. However, some insulin-dependent employees may have to self-administer injections while at work.

Accommodation Ideas. Although most diabetic employees need no accommodations, some will. As with other disabilities, possible job accommodations should be discussed with the job applicant or employee who will know best what he or she needs as an individual. However, some common accommodations include allowing the person to work day shifts only, or at least to work a regularly scheduled shift rather than rotating shifts. Changes in schedules can upset the balance the individual has achieved in regulating blood sugar levels. Consistency in meal times is also important.

Allowing the employee some flexibility at work in order to eat a snack is helpful in the occasional situations where the person's blood sugar is running low (hypoglycemia). Consideration should be given to adjusting rest breaks to fit the needs of insulin-dependent employees for testing their blood sugar and injecting any necessary insulin (it only takes a few minutes).

Insulin-dependent diabetics do not have to have a refrigerator to store their insulin, but it must be stored in an area of normal temperatures—about 60 to 75 degrees is best. Insulin and other diabetic supplies should be kept in a dry, secure, and clean location. One especially helpful accommodation to insulin-dependent employees is a clean restroom or other location in which to test their blood sugar and inject insulin. A clean shelf located in the handicapped stall of restrooms allows a person to place their diabetic supplies in a manner that will allow effective blood sugar testing or injection.

Employers with diabetic employees should prepare a plan to handle the extremely rare times a diabetic employee has a coma resulting from very high blood sugar, or severe hypoglycemia resulting from blood sugar that is too low. If the company does not have a medical staff, information concerning emergency action may be obtained from the American Diabetes Association, P.O. Box 25757, Alexandria, VA 22313, phone (703) 549-1500. Interestingly, employees having these reactions may be those who do not know they have diabetes, since those that do know their medical condition are usually controlling it.

There are very few jobs that should be denied diabetic individuals. Most are able to adjust their diabetes to accommodate their jobs. However, a limited number of people with diabetes may have problems with hazardous work or work involving unplanned, irregular hours.

Diabetic individuals who cannot successfully regulate their blood sugar levels, leading to altered states of consciousness, should not work where this can cause a physical danger to the individual or others. For example, diabetic individuals who are subject to periodic bouts of hypoglycemia (low blood sugar) and who work with hazardous machinery may pose a safety hazard if the machinery cannot be shut down for a few minutes. Such individuals will need a few minutes to ingest sugar and wait for it to raise their blood sugar level. However, employers should remember that this extreme condition is uncommon.

Conversely, some diabetics with hyperglycemia (uncontrolled high blood sugar that can lead to a coma)—while rare—are equally dangerous. Other types of jobs where these employees *may* be dangerous include, but are not limited to, bus driving, working directly with hazardous chemicals, construction (where placed in dangerous positions such as steelworkers walking girders), and forklift operators.

However, each case must be looked at individually. One should *not* refuse to place all diabetics or all insulin-dependent diabetics in dangerous jobs. Employees with diabetes are unqualified to work in hazardous jobs only if their own individualized medical conditions make working dangerous. This must be determined on a case-by-case analysis. Generally, freedom from hypoglycemia and hyperglycemia leading to loss of consciousness or convulsions for a period of one year is proof that the individual can effectively control the diabetes and safely deal with dangerous equipment, drive vehicles, and undertake other hazardous jobs.

Diabetes is one health problem in which a company cannot necessarily rely on the medical opinion of the company doctor or the physician conducting a company medical examination. The following fact situation, based upon a real lawsuit, illustrates the problem:

John Jones voluntarily stated in a job interview that he had diabetes. The position was that of a building repairer, which required work in some dangerous areas such as on roofs. The employer had its physician give a medical exam and opinion. The physician recommended against hiring Jones because his blood sugar after fasting was 190, a level the physician thought to show a lack of proper control. The company followed the physician's recommendation. Jones sued the company and produced evidence from two physicians stating that fasting blood sugars of less than 250 usually cause no detectable problems, and levels of under 200 (as with Jones) were reasonably well controlled. The court found the company had illegally discriminated against Jones.

The problem is a split in medical opinion. Some physicians believe that fully controlled diabetics should have fasting blood sugar levels under 120. Other expert physicians feel that 120–150 is desirable in some patients, and that 120–200 is acceptable, while levels under 250 will help avoid current and future health problems. Although it can be argued that fasting blood sugar levels above 150 may increase the chance of later medical problems such as blindness and circulatory disease, the courts say these chances are too speculative to use as a job requirement (see Chapter 3, "Determining Who Is Disabled," and Chapter 6, "Risk of Future Injury: Epilepsy, Diabetes, and Bad Back," concerning the legal standards applied to diabetic job applicants and employees).

The lesson from the above-stated case is that a company cannot safely rely upon the conclusions of any one physician who finds a person unqualified for a job because of diabetes. If the employee disputes the finding, additional medical opinion should be obtained.

Discovery of Diabetes. Progressive companies may benefit themselves and their employees by conducting diabetes screening tests and encouraging self-identification of the disability by those who realize they have diabetes. While diabetes itself may cause no lost time from work, the complications and side effects of diabetes can be costly to the employer and dangerous to the employee. Untreated and uncontrolled diabetes can cause heart and kidney disease, stroke, tooth and gum problems, vision problems, and other conditions that require sick leave, health insurance claims, or other employer expenses. Discovery of the unknown diabetic individuals in the workplace can help reduce these future costs.

A voluntary, well-explained diabetes testing program can save the employer money and the employee his or her health. However, to avoid employee suspicion and invasion of privacy, the program must be carefully and fully thought out, explained, and monitored.

Sources of Information Used in This Section:

Facts About Insulin-Dependent Diabetes, Noninsulin-Dependent Diabetes, The Diabetes Dictionary, and *Diabetes Mellitus,* Public Health Service, National Institutes of Health, U.S. Department of Health & Human Services, available from the National Diabetes Clearinghouse, Box NDIC, Bethesda, MD 20892.

Amanda Patterson, *Employment, the Law, and You,* Diabetes Forecast 28–36 (Aug. 1988). American Diabetes Association, National Service Center, 1660 Duke Street, P.O. Box 25757, Alexandria, VA 22313, phone (800) 232-3472 or (703) 549-1500.

Putting Disabled People in Your Place: Focus on Individuals with Diabetes, Mainstream, Inc., 3 Bethesda Metro Center, Suite 830, Bethesda, MD 20814, phone (301) 654-2400.

Bentivegna v. City of Los Angeles, 694 F.2d 619, 30 FEP Cases 875 (9th Cir. 1982).

Other General Sources of Information: *(See also pp. 231–32)*

American Diabetes Association
P.O. Box 25757
Alexandria, VA 22313
(800) 232-3472 or (703) 549-1500
    Provides information on all types of diabetes.

Juvenile Diabetes Foundation International
432 Park Ave., South
New York, NY 10016

(800) 223-1138 or (212) 889-7575
Provides information on Type I diabetes.

DIGESTIVE DISEASES

The Problem. Digestive diseases, while fairly common, are unknown to persons without the disease because intestinal functions and bowel movements are not socially acceptable topics of conversation. However, reasonable accommodations and job assignments cannot be made until one generally understands some of the major digestive diseases and their effects on people.

The most serious, long-term disabilities include ulcerative colitis, Crohn's disease, diverticulitis, and colon cancer. In addition, a significant number of Americans suffer from irritable bowel syndrome. Complications known as ileus, intestinal obstruction, and peritonitis may be caused. Fissures (cracks in the skin, often near the anus), fistulas (small channels from the intestine that break through the skin), and small open wounds on the abdomen may result. Other diseases, usually more minor, such as diverticular diseases and irritable colon may sometimes turn into a more serious permanent disability.

Inflammatory Bowel Disease (IBD) is a term used to describe two types of serious digestive diseases: ulcerative colitis and Crohn's disease. Ulcerative colitis is a long-term condition in which raw, inflamed ulcers and small abscesses (collections of pus) develop in the inner lining of the large intestine. Crohn's disease is a chronic condition causing inflammation of the digestive system. The inflammation may occur anywhere from the mouth to the anus, but most frequently occurs in the small intestine. These diseases may have similar symptoms. There is no known cause for either disease; however, it is known that they are not communicable diseases.

Diverticulitis, another digestive disease, occurs when small sac-like swellings in the intestinal walls, most commonly in the large intestine, become inflamed. While not as serious as inflammatory bowel disease, it can be a chronic, disabling condition.

Colon cancer may cause some of the same symptoms as IBD. In IBD or cancer the individual may have intestinal pain, cramps, diarrhea, and a general sense of feeling bad. Both colon cancer and IBD may create a blockage of the intestines. Severe cases can cause vomiting, extreme pain, and a rupture of the intestine, causing peritonitis, a life-threatening emergency.

Most colon cancers, many cases of IBD, and some cases of diverticulitis are treated surgically by cutting away the diseased part of the intestine and sewing together the remaining parts (called a resection). In many cases, this causes only a few weeks of hospitalization and recovery with no major symptoms occurring thereafter. The accommodations made by the employer may be limited to a reasonable amount of sick leave and, as given to other returning surgery patients, light work for a temporary period.

Long-term accommodations at work may be necessary when a large part of the individual's digestive system must be removed and an ostomy is created, or when surgery is not performed and the medical condition becomes a serious, long-term, but not life-threatening problem. These are the two conditions employers need to understand.

About one million Americans have an ostomy, and most are fully employable. Because ostomies involve the elimination process for the human body, little is said about them and little is understood by those without an ostomy. An ostomy is created by placing the end of the intestine through an opening in the abdominal wall (called a stoma). Fecal material (body waste) then exits the stoma and empties into an ostomy bag that is attached to the abdomen, rather than by way of the rectum. The bag is necessary since most ostomies do not allow one to control the expulsion of the wastes. The ostomy may be either a colostomy where the end of the intestine placed through the abdominal wall is the large intestine, or an ileostomy where the large intestine has been removed and the small intestine is placed through the abdominal wall. Many urinary ostomies are also created for the expulsion of urine directly into an ostomy bag.

Since the introduction of new bags and devices to hold the bags in place, people with ostomies need little or no accommodation if the surgery has remedied their underlying problems. In fact, while people with ostomies fit the legal definition of a disabled person, you probably know several people with ostomies—you just don't know who they are because they act and appear no different from other people. However, some people with ostomies can be aided by some simple accommodations given later in this section.

Accommodations are most needed by people who have chronic cases of IBD without surgery, or where the surgery does not alleviate the underlying problem, or where multiple surgeries are necessary. IBD is a frustrating disease to the person who has it and may be equally frustrating to the employer. The individual may have constant or periodic bouts of diarrhea, constipation, pain, and fever. The periodic bouts may occur frequently, or just every few months or years, or simply occur two or three times and never be repeated. Sick leave may involve a large amount of time or a number of shorter times. The employee may be hospitalized several times. Sometimes the person will appear sick, and other times the IBD victim will look perfectly healthy.

Although no employer is required to continue employment of a person who misses work so often they violate the company's own sick leave policies and are not doing the work for which they were hired, employers may be able to save the employment of a valuable employee by being as accommodating as possible.

Accommodation Ideas. Colon cancer patients may need the same types of accommodations as general cancer victims if additional radiation or treatment is required (see the section on Cancer). However, most colon cancer patients need no accommodation beyond that needed for normal recovery from a major operation if they have undergone a resection that removed the cancerous area.

Employees with ostomies who have no further serious symptoms of the underlying disease normally can work at any position for which they are qualified. However, many people with ostomies should not engage in heavy lifting because of the danger of hernias occurring at the place of their surgical scars or the stoma area. If the job involves heavy lifting an employer should, with the individual's permission, contact the attending physician, explain the job requirements, and obtain a written statement releasing the individual to do heavy lifting.

People with ostomies may also need a private area in which to empty or change their ostomy bag. Restrooms with at least one closed stall with a shelf are usually sufficient.

Employees with continuing IBD problems must have access to a restroom, and they should be allowed to take short breaks at times of their choosing because diarrhea may be a serious problem. If the job position requires constant attention, such as on an assembly line, the employee may not be qualified. However, before making this determination, one should talk with the individual to determine their need for frequent short breaks and try to work out reasonable arrangements that might be possible. For instance, it may be possible for a supervisor or other worker to substitute for the employee when a break is necessary.

Some employees with IBD may need to take oral medications while on the job, and others will become ill without appearing to be sick. Therefore, the employee's supervisor should be informed of these problems. Supervisors also need to understand that the symptoms of the disease occur at random and without warning. An employee who looks and feels fine today may be sick tomorrow. The employee is not "goofing-off."

Both those with ostomies and those with continuing IBD problems sometimes have more trouble working one shift than another and may have special problems in regulating themselves if their shifts or work times are frequently changed. Although stress does not cause IBD, it may exacerbate the symptoms.

Inappropriate jobs for *some* people with IBD or ostomies may include those involving extensive travel, outdoor work, heavy lifting, strong physical exertion, irregular hours, exposure to extreme heat, and other unusual conditions. However, never assume this to be true. Each case is different. If the job involves any of these factors, ask the individual if he or she can perform without problems. If the individual is unsure, ask if you can contact the individual's physician for advice. An examination and recommendation by a company doctor is not sufficient. Only the individual and the individual's physician who has worked with the patient can really know how the disease affects that individual.

Sources of Information Used in This Section:

Employment of the Ostomate: Well-Adjusted, Healthy Ostomates are Fully Employable, published by the United Ostomy Association, Inc., 36 Executive Park, Suite 120, Irvine, CA 92714.

Questions & Answers about Crohn's Disease and Ulcerative Colitis, and *A Teacher's Guide to Crohn's Disease and Ulcerative Colitis*, Crohn's & Colitis Foundation of America, 444 Park Avenue, South, 11th Floor, New York, NY 10016, phone (800) 343-3637 or (212) 685-3440.

Other General Sources of Information: *(See also pp. 231–32)*

National Digestive Diseases Information Clearinghouse
Box NDDIC
Bethesda, MD 20892
(301) 468-6344

DIVERTICULAR DISEASE: See Digestive Diseases.

DOWN SYNDROME: See Retardation.

DRUG ABUSE: See Alcohol and Drug Abuse.

DUODENAL ULCER: See Ulcer.

DYSCALCULIA: See Learning Disabilities.

DYSGRAPHIA: See Learning Disabilities.

DYSLEXIA: See Learning Disabilities.

DYSPHASIS: See Learning Disabilities.

EMBOLISM: See Heart and Circulatory Problems.

EPILEPSY

   The Problem. Because of numerous misconceptions and out-of-date information, people with epilepsy suffer more from employer and co-worker bias than from the condition itself. Therefore, education of managers, supervisors, and co-workers can be the best accommodation. Because of the confidentiality requirements of the Americans with Disabilities Act, co-worker education should not be given in reference to any specific epileptic employee, but rather as a general subject. The following materials outline some of the *facts* about epilepsy.
   Approximately two million Americans have epilepsy. Although workers with epilepsy seldom need special accommodations and the condition has nothing to do with one's intelligence, aptitude, or vocational ability, several studies show that of any disability, epilepsy is the greatest barrier to employment. Unemployment rates among epileptic persons run as high as 25 percent, with many more underemployed.
   Epilepsy is not a disease, but rather a problem in communication among the brain's nerve cells. Often no cause is known, but sometimes epilepsy is the result of a birth defect, childhood fever, infectious disease, or other identifiable cause.
   Employment discrimination against persons with epilepsy often results from the belief that a person with epilepsy will have a "fit" at work, causing injury to the individual, co-workers, or cus-

tomers, or will have a series of "fits" and medical problems that disrupt work and increase medical bills or workers' compensation premiums.

The truth is that most epileptic employees will *never* have a "fit" or seizure at work. At least 80 percent of all people with epilepsy have the condition completely under control by the use of medication. Many of the 20 percent who occasionally have seizures will tend to have them at night, and even if they occur at work, most seizures are quite mild.

As with many other disabilities, studies prove that workers with epilepsy have slightly better than average safety records. These studies also show good productivity records and good attendance records. All states now allow people with epilepsy to operate a motor vehicle if they are seizure free.

In addition to the moral obligation to avoid discrimination, there is also a legal one. An examination of lawsuits successfully prosecuted under the 1973 Rehabilitation Act and similar state laws show epilepsy to be the single largest category type of impairment leading to a lawsuit. Therefore, employers must be careful in dealing with individuals who have epilepsy. (See Chapter 6, "Risk of Future Injury: Epilepsy, Diabetes, and Bad Back," for additional legal information concerning epilepsy lawsuits.)

Information Concerning Seizures Necessary for Proper Placement and Accommodation. Those who interview and hire new employees need to understand what occurs when seizures happen. Supervisors also need to understand epilepsy so that proper treatment is given if a worker suffers a seizure. Seizures may be classified as one of four types.

Generalized Tonic-Clonic (Grand Mal). This is the type of seizure or "fit" that most people mistakenly think is typical. An individual experiencing a tonic-clonic will become rigid, and if standing, will fall to the ground. Jerking movements usually occur. Urinary incontinence or tongue biting may occur. The entire episode normally lasts 3–5 minutes, but can last from 1–20 minutes. Often the individual returns to complete normalcy at the end of the seizure, except for a very brief period of confusion. However, if the seizure lasts for 10–20 minutes, it may be followed by a few hours of deep sleep or coma. During a seizure the person may appear to turn blue and have breathing problems. However, these problems will rapidly go away at the end of the seizure.

Some people will experience an "aura" or special feeling before the onset of a seizure; therefore, they have a warning whereby they avoid danger by stepping away from a machine or putting down a dangerous instrument.

First Aid.

- Let the seizure run its course. There is nothing that can be done to avoid or stop the seizure.
- Remain calm.
- Remove sharp or hard objects from the person's reach.
- If the person is not on the floor, place him there. Roll the person on his side and place a pillow or rolled up coat under his head.
- Be sure that nothing obstructs the person's mouth. But do *not* place a pencil or any other object in the person's mouth or hold the person's tongue.
- Do *not* give liquids or attempt to restrain the person.
- If the person is unconscious, loosen any tie or other restrictive clothing.
- There is no need to take the person to an emergency room after a seizure unless it lasted over 10 minutes or caused some other injury to the individual.

Generalized Absence (Petit Mal) Seizures. These seizures can be difficult to spot. They consist of brief lapses of attention, sometimes accompanied by a blank stare or rapid eye blinking. Absence seizures last only seconds and require no first aid. The person simply appears to be daydreaming. This condition is rare in adults and more common in children under the age of 15.

Simple Partial Seizures. Consciousness is not lost, but there may be a brief loss of motor control and some minor twitching of the head, legs, arms, fingers, or toes. In other cases the person simply "feels funny" or has some change in their sensory perceptions such as a strange smell or seeing a strange color. These seizures last no more than a few minutes and require no first aid.

Complex Partial Seizures. This type is the most common among adults with epilepsy. The individual will not lose consciousness, and they usually will not twitch or show other physical symptoms. Rather the person will seem disoriented and dazed and may pick at their clothes, chew, mumble, or wander around. The seizure will last only a few minutes.

First Aid. Guide the person away from obvious hazards without using any physical restraint. Stay with the person and talk calmly until the seizure passes.

Remember that not all seizures are the result of epilepsy. If the person is not identified as having epilepsy the chances increase that a seizure is the result of a tumor, heart attack, stroke, diabetes, heat exhaustion, or other cause.

Interview and Job Placement. If it is known that a job applicant has epilepsy, the following questions may be asked to determine if the applicant is qualified for the job and to decide upon proper placement and accommodations:

1. What kind(s) of seizures do you have, and what happens when there is a seizure? A detailed description will help the interviewer understand the individual's problems, rather than relying upon a stereotype.
2. When was your last seizure? Medical opinion, judicial case decisions, and even driver's license requirements normally assume that complete control of seizures for one year prove that no restrictions on the individual's activities or work should be imposed.
3. Do you take medicine to control seizures, and if so, are there any side effects to the medicine that may affect your work or need to be accommodated?

If the person has suffered recent seizures, the following additional questions may be asked:

1. When do the seizures occur? Many people with epilepsy who continue to have seizures have them only while sleeping or just after awakening; thus, no job restrictions should be imposed on them.
2. If the person has daytime or at-work seizures, ask if there is an "aura" or warning so that the individual can step away from dangerous instruments or equipment.
3. Can environmental factors such as flashing lights, certain sounds, or stressful situations cause a seizure? Answers to this question may be useful in job placement.
4. Are you aware of any types of jobs or situations you think you need to avoid?
5. If still unsure as to the individual's abilities and limitation, ask if you can contact the individual's physician. If the answer is yes, have the applicant sign a statement giving permission (a release).

Additional information concerning interviewing job applicants with epilepsy may be obtained by ordering a pamphlet entitled "Interviewing Guide for the Epileptic" from the Epilepsy Foundation of America, 4351 Garden City Drive, Suite 406, Landover, MD 20785, phone (301) 459-3700.

Accommodation Ideas. Although most people with epilepsy have it controlled and need no accommodations, the following ideas may be useful in appropriate cases:

1. Under OSHA standards the company safety officer, if any, and the individual's supervisor must be informed of the epilepsy if it is not under control and a seizure may occur at work. The supervisor should be informed of the different types of seizures and first aid procedures (see the list given above).

2. The supervisor should be encouraged to minimize the worker's stress for the first few days on the job if it is known that stress sometimes causes the person's seizures.

3. Consider assigning the worker to day shifts only if the seizures tend to happen at night or when irregular hours are worked.

4. If seizures are sometimes caused by environmental factors, analyze the job to which the worker will be assigned so as to avoid such factors as flashing lights or other circumstances that induce seizures.

5. Avoid hiring or placing a person to work with dangerous equipment, climb ladders, drive vehicles, and be placed in other situations that might cause danger to the individual or others *only if* the person continues to suffer work time seizures that cause danger without a warning "aura."

6. Ask workers who are likely to suffer noticeable seizures at work to voluntarily inform co-workers of their epilepsy so that the company can give the co-workers facts about epilepsy and seizures. The employer should not, on its own, inform anyone other than safety personnel and supervisors about the individual's epilepsy.

If a seizure does occur without prior notice to and education of co-workers, serious problems can develop that harm both the company work environment and the person with epilepsy. Co-workers who are educated about epilepsy can be helpful and understanding. Those who are not may rely upon old stereotypes and discriminate against the worker. The Epilepsy Foundation of America has several brochures and films that may be used in educating co-workers.

Sources of Information Used in This Section:

Employment Action on Epilepsy, Management by Common Sense, and *Seizure Recognition and First Aid,* Epilepsy Foundation of America, 4351 Garden City Drive, Landover, MD 20785, phone (301) 459-3700 or the Epilepsy Information Line (800) 332-1000.

Putting Disabled People in Your Place: Focus on Individuals With Epilepsy, Mainstream, Inc., 3 Bethesda Metro Center, Suite 830, Bethesda, MD, phone (301) 654-2400.

Other Sources of Information: See Pages 231–32.

FISTULA: See Digestive Diseases.

GALLSTONES

The Problem: The gallbladder is a small, pear-shaped sack located below the liver on the right side of the abdomen. Its function is to store and secrete bile into the intestine to aid in digestion. Gallstones are clumps of solid matter that range from the size of a piece of sand to an egg. Millions of people have gallstones, and many will never have any problems from them. However, others develop problems when the stones travel into the bile ducts, causing severe pain. Blockages may also occur that may be life threatening if not removed.

Treatment and Accommodations. Gallstones may be treated by surgery, endoscopic manipulation, drugs, and shock wave therapy. There is some medical controversy about the use of drugs and shock wave therapy. Although patients subjected to these treatments will miss no work, or only a very few days of work, the efficiency of these methods is questionable.

The standard procedure, surgery, often requires a hospital stay of five to seven days, and a home recovery period of one or two months.

The only accommodations employees need for gallstone problems is understanding and some temporary flexibility in work time when the first attacks of severe pain occur. The attacks can last several hours and come at unexpected times, and they are normally so severe that the person cannot work. While sick leave of a few days to a couple of months may be needed for medical treatment, there are no additional accommodations needed after the employee returns to work.

Sources of Information Used in This Section:

Hall, *Gallstones* (1987), National Institute of Diabetes and Digestive and Kidney Disease, National Institutes of Health, U.S. Department of Health and Human Services, Building 31, Room 9A04, 9000 Rockville Pike, Bethesda, MD 20892.

Other Sources of Information: See Pages 231–32.

GASTRIC ULCER: See Ulcer.

GRAVES DISEASE

The Problem. Graves disease, also referred to as hyper-thyroidism, is a disorder causing the thyroid gland to continuously produce large quantities of its own hormones. This may result in a person becoming fidgety and anxious, tired but unable to sleep, and have trembling hands. It may also cause one to become insensitive to cold, perspire most of the time, and lead to arguments about the proper temperature of a room. The heartbeat may become irregular and much faster, causing palpitations and fluttering in the chest. Attacks of diarrhea also may occur as well as muscular weakness and eye problems.

Treatment and Accommodations. There are three possible treatments: (1) Take tablets that contain antithyroid drugs for up to one year. Future relapses are common and require additional periods of taking the tablets. (2) Have an operation to remove the thyroid gland. While this usually cures the problem, it may result in hypothyroidism. The symptoms are the exact opposite of Graves disease—body processes, including the heartbeat slow down, a person feels cold even in warm temperatures, etc. Treatment consists of taking pills containing synthetic thyroid hormones. (3) The most common remedy consists of taking radioactive iodine that concentrates in the thyroid gland and slows the overactivity. Occasionally, too much iodine collects in the gland, requiring the individual to take the synthetic thyroid pills.

Graves disease requires no employer accommodations other than temporary flexibility in work time to allow the employee to undergo medical tests, receive an injection of iodine, or undergo surgery. Surgery patients can be expected to return to work in a very short time.

Once the diagnosis and treatment of Graves disease or its opposite condition, hypothyroidism, have begun, there should be no stoppage of work performance and no restrictions on the type of work performed.

HARDENING OF THE ARTERIES: See Heart and Circulatory Problems.

HEADACHE, CHRONIC

The Problem. Because almost everyone has headaches, many of which are not severe or long-lasting, people with severe headaches are sometimes treated with little sympathy or concern. However, like other medical problems, headaches vary greatly in intensity, frequency, and cause. A Harris Poll found that 45 million Americans suffer from chronic, recurrent headache and industry loses at least $55 million a year due to absenteeism and medical expenses.

Headaches may be classified into three main types:

Migraine. Normally beginning as a dull pain, it may progress to a severe, throbbing pain that usually occurs on just one side of the head. Ten to 15 percent of the cases are preceded by an "aura," consisting of vision problems that occur 10 to 15 minutes before the onset of the headache. Migraine headaches often first occur between the ages of 12 and 30. Classic migraines usually last up to four hours, while common migraines last from 24 to 72 hours. More women suffer from migraine headaches than do men. Migraines can be totally disabling during the period of the headache. They may cause nausea and vomiting, as well as visual problems.

Tension. Although this is most common type of headache, many are not disabling. However, some do cause a substantial impairment. Tension headaches are usually dull; however, some people will experience sharp, knife-like pains. Beginning any time of the day, the headaches can last from a few hours to a few weeks. Tension headaches may be accompanied by nasal stuffiness and redness of the eyes (often just one eye).

Cluster. This is the least common of the types of headaches, but one of the most disabling. The condition is rarely found in women. The onset of cluster headaches often occurs between the ages of 25 and 40. Frequently occurring at night, the pain is deep, burning, and excruciating—so much so that some victims may be suicidal. The attacks may occur only one or twice a day for just a few days each year, or they may occur four times a day for four to eight weeks at a time. Extreme cases range up to 14 attacks per day for an extended period of time. People with cluster headaches may also have stiffness of the neck and shoulder aches. During the period of attack, usually from 15 to 45 minutes, the person will probably be unable to engage in effective job performance.

Treatment and Accommodation. Although common headaches may be successfully treated with over-the-counter painkillers, other cases may require rehabilitative treatment and various drugs. Because headaches have little or no physical evidence that can be detected in a brain scan or other diagnostic procedures, the medical community still knows relatively little about the exact causes of various headaches.

It is generally agreed that migraine headaches may be caused by fatigue, stress, hypoglycemia, diet, bright sunlight, or hormonal changes. Cluster headaches may be caused by alcohol and some chemicals. Tension headaches may occur because of stress, fatigue, emotional state, or for no obvious reason. In addition to drugs, treatment consists of removing or lessening the possible causes of the headache.

Successful employer accommodations may include being flexible when employees suffer attacks of severe headaches. Work schedule adjustments, temporary part-time work, flexible day-to-day working hours, and similar arrangements may be helpful.

Migraine and tension headaches may be reduced in severity or frequency by taking steps to reduce fatigue and stress resulting from the employee's job. Some example actions include the following:

- Transferring the worker to a less competitive, stressful position
- Changing the employee's location at work to a quiet area of the workplace
- Allowing the worker to go on flextime, giving them some control over their work schedule
- Referring the employee to a pain clinic or other medical facility
- Allowing release time for stress therapy and counseling services

Exposure to workplace chemicals or other substances may be a suspected cause of any type of headache that begins after the worker is originally hired by the employer. Work exposure may be particularly suspect if the headaches tend to occur only at work, or began after introduction of new substances such as paints or chemicals. Temporarily changing the employee's work location or exposure to various chemicals and other substances might pinpoint the problem. If a workplace exposure is suspected, employers should engage in extensive work to locate and remove the source because the headaches may not only cause absenteeism and health insurance claims, but also result in a workers' compensation claim.

Sources of Information Used in This Section:

Spunt, *Headache: Classification, complications, and treatment*, Drug Topics (Apr. 9, 1990), pp. 66–75.

Derman, *Old, Newer, and New Treatments*, Consultant (Sept. 1988), pp. 31–39.

Clark, *Headaches*, Newsweek (Dec. 7, 1987), pp. 76–82.

Other Sources of Information: See Pages 231–32.

HEARING IMPAIRMENTS: See Deafness and Hearing Impairments.

HEART ATTACK: See Heart and Circulatory Problems.

HEART AND CIRCULATORY PROBLEMS

The Problem. Although there are many different types of heart and circulatory problems, the considerations employers must apply in hiring an applicant, returning an employee to work, and making accommodations are similar. A few of the most common heart and circulatory problems include the following:

Coronary Artery Disease (hardening of the arteries). Fatty deposits form in the arteries that supply blood to the heart, thus narrowing the passageways. Also, the blood may form a clot (thrombus) that blocks the artery. The resulting strain causes angina (heart pain) or, with total blockage, a heart attack.

Heart Attack. The most common cause of a heart attack is a blockage of one of the coronary arteries (see above). Two out of three who have heart attacks recover, and if the patient lives over two hours, chance of recovery is very high. Treatment with medicine or surgery may be necessary to reduce the risk of future heart attacks.

High Blood Pressure (Hypertension). Abnormalities in the blood vessels cause the blood to be pumped through the circulatory system under high pressure, thus causing damage leading to a number of serious arterial problems. Although it is important to monitor and control to avoid future arterial problems, high blood pressure has no symptoms, and thus necessary treatment may be delayed.

Cardiac Arrest (Ventricular Fibrillation). In cardiac arrest the heart stops and the brain no longer gets a supply of blood. The cause is normally some other disease, especially coronary artery disease. With quick response by trained medical personnel, there should be no permanent damage or disability.

Heart Failure. This medical term refers to a heart that is not working effectively, not a heart that has completely shut down. This is normally a complication of some other heart or circulatory problem such as coronary artery disease, hypertension, or heart valve disorders.

Hardening of the Arteries (arteriosclerosis). Noncoronary hardening of the arteries may occur in any part of the body, but is most frequent in the legs. The tendency to have a build up of fatty deposits sufficient to cause hardening of the arteries appears more in older people. It may cause severe leg pain and may result in amputation of the limb if not treated.

Pulmonary Embolism. A blood clot breaks loose, often from a deep-vein thrombosis (an area of blood clotting that is often in the leg), and travels through the blood stream. If large, it may become lodged in an artery in the lung, cutting the supply of fresh, oxygen-rich blood to the heart and other organs. Almost 30 percent of patients die. However, after recovering from medical treatment, the remaining patients should be able to lead normal lives.

Phlebitis. An inflammation of a vein, it is usually caused by infection or injury. Blood clots form and attach to the side of veins, often in the legs. Although it can lead to blood poisoning, and there is a slight chance the clot might break off and enter the heart or lungs, most conditions clear up in a week or so. Prolonged cases may require drugs or surgery.

Aneurysms. A permanent swelling of an artery due to a weakness in the wall, aneurysms are most common in the aorta and arteries of the brain. They lead to poor blood circulation, possible bursting, or pressure on nearby organs.

Raynaud's Disease. The disease affects the fingers, and occasionally toes, causing them to become extra sensitive to cold. The condition gradually worsens, sometimes causing loss of feeling. It may also lead to the complete loss of blood supply, creating gangrene that requires amputation.

Temporal Arteritis. A chronic inflammation of the arteries, it blocks the flow of blood. When this occurs in the arteries beside the brain, a stroke may result.

Stroke. Considered medically to be a disorder of the neurological system, it is covered in this section because it is caused by circulatory problems, and the recovery and accommodation process may be similar to some types of heart and circulatory problems. There are two types of strokes. The first is caused by an arterial blockage, depriving blood supply to part of the brain. The second is a cerebral hemorrhage, where blood seeps into the brain from a burst artery. Surgery and anticoagulant drugs are common treatments.

Many other heart and circulation problems may occur. The causes are many, including high blood pressure, smoking, high cholesterol, infections, syphilis, and inherited traits.

Most people who recover from heart and circulatory problems can enter or return to the workforce. One study showed that 85 percent of employed people who had mild to moderate heart attacks returned to work. Even some of the most serious stroke victims can return to work after rehabilitation. (See Chapter 5, "Making Accommodations for Disabled Employees," for a story of a blue collar worker with a severe stroke returning to work.)

Accommodations. The crucial phase of an employer's accommodation to a person who has recently suffered serious heart, circulatory, or stroke problems concerns the timing of a return to work and the work conditions during the first few weeks. Employers should do the following:

1. Remember that many people with heart surgery are in much better physical shape after surgery than before. Don't assume they will have future medical problems.
2. Contact the patient's family or doctor shortly after any medical problem develops to determine the best time to talk with or visit the patient.

3. At an appropriate, but early time, call or visit the patient, explaining any company fringe benefits such as medical care, disability leave, etc. Tell the individual that the company is expecting a return to work, if possible. Informing the patient of the company's concern and desire to return the patient to work can do wonders for the individual's recovery.

4. In consultation with the patient, attending physician, and other relevant people such as a rehabilitation specialist, project a planned date for the employee's return.

5. If possible, offer a phased-in return to work. For example, working half-days the first two weeks, full time with no overtime for a few weeks, then full return.

6. Consider any temporary or permanent work duty changes that might lessen tension and stress. However, if this changes the job position, status, or pay of the employee, don't do this without the complete (and signed) agreement of the employee. Otherwise, it may be illegal discrimination based on the employee's disability.

7. If the job involves manual labor, heavy lifting, extensive travel, or other unusual physical demands, consult with the employee's doctor as to work limitations.

8. Before the actual date of a return to work, be sure to explain the exact duties of the job to the employee's physician and have the employee obtain a physician's statement authorizing a return to work.

9. Learn from the patient and physician of any warning signs of future problems.

10. Educate the employee's supervisor as to activity restrictions and signs of future medical problems.

Sources of Information Used in This Section:

Underhill, Woods, Sivarajas & Halfpenny, *Cardiac Nursing* (2d ed. 1989), p. 752.

Putting Disabled People in Your Place: Focus on Individuals with Heart Disease, Mainstream, Inc., 3 Bethesda Metro Center, Suite 830, Bethesda, MD 20814, phone (301) 654-2400.

Other General Sources of Information: *(See also pp. 231–32)*

American Heart Association
7320 Greenville Ave.

Dallas, TX 75231
(214) 750-5300
Offers numerous publications and conducts educational training on the diagnoses and treatment of cardiovascular diseases.

HEART FAILURE: See Heart and Circulatory Problems.

HEMOLYTIC ANEMIA: See Anemia.

HEMOPHILIA

The Problem. Hemophilia is an inherited disease in which the person has a marked reduction in the production of antihemophilic globulin that is vital in causing blood to clot. About one male per 10,000 has the disease. Females do not suffer from hemophilia; however, they may pass the genes that cause this condition to male offspring. Unfortunately, there is no cure.

Treatment and Accommodation. Diagnoses of hemophilia are made during childhood, so any job applicant or employee will know if they have the medical condition. After the condition is known, by voluntary disclosure or a post-hiring medical screening, employers should consider excluding the individual from jobs that have a high risk of physical injury, including cuts and bruises, if reasonable accommodations cannot be made. The decision to exclude should be based upon the legal factors listed in Chapter 6, "Risk of Future Injury: Epilepsy, Diabetes, and Bad Back," concerning risk of future injury; for example, the risk must be both substantial and serious.

Employees in dangerous jobs should be given the option to transfer to any open position for which they are qualified that does not pose the danger of cuts and bruises.

About the only accommodation needed by employees in nondangerous jobs is some understanding during the rare times they suffer accidents that require medical treatment and hospitalization. Blood transfusions are often given during hospitalization. Because blood to be used in transfusions was not checked for HIV during the first few years of the epidemic of AIDS, many people with hemophilia have also contracted the virus of AIDS (see the section on AIDS). Blood transfusions in the past few years are extremely unlikely to have transmitted the HIV infection.

HEMORRHAGES: See Brain Injury.

HERNIAS

The Problem. A hernia is a bulge or protrusion of soft tissue, often a piece of intestine, that forces its way through or between the muscles. The bulge may occur suddenly after physical exertion, coughing, or crying; or more slowly over a period of days or weeks. They are most common in the abdominal wall; however, they can occur almost anywhere.

Contrary to popular opinion, the first symptom of a hernia is usually not pain, but rather a simple bulge or swelling. However, if a part of the intestine becomes squeezed into the abdominal wall, severe pain may occur. An emergency operation may be needed if the intestine is strangulated, thus obstructing it or cutting off its blood supply.

There is only one cure for hernias—surgery. Trusses or supportive corsets that help firm up the outside of the abdomen are temporary measures only. They will not cure the hernia. Prolonged use of trusses may actually cause the problem to become worse. With few exceptions, hernias get worse as time progresses, not better.

Accommodations. An employee with a hernia may require light duty (no heavy lifting or straining) for a temporary time until surgery can be performed. Most employees will miss little or no work for a hernia operation. Many hernia surgeries are performed on an out-patient basis. The patient comes to the hospital a day before surgery for some blood work and tests. The surgery is often done under a local anesthetic and the patient is allowed to leave the hospital within hours.

Although recovering hernia surgery patients used to take a month or more before returning to work, most physicians now allow a return to work just as soon as the patient feels like it, often a day or two after surgery. Many physicians recommend against strenuous activity or heavy lifting for three to six weeks. The overall physical condition of the patient might also be a factor in determining the period of activity restriction. Overweight people or those with other medical problems such as diabetes may take longer to recover.

A growing minority of physicians place little or no post-operative physical limitations on patients. This is possible because of new types of tension-free, unbreakable sutures. This approach is controversial; therefore, it may be advisable to obtain a written statement from any physician who suggests no work restrictions.

Sources of Information Used in This Section:

Kingsley, Lichtenstein & Seiber, *Common hernias in primary care*, Patient Care (Apr. 15, 1990), pp. 98–115.

The Do's and Don'ts of Dealing with a Hernia, Business Week (Aug. 20, 1984), pp. 143–4.

Other Sources of Information: See the List on Pages 231–32.

HIGH BLOOD PRESSURE: See Heart and Circulatory Problems.

HODGKIN'S DISEASE: See Cancer.

HUNTINGTON'S CHOREA: See Nerve Disease.

HYPERTENSION: See Heart and Circulatory Problems.

HYPERTHYROIDISM: See Graves Disease.

HYPOCHONDRIA: See Mental Diseases.

HYPOGLYCEMIA: A condition almost entirely caused by diabetic people giving themselves too much insulin (see the section on Diabetes).

HYPOTENSION

The Problem. Hypotension is low blood pressure, and it rarely causes any problem or work restriction. However, if it occurs abruptly and results in dizziness or faintness, it may be postural hypotension. Postural hypotension may be due to medicines taken for high blood sugar (diabetes), a complication of pregnancy, a symptom of other illness, or a reaction to a sudden emotional event.

Treatment and Accommodation. A person with continuing episodes of dizziness or faintness should consult a physician. There should be no needed work accommodations.

HYPOTHYROIDISM: See Graves Disease.

HYSTERIA: See Mental Illness or Disease.

ILEOSTOMY: See Digestive Diseases.

INFLAMMATORY BOWEL DISEASE (IBD): See Digestive Diseases.

INTESTINAL OBSTRUCTION: See Digestive Diseases.

IRRITABLE COLON: See Digestive Diseases.

LARYNX: See Speech Impairments.

LEARNING DISABILITIES

The Problem. The term "learning disability" covers a wide range of problems caused by a disorder in one or more of the basic processes involved in understanding or using language: spoken, written, or expressed in mathematical symbols. The condition results in one or more problems in:

- Oral comprehension
- Oral communication
- Academic skills
- Sustained attention span
- Ability to organize
- Mental (and sometimes physical) coordination
- Ability to correctly perceive others' intentions
- Social judgment

Included in the term "learning disabilities" are dyslexia (inability to read), dyscalculia (inability to do math), dysgraphia (inability to write), and dysphasia (impairment in the ability to speak or understand oral language).

Learning disabilities are not to be confused with mental illness or mental impairment. Most people with learning disabilities have average to high intelligence. Some famous people with serious learning disabilities include former Olympics champions Bruce Jenner and Greg Louganis, Cher, Albert Einstein, Thomas Edison, Hans Christian Anderson, and Leonardo Da Vinci. Einstein flunked math, leading his teacher to believe he was retarded, while a long succession of tutors attempted unsuccessfully to teach Hans Christian Anderson to read (he later dictated his stories since he could not read or write).

A learning disability severe enough to be considered a legal disability in employment will normally have a cluster of symptoms that do not improve with age or education. Typically the cluster may include several of the following symptoms:

- Short attention span
- Poor memory
- Difficulty following directions
- Inadequate ability to discriminate among different letters of the alphabet, numbers, or sounds
- Poor reading ability
- Poor eye-hand coordination
- Difficulty in sequencing

Many symptoms of learning disabilities are common to all people at some time, to some degree. A learning disability may be present when a person has severe problems with several of the following symptoms:

- Work performance varies from day-to-day
- Inappropriate responses, such as acting happy when criticized or sad when complimented
- Restlessness and inability to stay interested in one subject for more than a short time
- Often says one thing but means another
- Fails to adjust to change
- Immature speech
- Does not listen well or remember
- Cannot follow multiple directions
- Has difficulty telling right from left
- Has trouble naming familiar people or things
- Has difficulty in sounding out words
- Writes poorly
- Reverses letters or places them in incorrect sequences such as reading or writing "b" instead of "d", or "gril" instead of "girl"
- Is impulsive

It is believed that as many as one of ten Americans have a learning disorder, many of them of such seriousness that it constitutes an employment disability. Because learning disabilities were not recognized as a specific medical or learning problem until the 1940s, many older workers with the disability, as well as some younger ones, have never been diagnosed or treated. Your work force may contain a number of learning disabled employees at every level of the business. Several top executives of major corporations have learning disabilities, proving that people with such disabilities are not prevented from performing in business.

Treatment. Because learning disabilities are numerous in types and results and the entire area is a relatively new medical field, there are only a few, limited methods of treatment.

Clinical or group therapy and specialized training in reading, writing, math, and other subjects are available. However, the programs are sometimes difficult to find. Referrals to local sources of aid may be obtained from the Association for Children and Adults With Learning Disabilities, 4156 Library Road, Pittsburgh, PA 15234, phone (412) 341-1515; the Orton Dyslexia Society, 724 York Road, Baltimore, MD 21204, phone (800) 222-3123 or (301) 296-0232; or your local vocational training agency.

Testing. Test-taking may present a special problem for job applicants with learning disabilities. Although the range of learning disabilities is so broad that testing accommodations should be made on a case-by-case basis, the following are some general guidelines:

1. Applicants with dyslexia should be offered the option of having the test given by cassette tape or being read aloud by the examiner.
2. Extra time to complete the test should be considered for learning disabled persons. Extra time is absolutely necessary if a cassette tape or reader is used.
3. Examiners should be sure multiple choice questions are answered in the correct format. Check to see if the applicant is filling out the exam correctly, darkens the correct spaces, etc. Allowing the applicant to use a ruler may be helpful.
4. Extra care should be taken when giving oral or written test instructions. It may be necessary to repeat the instructions.

Accommodation Ideas. As with most disabilities, each person is different and has different needs. As a general rule, the strengths, rather than the weaknesses, of learning disabled job applicants and employees should be addressed. Proper job placement based upon the person's strengths can be crucial, as is training. While employers have found training of learning disabled persons to require longer periods of time than normal, many have found learning disabled persons to be excellent employees. Many are eager workers who have already learned to overcome substantial obstacles, showing the intelligence and drive that makes a good employee.

Some practical accommodations for various learning disabilities include the following:

Reading problems:

- Use verbal instructions.
- Have fellow employees read important memos.
- Provide and encourage employees to use tape recorders when attending meetings, receiving oral instructions, etc. Tape recorders with variable speed playback are useful so that the employee can set the speed best suited to his or her needs.
- Allow the use of telephone calls to replace written letters.
- Allow extra time for reading written materials.

Listening problems:

- If possible, provide a quiet environment.
- Furnish written instructions.
- Demonstrate new tasks or job duties.
- Provide a tape recorder and encourage the employee to tape oral instructions, important meetings, and phone calls. A variable speed recorder allows the employee to play back taped material at a rapid speed.
- Speak clearly in short, simple sentences.
- Encourage note taking.

Writing problems:

- Allow dictation.
- Assign someone to proofread written materials.
- If the employee is to do much writing, provide for the use of a computer and word processing program.
- Obtain computer software word processing programs that include spelling checkers, grammar checkers, dictionaries, and thesauruses that can catch mistakes. Cost: $49 to $500, depending upon name-brand and desired features.

Memory problems:

- Employ backup reminder systems to give notice of meetings and other special times and dates.

- In job positions requiring meetings, appointments, special events, and changing schedules, give the employee a typed, daily reminder of his or her schedule.
- Provide employee with a portable electronic schedule reminder. Cost: $25 to $200, depending upon brand and features desired.
- If a white collar or professional employee, provide a daily planner and a clock.
- Encourage (and possibly pay for) the employee to attend memory training programs.

Math problems:

- If any math, simple or complex, must be used on the job, provide a calculator with a print out or voice synthesizer. Cost: $39.95 to $100.
- If any mathematical terms will be used by the employee, furnish a calculator with a voice synthesizer. For example, a dyslexic employee filling out a purchase order for 2,600 cases of goods may actually state the amount as 6,200. A "talking" calculator may allow the employee to type in the figure and check it by hearing it spoken. Cost: $39.50.

Social Problems:

- Say what you mean in a direct way.
- Avoid sarcasm.
- Don't hint; state clearly what is desired.
- Help the employee learn the unwritten rules of the organization. Appointment of a mentor to help new employees may be useful. However, under the ADA the disabled employee must first disclose his or her disability to the co-worker who will serve as a mentor.
- Provide feedback to the employee as to job performance evaluations.
- Give encouragement and complement the employee when work is good. Remember that the employee may have been constantly criticized in school, at home, and at work. Positive feedback when the employee overcomes the disability is important in order to create a good, permanent employee.

Employers may desire to aid employees with learning disability problems by encouraging and even financing additional education or rehabilitation. Information concerning over 900 institutions of higher education that offer programs for the learning disabled is available in *Peterson's Colleges With Programs for Learning-Disabled Students* (2d ed. 1991), a book found in most larger bookstores and libraries.

Sources of Information Used in This Section:

For Employers: A Look at Learning Disabilities; Learning Disabilities—What Is It? and *Finding Ways to Assist Learning-Disabled Workers*, Association for Children & Adults with Learning Disabilities, 4156 Library Rd., Pittsburgh, PA 15234, phone (412) 341-1515.

Learning Disability: Not Just a Problem Children Outgrow, The President's Committee on Employment of People With Disabilities, 1111 20th Street, NW, Suite 636, Washington, DC 20036, phone (202) 653-5044 or FAX (202) 653-7386.

What is Dyslexia and *Guidelines for Seeking Help*, The Orton Dyslexia Society, 724 York Road, Baltimore, MD 21204, phone (800) 222-3123 or (301) 296-0232.

Testing Applicants with Specific Learning Disabilities, In the Mainstream, MIN Report #5 (Sept.–Oct., 1988), 3 Bethesda Metro Center, Suite 830, Bethesda, MD 20814, phone (301) 654-2400.

Other General Sources of Information: *(See also pp. 231–32)*

IBM National Support Center for Persons With Disabilities
P.O. Box 2150
Atlanta, GA 30055
(800) 426-2133
    Provides information on technical devices to accommodate disabled employees, the large majority of which are not IBM products.

LEUKEMIA: See Cancer.

LOW BLOOD PRESSURE: See Hypotension.

LUNG CANCER: See Cancer.

LYMPHOMA: See Cancer.

MANIC-DEPRESSION: See Mental Illness or Disease.

MENTAL ILLNESS OR DISEASE

The problem. Mental illness is a term used to describe a large group of disorders that cause serious disturbances in thinking, feeling, relating, and working. Mental illness affects people of all ages, but most often occurs first in young to middle-aged adults. Mental illness is not related to mental retardation.

Many mental illnesses are temporary, and most can be successfully treated. After successful treatment for mental illness the person may be considered "mentally restored." However, the person continues to be covered by the ADA because he or she has a history of a disability.

The most common types of mental illness are as follows:

Schizophrenia. Contrary to popular opinion, schizophrenia is not synonymous with a split personality. Instead, symptoms may include problems in concentration, illogical thought processes, incoherence, and inappropriate vocal statements. Emotional problems, withdrawal, and delusions may accompany the disease. The condition may last for a very short time, for a very long time, or for short, but recurring times. Most frequently it is a lifetime illness whose symptoms may be exacerbated or in remission at different times.

Manic-Depressive Disorder. Generally occurring first before the age of 35, one of every 100 people will eventually experience this condition. Some people only experience the manic phase, exhibiting excessively good moods, expressing unwarranted optimism, hyperactivity, flights of ideas, and a decreased need for sleep. However, these symptoms may be accompanied by sudden irritability, rage, or paranoia. Others will experience only the depressive phase, having feelings of hopelessness, inappropriate guilt, crying spells, withdrawal from society, inability to concentrate, loss of appetite, and various other symptoms. No one person will exhibit all the listed symptoms. People who swing from manic to depressive are said to be bipolar.

Depression. Minor depression is common and no cause for concern if connected to adverse events in one's life where the depression lasts for only a short time. Minor depression that will not go away, moderate depression for more than a few days, and serious depression will require treatment. Moderate depression results in a hopeless feeling that may seriously affect eating, sleeping, and working. Thoughts of suicide are common. Serious depression will affect 20 percent of the population at some time in their lives. It consists of the same problems of minor or moderate depression, but with greater severity. There also may be hallucinations, delusions, and other misconceptions. It is a life-threatening disease.

Obsessive-Compulsive Disorders. The illness afflicts 2.4 million Americans of every age, race, and social status. The obsessive part of the problem consists of prolonged, irrational thoughts and fears. Some may constantly worry about harming other people or constantly worry about their actions violating social norms. Individuals may excessively worry about their house (or dishes, or their hands) being unclean, or they may have a number of other irrational obsessions. Most with obsessions also become compulsive in an irrational, constant, repetitive ritual in acting on their fears. A person with a compulsion about clean teeth may brush his teeth over and over and over again. Another with a compulsive anxiety about locking the front door of her house may check it dozens of times before leaving. Other physical actions may include over-meticulous neatness, hoarding of useless items, avoiding common situations, slowness in actions, and constant repeating of statements or actions.

Phobias. The most common of the various forms of anxiety, phobias are the irrational fear of common events, situations, products, or substances. The National Institute of Mental Health estimates that between 5 and 12.5 percent of Americans have phobias. It is the most common mental illness of women and the second most common for men over the age of 25. The most common phobia is agoraphobia, the fear of being alone in a crowd. Other common phobias include the irrational fear of being in a social or employment situation where others can observe the person's performance, or fear of specific objects such as animals, insects, water, heights, or closed spaces.

Phobias cause psychological and physical reactions. The victim may feel total panic, dread, or horror. All the physical symptoms of complete fear may occur: rapid heartbeat, shortness of breath, trembling, and faintness. The victim knows the reaction is not appropriate but cannot stop it. Therefore the item or event that caused the phobia is avoided in the future.

Panic Disorders. Affecting 1.2 million Americans, the symptoms are similar to phobias. However there is a big difference: panic causes an intense, overwhelming terror *for no apparent reason*. People experiencing their first panic attack will often rush to the hospital, convinced they are having a heart attack. Because panic attacks occur without reason, the victim cannot predict when they will occur.

Posttraumatic Stress Disorder. Sometimes referred to as posttraumatic stress syndrome, it is best known as a condition afflicting many Vietnam war veterans. However, it can affect anyone who has survived a severe and unusual physical or mental trauma such as witnessing a plane crash, being in a car wreck, being raped or mugged, and other unexpected, traumatic events. The symptoms may include nightmares, night terrors, flashbacks that last from seconds to days, a psychic numbing (decreased interest and involvement with life), or excessive alertness that causes one to be easily startled by common noises.

Treatment. Most mental illnesses can be cured or managed with proper medicines, counseling, and other treatment. Once cured or appropriately managed, individuals can function in much the same way as any nondisabled person. However, sometimes there are relapses, just as a recovering alcoholic or drug abuser may relapse. Some of the relapses are caused by a failure to continue taking prescribed drugs, or stopping recommended therapy. However, many relapses are due to situations beyond the control of the individual.

Accommodations. The most important accommodations employers can take toward job applicants and employees with present or past mental illnesses is to avoid myths about mental illness and replace them with knowledge. With the possible exception of epilepsy and AIDS, people with current or past mental illness experience the most discrimination of any disabled group. Managers must make extra efforts to understand that mental illness is a medical disease in the same manner as is diabetes or arthritis. The first step in removing discrimination is to remove some common myths about mental illness.

Myth 1. Recovered mental patients are potentially dangerous. "They could go berserk at any time." Most mentally ill individuals never went berserk at the height of their mental illness and will not do so in the future. Mental patients more typically become quiet and withdrawn. There is no reason to believe a mentally restored person is any more likely to "go wild" than any other individual. One East Coast employer with a history of hiring mentally restored employees reports that he has never had any hint of any employee becoming wild, uncontrollable, or hard to handle.

Myth 2. Mentally restored people are suitable only for routine jobs under close supervision. People who have had mental illness have all types of knowledge and all levels of intelligence, training, desire, and ability. They include U.S. presidents, senators, great athletes, entertainers, and even astronauts.

Myth 3. Fellow employees will not accept a mentally restored co-worker. In most cases co-workers will have no reason to know the individual has had mental problems. However, the experiences of several employers show that when the mental problem is known, co-workers usually sympathize with and help the employee.

The return to work after treatment for mental illness is one of the most crucial times in an individual's restoration to a normal life. Additionally, the return to work may cause great stress and fear. Specific steps employers should take to help an employee return to work after treatment for mental illness include:

1. Inform the attending physician of the exact duties of the job before the physician makes a final decision on return to work.
2. In consultation with the individual's physician, encourage an early return to work. The longer an employee is out of work due to treatment, the more the employee will worry about losing his or her job. Furthermore, the longer a person is away from the job the more mentally detached from it they will become. An early return is best if for no other reason than decreased disability pay, health insurance payments, or workers' compensation payments.
3. Consider a gradual return to work. Allowing part-time work for several weeks may help reduce stress, leave time for additional medical counseling, and allow the worker to quickly get back into a normal routine. Flextime, temporarily changed duties that involve less job-related stress, or other flexible arrangements may be helpful. However, there should be a clear understanding between the employee and the employer as to the details of the return to work program: the expected length of time special accommodations will be granted, what day-to-day flexibility is allowed, the exact duties of the employee, and who will supervise the worker.

Some other possible accommodations that might reduce the stress of starting or returning to a job after a mental illness include:

-   Altering the pace of work.
-   Lowering the noise level at work.

- Providing water, tea, or soda and crushed ice to combat a dry mouth caused by some medications for mental illness.
- Extra encouragement and praise of job performance, but only if warranted and not obviously excessive.
- Avoiding mention or discussion of the mental illness or its aftermath. The past is past. Let the employee have a fresh start.
- While taking steps to reduce stress, avoid babying the employee. Over-protection or excessive concern may harm the person's mental adjustment even more than a lack of caring and concern.
- Be sure the employee is treated as a member of the team and not excluded from social events, business meetings, or other activities relevant to the employee's job position.

Recruiting and Hiring. An employer normally will have no knowledge of past mental problems of employees who are recruited in the usual ways such as through newspaper advertising, employment agencies, and walk-ins. Because the Americans with Disabilities Act does not allow job applicants to be asked about disabilities, including mental illness, they will be hired in the normal fashion.

However, employers may wish to contact private or state agencies to refer mentally restored individuals, or the agencies may call upon the business to interview their patients. In these cases where the disability is known, it is still illegal to ask about the severity of the illness. An employer can ask job-related questions of the agency, counselor, or applicant, such as:

1. Will the individual need time off from work for future counseling or therapy?
2. Are there any accommodations needed in order for the person to successfully perform the job in question?
3. What arrangements, if any, will be needed to allow the individual to take medication while on the job?
4. Do you have any concerns about the individual's ability to do the job?

Employers can reassure themselves concerning the job applicant by making observations during the interview that should be made with all job applicants, disabled or nondisabled. Ask yourself the following questions:

1. Did the applicant arrive on time for the interview? If not, was an acceptable excuse given?
2. Did the applicant miss any scheduled interviews? If so, was the company notified in advance and given an acceptable excuse?
3. Is the applicant pleasant in appearance and behavior?
4. Did the applicant's grooming and dress appear appropriate for the interview?
5. Did the applicant make appropriate responses to questions, considering the applicant's education and the type of job involved?

Sources of Information Used in This Section:

Accommodating Workers with Mental Disabilities, BNA Policy and Practice Series, *Fair Employment Practices*, (May 26, 1988), p. 66.

Work Return for Mentally Ill an Arduous Task, Employee Benefit Plan Review, Vol. 39 (1984), pp. 104–6.

Putting Disabled People in Your Place: Focus on Individuals With a History of Mental Illness, Mainstream, Inc., 3 Bethesda Metro Center, Suite 830, Bethesda, MD 20814, phone (301) 654-2400.

Eight Questions Employers Ask About Hiring the Mentally Restored, National Institute of Mental Health, U.S. Department of Health and Human Services (1981).

Honberg, *Persons with Mental Illnesses*, In the Mainstream (Jan.–Feb. 1990), pp. 11–12.

Phobias, Obsessive-Compulsive Disorder, Anxiety Disorders, Depression, Manic-Depressive Disorder, a series of pamphlets published by the American Psychiatric Association, 1400 K St., NW, Washington, DC 20005.

Other General Sources of Information: *(See also pp. 231–32)*

National Institute of Mental Health
5600 Fishers Lane
Rockville, MD 20857

Publishes a variety of booklets including *Schizophrenia: Questions and Answers, Useful Information on Phobias and Panic, The Mentally Restored and Work: A Successful Partnership*, and *Affirmative Action to Employ Mentally Restored People*.

Local Chapter of the National Alliance for the Mentally Ill; or contact the National Alliance for the Mentally Ill
1901 North Fort Meyer Drive
Suite 500
Arlington, VA 22209
(703) 524-7600
Promotes public education on mental illness, including practical guidance and case management.

State Vocation Rehabilitation Agencies

Mental Health Association
1800 North Kent Street
Arlington, VA 22209
(703) 528-6405
Publishes a variety of materials on mental illness and can refer people to one of the 850 local chapters of the association.

MIGRAINE: See Headache, Chronic.

MULTIPLE MYELOMA

The Problem. Plasma cells in the bone marrow undergo a malignant change and multiply. In simple terms, the result is the loss of many red blood cells, bone tissue, and the body's ability to produce antibodies to fight infection. It is a fairly rare disease and occurs primarily in people over the age of 50.

Treatment and Accommodation. Although the disease cannot be cured, modern medicine allows people with multiple myeloma to continue their major activities for years. Since most employees are 50 or older and will normally retire within a decade, the disease, while very serious, may have little or no effect on the employee's ability to work.

Only two accommodations may be needed: First, sufficient medical leave to receive treatment. However, standard company leave policies may be followed. Second, activities should be avoided that increase the chance of the employee catching the flu or other viruses because of the person's decreased amount of antibodies.

For Additional Information: See the Listing on Pages 231–32.

MULTIPLE SCLEROSIS: See Nerve Disease.

NARCOLEPSY

The Problem. Narcolepsy is a sleep disorder that can be chronic and very dangerous. It may involve a serious inability to obtain sufficient restful sleep, or it may cause repeated cessation of breathing and a struggle to re-open the upper air passages to the lungs (called "sleep apnea"). Narcolepsy affects 1 of every 50 men and a somewhat lower ratio of women. The problem usually first develops between the ages of 40 and 60. Potential complications include heart failure, hypertension, heart attack, stroke, and sudden death. However, the major complication affecting an employer is decreased work performance.

The serious effect of this disease on employment is illustrated by a recent survey that showed that 84 percent of working age adults with narcolepsy have experienced decreased work performance, while 57 percent have changed jobs and 38 percent have lost one or more promotions.

Identification of Employees With Narcolepsy. Many people with narcolepsy do not realize it. Those afflicted with narcolepsy may attribute their loss of memory, confusion, and poor mental processes to Alzheimer's disease, rather than sleep problems. Supervisors and managers often believe the employee is lazy, apathetic, stupid, or on drugs.

Because the condition is chronic, employee productivity will not improve unless employees with narcolepsy are identified and treated. Symptoms observable on the job include decreased performance in the latter part of a work shift, dozing off during meetings, increased physical clumsiness, partial eyelid closure, rambling speech—especially if these symptoms occur in employees over 40 years of age and become progressively worse. Increased irritability and malaise, as well as constant worrying about the competition from younger workers, may also indicate narcolepsy.

Treatment. In the large majority of cases treatment is successful in avoiding complications that may include heart attacks or stroke. Treatment almost always improves the basic condition to the point that the employee will exhibit little or no job performance problems. However, it is important that the employee see a physician who is familiar with narcolepsy. Otherwise, the employee may be told he has no medical problems or is suffering from depression. Although narcolepsy is a physical condition, not a mental disease, psychological counseling may be needed to deal with the frustrations caused by the disease.

Possible Accommodations. Work situations that should be *avoided* if possible include:

- Lengthy workdays and overtime.
- Frequent shift changes.
- Long work shifts ending after nightfall (these are very dangerous if the employee continues to have narcolepsy symptoms and will drive home after work).
- A desk job without the freedom to get up and walk around.
- A job with dull, repetitive motions.

If the employee's job performance directly involves the health and safety of the employee or others—aircraft pilot, bus driver, use of dangerous substances or machines, etc.—it may be necessary to remove that person from the job, at least until valid medical opinion shows successful treatment and a lack of on-going problems.

Sources of Information Used in This Section:

Clark, *Recognize "Sleepy" Workers by Asking the Right Questions Early in the Rehabilitation Process*, Journal of Rehabilitation (Jan.–Feb. 1989), pp. 9–12.

Other General Sources of Information: *(See also pp. 231–32)*

American Narcolepsy Association
335 Quarry Road
Belmont, CA 94002

American Sleep Disorders Association
604 Second Street, SW
Rochester, MN 55902

NERVE DISEASE

The Problem. Several major disabilities result from nervous system disorders, including cerebral palsy, multiple sclerosis, Tourette syndrome, amyotrophic lateral sclerosis (ALS), Parkinson's disease, Huntington's chorea, Bell's palsy, and peripheral neuropathy. Although they are basically nervous system disorders, they often result in loss of muscle control and paralysis. None of these diseases are communicable.

Cerebral Palsy. The result of damage or malformation of the part of the brain that controls motor functions, it may cause paralysis, weakness, tremors, stiffness, involuntary motions, and a lack of coordination. People with mild cases can walk and handle things; however, precision movements may be very difficult. A moderate or severe case can restrict individuals to the use of a wheelchair and cause problems in talking, seeing, hearing, smelling, and touching. Some severe cases involve people who have additional birth defects that cause mental retardation and emotional problems. Others with cerebral palsy may be highly intelligent.

Multiple Sclerosis. Another chronic disease, it affects the central nervous system. It is neither infectious nor inherited, and it often first occurs in young adults, although the age range tends to be from 15 to 50. Because the condition often progresses slowly, most people with multiple sclerosis can work for many years. Symptoms vary greatly and may include blurred or double vision, numbness or a tingling sensation, fatigue, and difficulty in coordination. Other cases produce no outward symptoms, but rather general weakness, sensitivity to heat, and possible bladder problems.

Tourette Syndrome. A neurological disorder that usually first occurs between the ages of 2 and 16, the disease affects males three times as often as females. The cause is not known. Symptoms are rather strange and disturbing. Facial tics are most common. These include excessive blinking of eyes and grimaces. The symptoms may later include constant clearing of the throat, coughing, sniffing, grunting, barking, or shouting, and in some cases, involuntary shouting of obscenities. The cause is unknown and it is usually a chronic, lifelong condition, although some people experience a remission in early adulthood.

Amyotrophic Lateral Sclerosis. Also known as Lou Gehrig's disease, it is fairly rare. It normally strikes adults between the ages of 35 and 65, and it is fatal. However, the progress of the disease varies from person to person. Some cases result in a rapid degeneration of muscle control leading to an early onset of muscle twitches, spasms, and loss of muscle control. Death may occur within two or three years. In other cases, the physical symptoms slowly develop over a period of many years. The disease does not cause pain, and there is no loss of mental ability or vision.

Parkinson's Disease. Parkinson's disease causes a gradual deterioration of certain areas in the brain that control physical movements, particularly semi-automatic movements such as swinging one's arms while walking. The disease may be caused by occupational exposure to certain metals such as magnesium, substances such as carbon monoxide, or by brain injury. Often the cause is unknown.

Physical symptoms often become increasingly serious. They include tremors, involuntary movement of hands or head, and problems in writing legibly and speaking clearly. There is no deterioration of mental ability until the very late stages of the disease, often many years from the outset of the problem. Parkinson's disease is not fatal and it can often be kept under reasonable control by modern drugs.

Huntington's Chorea. This is a rare inherited disease normally appearing only after a person is over 20 years of age. Symptoms include uncontrolled, rapid body movements, lack of coordination, and decline in mental function. It is a progressive disease that ends in insanity and death.

Bell's Palsy. This is the only disease listed in this section that is usually not permanent nor extremely serious. The physical result, however, is very noticeable. Typically, the nerves controlling one side of the person's face become paralyzed and the face becomes distorted. It is not a dangerous condition and it seldom lasts for more than several weeks, although rare cases persist and may have to be treated surgically. During the time the person has Bell's palsy, the eye on the paralyzed side of the face must be protected against exposure and dust. Eye drops may be prescribed, and the physician may advise that an eye patch be worn.

Peripheral Neuropathy. The term describes damage to the nervous system other than in the brain and spinal cord. Sometimes it is a complication of another disease such as diabetes. It may also be caused by alcoholism, a Vitamin B_{12} deficiency, or exposure to certain chemicals such as arsenic, mercury, lead, and compounds found in insecticides. The disease is not fatal, but may result in tingling sensation, numbness, and a gradual reduction in muscle strength. In rare cases, paralysis may result.

Rehabilitation and Return to Work. At present there are no cures for most of these diseases. However, some drugs are effective in reducing their symptoms. Other devices such as wheelchairs, leg braces, and other body supports can help. Typically, by the time an employer first sees a person with such conditions, during a job interview or return to work, the employee has undergone substantial rehabilitation. Because of this, information concerning the person's true job abilities, as well as possible accommodations, can be obtained from the person or agency that worked with the individual.

A promising rehabilitation and employability program is "Job Raising," a trademarked name for nonprofit programs established in over 20 geographic areas to help persons with multiple sclerosis and similar problems to obtain or return to work. Outreach, employee screening, and job readiness training is given by a staff of professional rehabilitation employees and volunteer business people.

Careful attention must be paid to the placement process of job applicants and returning workers. Those who interview, hire, or decide upon rehiring may easily denigrate the intelligence and ability of an individual because the person *appears* unintelligent or mentally retarded. Keep in mind that physical appearance and manner of speech do not relate to intelligence. Because people with these conditions often have communication problems, one must allow the person to speak at his or her own pace.

Accommodation Ideas. Most people with these diseases can work. Frequently the largest obstacles to overcome are resistance of employers in hiring or returning workers to the workplace and co-worker attitudes. Successful employment depends both on a good match between the individual's ability and the job duties, and cooperation and understanding by the employer and other employees.

A job analysis must be made whereby the exact functional requirements of a job are determined. The individual's abilities, physical and sometimes mental, must then be matched with the job. In determining the individual's ability one can rely upon the ideas of the disabled person, reasonable job skill tests, and most importantly, information from vocational rehabilitation people and agencies who have worked with the individual. However, the vocational rehabilitation experts cannot give aid in deciding upon placement and accommodations unless they are given the exact job duties to be performed. This makes the job analysis the key to a successful matching of employer needs and employee abilities.

Typical accommodations include flexible working hours, parking spaces near the entrance to work, a work location near a restroom, and especially for those with multiple sclerosis, air conditioning. Other accommodation ideas are covered in the section entitled **SPINAL CORD INJURY AND WHEELCHAIR USERS.**

Because many people feel uncomfortable around individuals with obvious problems in physical control and movement, the aid of a person's supervisor and co-workers should be obtained before placing the disabled person in the job. Although the Americans with Disabilities Act does not provide for employers disclosing disabilities to co-workers, there should be no danger in doing so when the disability is obvious and will be immediately apparent to co-workers. Education must accompany these requests if a favorable response is to be expected. The American Cancer Society and the others listed below have excellent sources of material for the education of management and employees.

Sources of Information Used in This Section:

Putting Disabled People in Your Place: Focus on Individuals with Cerebral Palsy, Mainstream, Inc., 3 Bethesda Metro Center, Suite 830, Bethesda, MD, phone (301) 654-2400.

Cerebral Palsy: Hope Through Research, Office of Scientific & Health Reports, National Institute of Neurological & Communicative Disorders & Strokes, National Institutes of Health, Bethesda, MD 20205.

Facts & Issues and *Job Raising*, National Multiple Sclerosis Society, 205 East 42d Street, New York, NY 10017, phone (800) 624-8236 or (212) 986-3240. *Job Raising* includes the names, addresses, and phone number of over 20 agencies engaged in this program.

Fact Sheet: Tourette Syndrome, Tourette Syndrome Association, Inc., 41-02 Bell Blvd., Bayside, NY 11361, phone (212) 224-2999.

Other General Sources of Information: *(See also pp. 231–32)*

United Cerebral Palsy Assocation
66 East 34th St.
New York, NY 10016
(800) 872-1872 or (212) 481-6300

State United Cerebral Palsy Organizations

State Vocational Rehabilitation Agencies

IBM National Support Center for Persons With Disabilities
P.O. Box 2150
Atlanta, GA 30055
(800) 426-2133

Provides information on technical devices to accommodate disabled employees, the large majority of which are not IBM products.

NERVOUS BREAKDOWN: See Mental Illness or Disease.

OSTOMY: See Digestive Diseases.

PARKINSON'S DISEASE: See Nerve Disease.

PEPTIC ULCER: See Ulcer.

PERIPHERAL NEUROPATHY: See Nerve Disease.

PHLEBITIS: See Heart and Circulatory Problems.

PHOBIAS: See Mental Illness or Disease.

PULMONARY EMBOLISM: See Heart and Circulatory Problems.

RAYNAUD'S DISEASE: See Heart & Circulatory Problems. See Repetitive Motion Injury for occupationally caused Raynaud's Syndrome.

REPETITIVE MOTION INJURY

The Problem. Repetitive motions, often caused by required work procedures, may cause damage to the joints, hands, fingers, or other body parts. Tendinitis, sometimes called tennis elbow or golf elbow, is more likely to result from jobs requiring repetitive acts such as driving screws to lifting bags. Raynaud's syndrome, also called vibration white finger (VWF), is associated with the use of heavy, vibrating equipment, especially when temperatures are low.

This section will discuss the most common repetitive motion injury—carpal tunnel syndrome (CTS), although some suggestions for handling CTS cases are equally useful in other repetitive injury cases. CTS is a disorder caused by injury to the median nerve where it passes through the wrist from the forearm to the hand. Its name comes from the eight bones in the wrist, called carpals, that form a tunnel-like structure. The tunnel is filled with tendons and the median nerve. The median nerve controls the sensory and motor control of the hand and fingers.

Compression of the nerve may occur as the result of wrist fractures, tumors, arthritis, and diabetes. The most common cause, however, is repetitive motion that places a strain upon the wrist and the median nerve. The first symptom of CTS is a tingling or numbness in the hand. The condition may progress to a loss of feeling, loss of gripping power, and finally, a general loss of hand functions. In the most serious cases, substantial pain and almost complete inability to use the hand can result.

A person may first notice CTS when reoccurring tingling, numbness, and "pins and needles" sensations begin. Although everyone has these symptoms occasionally, it will persist in people with CTS. The sensations usually begin at night, sometimes waking the individual in the middle of the night. The early symptoms may be incorrectly attributed to arthritis or aging. As the syndrome progresses, the sensations become more frequent and start occurring during the daytime. Eventually, clumsiness and weakness become obvious.

CTS often occurs in workers between the ages of 30 and 60. Women workers are three to ten times more likely to develop CTS than male employees. Researchers report an increased risk of CTS when an individual has one of the following states or conditions: diabetes, pregnancy, arthritis, oral contraceptive use, menopause, surgical removal of one or both ovaries, dialysis, gout, hypothyroidism, or small wrist size. However, none of the studies reporting this information are comprehensive enough to exclude female workers or people with the above-listed conditions from jobs requiring repetitive motion. Nor may they be used to deny specific individuals jobs. As covered in Chapter 6, "Risk of Future Injury: Epilepsy, Diabetes, and Bad Backs," there must be a substantial probability of future injury in order to disqualify a person from a job, not just an increased statistical likelihood of danger.

Even if diabetes, pregnancy, or other factors contribute to CTS, workplace activities are often the major cause of disabling CTS. The most harmful job activities are those that cause frequent deviations from neutral wrist positions, frequent use of pinching or grabbing items, and repetitive wrist or hand movements. Office workers may be as likely to develop problems as assembly-line employees.

Accommodation and Rehabilitation. Many accommodations and rehabilitative ideas involve the same methods by which CTS may be prevented. These include the following:

1. Purchase and use of ergonomically designed tools. These tools, sometimes referred to as having the "Bennett Bend," or "Bionic Curve," incorporate a 19-degree bend in otherwise straight handles. These are beginning to be extensively used in poultry and meat processing industries and may be useful in other types of work.
2. Provision of training in proper use of tools, word processors, or other equipment.
3. Provision of cushioned arm rests to support the forearm, thus increasing the manipulative ability of the hand.
4. Storage of parts or supplies so that employees can reach them with a minimum of hand flexing or extension.
5. Use of a touch-sensitive control button, or a control button of a different configuration when it must be repetitively used. For instance, change switches that require pressure, especially if the hand must be in an unnatural position, to a large control activated by the palm or fist.
6. If lifting is involved, consider reducing the size of each packet or amount lifted to reduce strain.
7. Provision of wrist splints to avoid further injury. Various splints are sold for $12 to $35.
8. Provision of antivibration gloves. Cost: $15 to $30.
9. Application of rubber-backed low pile carpeting on work tables where vibrating tools are used in order to dampen the vibrations.
10. Elimination of sharp edges, such as rounding the edge of a table where typists or assemblers rest their hands or arms.
11. Suspension of power tools on balances to support the tool's weight.
12. Minimize exposure to cold temperatures. Whether by use of heaters or gloves, try to maintain normal room temperature around the hands.

Employment of an ergonomic engineer or rehabilitation specialist may be cost effective in reducing CTS claims and accommodating returning workers. For example, a rehabilitation specialist may use the Baltimore Therapeutic Equipment (BTE) work-hardening machine to diagnose employee problems and prepare for return to work. The BTE is a computerized work simulator that measures functional capabilities for 100 different types of job tasks. Once a specialist visits the job site to determine the work that will be done by a returning worker and tests the worker for required job motions on the BTE, a course of exercise and a decision on accommodations, such as wrist splints, can allow the worker to successfully return to work.

Surgery may be an effective alternative for people with serious CTS problems that cannot be solved by rehabilitation and the use of accommodation devices. However, it should be a last resort. Significant complications have been discovered following surgery. Weak grip strength occurs in 23 percent of surgical patients, persistent pain and decreased sensation in the fingers by 8 percent, and 19 percent find a persistent deterioration of hand muscles.

Even successful surgeries often result in a reduction of hand strength of around 10 percent, and some pain usually continues. Most importantly, if a worker is returned to the same job, done the same way, CTS is likely to reappear.

Accommodations that do not require the use of new equipment may be most effective in reducing CTS and accommodating workers who already have the problem. These changes include the following:

1. Providing a rest break once per hour. A five-minute rest break every hour for a word processor is better than a 15-minute break every three hours.
2. Allowing an employee to frequently change job duties. For example, avoid hiring separate word processors and filing clerks. Let each worker mix the two duties, thus relieving the strain of both types of repetitive motion—typing and filing. Or use a team approach to assembly operations. Rather than having one person spend the day using a screwdriver, another a wrench, and still another a drill, have the employees switch jobs every hour or so.
3. Using an ergonomic engineer to change the way jobs are done. A less expensive alternative is to ask some experienced workers how they have personally modified the methods they use in working. Often these workers have unknowingly used practical ergonomic principles in devising work habits that reduce pain or pressure.

Sources of Information Used in This Section:

Carpal Tunnel Syndrome: Selected References, National Institute for Occupational Safety and Health, 4676 Columbia Parkway, Cincinnati, OH 45226, March, 1989. The following additional information may be obtained from the Institute or a local or university library:

Armstrong, Radwin, Hanson & Kennedy, *Repetitive Trauma Disorders: Job Evaluation and Design*, Human Factors, Vol. 28(3), pp. 325–336.

Bernard, *Carpel Tunnel Syndrome: Identification and Control*, Occupational Health Nursing, Vol. 27(6), pp. 15–17.

The Institute also has a videotape, *The Finest Tools*, for sale ($100) or loan.

Other General Sources of Information: See Pages 231–32.

RETARDATION

The Problem. Over six million Americans are mentally retarded. Mental retardation affects 15 times the number of people who are blind, and 10 times as many people as polio did before immunizations became effective. There is no correlation between retardation and race, sex, or family income.

Experts (and vocational rehabilitation workers a business person is likely to deal with) define the degrees of retardation as follows:

Mild: An IQ of 51–70. Ninety percent of all retarded people fall into this category. Most can perform all types of work, and many adults work without anyone even recognizing their retardation.

Moderate: An IQ of 36–50. Less than 400,000 people fall into this category (about 6 percent of total retarded people). Some work in sheltered workshops; however, many can work in a competitive environment.

Severe: An IQ of 21–35. Less than 250,000 come under this category (approximately 3.5 percent of all retarded people). Severely retarded people can seldom work in a competitive environment; however, they have successfully worked in sheltered workshops and "enclaves." An enclave refers to direct employment by a private company. However, the workers are placed in a special area of the company under a trained supervisor, usually to do simple, repetitive work.

Profound: IQ under 20. Less than 99,000 Americans are profoundly retarded (or about 1.5 percent of all retarded people). They may be able to engage in structured workshops.

Although over 250 causes of mental retardation have been discovered, the leading causes are genetic irregularities (including Down syndrome), problems during pregnancy or birth, and environmental factors such as malnutrition, disease, lead poisoning, and inadequate health care while young.

With the exception of the most severely retarded people, almost all retarded people can work in a variety of jobs. Unfortunately, a vast majority are not employed. The President's Committee on Mental Retardation reports that society spends an average $29,220 for each institutionalized person with mental retardation, and a smaller, yet substantial sum for nonemployed, noninstitutionalized people. In addition, the government loses tax dollars because of income taxes not paid, and employers lose a large and valuable pool of potential employees.

The major reasons why retarded people are not more often employed include employers' misunderstandings concerning retarded people, a lack of a good referral source, and the need for extra training of retarded workers.

In addition to the myths concerning all disabled people given in Chapter 2, "Major Changes to Conform to the Law," several other myths apply to retarded people.

Myth #1. Mental illness and mental retardation are essentially the same thing. Mentally retarded people simply have a learning problem; i.e., they learn more slowly. Just like the rest of the population, they may or may not have a mental illness. There is no increase in mental disease caused by mental retardation.

Myth #2. Because mentally retarded persons are slow, they will harm productivity. Although retarded persons may be slower in learning the job, they are usually not slower in performing the job. A manager of a plating company in Wisconsin who added a number of mentally retarded workers found that he did get complaints from the other workers. However, when he investigated, he found the "problem" was that the other employees were mad because the newer retarded workers were outperforming them.

Myth #3. Retarded workers need more supervision. Once a successful training program has been completed, this is untrue. A manager of a large department store who has hired retarded workers for a decade found supervisory problems to be the same for mentally retarded and nondisabled employees.

Myth #4. Hiring retarded workers will cause expensive modifications to the workplace. Retarded employees normally need no special physical accommodation devices or structural changes.

Myth #5. They are good workers, but they should not be mixed with other employees. Thousands of examples exist where mentally retarded and nondisabled employees work side-by-side without difficulty. However, many retarded workers lack basic social skills and will be slow to socialize with co-workers.

Myth #6. Training new retarded employees is too expensive. Mentally retarded workers are usually more difficult to train; however, various public and private organizations can make major contributions. State vocational rehabilitation agencies train potential workers in social and business skills before the retarded person enters the labor market. Some agencies also contribute financial support toward employer training. Others may furnish "job coaches" who come to work with the retarded person for the first few weeks in order to carefully train and observe the new employee. Where offered, this is at no cost to the employer. Tax deductions or credits are also possible (see Chapter 5, "Making Accommodations for Disabled Employees").

Several private organizations are also available to help place and train disabled workers. One of the largest, the Association for Retarded Citizens (ARC), National Employment and Training Program, P.O. Box 6109, Arlington, TX 56005, phone (817) 640-0204, is funded by the federal government and has a national program. There are nearly 1,300 state and local chapters, as well as 20 major centers. Some of their programs include:

- Placement aid in identifying appropriate jobs for various retarded people. The ARC may reimburse companies hiring retarded workers for up to one-half the entry wages for the first 160 hours of employment, and up to one-fourth of the wages for an additional 160 working hours.
- Local supported employment programs using job coaches supplied and paid by the ARC or other nonemployer agency.
- Technical assistance in holding seminars, providing films, teaching job coaches, and other matters.

People with Down syndrome have added problems. Although the primary result of Down syndrome is mental retardation (again ranging from mild to severe), they have physical features such as a flat face, abnormal development of the ears, and abnormal development of the pelvis. Although their physical appearance is not a health problem, it does physically identify the person. As a result, people with Down syndrome who may be just as capable as others with similar retardation may face more job discrimination. This is particularly unfortunate because many people with Down syndrome are much more socially adept than others with different types of mental retardation. However, they may have hearing problems, as well as a slightly increased chance of leukemia.

Recruiting and Hiring. To increase the pool of persons available for employment companies should contact local vocational schools, rehabilitation agencies (government and nongovernment), any local ARC, or the national office of ARC (cited above), and inform them of the jobs that might be available—now or in the future—plus any special training needs. Agencies are usually listed in the phone book under headings such as "Opportunity Center," "Vocational Rehabilitation," "Rehabilitative Agencies," "Occupational Training," "Work Activity Center," or under state or local government listings. Ideally, the first inquiry should lead to an ongoing relationship so the agencies can continue to learn your company's needs and refer appropriate job applicants.

Before interviewing a job applicant sent by one of the agencies listed above, ask their job placement specialist about the following areas:

1. The type of education and training the applicant received.
2. The applicant's general adjustment during training.
3. The functional level of the applicant, including ability to follow sequential instructions and language ability.
4. The applicant's skills and general background.
5. Whether any incentive programs such as tax credits, on-the-job training reimbursement program, job coaching, or other aids will apply.

When interviewing an applicant it may be helpful to allow the person's employment placement specialist or job coach to be present. However, most questions and statements should be made directly to the job applicant. The following suggestions may be helpful in interviewing retarded job applicants:

- Talk directly to the applicant.
- Explain the job position in simple, clear terms, but do not use a tone of voice or words you would use with a child. Speak in a normal tone of voice.
- Explain the job benefits—pay, medical insurance, pension, etc.
- If practical, give the applicant a tour of the workplace and introduce the supervisor under which the applicant will work, if hired.

- State the time at which you will later contact the applicant.
- If job placement specialist is present, ask for assistance in completing necessary tax or pay reimbursement forms.

Once a decision to hire is made, employers should do the following:

1. Inform the appropriate supervisor, explain the facts of retardation, possible problems it might cause, and enlist the supervisor's support for hiring and training the employee. Placement of a person with Down syndrome may require additional explanation to convince the supervisor of the person's ability.
2. If the new employee will not be accompanied by a job coach, the supervisor should be encouraged to talk with the retarded person's placement specialist to understand how to work with the new employee.
3. On the first day of employment, the supervisor or other person should
   a. Introduce co-workers.
   b. Show the worker where the sign in/time clock is and how to use it, as well as showing the location of any cafeteria/lunch room, and bathrooms.
   c. Be specific in explaining rest breaks, lunch time, and quitting time.
   d. Identify the person to whom the new employee should go if a problem arises, and where appropriate, who to go to if the employee runs out of work and wants more.
   e. Be prepared to repeat these instructions.
   f. Allow extra time for training and be sure to periodically check on the employee's progress.
   g. Introduce new responsibilities gradually—don't overload the employee with too many facts and directions in a short space of time.
4. Consider setting up a "buddy system" where a co-worker can help answer questions and make suggestions during the first few weeks of employment. Technically this may violate the Americans with Disabilities Act's restriction on confidentiality of employee disabilities. However, where the disability is obvious to the co-worker who will serve as the "buddy," no real legal danger exists in asking the person to become a "buddy."

5. Praise the new worker when you notice good job performance.
6. Keep an eye on the employee and don't hesitate to point out mistakes. However, be constructive in explaining how the work should be done—even if it has been explained before.

During and after the initial employment training period, the following ideas may be helpful:

- Remember that not all retarded people are the same. They vary in personality, job skills, and other factors, just as do nonretarded people.
- Let retarded employees know what is expected of them.
- Evaluate frequently to spot any new problems.
- Continue to praise or criticize job performance.
- Attempt to slowly bring the retarded worker into the social aspects of working, such as sharing stories, eating together, etc. Many retarded persons are socially immature.
- If possible, have only one supervisor deal with any one retarded person. Multiple supervisors can be confusing.
- Be aware of and stop any harassment of the worker by co-workers.

Sources of Information Used in This Section:

Working Together and various handouts supplied by the Association for Retarded Citizens (ARC), 2501 Avenue J, Arlington, TX 76006, phone 817-640-0204.

Putting Disabled People in Your Place: Focus on Mentally Retarded Individuals, Mainstream, Inc., 3 Bethesda Metro Center, Suite 830, Bethesda, MD, phone (301) 654-2400.

Report to the President: The Mentally Retarded Worker An Economic Discovery, President's Committee on Mental Retardation, U.S. Department of Health and Human Services, Office of Human Development Services, Washington, DC 20201.

Questions and Answers About Down Syndrome and other materials from the National Down Syndrome Society, 666 Broadway, New York, NY 10012, phone (800) 221-4602 or (212) 460-9330.

Other Sources of Information: See Pages 231–32.

RHEUMATOID ARTHRITIS: See Arthritis.

SCHIZOPHRENIA: See Mental Illness or Disease.

SICKLE-CELL ANEMIA: See Anemia.

SLEEP DISORDERS OR SLEEP APNEA: See Narcolepsy.

SLIPPED DISK: See Back Problems.

SPEECH IMPAIRMENTS

The Problem. Speech and language disorders include severe stuttering, complete loss of voice, adult aphasia, and dysarthria.

A severe stuttering problem still present after one has become an adult is unlikely to be cured or substantially improved. However, some adults are helped by therapists.

A complete loss of voice is often caused by the removal of the larynx because of cancer or other problems. In many cases, the person can be taught to talk by use of an artificial larynx.

Adult aphasia often is the result of a stroke. The person may have a reduced ability to understand what others are saying, as well as problems in coordinating the movements of the lips, tongue, palate, and larynx. This may be only a minor problem, causing a little slurring of sounds. Or it may almost completely prevent effective communication. It is estimated that there are over one million Americans with aphasia.

Dysarthria interferes with normal control of the speech mechanism. Speech may be slurred or otherwise difficult to understand because of a lack of the ability to coordinate the movement of the lips, tongue, palate, and larynx. Diseases such as multiple sclerosis, Parkinson's disease, or Bell's palsy are often the cause of the disorder, as are strokes and accidents. The degree of speaking impairment varies greatly from one individual to another.

Accommodations. When talking to a job applicant or employee who has difficulty speaking, the following suggestions may be helpful:

- Be patient. It may take the person extra time to answer or orally respond.
- Give the individual your undivided attention, even if the slowness of speech is irritating.
- Ask the person for help in communicating. Often, the person has printed instructions on any communication devices they might have that explain the method of communication.

- Speak in your regular tone of voice. Speaking problems usually have nothing to do with hearing or intelligence.
- Inform the person if you do not understand what they are trying to say. Ask them to repeat their message or restate it by using different words.
- To obtain information quickly, ask short questions that require no more than a brief answer or nod of the head.
- Talk to the person as you would any person of their chronological age.

Technical devices that may be used to communicate by people with speaking impairments are diverse both in types and costs. Some examples include the following:

- Speech synthesizers for attachment to computers and word processors to allow person to type messages that will then be spoken by the synthesizer. Cost: $60 to $450, depending upon features and computer to be used.
- Portable word processor-voice synthesizer that allows user to type sentences to be spoken, or put into storage several hundred complete sentences that may be recalled and spoken instantly. Cost: $2,695.
- Portable voice synthesizer that allows customizing of 128 sections by choosing picture keys, rather than spelling the words as in a word processor. Cost: $2,999 to $3,999, depending upon special features.
- Software to be used in computers that allows one to select pictures which then are printed in words on a computer printout. Cost: $150.
- Artificial larynx that allows people without vocal cords to speak. Cost: $450.
- Speech amplifier. Cost: $320.
- Computer, voice synthesizer, extra-large keyboard, and software to allow picture use that is converted to voice output. Cost: $3,935.

Sources of Information Used in This Section:

Recognizing Communicative Disorders, Communication Disorders and Aging, Answers About Adult Aphasia, and *Augmentative Communication,* pamphlets published by The National Association for Hearing and Speech Action, 10801 Rockville Pike, Rockville, MD 20852, phone (800) 638-8255 or (301) 897-8682.

Other General Sources of Information: *(See also pp. 231–32)*

IBM National Support Center for Persons With Disabilities
P.O. Box 2150
Atlanta, GA 30055
(800) 426-2133

Provides information on technical devices to accommodate disabled employees, the large majority of which are not IBM products.

SPINA BIFIDA

The Problem. The result of a birth defect, a part of the bony spine that helps protect the spinal cord fails to develop. Although operations may result in covering the exposed spine, a cure is normally not possible. The individual will usually experience some degree of paralysis of the legs, bladder, and bowels. The extent of impairment differs greatly. Some people with spina bifida may even be able to walk; however, most will use walkers, crutches, or wheelchairs.

Accommodations. By the time a person with spina bifida enters the work force the condition is stable. Because the major problem is lack of mobility, accommodations listed in **SPINAL CORD INJURY AND WHEELCHAIR USERS**, given below, should be considered.

SPINAL CORD INJURY AND WHEELCHAIR USERS

The Problem. People who use wheelchairs do so as a result of many conditions including cerebral palsy, multiple sclerosis, spina bifida, and arthritis. However, the leading cause necessitating wheelchair use is a spinal cord injury resulting from an auto accident, gunshot wound, war injury, diving mishap, or a fall. About 80 percent of all paraplegics and quadriplegics are males who first became paralyzed between the ages of 15 and 30.

Paraplegia refers to paralysis approximately from the waist down. Quadriplegia refers to a paralysis from approximately the shoulders down. As is true with many disabilities, companies are likely to have more employees become paralyzed after initial employment, as compared to paralyzed job applicants. Approximately 60 percent of injuries occur to people who are already in the labor force, while only 20 percent occur before first employment.

People who return to work within one year of the injury usually return to the same job held before the injury.

Slightly over one half of all spinal cord injuries are incomplete, meaning that some feeling or function remains. Before the enactment of the Americans with Disabilities Act, only about a quarter of those whose injury caused paraplegia were still in the labor force five years from the date of accident, while less than one-fifth of quadriplegics remained employed. However, the ADA's employment and transportation sections are expected to substantially increase the number who return to or enter the labor force.

Some paraplegic individuals may not require the use of a wheelchair, but rather a cane, walker, or crutches. And some people with wheelchairs may not have to use them all of the time. Depending upon the circumstances, they may leave the wheelchair for short periods of time. This is particularly true for people with severe arthritis and other nonspinal cord problems.

In addition to the obvious problems in mobility, and sometimes dexterity, damage to the spinal cord usually results in incontinence. This requires a urinary collection bag or catheterization. Many paralyzed wheelchair users also employ laxatives to control bowel movements.

Another less obvious problem is temperature. If it is too cold the person's muscles may tighten and arms may not move properly. On the other hand, too much heat may cause perspiration problems that are compounded by the lack of sensation and constant confinement to the wheelchair.

Three major irritants to many people in wheelchairs are the level of eye contact, people who are too helpful, and a tendency to overlook people in wheelchairs when dealing with a group. Eye contact between people in wheelchairs and nondisabled persons is often unequal. A person in a wheelchair is sitting, while a nondisabled person is often standing. The result can be a psychological disadvantage to the sitting person.

Also psychologically disabling is the tendency of some people to be overly sympathetic and helpful. People in wheelchairs often want—just like other people—to act independently and remain in control of their own actions.

People in wheelchairs report they are too often ignored in group settings. A business meeting of six nondisabled people and one in a wheelchair may often develop into a discussion that subconsciously excludes the disabled person. Because of the individual's exclusion from various activities and groups in the past, the person in the wheelchair may not feel comfortable in joining in without being asked for his or her opinion.

People with a congenital impairment, or one occurring early in life, have fewer adjustments to make than those involved in accidents. Spinal cord accidents are sudden, often occurring to younger men to whom physical prowess is important. Although there are major variations, many accidents will result in hospitalization of four to eight months, followed by extensive rehabilitation. The mental adjustment may be more difficult than the physical adjustment.

Most job applicants have been paralyzed for a lengthy time, therefore, one should not assume they are frustrated or suffering. Although they may have felt like this at one time, most often they are now in a stable condition, both physically and mentally. Pity is more annoying than having to use a wheelchair.

Accessibility. The first and most important accommodation for people in wheelchairs is physical accessibility of the premises. As explained in Chapter 2, "Major Changes to Conform to the Law," newly built and renovated work sites will have to meet the regulations of the U.S. Attorney General. Physical modifications to preexisting work sites to increase accessibility are required only if the changes are reasonable accommodations, as explained in Chapter 5, "Making Accommodations for Disabled Employees." However, accessibility problems that prevent a person in a wheelchair from applying and interviewing for a job can be illegal discrimination. Therefore, the guidelines for accessibility listed in Chapter 2 should be followed in insuring an accessible route of entry to the human relations department, personnel office, or other site where job seekers apply or interview for a job. Accessibility of the remaining portion of an employer's work site can await a specific need to accommodate a disabled employee.

Interviewing. Interviewing a person with mobility problems should normally be done in the same manner as interviewing other job applicants. However, some paraplegic and quadriplegic persons may have speech problems. See the section entitled **SPEECH IMPAIRMENTS** for information.

Once the disability becomes obvious or has been disclosed by the applicant, it may be helpful to follow these recommendations:

1. Shake hands, even if the applicant appears to have arm or hand problems.
2. Offer assistance, but do not give without asking first.

3. Sit down before talking to the applicant. Without becoming obvious, minimize the times you communicate with a person in a wheelchair while they are sitting and you are standing.

4. Relax and talk naturally. Don't avoid words such as "walk" or "run." Persons in wheelchairs use the English language just like other people. They are just as likely to say "I have to run" as anyone else.

5. Do *not* ask the cause of the applicant's problem. It is none of your business and is too personal to ask of a new acquaintance.

6. Do go over the duties of the job. If you are unsure the applicant can perform a listed duty, ask them how they would perform it.

7. If the person appears otherwise qualified for the job, except for the disability, ask the applicant to suggest reasonable accommodations (remember, you don't have to comply with the suggestions if they are not reasonable accommodations or if you discover alternatives that are less costly, but equally effective).

8. If possible, give the applicant a tour of the workplace. This is a good time to discuss possible accommodations.

9. Refrain from assuming certain jobs cannot be done by paralyzed or mobility impaired people.

Testing. Mobility impaired people, especially quadriplegics and those with nerve diseases, may have difficulty in taking tests because of limitations on motor functions such as using their arms or hands. Some may have problems communicating orally because of a lack of muscle control in and around the mouth. Consider adjusting the testing procedures to make allowances for these impairments. Some modifications can include the following:

• Extension of test time limits.
• Providing a page turner or someone to mark answers.
• Providing answer sheets with enlarged answering blocks to mark.
• Allowing the applicant to give oral answers to written tests.

The best source of testing modification ideas can come from the job applicant. Ask what testing accommodations are needed.

Work Site Modifications. Many accommodations are less costly than first imagined. An example of this occurred to a New York City business several years ago. When the company learned that an employee recently paralyzed as a result of an auto accident was planning to return to work, a committee was created to plan workplace accommodations. The committee recommended changes that cost almost one million dollars, including electric-eye doors and substantial renovations of the office areas where the employee worked. Luckily, someone thought to ask the disabled employee what he needed. His only requests: a doorbell at the entrance he could ring so someone would open the door in the morning, and some blocks placed under his desk legs to raise the level so he could wheel himself up to the desk.

This story illustrates two important points in making accommodations. First, keep it simple. Ingenuity and common sense can solve many problems cheaply. Second, ask the disabled person what he or she needs. Often, as in the example, just a few simple, inexpensive modifications need be made. These may include:

- Rearranging files or shelves for wheelchair accessibility;
- Widening aisles between desks, files, and other fixtures to allow access;
- Raising or lowering desks, tables, and workspaces;
- Modifying foot-controlled equipment to hand controlled;
- Providing personal assistance in entering or leaving the workplace;
- Determining if some minor job redesign and job duty swapping with nondisabled workers will allow the disabled person to adequately perform the essential duties of the job.

Accommodations. When hiring or returning a person to work who uses a wheelchair or has other serious mobility problems, be sure the supervisor is briefed in advance. This is the time to explain that the disabled worker is not to get special treatment, but rather reasonable accommodations to allow an equal chance to work.

The most basic accommodation is to provide at least one accessible restroom that is usable by persons in wheelchairs. At a minimum, doors should be at least 32 inches wide, the restroom should be large enough to turn a wheelchair around (an unobstructed circle with a radius of 5 feet is preferable). Stall doors should also be at least 32 inches wide. Grab bars should be on both sides of the toilets. Wash basin controls should be reachable, and towel racks and dispensers should be no more than 48 inches from the floor. See Chapter 2, "Major Changes to Conform to the Law," for more information on physical accessibility.

The following are examples of other accommodation devices:

- Universal holder using a Velcro strap to allow those with poor gripping strength to hold tools or other objects. Cost: $13.50.
- A product also using Velcro that allows a pencil to be inserted to use as a pointing, marking, or keyboard input device. Cost: $5.50.
- Door knob lever for easily turning a round door knob. Cost: $7.50.
- Automatic door shutter so those in wheelchairs need not twist around to close door after going through. Cost: $16.
- Electric automatic swinging door operator. Cost: $1,000 plus installation.
- Wheelchair tray to allow one to work without a table or desk. Cost: $44.50.
- Three-wheeled, motorized chair. Cost: $2,000 to $4,000.
- Basic or battery-powered wheelchairs with devices that allow the paralyzed person to stand. Cost: $4,000 to $11,500.
- A stationary, hydraulic lift unit that allows the user to rise from a wheelchair into a standing position. Cost: $1,995.
- A "Rollator" that looks like a walker with wheels and a basket to carry things. Cost: $345.
- Do-it-Yourself system for marking handicapped parking, accessible entrances, lines, and directional arrows. Cost: $24 and up, depending upon number and type.
- Driving aids that fit on existing vehicles to allow driving without the use of legs. Cost: $300.
- Powered wheelchair lift for stairways up to 18 feet in length. Cost: $6,295.
- Wheelchair lift to avoid short flight of steps (48 inch vertical rise) as is often found at building entrances. Cost: $4,410 plus installation.
- Powered lift with swing-away chair for stairways up to 19 feet. Cost: $2,195.
- Portable, electric-powered wheelchair lift device that allows a person in a wheelchair to be lifted up any flight of stairs (requires another person to guide it). Cost: $5,500.
- Commercial-grade wheelchair lift on track attached to stairway. Cost: $13,000 to $18,000.
- One-story elevator to lift wheelchair that requires no shaft (operates on rail on wall through a cut in the second floor). Cost: $12,000 to $14,000 installed.

- One-story elevator installed into an elevator shaft. Cost: $20,000 and up.
- Complete modular computer desk with turntable. Cost: $575.
- Motorized, swing-away portable desk to be attached to wheelchair. Cost: $550.
- Disk-loading device that allows retrieval and insertion by use of mouth only. Cost: $60.
- Universal telephone adapter for paralyzed people: $96.
- Complete control kit for mouth operation of computers, light switches, and other equipment. Cost: $473.
- Computer access system including optical head pointer, software, connection devices, manual. Cost: $1,395.

As covered in more detail in Chapter 5, "Making Accommodations for Disabled Employees," generally the employer is not required to provide for normal, everyday living aids. So the provision of a wheelchair would usually not be required (but may be voluntarily given). The employer is responsible for obtaining devices that go beyond everyday living aids such as desks, devices used only at work, and even specialized wheelchairs or standing devices, if necessary for good job performance and a reasonable accommodation. Also see Chapter 5 for information about agencies who may pay for wheelchairs, standers, and other devices, and tax advantages that may help reduce the net cost of accommodations to employers.

Accommodating employees in wheelchairs and those using crutches requires that meeting and conference sites, on or off the premises, be accessible. Meeting locations accessible only by stairways should be avoided, while chairs and tables should be arranged to allow physical access through the room. If it is known that a disabled person or persons will attend, chairs should be removed from some tables or other areas to allow wheelchairs to be placed in a proper location.

When planning meetings in hotels, restaurants, country clubs, or any other off-premise location, determine if it is accessible to all attendees.

Sources of Information Used in This Section:

Putting Disabled People in Your Place: Focus on Paraplegia and Quadriplegia, Mainstream, Inc., 3 Bethesda Metro Center, Suite 830, Bethesda, MD 20814, phone (301) 654-2400.

Revised Manual for Accessibility, National Rehabilitation Association, 633 South Washington Street, Alexandria, VA (1988), phone (703) 715–9090.

Gething, Leonard & O'Loughlin, *Person to Person: Community Awareness of Disability* (1989).

Other General Sources of Information: *(See also pp. 231–32)*

National Spinal Cord Injury Association
600 West Cummings Park—Suite 2000
Woburn, MA 01801
(800) 962-9629
    Offers a variety of pamphlets.

IBM National Support Center for Persons With Disabilities
P.O. Box 2150
Atlanta, GA 30055
(800) 426-2133
    Provides information on technical devices to accommodate disabled employees, the large majority of which are not IBM products.

STOMACH ULCER: See Ulcer.

STROKE: See Heart and Circulatory Problems.

TEMPORAL ARTERITIS: See Heart and Circulatory Problems.

THALASSEMIA: See Anemia.

THROMBOPHLEBITIS: See Heart and Circulatory Problems.

THROMBOSIS: See Heart and Circulatory Problems.

TOURETTE SYNDROME: See Nerve Disease.

ULCER

    The Problem. Some 500,000 people are diagnosed with ulcers each year. Gastric ulcers form in the stomach, while peptic ulcers may occur in the esophagus, stomach, or duodenum (the first part of the small intestine).

Gastric ulcers are sores that form in the inner lining of the stomach. Contrary to popular belief, special diets are not usually recommended. Antacids can provide temporary relief from pain, but they do not help cure the problem. Restricting the intake of alcohol and caffeine will be helpful in decreasing the symptoms of a stomach ulcer.

Peptic ulcers affect one of every 100 Americans at some time in their lifetimes. Duodenal ulcers often appear during the ages from 20 to 40. Environmental factors causing peptic ulcers include the ingestion of aspirin, smoking, and drinking caffeine. Drinking alcohol does not appear to be a major cause. Increasingly, physicians are also discounting stress as a cause of ulcers.

Treatment and Accommodation. Medical treatment may be by drugs or surgery. Few, if any, employer accommodations will normally be needed, except for release time to see a doctor and medical leave time if an operation is necessary.

Sources of Information Used in This Section:

The Inside Story on Ulcers, Current Health (Jan. 1988), pp. 20–1.

Clearfield & Wright, *Update on peptic ulcer disease*, Patient Care (Feb. 15, 1990), pp. 28–40.

Malagelada, *About Stomach Ulcers* and *Peptic Ulcers*, National Digestive Diseases Clearinghouse, National Institute of Arthritis, Diabetes and Digestive Diseases, National Institutes of Health, 1255 23d St., N.W., Suite 277, Washington, DC 20037, phone (202) 296-1138.

Additional Sources of Information: See Pages 231–32.

THYROID PROBLEMS: See Graves Disease.

ULCERATIVE COLITIS: See Digestive Diseases.

Appendix A

Americans With Disabilities Act (1990)
(P.L. 101–336, approved July 26, 1990)

Preface and Part I. Employment

Chapter 126 [of 42 U.S. Code]. Americans With Disabilities

§ 12101. Short title; Table of contents

[Sec. 1] (a) This act may be cited as the "Americans With Disabilities Act of 1990."
(b) Table of Contents [Omitted.]

§ 12102. Findings and purposes

[Sec. 2] (a) The Congress finds that—
(1) some 43,000,000 Americans have one or more physical or mental disabilities, and this number is increasing as the population as a whole is growing older;
(2) historically, society has tended to isolate and segregate individuals with disabilities, and, despite some improvements, such forms of discrimination against individuals with disabilities continue to be a serious and pervasive social problem;
(3) discrimination against individuals with disabilities persists in such critical areas as employment, housing, public accommodations, education, transportation, communication, recreation, institutionalization, health services, voting, and access to public services;
(4) unlike individuals who have experienced discrimination on the basis of race, color, sex, national origin, religion, or age, individuals who have experienced discrimination on the basis of disability have often had no legal recourse to redress such discrimination;
(5) individuals with disabilities continually encounter various forms of discrimination, including outright intentional exclusion, the discriminatory effects of architectural, transportation, and communication barriers, overprotective rules and policies, failure to make modifications to existing facilities and practices, exclusionary qualification standards and criteria, segregation, and regulation to lesser services, programs, activities, benefits, jobs, or other opportunities;

347

(6) census data, national polls, and other studies have documented that people with disabilities, as a group, occupy an inferior status in our society, vocationally, economically, and educationally;

(7) individuals with disabilities are a discrete and insular minority who have been faced with restrictions and limitations, subjected to a history of purposeful unequal treatment, and regulated to a position of political powerlessness in our society, based on characteristics that are beyond the control of such individuals and resulting from stereotypic assumptions not truly indicative of the individual ability of such individuals to participate in, and contribute to, society;

(8) the Nation's proper goals regarding individuals with disabilities are to assure equality of opportunity, full participation, independent living, and economic self-sufficiency for such individuals; and

(9) the continuing existence of unfair and unnecessary discrimination and prejudice denies people with disabilities the opportunity to compete on an equal basis and to pursue those opportunities for which our free society is justifiably famous, and costs the United States billions of dollars in unnecessary expenses, resulting from dependency and nonproductivity.

(b) It is the purpose of this Act—

(1) to provide a clear and comprehensive national mandate for the elimination of discrimination against individuals with disabilities;

(2) to provide clear, strong, consistent, enforceable standards addressing discrimination against individuals with disabilities;

(3) to ensure that the Federal Government plays a central role in enforcing the standards established in this Act on behalf of individuals with disabilities; and

(4) to invoke the sweep of congressional authority, including the power to enforce the fourteenth amendment and to regulate commerce, in order to address the major areas of discrimination faced day-to-day by people with disabilities.

§ 12103. Definitions

[Sec. 3] As used in this Act:

(1) The term "auxiliary aids and services" includes—

(A) qualified interpreters or other effective methods of making aurally delivered materials available to individuals with hearing impairments;

(B) qualified readers, taped texts, or other effective methods of making visually delivered materials available to individuals with visual impairments;

(C) acquisition or modification of equipment or devices; and

(D) other similar services and actions.

(2) The term "disability" means, with respect to an individual—

(A) a physical or mental impairment that substantially limits one or more of the major life activities of such individual;

(B) a record of such an impairment; or

(C) being regarded as having such an impairment.

(3) The term "State" means each of the several States, the District of Columbia, the Commonwealth of Puerto Rico, Guam, American Samoa, the Virgin Islands, the Trust Territory of the Pacific Islands, and the Commonwealth of the Northern Mariana Islands.

Title I. Employment

§ 12111. Definitions

[Sec. 101] As used in this title:

(1) The term "Commission" means the Equal Employment Opportunity Commission established by section 705 of the Civil Rights Act of 1964 (42 U.S.C. 2000e–4).

(2) The term "covered entity" means an employer, employment agency, labor organization, or joint labor-management committee.

(3) The term "direct threat" means a significant risk to the health or safety of others that cannot be eliminated by reasonable accommodation.

(4) The term "employee" means an individual employed by an employer.

(5)(A) The term "employer" means a person engaged in an industry affecting commerce who has 15 or more employees for each working day in each of 20 or more calendar weeks in the current or preceding calendar year, and any agent of such person, except that, for two years following the effective date of this title, an employer means a person engaged in an industry affecting commerce who has 25 or more employees for each working day in each of 20 or more calendar weeks in the current or preceding year, and any agent of such person.

(B) The term "employer" does not include—
  (i) the United States, a corporation wholly owned by the government of the United States, or an Indian tribe; or
  (ii) a bona fide private membership club (other than a labor organization) that is exempt from taxation under section 501(c) of the Internal Revenue Code of 1986.

(6)(A) The term "illegal use of drugs" means the use of drugs, the possession or distribution of which is unlawful under the Controlled Substances Act (21 U.S.C. 812). Such term does not include the use of a drug taken under supervision by a licensed health care professional, or other uses authorized by the Controlled Substances Act or other provisions of Federal law.

(B) The term "drug" means a controlled substance, as defined in schedule I through V of section 202 of the Controlled Substances Act.

(7) The terms "person", "labor organization", "employment agency", "commerce", and "industry affecting commerce", shall have the same meaning given such terms in section 701 of the Civil Rights Act of 1964 (42 U.S.C. 2000e).

(8) The term "qualified individual with a disability" means an individual with a disability who, with or without reasonable accommodation, can perform the essential functions of the employment position that such individual holds or desires. For the purposes of this title, consideration shall be given

to the employer's judgment as to what functions of a job are essential, and if an employer has prepared a written description before advertising or interviewing applicants for the job, this description shall be considered evidence of the essential functions of the job.

(9) The term "reasonable accommodation" may include—

    (A) making existing facilities used by employees readily accessible to and usable by individuals with disabilities; and

    (B) job restructuring, part-time or modified work schedules, reassignment to a vacant position, acquisition or modification of equipment or devices, appropriate adjustment or modifications of examinations, training materials or policies, the provision of qualified readers or interpreters, nad other similar accommodations for individuals with disabilities.

(10)(A) The term "undue hardship" means an action requiring significant difficulty or expense, when considered in light of the factors set forth in subparagraph (B).

    (B) In determining whether an accommodation would impose an undue hardship on a covered entity, factors to be considered include—

        (i) the nature and cost of the accommodation needed under this Act;

        (ii) the overall financial resources of the facility or facilities involved in the provision of the reasonable accommodation; the number of persons employed at such facility; the effect on expenses and resources, or the impact otherwise of such accommodation upon the operation of the facility;

        (iii) the overall financial resources of the covered entity; the overall size of the business of a covered entity with respect to the number of its employees; the number, type, and location of its facilities; and

        (iv) the type of operation or operations of the covered entity, including the composition, structure, and functions of the workforce of such entity; the geographic separateness, administrative, or fiscal relationship of the facility or facilities in question to the covered entity.

§ 12112. Discrimination

[Sec. 102] (a) No covered entity shall discriminate against a qualified individual with a disability because of the disability of such individual in regard to job application procedures, the hiring, advancement, or discharge of employees, employee compensation, job training, and other terms, conditions, and privileges of employment.

(b) As used in subsection (a), the term "discriminate" includes—

(1) limiting, segregating, or classifying a job applicant or employee in a way that adversely affects the opportunities or status of such applicant or employee because of the disability of such applicant or employee;

(2) participating in a contractual or other arrangement or relationship that

has the effect of subjecting a covered entity's qualified applicant or employee with a disability to the discrimination prohibited by this title (such relationship includes a relationship with an employment or referral agency, labor union, an organization providing fringe benefits to an employee of the covered entity, or an organization providing training and apprenticeship programs);

(3) utilizing standards, criteria, or methods of administration—

   (A) that have the effect of discrimination on the basis of disability; or

   (B) that perpetuate the discrimination of others who are subject to common administrative control;

(4) excluding or otherwise denying equal jobs or benefits to a qualified individual because of the known disability of an individual with whom the qualified individual is known to have a relationship or association;

(5)(A) not making reasonable accommodations to the known physical or mental limitations of an otherwise qualified individual with a disability who is an applicant or employee, unless such covered entity can demonstrate that the accommodation would impose an undue hardship on the operation of the business of such covered entity; or

   (B) denying employment opportunities to a job applicant or employee who is an otherwise qualified individual with a disability, if such denial is based on the need of such covered entity to make reasonable accommodation to the physical or mental impairments of the employee or applicant;

(6) using qualification standards, employment tests or other selection criteria that screen out or tend to screen out an individual with a disability or a class of individuals with disabilities unless the standard, test or other selection criteria, as used by the covered entity, is shown to be job-related for the position in question and is consistent with business necessity; and

(7) failing to select and administer tests concerning employment in the most effective manner to ensure that, when such test is administered to a job applicant or employee who has a disability that impairs sensory, manual, or speaking skills, such test results accurately reflect the skills, aptitude, or whatever other factor of such applicant or employee that such test purports to measure, rather than reflecting the impaired sensory, manual, or speaking skills of such employee or applicant (except where such skills are the factors that the test purports to measure).

(c)(1) The prohibition against discrimination as referred to in subsection (a) shall include medical examinations and inquiries.

(2)(A) Except as provided in paragraph (3), a covered entity shall not conduct a medical examination or make inquiries of a job applicant as to whether such applicant is an individual with a disability or as to the nature or severity of such disability.

   (B) A covered entity may make preemployment inquiries into the ability of an applicant to perform job-related functions.

(3) A covered entity may require a medical examination after an offer of employment has been made to a job applicant and prior to the commencement of the employment duties of such applicant, and may condition an offer of employment on the results of such examination, if—

(A) all entering employees are subjected to such an examination regardless of disability;

(B) information obtained regarding the medical condition or history of the applicant is collected and maintained on separate forms and in separate medical files and is treated as a confidential medical record, except that—

    (i) supervisors and managers may be informed regarding necessary restrictions on the work or duties of employee and necessary accommodations;

    (ii) first aid and safety personnel may be informed, when appropriate, if the disability might require emergency treatment; and

    (iii) government officials investigating compliance with this Act shall be provided relevant information on request; and

(C) the results of such examination are used only in accordance with this title.

(4)(A) A covered entity shall not require a medical examination and shall not make inquiries of an employee as to whether such employee is an individual with a disability or as to the nature or severity of the disability, unless such examination or inquiry is shown to be job-related and consistent with business necessity.

(B) A covered entity may conduct voluntary medical examinations, including voluntary medical histories, which are part of an employee health program available to employees at that work site. A covered entity may make inquiries into the ability of an employee to perform job-related functions.

(C) Information obtained under subparagraph (B) regarding the medical condition or history of any employee are subject to the requirements of subparagraphs (B) and (C) of paragraph (3).

§ 12113. Defenses

[Sec. 103] (a) It may be a defense to a charge of discrimination under this Act that an alleged application of qualification standards, tests, or selection criteria that screen out or tend to screen out or otherwise deny a job or benefit to an individual with a disability has been shown to be job-related and consistent with business necessity, and such performance cannot be accomplished by reasonable accommodation, as required under this title.

(b) The term "qualification standards" may include a requirement that an individual shall not pose a direct threat to the health or safety of other individuals in the workplace.

(c)(1) This title shall not prohibit a religious corporation, association, educational institution, or society from giving preference in employment to individuals of a particular religion to perform work connected with the carrying on by such corporation, association, educational institution, or society of its activities.

(2) Under this title, a religious organization may require that all applicants and employees conform to the religious tenets of such organization.

(d)(1) The Secretary of Health and Human Services, not later than 6 months after the date of enactment of this Act, shall—

    (A) review all infectious and communicable diseases which may be transmitted through handling the food supply;

    (B) publish a list of infectious and communicable diseases which are transmitted through handling the food supply;

    (C) publish the methods by which such diseases are transmitted; and

    (D) widely disseminate such information regarding the list of diseases and their modes of transmissability to the general public.

Such list shall be updated annually.

(2) In any case in which an individual has an infectious or communicable disease that is transmitted to others through the handling of food, that is included on the list developed by the Secretary of Health and Human Services under paragraph (1), and which cannot be eliminated by reasonable accommodation, a covered entity may refuse to assign or continue to assign such individual to a job involving food handling

(3) Nothing in this Act shall be construed to preempt, modify, or amend any State, county, or local law, ordinance, or regulation applicable to food handling which is designed to protect the public health from individuals who pose a significant risk to the health or safety of others, which cannot be eliminated by reasonable accommodation, pursuant to the list of infectious or communicable diseases and the modes of transmissability published by the Secretary of Health and Human Services.

§ 12114. Illegal use of drugs and alcohol

[Sec. 104] (a) For purposes of this title, the term "qualified individual with disability" shall not include any employee or applicant who is currently engaging in the illegal use of drugs, when the covered entity acts on the basis of such use.

(b) Nothing in subsection (a) shall be construed to exclude as a qualified individual with a disability an individual who—

(1) has successfully completed a supervised drug rehabilitation program and is no longer engaging in the illegal use of drugs, or has otherwise been rehabilitated successfully and is no longer engaging in such use;

(2) is participating in a supervised rehabilitation program and is no longer engaging in such use; or

(3) is erroneously regarded as engaging in such use, but is not engaging in such use;

except that it shall not be a violation of this Act for a covered entity to adopt or administer reasonable policies or procedures, including but not limited to drug testing, designed to ensure that an individual described in paragraph (1) or (2) is no longer engaging in the illegal use of drugs.

(c) A covered entity—

(1) may prohibit the illegal use of drugs and the use alcohol at the workplace by all employees;

(2) may require that employees shall not be under the influence of alcohol or be engaging in the illegal use of drugs at the workplace;

(3) may require that employees behave in conformance with the requirements

established under the Drug-Free Workplace Act of 1988 (41 U.S.C. 701 et seq.);

(4) may hold an employee who engages in the illegal use of drugs or who is an alcoholic to the same qualification standards for employment or job performance and behavior that such entity holds other employees, even if any unsatisfactory performance or behavior is related to the drug use or alcoholism of such employee; and

(5) may, with respect to Federal regulations regarding alcohol and the illegal use of drugs, require that—

(A) employees comply with the standards established in such regulations of the Department of Defense, if the employees of the covered entity are employed in an industry subject to such regulations, including complying with regulations (if any) that apply to employment in sensitive positions in such an industry, in the case of employees of the covered entity who are employed in such positions (as defined in the regulations of the Department of Defense);

(B) employees comply with the standards established in such regulations of the Nuclear Regulatory Commission, if the employees of the covered entity are employed in an industry subject to such regulations, including complying with regulations (if any) that apply to employment in sensitive positions in such an industry, in the case of employees of the covered entity who are employed in such positions (as defined in the regulations of the Nuclear Regulatory Commission); and

(C) employees comply with the standards established in such regulations of the Department of Transportation, if the employees of the covered entity are employed in a transportation industry subject to such regulations, including complying with such regulations (if any) that apply to employment in sensitive positions in such an industry, in the case of employees of the covered entity who are employed in such positions (as defined in the regulations of the Department of Transportation).

(d)(1) For purposes of this title, a test to determine the illegal use of drugs shall not be considered a medical examination.

(2) Nothing in this title shall be construed to encourage, prohibit, or authorize the conducting of drug testing for the illegal use of drugs by job applicants or employees or making employment decisions based on such test results.

(e) Nothing in this title shall be construed to encourage, prohibit, restrict, or authorize the otherwise lawful exercise by entities subject to the jurisdiction of the Department of Transportation of authority to—

(1) test employees of such entities in, and applicants for, positions involving safety-sensitive duties for the illegal use of drugs and for on-duty impairment by alcohol; and

(2) remove such persons who test positive for illegal use of drugs and on-duty impairment by alcohol pursuant to paragraph (1) from safety-sensitive duties in implementing subsection (c).

§ 12115. Posting notices

[Sec. 105] Every employer, employment agency, labor organization, or joint labor-management committee covered under this title shall post notices in an accessible format to applicants, employees, and members describing the applicable provisions of this Act, in the manner prescribed by section 711 of the Civil Rights Act of 1964 (42 U.S.C. 2000e–10).

§ 12116. Regulations

[Sec. 106] Not later than 1 year after the date of enactment of this Act, the Commission shall issue regulations in an accessible format to carry out this title in accordance with subchapter II of chapter 5 of title 5, United States Code.

§ 12117. Enforcement

[Sec. 107] (a) The powers, remedies, and procedures set forth in sections 705, 706, 707, 709, and 710 of the Civil Rights Act of 1964 (42 U.S.C. 2000e–4, 2000e–5, 2000e–6, 2000e–8, and 2000e–9) shall be the powers, remedies, and procedures this title provides to the Commission, to the Attorney General, or to any person alleging discrimination on the basis of disability in violation of any provision of this Act, or regulations promulgated under section 106, concerning employment.

(b) The agencies with enforcement authority for actions which allege employment discrimination under this title and under the Rehabilitation Act of 1973 shall develop procedures to ensure that administrative complaints filed under this title and under the Rehabilitation Act of 1973 are dealt with in a manner that avoids duplication of effort and prevents imposition of inconsistent or conflicting standards for the same requirements under this title and the Rehabilitation Act of 1973. The Commission, the Attorney General, and the Office of Federal Contract Compliance Programs shall establish such coordinating mechanisms (similar to provisions contained in the joint regulations promulgated by the Commission and the Attorney General at part 42 of title 28 and part 1691 of title 29, Code of Federal Regulations, and the Memorandum of Understanding between the Commission and the Office of Federal Contract Compliance Programs dated January 16, 1981 (46 Fed. Reg. 7435, January 23, 1981) in regulations implementing this title and Rehabilitation Act of 1973 not later than 18 months after the date of enactment of this Act.

§ 12118. Effective date

[Sec. 108] This title shall become effective 24 months after the date of enactment.

Appendix B

EEOC: Americans With Disabilities Act Employment Regulations

Following is the text of the rules issued by EEOC to implement Title I, the employment provisions, of the 1990 Americans with Disabilities Act. Codified as 29 CFR Part 1630, the final rules were published and became effective on July 26, 1991, at 56 FR 35734.

PART 1630—REGULATIONS TO IMPLEMENT THE EQUAL EMPLOYMENT PROVISIONS OF THE AMERICANS WITH DISABILITIES ACT

Table of Contents

Section 1630.1. Purpose, Applicability, and Construction

(a) *Purpose.* The purpose of this part is to implement title I of the Americans with Disabilities Act (42 U.S.C. 12101, *et seq.*) (ADA), requiring equal employment opportunities for qualified individuals with disabilities, and sections 3(2), 3(3), 501, 503, 506(e), 508, 510, and 511 of the ADA as those sections pertain to the employment of qualified individuals with disabilities.

(b) *Applicability.* This part applies to "covered entities" as defined at Sec. 1630.2(b).

(c) *Construction.*—(1) *In general.* Except as otherwise provided in this part, this part does not apply a lesser standard than the standards applied under title V of the Rehabilitation Act of 1973 (29 U.S.C. 790-794a), or the regulations issued by Federal agencies pursuant to that title.

(2) *Relationship to other laws.* This part does not invalidate or limit the remedies, rights, and procedures of any Federal law or law of any State or political subdivision of any State or jurisdiction that provides greater or equal protection for the rights of individuals with disabilities than are afforded by this part.

Sec. 1630.2. Definitions

(a) *Commission* means the Equal Employment Opportunity Commission established by section 705 of the Civil Rights Act of 1964 (42 U.S.C. 2000e-4).

357

(b) *Covered Entity* means an employer, employment agency, labor organization, or joint labor management committee.

(c) *Person, labor organization, employment agency, commerce and industry affecting commerce* shall have the same meaning given those terms in section 701 of the Civil Rights Act of 1964 (42 U.S.C. 2000e).

(d) *State* means each of the several States, the District of Columbia, the Commonwealth of Puerto Rico, Guam, American Samoa, the Virgin Islands, the Trust Territory of the Pacific Islands, and the Commonwealth of the Northern Mariana Islands.

(e) *Employer.*—(1) *In general.* The term employer means a person engaged in an industry affecting commerce who has 15 or more employees for each working day in each of 20 or more calendar weeks in the current or preceding calendar year, and any agent of such person, except that, from July 26, 1992 through July 25, 1994, an employer means a person engaged in an industry affecting commerce who has 25 or more employees for each working day in each of 20 or more calendar weeks in the current or preceding year and any agent of such person.

(2) *Exceptions.* The term employer does not include—

(i) The United States, a corporation wholly owned by the government of the United States, or an Indian tribe; or

(ii) A bona fide private membership club (other than a labor organization) that is exempt from taxation under section 501(c) of the Internal Revenue Code of 1986.

(f) *Employee* means an individual employed by an employer.

(g) *Disability* means, with respect to an individual—

(1) A physical or mental impairment that substantially limits one or more of the major life activities of such individual;

(2) A record of such an impairment; or

(3) being regarded as having such an impairment.
(See Sec. 1630.3 for exceptions to this definition).

(h) *Physical or mental impairment* means:

(1) Any physiological disorder, or condition, cosmetic disfigurement, or anatomical loss affecting one or more of the following body systems: neurological, musculoskeletal, special sense organs, respiratory (including speech organs), cardiovascular, reproductive, digestive, genito-urinary, hemic and lymphatic, skin, and endocrine; or

(2) Any mental or psychological disorder, such as mental retardation, organic brain syndrome, emotional or mental illness, and specific learning disabilities.

(i) *Major Life Activities* means functions such as caring for oneself, performing manual tasks, walking, seeing, hearing, speaking, breathing, learning, and working.

(j) *Substantially limits*—(1) The term *substantially limits* means:

(i) Unable to perform a major life activity that the average person in the general population can perform; or

(ii) Significantly restricted as to the condition, manner or duration under which an individual can perform a particular major life activity as compared to the condition, manner, or duration under which the average person in the general population can perform that same major life activity.

(2) The following factors should be considered in determining whether an individual is substantially limited in a major life activity:

(i) The nature and severity of the impairment;

(ii) The duration or expected duration of the impairment; and

(iii) The permanent or long term impact, or the expected permanent or long term impact of or resulting from the impairment.

(3) With respect to the major life activity of *working*—

(i) The term *substantially limits* means significantly restricted in the ability to perform either a class of jobs or a broad range of jobs in various classes as compared to the average person having comparable training, skills and abilities. The inability to perform a single, particular job does not constitute a substantial limitation in the major life activity of working.

(ii) In addition to the factors listed in paragraph (j)(2) of this section, the following factors may be considered in determining whether an individual is substantially limited in the major life activity of "working":

(A) The geographical area to which the individual has reasonable access;

(B) The job from which the individual has been disqualified because of an impairment, and the number and types of jobs utilizing similar training, knowledge, skills or abilities, within that geographical area, from which the individual is also disqualified because of the impairment (class of jobs); and/or

(C) The job from which the individual has been disqualified because of an impairment, and the number and types of other jobs not utilizing similar training, knowledge, skills or abilities, within that geographical area, from which the individual is also disqualified because of the impairment (broad range of jobs in various classes).

(k) *Has a record of such impairment* means has a history of, or has been misclassified as having, a mental or physical impairment that substantially limits one or more major life activities.

(l) *Is regarded as having such an impairment* means:

(1) Has a physical or mental impairment that does not substantially limit major life activities but is treated by a covered entity as constituting such limitation;

(2) Has a physical or mental impairment that substantially limits major life activities only as a result of the attitudes of others toward such impairment; or

(3) Has none of the impairments defined in paragraphs (h) (1) or (2) of this section but is treated by a covered entity as having a substantially limiting impairment.

(m) *Qualified individual with a disability* means an individual with a disability who satisfies the requisite skill, experience, education and other job-related requirements of the employment position such individual holds or desires, and who, with or without reasonable accommodation, can perform the essential functions of such position. (See Sec. 1630.3 for exceptions to this definition).

(n) *Essential functions.*—(1) *In general.* The term *essential functions* means the fundamental job duties of the employment position the individual with a disability holds or desires. The term "essential functions" does not include the marginal functions of the position.

(2) A job function may be considered essential for any of several reasons, including but not limited to the following:

(i) The function may be essential because the reason the position exists is to perform that function;

(ii) The function may be essential because of the limited number of employees available among whom the performance of that job function can be distributed; and/or

(iii) The function may be highly specialized so that the incumbent in the position is hired for his or her expertise or ability to perform the particular function.

(3) Evidence of whether a particular function is essential includes, but is not limited to:

(i) The employer's judgment as to which functions are essential;

(ii) Written job descriptions prepared before advertising or interviewing applicants for the job;

(iii) The amount of time spent on the job performing the function;

(iv) The consequences of not requiring the incumbent to perform the function;

(v) The terms of a collective bargaining agreement;

(vi) The work experience of past incumbents in the job; and/or

(vii) The current work experience of incumbents in similar jobs.

(o) *Reasonable accommodation.* (1) The term *reasonable accommodation* means:

(i) Modifications or adjustments to a job application process that enable a qualified applicant with a disability to be considered for the position such qualified applicant desires; or

(ii) Modifications or adjustments to the work environment, or to the manner or circumstances under which the position held or desired is customarily performed, that enable a qualified individual with a disability to perform the essential functions of that position; or

(iii) Modifications or adjustments that enable a covered entity's employee with a disability to enjoy equal benefits and privileges of employment as are enjoyed by its other similarly situated employees without disabilities.

(2) *Reasonable accommodation* may include but is not limited to:

(i) Making existing facilities used by employees readily accessible to and usable by individuals with disabilities; and

(ii) Job restructuring; part-time or modified work schedules; reassignment to a vacant position; acquisition or modifications of equipment or devices; appropriate adjustment or modifications of examinations, training materials, or policies; the provision of qualified readers or interpreters; and other similar accommodations for individuals with disabilities.

(3) To determine the appropriate reasonable accommodation it may be necessary for the covered entity to initiate an informal, interactive process with the qualified individual with a disability in need of the accommodation. This process should identify the precise limitations resulting from the disability and potential reasonable accommodations that could overcome those limitations.

(p) *Undue hardship*—(1) *In general.* *Undue hardship* means, with respect to the provision of an accommodation, significant difficulty or expense incurred by a covered entity, when considered in light of the factors set forth in paragraph (p)(2) of this section.

(2) *Factors to be considered.* In determining whether an accommodation would impose an undue hardship on a covered entity, factors to be considered include:

(i) The nature and net cost of the accommodation needed under this part, taking into consideration the availability of tax credits and deductions, and/or outside funding;

(ii) The overall financial resources of the facility or facilities involved in the provision of the reasonable accommodation, the number of persons employed at such facility, and the effect on expenses and resources;

(iii) The overall financial resources of the covered entity, the overall size of the business of the covered entity with respect to the number of its employees, and the number, type and location of its facilities;

(iv) The type of operation or operations of the covered entity, including the composition, structure and functions of the workforce of such entity, and the geographic separateness and administrative or fiscal relationship of the facility or facilities in question to the covered entity; and

(v) The impact of the accommodation upon the operation of the facility, including the impact on the ability of other employees to perform their duties and the impact on the facility's ability to conduct business.

(q) *Qualification standards* means the personal and professional attributes including the skill, experience, education, physical, medical, safety and other requirements established by a covered entity as requirements which an individual must meet in order to be eligible for the position held or desired.

(r) *Direct Threat* means a significant risk of substantial harm to the health or safety of the individual or others that cannot be eliminated or reduced by reasonable accommodation. The determination that an individual poses a "direct threat" shall be based on an individualized assessment of the individual's present ability to safely perform the essential functions of the job. This assessment shall be based on a reasonable medical judgment that relies on the most current medical knowledge and/or on the best available objective evidence. In determining whether an individual would pose a direct threat, the factors to be considered include:

(1) The duration of the risk;

(2) The nature and severity of the potential harm;

(3) The likelihood that the potential harm will occur; and

(4) The imminence of the potential harm.

Section 1630.3. Exceptions to the Definitions of "Disability" and "Qualified Individual with a Disability"

(a) The terms *disability* and *qualified individual with a disability* do not include individuals currently engaging in the illegal use of drugs, when the covered entity acts on the basis of such use.

(1) *Drug* means a controlled substance, as defined in schedules I through V of Section 202 of the Controlled Substances Act (21 U.S.C 812)

(2) *Illegal use of drugs* means the use of drugs the possession or distribution of which is unlawful under the Controlled Substances Act, as periodically updated by the Food and Drug Administration. This term does not include the use of a drug taken under the supervision of a licensed health care professional, or other uses authorized by the Controlled Substances Act or other provisions of Federal law.

(b) However, the terms *disability* and *qualified* individual with a disability may not exclude an individual who:

(1) Has successfully completed a supervised drug rehabilitation program and is no longer engaging in the illegal use of drugs, or has otherwise been rehabilitated successfully and is no longer engaging in the illegal use of drugs; or

(2) Is participating in a supervised rehabilitation program and is no longer engaging in such use; or

(3) Is erroneously regarded as engaging in such use, but is not engaging in such use.

(c) It shall not be a violation of this part for a covered entity to adopt or administer reasonable policies or procedures, including but not limited to drug testing, designed to ensure that an individual described in paragraph (b) (1) or (2) of this section is no longer engaging in the illegal use of drugs. (See Sec. 1630.16(c) Drug testing).

(d) *Disability* does not include:

(1) Transvestism, transsexualism, pedophilia, exhibitionism, voyeurism, gender identity disorders not resulting from physical impairments, or other sexual behavior disorders;

(2) Compulsive gambling, kleptomania, or pyromania; or

(3) Psychoactive substance use disorders resulting from current illegal use of drugs.

(e) *Homosexuality* and *bisexuality* are not impairments and so are not disabilities as defined in this part.

Section 1630.4. Discrimination Prohibited

It is unlawful for a covered entity to discriminate on the basis of disability against a qualified individual with a disability in regard to:

(a) Recruitment, advertising, and job application procedures;

(b) Hiring, upgrading, promotion, award of tenure, demotion, transfer, layoff, termination, right of return from layoff, and rehiring;

(c) Rates of pay or any other form of compensation and changes in compensation;

(d) Job assignments, job classifications, organizational structures, position descriptions, lines of progression, and seniority lists;

(e) Leaves of absence, sick leave, or any other leave;

(f) Fringe benefits available by virtue of employment, whether or not administered by the covered entity;

(g) Selection and financial support for training, including: apprenticeships, professional meetings, conferences and other related activities, and selection for leaves of absence to pursue training;

(h) Activities sponsored by a covered entity including social and recreational programs; and

(i) Any other term, condition, or privilege of employment.

The term *discrimination* includes, but is not limited to, the acts described in Secs. 1630.5 through 1630.13 of this part.

Section 1630.5. Limiting Segregating, and Classifying

It is unlawful for a covered entity to limit, segregate, or classify a job applicant or employee in a way that adversely affects his or her employment opportunities or status on the basis of disability.

Section 1630.6. Contractual or Other Arrangements

(a) *In qeneral.* It is unlawful for a covered entity to participate in a contractual or other arrangement or relationship that has the effect of subjecting the covered entity's own qualified applicant or employee with a disability to the discrimination prohibited by this part.

(b) *Contractual or other arrangement defined.* The phrase *contractual or other arrangement or relationship* includes, but is not limited to, a relationship with an employment or referral agency; labor union, including collective bargaining agreements; an organization providing fringe benefits to an employee of the cov-

ered entity; or an organization providing training and apprenticeship programs.

(c) *Application.* This section applies to a covered entity, with respect to its own applicants or employees, whether the entity offered the contract or initiated the relationship, or whether the entity accepted the contract or acceded to the relationship. A covered entity is not liable for the actions of the other party or parties to the contract which only affect that other party's employees or applicants.

Section 1630.7. Standards, Criteria, or Methods of Administration

It is unlawful for a covered entity to use standards, criteria, or methods of administration, which are not job-related and consistent with business necessity, and:

(a) That have the effect of discriminating on the basis of disability; or

(b) That perpetuate the discrimination of others who are subject to common administrative control.

Section 1630.8. Relationship or Association With an Individual With a Disability

It is unlawful for a covered entity to exclude or deny equal jobs or benefits to, or otherwise discriminate against, a qualified individual because of the known disability of an individual with whom the qualified individual is known to have a family, business, social or other relationship or association.

Section 1630.9. Not Making Reasonable Accommodation

(a) It is unlawful for a covered entity not to make reasonable accommodation to the known physical or mental limitations of an otherwise qualified applicant or employee with a disability, unless such covered entity can demonstrate that the accommodation would impose an undue hardship on the operation of its business.

(b) It is unlawful for a covered entity to deny employment opportunities to an otherwise qualified job applicant or employee with a disability based on the need of such covered entity to make reasonable accommodation to such individual's physical or mental impairments.

(c) A covered entity shall not be excused from the requirements of this part because of any failure to receive technical assistance authorized by section 506 of the ADA, including any failure in the development or dissemination of any technical assistance manual authorized by that Act.

(d) A qualified individual with a disability is not required to accept an accommodation, aid, service, opportunity or benefit which such qualified individual chooses not to accept. However, if such individual rejects a reasonable accommodation, aid, service, opportunity or benefit that is necessary to enable the individual to perform the essential functions of the position held or desired, and cannot, as a result of that rejection, perform the essential functions of the position, the individual will not be considered a qualified individual with a disability.

Section 1630.10. Qualification Standards, Tests, and Other Selection Criteria

It is unlawful for a covered entity to use qualification standards, employment tests or other selection criteria that screen out or tend to screen out an individual with a disability or a class of individuals with disabilities, on the basis of disability, unless the standard, test or other selection criteria, as used by the covered entity, is shown to be job-related for the position in question and is consistent with business necessity.

Section 1630.11. Administration of Tests

It is unlawful for a covered entity to fail to select and administer tests concerning employment in the most effective manner to ensure that, when a test is administered to a job applicant or employee who has a disability that impairs sensory, manual or speaking skills, the test results accurately reflect the skills, aptitude, or whatever other factor of the applicant or employee that the test purports to measure, rather than reflecting the impaired sensory, manual, or speaking skills of such employee or applicant (except where such skills are the factors that the test purports to measure).

Section 1630.12. Retaliation and Coercion

(a) *Retaliation.* It is unlawful to discriminate against any individual because that individual has opposed any act or practice made unlawful by this part or because that individual made a charge, testified, assisted, or participated in any manner in an investigation, proceeding, or hearing to enforce any provision contained in this part.

(b) *Coercion, interference or intimidation.* It is unlawful to coerce, intimidate, threaten, harass or interfere with any individual in the exercise or enjoyment of, or because that individual aided or encouraged any other individual in the exercise of, any right granted or protected by this part.

Section 1630.13. Prohibited Medical Examinations and Inquiries

(a) *Pre-employment examination or inquiry.* Except as permitted by Sec. 1630.14, it is unlawful for a covered entity to conduct a medical examination of an applicant or to make inquiries as to whether an applicant is an individual with a disability or as to the nature or severity of such disability.

(b) *Examination or inquiry of employees.* Except as permitted by Sec. 1630.14, it is unlawful for a covered entity to require a medical examination of an employee or to make inquiries as to whether an employee is an individual with a disability or as to the nature or severity of such disability.

Section 1630.14. Medical Examinations and Inquiries Specifically Permitted

(a) *Acceptable pre-employment inquiry.* A covered entity may make pre-employment inquiries into the ability of an applicant to perform job-related functions, and/or may ask an applicant to describe or to demonstrate how, with or without reasonable accommodation, the applicant will be able to perform job-related functions.

(b) *Employment entrance examination.* A covered entity may require a medical examination (and/or inquiry) after making an offer of employment to a job applicant and before the applicant begins his or her employment duties, and may condition an offer of employment on the results of such examination (and/ or inquiry), if all entering employees in the same job category are subjected to such an examination (and/or inquiry) regardless of disability.

(1) Information obtained under paragraph (b) of this section regarding the medical condition or history of the applicant shall be collected and maintained on separate forms and in separate medical files and be treated as a confidential medical record, except that:

(i) Supervisors and managers may be informed regarding necessary restrictions on the work or duties of the employee and necessary accommodations;

(ii) First aid and safety personnel may be informed, when appropriate, if the disability might require emergency treatment; and

(iii) Government officials investigating compliance with this part shall be provided relevant information on request.

(2) The results of such examination shall not be used for any purpose inconsistent with this part.

(3) Medical examinations conducted in accordance with this section do not have to be job-related and consistent with business necessity. However, if certain criteria are used to screen out an employee or employees with disabilities as a result of such an examination or inquiry, the exclusionary criteria must be job-related and consistent with business necessity, and performance of the essential job functions cannot be accomplished with reasonable accommodation as required in this part. (See Sec. 1630.15(b) Defenses to charges of discriminatory application of selection criteria.)

(c) *Examination of employees.* A covered entity may require a medical examination (and/or inquiry) of an employee that is job-related and consistent with business necessity. A covered entity may make inquiries into the ability of an employee to perform job-related functions.

(1) Information obtained under paragraph (c) of this section regarding the medical condition or history of any employee shall be collected and maintained on separate forms and in separate medical files and be treated as a confidential medical record, except that:

(i) Supervisors and managers may be informed regarding necessary restrictions on the work or duties of the employee and necessary accommodations;

(ii) First aid and safety personnel may be informed, when appropriate, if the disability might require emergency treatment; and

(iii) Government officials investigating compliance with this part shall be provided relevant information on request.

(2) Information obtained under paragraph (c) of this section regarding the medical condition or history of any employee shall not be used for any purpose inconsistent with this part.

(d) *Other acceptable examinations and inquiries.* A covered entity may conduct voluntary medical examinations and activities, including voluntary medical histories, which are part of an employee health program available to employees at the work site.

(1) Information obtained under paragraph (d) of this section regarding the medical condition or history of any employee shall be collected and maintained on separate forms and in separate medical files and be treated as a confidential medical record, except that:

(i) Supervisors and managers may be informed regarding necessary restrictions on the work or duties of the employee and necessary accommodations;

(ii) First aid and safety personnel may be informed, when appropriate, if the disability might require emergency treatment; and

(iii) Government officials investigating compliance with this part shall be provided relevant information on request.

(2) Information obtained under paragraph (d) of this section regarding the medical condition or history of any employee shall not be used for any purpose inconsistent with this part.

Section 1630.15. Defenses

Defenses to an allegation of discrimination under this part may include, but are not limited to, the following:

(a) *Disparate treatment charges.* It may be a defense to a charge of disparate treatment brought under Secs. 1630.4 through 1630.8 and 1630.11 through 1630.12 that the challenged action is justified by a legitimate, nondiscriminatory reason.

(b) *Charges of discriminatory application of selection criteria*—(1) *In general.* It may be a defense to a charge of discrimination, as described in Sec. 1630.10, that an alleged application of qualification standards, tests, or selection criteria that screens out or tends to screen out or otherwise denies a job or benefit to an individual with a disability has been shown to be job-related and consistent with business necessity, and such performance cannot be accomplished with reasonable accommodation, as required in this part.

(2) *Direct threat as a qualification standard.* The term "qualification standard" may include a requirement that an individual shall not pose a direct threat to the health or safety of the individual or others in the workplace. (See Sec. 1630.2(r) defining direct threat.)

(c) *Other disparate impact charges.* It may be a defense to a charge of discrimination brought under this part that a uniformly applied standard, criterion, or policy has a disparate impact on an individual with a disability or a class of individuals with disabilities that the challenged standard, criterion or policy has been shown to be job-related and consistent with business necessity, and such performance cannot be accomplished with reasonable accommodation, as required in this part.

(d) *Charges of not making reasonable accommodation.* It may be a defense to a charge of discrimination, as described in Sec. 1630.9, that a requested or necessary accommodation would impose an undue hardship on the operation of the covered entity's business.

(e) *Conflict with other federal laws.* It may be a defense to a charge of discrimination under this part that a challenged action is required or necessitated by another Federal law or regulation, or that another Federal law or regulation prohibits an action (including the provision of a particular reasonable accommodation) that would otherwise be required by this part.

(f) *Additional defenses.* It may be a defense to a charge of discrimination under this part that the alleged discriminatory action is specifically permitted by Secs. 1630.14 or 1630.16.

Section 1630.16. Specific Activities Permitted

(a) *Religious entities.* A religious corporation, association, educational institution, or society is permitted to give preference in employment to individuals of a particular religion to perform work connected with the carrying on by that corporation, association, educational institution, or society of its activities. A religious entity may require that all applicants and employees conform to the religious tenets of such organization. However, a religious entity may not discriminate against a qualified individual, who satisfies the permitted religious criteria, because of his or her disability.

(b) *Regulation of alcohol and drugs.* A covered entity:

(1) May prohibit the illegal use of drugs and the use of alcohol at the workplace by all employees;

(2) May require that employees not be under the influence of alcohol or be engaging in the illegal use of drugs at the workplace;

(3) May require that all employees behave in conformance with the requirements established under the Drug-Free Workplace Act of 1988 (41 U.S.C. 701 et seq.);

(4) May hold an employee who engages in the illegal use of drugs or who is an alcoholic to the same qualification standards for employment or job performance and behavior to which the entity holds its other employees, even if any unsatisfactory performance or behavior is related to the employee's drug use or alcoholism;

(5) May require that its employees employed in an industry subject to such regulations comply with the standards established in the regulations (if any) of the Departments of Defense and Transportation, and of the Nuclear Regulatory Commission, regarding alcohol and the illegal use of drugs; and

(6) May require that employees employed in sensitive positions comply with the regulations (if any) of the Departments of Defense and Transportation and of the Nuclear Regulatory Commission that apply to employment in sensitive positions subject to such regulations.

(c) *Drug testing*—(1) *General policy.* For purposes of this part, a test to determine the illegal use of drugs is not considered a medical examination. Thus, the administration of such drug tests by a covered entity to its job applicants or employees is not a violation of Sec. 1630.13 of this part. However, this part does not encourage, prohibit, or authorize a covered entity to conduct drug tests of job applicants or employees to determine the illegal use of drugs or to make employment decisions based on such test results.

(2) *Transportation Employees.* This part does not encourage, prohibit, or authorize the otherwise lawful exercise by entities subject to the jurisdiction of the Department of Transportation of authority to:

(i) Test employees of entities in, and applicants for, positions involving safety sensitive duties for the illegal use of drugs or for on-duty impairment by alcohol; and

(ii) Remove from safety-sensitive positions persons who test positive for illegal use of drugs or on-duty impairment by alcohol pursuant to paragraph (c)(2)(i) of this section.

(3) *Confidentiality.* Any information regarding the medical condition or history of any employee or applicant obtained from a test to determine the illegal use of drugs, except information regarding the illegal use of drugs, is subject to the requirements of Sec. 1630.14(b) (2) and (3) of this part.

(d) *Regulation of smoking.* A covered entity may prohibit or impose restrictions on smoking in places of employment. Such restrictions do not violate any provision of this part.

(e) *Infectious and communicable diseases; food handling jobs*—(1) *In general.* Under title I of the ADA, section 103(d)(1), the Secretary of Health and Human Services is to prepare a list, to be updated annually, of infectious and communicable diseases which are transmitted through the handling of food. (Copies may be obtained from Center for Infectious Diseases, Centers for Disease Control, 1600 Clifton Road, NE., Mailstop C09, Atlanta, GA 30333.) If an individual with a disability is disabled by one of the infectious or communicable diseases included on this list, and if the risk of transmitting the disease associated with the handling of food cannot be eliminated by reasonable accommodation, a covered entity may refuse to assign or continue to assign such individual to a job involving food handling. However, if the individual with a disability is a current employee, the employer must consider whether he or she can be accommodated by reassignment to a vacant position not involving food handling.

(2) *Effect on state or other laws.* This part does not preempt, modify, or amend any State, county, or local law, ordinance or regulation applicable to food handling which:

(i) Is in accordance with the list, referred to in paragraph (e)(1) of this section, of infectious or communicable diseases and the modes of transmissibility published by the Secretary of Health and Human Services; and

(ii) Is designed to protect the public health from individuals who pose a significant risk to the health or safety of others, where that risk cannot be eliminated by reasonable accommodation.

(f) *Health insurance, life insurance, and other benefit plans*—(1) An insurer, hospital, or medical service company,

health maintenance organization, or any agent or entity that administers benefit plans, or similar organizations may underwrite risks, classify risks, or administer such risks that are based on or not inconsistent with State law.

(2) A covered entity may establish, sponsor, observe or administer the terms of a bona fide benefit plan that are based on underwriting risks, classifying risks, or administering such risks that are based on or not inconsistent with State law.

(3) A covered entity may establish, sponsor, observe, or administer the terms of a bona fide benefit plan that is not subject to State laws that regulate insurance.

(4) The activities described in paragraphs (f) (1), (2), and (3) of this section are permitted unless these activities are being used as a subterfuge to evade the purposes of this part.

Appendix C

List of Suppliers

The following list of companies that supply products for disabled persons have items of possible interest to employers making accommodations for disabled employees. Each company's catalog or sales literature has been examined and found to contain apparently useful accommodation devices. However, inclusion on this list does not imply endorsement of the company or its products or services. Exclusion from the list does not imply a recommendation against the company or its products or services. The list is divided into four sections: General, Hearing, Communication, and Mobility.

General Products and Services. Companies offering a wide assortment of products and services to accommodate various disabilities:

Able Net AccessAbility, Inc.
1081 Tenth Avenue, S.E.
Minneapolis, MN 55414
(800) 322-0956

Alda Industries, Inc.
292 Charles Street
Providence, RI 02904
(401) 751-9421

Arcoa Industries
A Division of Caliputer, Inc.
888 Rancheros Drive
San Marcos, CA 92069
(619) 489-1170

Crestwood Company
6625 N. Sidney Place
Wilwaukee, WI 53209
(414) 352-5678

DU-IT Control Systems Group
8765 TR 513
Shreve, OH 44676
(216) 567-2906

Enrichments
145 Tower Drive
P.O. Box 579
Hinsdale, IL 60521
(800) 323-5547

Fred Sammons, Inc.
145 Tower Drive
Burr Ridge, IL 60521
(800) 323-5547

Global Industrial Equipment
1070 Northbrook Parkway
Department 63
Suwanee, GA 30174
(800) 645-1232

Global Occupational Safety
7117 Hemlock Drive
Hempstead, NY 11550
(800) 433-4848

Guardian Products, Inc.
12800 Wentworth Street
Box C-4522
Arleta, CA 91331
(800) 255-5022

Hoyle Products, Inc.
302 Orange Grove
P.O. Box 606
Fillmore, CA 93016
(805) 524-1211

Independent Living Aids, Inc.
27 East Mall
Plainview, NY 11803
(800) 537-2118

Innovator of Disability
  Equipment and Adaptations,
  Inc.
1393 Meadowcreek Drive
Suite 2
Pewaukee, WI 53072

J. A. Preston Corp.
60 Page Road
Clifton, NJ 07012
(800) 631-7277

Liberty Mutual Research
  Center
71 Frankland Road
Hopkinton, MA 01748
(508) 435-9061

LS&S Group, Inc.
P.O. Box 673
Northbrook, IL 60065
(800) 468-4789

Maddak Inc.
6 Industrial Road
Pequannock, NJ 07440
(201) 628-7600

Medical Line Warehouse
6130 Clark Center Ave., #103
Sarasota, FL 34238
(800) 247-2256

Park Surgical Company, Inc.
5001 New Utrecht Avenue
Brooklyn, NY 11219
(718) 436-9200

Prab Command, Inc.
4100 E. Milham
P.O. Box 2121
Kalamazoo, MI 49003
(616) 329-1096

Radio Shack
Advertising Department
300 One Tandy Center
Fort Worth, TX 76102
(817) 390-2821

Resources For Industry
Prospect Avenue
R.D. 3, Box 12
Walton, NY 13856
(607) 865-7184

Sears Focus Health Care
  Catalog
(800) 366-3000

SelfCare Catalog
349 Healdsburg Avenue
Healdsburg, CA 95448
(800) 345-3371

Seton Name Plate Company
P.O. Box TB-1331
New Haven, CT 06505
(800) 243-6624

Support Plus/FashionAble
Division of Surgical Products,
    Inc.
99 West Street
Box 500
Medfield, MA 02052
(508) 359-2910

TASH, Inc.
Unit 1, 91 Station Street
Ajax, Ontario
Canada L1S 3H2
(416) 686-4129

Therafin Corporation
3800 South Union Avenue
Steger, IL 60475
(708) 755-1535

X-10 (USA), Inc.
185A LeGrand Avenue
Northvale, NJ 07647
(800) 526-0027

Vision Problems. Products or services for use in accommodating employees who are blind or have vision problems:

American Printing House for
    the Blind, Inc.
1839 Frankfort Avenue
P.O. Box 6085
Louisville, KY 40206
(502) 895-2405

Ann Morris Enterprises, Inc.
26 Horseshoe Lane
Levittown, NY 11756
(516) 796-4938

Blazie Engineering
105 East Jarrettsville Road
Forest Hill, MD 21050
(410) 893-9333

Covox, Inc.
675 Conger Street
Eugene, OR 97402
(503) 342-1271

Edroy Products Company, Inc.
P.O. Box 998
245 Midland Avenue
Nyack, NY 10960
(800) 233-8803

GW Micro
310 Racquet Drive
Fort Wayne, IN 46825
(219) 483-3625

HumanWare, Inc.
6245 King Road
Loomis, CA 95650
(916) 652-7253

LS&S Group, Inc.
P.O. Box 673
Northbrook, IL 60065
(800) 468-4789

Science Products
Box 888
Southeastern, PA 19399
(215) 296-2111

SkiSoft Publishing Corporation
1644 Massachusetts Avenue
Suite 79
Lexington, MA 02173

TeleSensory
455 North Bernado Avenue
P.O. Box 7455
Mountain View, CA 94039
(415) 960-0920

TIGER
Communication System, Inc.
155 East Broad Street
Suite 325
Rochester, NY 14604
(716) 454-5134

VisAids
102-09 Jamaica Avenue
P.O. Box 26
Richmond Hill, NY 11418
(800) 346-9579

Xerox Imaging Systems, Inc.
185 Albany Street
Cambridge, MA 02139
(617) 864-4700

Communication Problems. Products or services for use in accommodating employees with speech problems or other difficulties in communication:

Adaptive Communication
   Systems, Inc.
Box 12440
Pittsburgh, PA 15231
(800) 537-3260

AT&T Special Needs Center
2001 Route 46, Suite 310
Parsippany, NJ 07054
(800) 233-1222

Cacti Computer Services
130 9th Street, S.W.
Portage la Prairie, Manitoba
Canada R1N 2N4
(204) 857-8675

Canon U.S.A., Inc.
One Canon Plaza
Lake Success, NY 11042
(516) 488-6700

Developmental Equipment,
   Inc.
P.O. Box 639
1000 N. Rand Road
Bldg. 115
Wauconda, IL 60084
(800) 999-4660

D Q P
14167 Meadow Drive
Grass Valley, CA 95945
(800) 456-4979

GW Micro
310 Racquet Drive
Fort Wayne, IN 46825
(219) 483-3625

Mayer-Johnson Company
P.O. Box 1579
Solana Beach, CA 92075
(619) 481-2489

Prentke Romich Company
1022 Heyl Road
Wooster, OH 44691
(216) 262-1984

Sound Associates, Inc.
424 West 45th Street
New York, NY 10036
(212) 757-5679

Voice Connection
17835 Skypark Circle, Suite C
Irvine, CA 92714
(714) 261-2366

World Communications
245 Tonopah Drive
Fremont, CA 94539
(415) 656-0911

Words+, Inc.
P.O. Box 1229
44421 10th Street West,
 Suite L
Lancaster, CA 93584
(800) 869-8521

Zygo Industries, Inc.
P.O. Box 1008
Portland, OR 97207
(503) 684-6006

Mobility Problems. Products or services intended to aid people with mobility problems, including wheelchair users, people who use crutches or have problems in walking or climbing, and those with motor skills problems:

Able Walker, Inc.
1122 Fir Avenue
Blaine, WA 98230
(800) 663-1305

ACTIVEAID, INC.
One Activeaid Road
P.O. Box 359
Redwood Falls, MN 56283
(507) 644-2951

ALTimate Medical, Inc.
913 South Washington
Redwood Falls, MN 56283
(800) 342-8968

American Walker, Inc.
797 Market Street
Oregon, WI 53575
(608) 835-9255

American Stair-Glide Corp.
4001 E. 138th Street
Grandview, MO 64030
(800) 383-3100

Amigo Mobility International,
 Inc.
P.O. Box 402
Bridgeport, MI 48722
(800) 248-9130 or (517) 777-0402

Barrier Free Lifts
P.O. Box 4163
Manassas, VA 22110
(800) 582-8732 or
 (703) 361-6531

BC Research
3650 Wesbrook Mall
Vancouver, B.C.
Canada V6S 2L2
(604) 224-4331

The Braun Corporation
P.O. Box 310
Winamac, IN 46996
(800) THE-LIFT

Brown & Co., Inc.
P.O. Box 2443
South Hamilton, MA 01982
(508) 468-7464

Bruno Independent Living
  Aids
430 Armour Court
P.O. Box 84
Oconomowoc, WI 53066
(800) 882-8183 or
  (414) 567-4990

Burke Mobility Products
P.O. Box 1064
Mission, KS 66222
(800) 255-4147 [In Kansas, call
  collect: (913) 722-5658]

Cheney
2445 South Calhoun Road
P.O. Box 51188
New Berlin, WI 53151-0188
(800) 782-7442

Creative Concepts
P.O. Box 541
Fremont, OH 43420
(419) 334-4100

Citadel Asphalt Systems, Inc.
9241 Citadel Ct.
Affton, MO 63124
(314) 638-3888

Collins Mobile-Tech
  Corporation
P.O. Box 2326
Hutchinson, KS 67504
(800) 835-5007

Contact Technologies
11600 Western Avenue
Stanton, CA 90680
(714) 898-7838

DORMA Door Controls Inc.
Dorma Drive
Reamstown, PA 17567
(800) 523-8483

Drive-Master Corporation
9 Spielman Road
Fairfield, NJ 07006
(201) 808-9713

EKEG Electronics Co., Ltd.
P.O. Box 46199
Station G
Vancouver, B.C.
Canada V6R 4G5

Electric Mobility
Dept. 2943
1 Mobility Plaza
Sewell, NJ 08080
(800) 662-4548

ETAC USA
2325 Parklawn Drive
Suite P
Waukesha, WI 53186
(800) 678-ETAC

Everest & Jennings
3233 E. Mission Oaks Blvd.
Camarillo, CA 93012
(805) 987-6911

Extensions for Independence
555 Saturn Blvd. #B-368
San Diego, CA 92154
(619) 423-7709

Fleetwood Furniture Company
P.O. Box 1259
Holland, MI 49422-1259
(800) 257-6390

Flinchbaugh Co., Inc.
390 Eberts Lane
York, PA 17403
(717) 854-7720

Florklift of New Jersey, Inc.
41 Lawrence Street
East Orange, NJ 07017
(201) 429-2200

Fortress
P.O. Box 489
Clovis, CA 93613
(209) 323-0292

Frohock-Stewart, Inc.
455 Whitney Avenue
Northboro, MA 01532
(800) 343-6059

Garaventa (Canada) Ltd.
7505-134A Street
Surrey, B.C.
Canada V3W 7B3
(800) 663-6556

Gendron
Lugbill Road
P.O. Box 197
Archbold, OH 43502
(800) 537-2521

Gresham Driving Aids, Inc.
30800 Wixom Road
P.O. Box 405
Wixom, MI 48393

Handicaps, Inc.
4335 S. Santa Fe Drive
Englewood, CO 80110
(303) 781-2062

Handi-Ramp, Inc.
P.O. Box 745
1414 Armour Blvd.
Mundelein, IL 60060
(708) 816-7525

Homecare Products, Inc.
15824 S.E. 296th Street
Kent, WA 98042
(206) 631-4633

Horton Automatics
4242 Baldwin Blvd.
Corpus Christi, TX 78405
(800) 531-3111

Inclinator Company of Ameria
2200 Paxton Street
P.O. Box 1557
Harrisburg, PA 17105
(717) 234-8065

I. D. C. Medical Equipment
20 Independence Court
Folcroft West Business Park
Folcroft, PA 19032
(215) 586-0986

Independent Mobility Systems,
   Inc.
3900 Bloomfield Highway
Farmington, NM 87401
(800) 622-0623

Kroepke Kontrols, Inc.
104 Hawkins Street
Bronx, NY 10464
(212) 885-1100

KY Enterprises
Custom Computer Services
3039 East 2nd Street
Long Beach, CA 90803
(213) 433-5244

LEVO USA Distributor
21050 Superior Street
Chatsworth, CA 91311
(800) 882-6944

Lindustries, Inc.
21 Shady Hill Road
Weston, MA 02193
(617) 235-5452

Lumex
100 Spence Street
Bay Shore, NY 11706
(516) 273-2200

Mannesmann Demag Ltd.
Material Handling Division
2400 Royal Windsor Drive
Mississauga, Ontario L5J 1K7
(416) 823-4500

McIntyre Computer Systems
22809 Shagbark
Birmingham, MI 48010
(313) 645-5090

M.D.F. Technologies, Inc.
P.O. Box 17204
Pittsburgh, PA 15235
(800) 448-3159

Mobilectrics
4311 Woodgate Lane
Louisville, KY 40220
(800) 876-6846

The National Wheel-O-Vator
   Co., Inc.
P.O. Box 348
Roanoke, IL 61561
(800) 551-9095

NobleMotion, Inc.
2120 One Mellon Bank Center
Pittsburgh, PA 15219
(800) 234-9255

Ortho-Kinetics, Inc.
P.O. Box 1647
Waukesha, WI 53187
(800) 522-0992

Palmer Industries, Inc.
P.O. Box 707NC
Endicott, NY 13760

Permobil
30 Ray Avenue
Department P
Burlington, MA 01803
(800) 736-0925

Pointer Systems, Inc.
One Mill Street
Burlington, VT 05401

Power Access Corporation
Bridge Street P.O. Box 235
Collinsville, CT 06022
(203) 693-0751

Quest Technologies
   Corporation
766 Palomar Avenue
Sunnyvale, CA 94086
(408) 739-3550

Rand-Scot, Inc.
1418 West Oak
Fort Collins, CO 80521
(303) 484-7967

Richard C. Peterson, P.E.
RR1, 15 Highland Road
Eastham, MA 02642

Samhall
P.O. Box 739
25 Lindeman Drive
Trumbull, CT 06611
(203) 371-8070

Southworth Products Corp.
P.O. Box 1380
Portland, ME 04104
(207) 772-0130

Stand Aid of Iowa, Inc.
P.O. Box 386
Sheldon, IA 51201
(800) 831-8580

Ted Hoyer and Company, Inc.
2222 Minnesota Street
P.O. Box 2744
Oshkosh, WI 54903
(414) 231-7970

Temco Health Care
125 South Street
Passaic, NJ 07055
(201) 472-3173

T.F. Herceg, Inc.
33 Rector Street
New York, NY 10006
(212) 425-3355

Touch Turner
443 View Ridge Drive
Everett, WA 98203
(206) 252-1541

Tubular Specialties Mfg., Inc.
13011 South Spring Street
Los Angeles, CA 90061
(800) 421-2961

Index

ARC (AIDS related complex). *See* Acquired immune deficiency syndrome

ARC (Association for Retarded Citizens), 331

Architects
  new structures, contracts, 40–41
  practical tips on designing accessible facilities, 44–45
  renovations, contracts, 38–39

Architectural and Transportation Barriers Compliance Board regulations, 15

Architectural barriers, removal. *See* Accessibility of workplace

Arline; School Board of Nassau County v., 59–61, 66–67, 117, 150

Arneson v. Heckler, 98

Arterial embolism. *See* Heart and circulatory problems

Arteriosclerosis, 300. *See also* Heart and circulatory problems

Arthritis, 246–248

ASL. *See* American Sign Language

Assistive devices. *See* Auxiliary aids

Association for Retarded Citizens (ARC), 331

Association with disabled persons, discrimination based on, 4
  charges and defenses, 202

Asthma, 241–242. *See* Allergies

AT&T training program, 223

Atherosclerosis. *See* Heart and circulatory problems

Attitudes of co-workers toward disabled employees, 18, 25
  AIDS, fear of, 152, 158
  epilepsy, practical tips on dealing with, 130
  undue hardship not created by, 100

Attitudes of disabled employees, 26

Attitudes of public toward disabled employees, 26

Attorney General, U.S.
  compliance reviews, 15
  regulations governing renovations and new construction, 15, 40
  suits by, 207

Attorneys' fees, 208

Auxiliary aids. *See also* Wheelchair accommodation

deafness, for, 277–279
grab bars, 341
injunctions requiring, 15
leases and rental contract provisions, 42
repetitive motion injury, for, 326–328
speech impairments, 336
spinal cord injuries, 338, 342–343
telecommunication devices for the deaf (TDDs), 278–279

AZT, 153

B

Back pay, 208

Back problems, 134–140, 249–253
  accommodation, 250–252
  case law on employment discrimination, 119–120, 135–139
  practical tips for dealing with, 139–140
  reasonable accommodation, case law, 94, 96
  sources of information, 252–253
  workers' compensation claims due to, 134

Bad backs. *See* Back problems

Bell's palsy, 322. *See also* Nerve disease

Benefits. *See* Fringe benefits; specific type of benefit (e.g., Health insurance)

Bentivegna v. U.S. Department of Labor, 120–121, 131

Bisexuality, not covered by ADA as disability, 6–7, 49

Blanket rules
  back problems, disqualification of persons with, 139
  diabetes, disqualification of persons with, 131–132
    practical tips, 133
  epilepsy, disqualification of persons with; practical tips, 129
  qualified individual with disability, determination, 71–72
  risk of future injuries, practical tips for dealing with, 122

Deaf persons—*cont'd*
  problem for employers, 272–274
  reasonable accommodation, case
      law, 95
  sources of information, 279–281
  statistics, 272–273
  TDDs, 278–279
  testing of applicants, 78–80, 276
Defense Department, 163, 167
Defenses
  ADA charges, to, 201–206
  AIDS discrimination, 150–152
Definitions
  commercial facilities, 14
  disabled persons, 47–63
    ADA, 47–48
    Rehabilitation Act, 48
  physical or mental impairment, 48
  qualified individual with disability,
      6–7, 64
  undue hardship, 11
Department of. *See* specific
      department (e.g., Defense
      Department)
Depression, 312. *See also* Mental
      illness or disease
Diabetes, 130–133
  accommodation ideas, 282–284
  case law on employment
      discrimination, 120–121,
      131–133
  facts about, 130, 281–282
  increased risk from infectious
      diseases, 158
  practical tips for dealing with
      employees and job applicants
      with, 133–134
  qualified individual with disability,
      determination, 71–72
  testing programs sponsored by
      employers, 284–285
Digestive diseases, 286–289
  accommodation ideas, 288–289
  problem for employers, 286–288
  sources of information, 289
Disability
  accommodating specific disabilities,
      231–345. *See also* specific
      disability by name
  AIDS as, 145

alcohol abuse. *See* Alcohol abuse
ARC as, 145
case law
  determination of extent, 52–53
  disability found, 53–55
  disability not found, 55–59
  Supreme Court, 59–61
definition, 5–6, 47–63
  ADA, 5–6, 47–48
  Rehabilitation Act, 6, 48
determination, practical tips, 61
different treatment by employer of
      disabled persons than of
      nondisabled persons, 27–28
disclosure by employer, 17–19, 32
exclusions, 6–7, 49–50
HIV as, 145
infectious disease as, 158, 160
obvious vs. hidden, 26
practical tips for determination, 61
qualified individuals. *See* Qualified
      individual with disability
sexual harassment defense, rejected
      by court, 57
Disability insurance
  increased costs, illegal
      discrimination to reject
      disabled employee due to
      probability of, 13, 20, 117
Disability management programs,
      213–227
  disability management vendors,
      selecting, 221–222
  education and training, 223–224
  examples, 214–217
  practical tips for small businesses, 222
  principles of effective programs,
      217–221
  statistics, 213–214
Disclosure, 17–19, 32. *See also*
      Confidentiality
  AIDS, 154–155
  charges of unlawful disclosure of
      disability and defenses, 204
  drug test results, legal prescription
      drugs, 163
  voluntary by employee
    policy statement, sample
        provision, 175–176
    sample forms, 194–195

About the Author

James G. Frierson is an attorney and professor in the College of Business of East Tennessee State University. He is also an adjunct faculty member of the James H. Quillen College of Medicine.

Professor Frierson received his B.S. degree in Economics from Arkansas State University, and his M.B.A. and J.D. degrees from the University of Arkansas. He was named as his university's Distinguished Faculty Member in 1977 and received the university's research award in 1986.

Professor Frierson has published over 150 journal articles in publications such as the *American Bar Association Journal, Employee Relations Law Journal, Personnel Journal, The Judges Journal, Labor Law Journal, Journal of Accountancy*, and the *Advanced Management Journal*. He is co-author of BNA's special report, *The Americans with Disabilities Act: A Practical and Legal Guide to Impact, Enforcement and Compliance* (1990).

Professor Frierson frequently conducts seminars and gives speeches on employment law for human resource managers, attorneys, accountants, rehabilitation and social support agencies, business managers, and various corporations. He has served as a consultant to numerous attorneys, accountants, and businesses.